Birds of the Middle East

and North Africa

Birds of the Middle East and North Africa

A companion guide

by P. A. D. HOLLOM, R. F. PORTER

S. CHRISTENSEN and IAN WILLIS

Illustrated by

IAN WILLIS

T & A D POYSER

Calton

ISBN 0 85661 047 X

First published 1988 by T & A D Poyser Ltd
Town Head House, Calton, Staffordshire, England

British Library Cataloguing in Publication Data
Birds of the Middle East and North Africa.
  1. Middle East. Birds   2. North Africa. Birds
  I. Hollom, P. A. D. (Philip Arthur Dominic),
  1912–   II Willis, Ian
  598.2956
  ISBN 0–85661–047–X

Text set in Monophoto Photina, printed and bound
in Great Britain by Butler & Tanner Ltd, Frome and London
Colour plates by Lawrence-Allen Ltd, Weston-super-Mare

Contents

Colour plates (1–40) are between pages 160 and 161

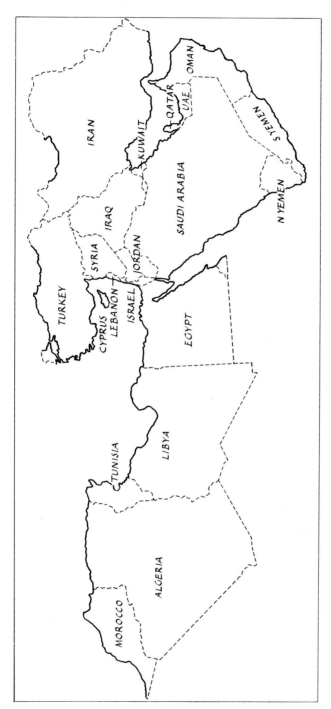

The area covered by the guide

Introduction

This book is intended as a companion to those guides which primarily cover the birds of Europe, notably *A Field Guide to the Birds of Britain and Europe* by Peterson, Mountfort and Hollom (PMH in the text). Where that work already describes a species adequately we generally omit identification details but give information on distribution, status and habitat in the Middle East and North Africa.

The need for a book such as this was brought home to the book's oldest author during the 1940s when he was having to visit at short notice places in and around the Mediterranean, and occasionally as far afield as Warsaw, Baghdad and Riyadh. This contributed to the coverage of the northern parts of the general area in *A Field Guide to the Birds of Britain and Europe* (1954), but the southern and eastern parts were – and to a large extent remain – more inscrutable.

Great help has been generously provided by many ornithologists and other observers over the years, starting in the 1950s with the preparation of some distribution maps for the project by Col. Richard Meinertzhagen who was at that time the outstanding authority on the birds of the Middle East; his interest and support were encouragement indeed. Since then, foreign travel by European birdwatchers has become commonplace, Israeli ornithology has come into being, a number of bird clubs have been formed in Arabia, nature reserves established in, for example, Iran and Libya. Trail-blazing books have been published in several languages. Knowledge has increased enormously.

The authors have undertaken much independent travel and have personally accumulated years of ornithological experience within the region, between them visiting (often repeatedly) all the countries concerned except Libya, South Yemen and Oman; acquaintance with some of the scarcer migrants or accidental visitors to the region has also been gained during journeys to the Canary Islands, Afrotropics, Oriental area and Siberia.

What the book covers. The project now emerges as a guide dealing with the birds of the southern part of the Western Palearctic, covering the countries which reach into the deserts near its southern fringe. These territories comprise, in North Africa, all the countries lying between the Mediterranean and the Sahara, and, in South-west Asia, Turkey and Iran and all countries southwards. This includes the whole of the Arabian peninsula where, especially in the south, some Oriental and Afrotropical species appear, but it is difficult to draw a clean, comprehensible line further north than Arabia's southern coastline. Thus, geographically, this book takes over where *A Field Guide to the Birds of Britain and Europe* leaves off.

There is of course an authorship link between the two books, and much of the style of presentation adopted in the earlier book has been followed here. In order to reduce duplication and costs, and to provide additional space for lesser-known species, the present book does not include illustration or description of most of the species already treated in the European Field Guide, and for these particulars the reader is advised, under the relevant species-headings, to 'see PMH', these initials indicating the authors of *A Field Guide to the Birds of Britain and Europe*, Roger Peterson, Guy Mountfort and P. A. D. Hollom. However, in some cases, such as Blue Tit and Chaffinch, where in our area there are races with field characters perceptibly different from those of their European counterparts, illustrations and descriptions have also been included here. In North Africa and the Middle East, therefore, this book should be used in conjunction with the Field Guide or one of the other identification guides to European birds.

There is also a link with the editors of *The Birds of the Western Palearctic*, and grateful acknowledgement is made of the great help provided by the chief editor of that work, Stanley Cramp, in allowing unrestricted access to all material in his possession, both published and unpublished, and in particular that relating to distribution.

Maps. Maps are included for all species nesting in the region, with breeding distribution marked in red, and in some cases additional areas, where breeding is likely but uncertain, are indicated by red question-marks; winter range is not shown, and no maps are included for species which do not breed in the region. Generally speaking, the mapping consists of red spots or relatively small patches in places where breeding is known or said to occur, rather than the more usual broad sweeps of colour to show potential breeding range within which the bird may occur in places where suitable habitat is available, disturbance levels are acceptable, etc. Our more exacting approach inevitably means that we must often have understated the present-day range (although doubtless at other times we have exaggerated or in some other way mis-stated it). Accordingly, proposals for amendments would be welcomed – to be sent, please, to the authors, c/o the publishers – for example the finding of an occupied nest, the draining of a lake, the effects of pollution or war, or intrusive recreation. Perhaps some adventurous readers may feel encouraged to explore areas where to the best of their knowledge other birdwatchers have not preceded them.

Taxonomy. The sequence and scientific nomenclature conform generally to those employed by Voous (in *List of Recent Holarctic Bird Species*), and in turn by the editors of *The Birds of the Western Palearctic* and the authors of *A Field Guide to the Birds of Britain and Europe*. There are however a few changes of classification. Tawny and Steppe Eagles have been treated here as though they were separate species, each with its own separate description, map and illustrations. Similarly we have treated Lesser Whitethroat, Hume's Lesser Whitethroat and Desert Lesser Whitethroat as though they were three different species, and we are likewise dividing the Lesser Golden Plovers. Opinion seems to be growing in support of revision of the Herring/Lesser Black-backed Gull group, including the introduction of new species; we give, under Herring Gull, a few details of some of the forms (or species) currently proposed, but until further study has been made, and a consensus reached, we prefer to treat these birds on the old basis.

We have no wish to review the records of any birds accepted by national, local or individual authorities within the region, and it is without in any way intending to suggest that past records should be reconsidered, that we have included descriptions of a few species which might occur, such as Great Frigatebird, in the hope that this may help observers to establish or discard any future possible sightings.

Problems caused by escapes. Particularly in Arabia, where the keeping of cage birds and, recently, some ornamental waterfowl, is becoming increasingly popular, escapes can cause confusion, but it is impractical to describe the many birds potentially involved. We have however included species of which instances of feral breeding have come to our notice. The groups most frequently recorded as escapes are the Mynahs and seed-eating finches, such as Manakins and Munias.

Habitat. Only those habitats relevant to the region are given.

Status. Every species-account contains a paragraph on status, indicating whether the bird is resident, summer visitor, winter visitor, partial migrant, passage migrant, or vagrant, as the case may be, or some combination of these. The terms 'resident' and 'summer visitor' relate to the areas where the bird breeds, as shown on its accompanying map. To have said e.g. 'Summer visitor to breeding areas in the region' in all such appropriate cases might have been more explicit, but was considered superfluous. The term 'partial migrant' means, for example, that some individuals are resident, others migratory, within a particular area or country, or that the species occurs only as a summer visitor in some (northern) part of the region while it remains throughout the year, or occurs as a winter visitor, in some other (southern) part.

In indicating the countries or areas in which a bird occurs, the following groupings have been used: NW Africa (Morocco, Algeria, Tunisia), N Africa (Morocco, Algeria, Tunisia, Libya, Egypt), Near East (Israel, Jordan, Syria, Lebanon), Arabia (all countries/states in the Arabian peninsula including Kuwait), E Arabia (the easterly parts of the Arabian peninsula from Kuwait to Oman inclusive), UAE (United Arab Emirates = Trucial States; part of E Arabia occupying a southerly position on the Arabian Gulf between north Oman and the Qatar peninsula), S Arabia (Oman, South Yemen, North Yemen, and adjoining parts of Saudi Arabia), SW Arabia (South Yemen, North Yemen and SW Saudi Arabia), Yemen (North Yemen and South Yemen), W Arabia (a band to the east of the Red Sea between Aqaba and Aden).

Knowledge of distribution and status is of course uneven over such a region. This particularly applies to Arabia and Iran, where the historical record is sketchy at best, neither of which falls within the scope of *The Birds of the Western Palearctic*. In both these areas, however, vast strides have been made in the last couple of decades or so, chiefly owing to the presence throughout the year of a few ornithologists of western origin. Nevertheless, in the main, these territories remain outside the experience, and even beyond the scope of the reading, of most birdwatchers, and in an attempt to compensate somewhat for this imbalance places like Oman, North Yemen and parts of Iran have perhaps received more than their fair share of mention in the details of status.

Even now, one's own previous misconceptions of the absence of precipitous and sometimes chilly mountains, woodland, plantations, still and running water, and marshes make it hard to credit the presence in southern Arabia of breeding accentors, woodpeckers, nectar-feeding sunbirds, kingfishers and grebes, and flocks of wintering ducks. Equally to be wondered at, and hopefully preserved, there and widely in Iran, is the apparent freedom of most species from shooting, netting or more casual forms of disturbance.

Acknowledgements

In the course of the preparation of this book we have received help from a number of observers and consultants. The contribution by Mrs F E Warr has been outstanding; she has carefully checked many reference sources as well as typing and commenting on the status sections and making available compilations of her own records and those of her many correspondents in Arabia.

In the preparation of the status notes and maps we have received great help from:

M D Gallagher (Oman)
M C Jennings (Saudi Arabia)
A M Macfarlane (Syria and Lebanon)
R P Martins (Turkey)
P L Meininger (Egypt)
D A Scott (Iran)

Others have assisted in a variety of ways in either giving freely of their comments and advice or providing moral support during our numerous visits to North Africa or the Middle East:

M Aaviv, P Alström, S Vere Benson, R Bijlsma, P Boyes, K Brockie, D J Brooks, G Bundy, L Cornwallis, S Cramp, G R Cunningham-van Someren, P. Doherty, C Erard, R D Etchecopar, M I Evans, M J Everett, R Fairbanks, J Finch, R N Fryer, S Goodman, C M Greaves, P Schiermacher Hansen, J G Harrison, P Harrison, M J Helps, S Howe, J and B Hulbert, E D H Johnson, L R Johnson, J Karpowicz, P Kennerley, B King, A R Kitson, E Krabbe, H Kumerloeve, L J Laine, W Laird, Y Leshem, Leverhulme Trust, I H J Lyster, R McGowan, J H McNeile, S C Madge, K Malling Olsen, H P Medhurst, R Meinertzhagen, B A E Marr, R McGregor, P Meeth, H Meilstrup, B U Meyburg, N Montfort, M Müller, K Mullarney, W C Mullie, C Muringo, J B Nelson, U Olsson, R E Passburg, I Petersen, N R Phillips, B O Poulsen, J F Reynolds, T J Roberts, M C Robinson, T Rogers, P D Round, F De Roder, V A D Sales, P Schlütter, D Scott, C Seton-Browne, H Shirihai, K E L Simmons, E Smith, A Stagg, W Stanford, L Svensson, U G Sorensen, K H Voous, F Walker, D I M Wallace, D Watson, Mrs D L Willis, J Wittenberg and H Wohlmuth.

The following museums have allowed us to examine study skins: British Museum (Natural History); Royal Museum of Scotland (Natural History Department); Zoological Museum, Copenhagen; and National Museums of Kenya.

Ostrich, male

Ostrich *Struthio camelus*

Identification: 180–240 cm. Sexes differ. Unmistakable due to *huge size*, very long, pinkish neck, small flat head and *very long, powerful, flesh-coloured legs*. Larger male has black body and wings, white ornamental primaries and tail-feathers. Female greyish-brown and lacks white. Immature like female. Mostly gregarious; can run very fast for long distances.
Voice: usually silent. In breeding season males have deep booming call, often compared to lion's roar.
Status: see map. May not breed in Egypt every year. Apparently extinct in Arabia since 1930s. Re-introduction attempt S Israel.
Habitat: semi-deserts in broken and rolling country, along sandy wadi beds and in arid steppes and savannas, but not sand-dunes. Nests on ground.

Red-throated Diver *Gavia stellata*

Identification: 54–58 cm. See PMH.
Status: rare winter visitor N and W coasts of Turkey and S Caspian. Vagrant Mediterranean, Atlantic and Gulf of Aqaba.
Habitat: mainly coastal waters.

Black-throated Diver *Gavia arctica*

Identification: 59–68 cm. See PMH.
Status: winter visitor. Widespread N coast of Turkey, fewer on W coast. Scarce S Caspian. Vagrant E Turkey, Israel, Gulf of Aqaba, Algeria and Morocco.
Habitat: mainly coastal waters.

Great Northern Diver *Gavia immer*

Identification: 69–81 cm. See PMH.
Status: vagrant Mediterranean.
Habitat: coastal waters.

13

Little Grebe *Tachybaptus ruficollis*

Identification: 27 cm. See PMH.

Status: see map; in Arabia readily colonises new waters. Partial migrant. Winters most breeding areas, also Black Sea, Mediterranean and Atlantic coasts, and Arabia.

Habitat: lakes and pools sometimes densely vegetated; in winter also estuaries. Nests in water on heap of vegetation.

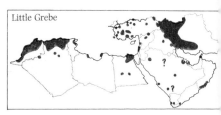

Great Crested Grebe *Podiceps cristatus*

Identification: 48 cm. See PMH.

Status: see map. Partial migrant. Winter range includes N African coast (inland waters mainly vacated), Turkey (especially Black Sea coast), south to Egypt and central Red Sea, east to Iran and Arabian Gulf; sometimes Oman. Vagrant Jordan.

Habitat: occurs in open areas of freshwater throughout year, also coastal waters in winter. Nest in water generally anchored to vegetation.

Red-necked Grebe *Podiceps grisegena*

Identification: 43 cm. See PMH.

Status: see map. Partial migrant. Winters SW Turkey, S Caspian (uncommon). Vagrant NW Africa, Egypt, Arabian Gulf.

Habitat: like Great Crested Grebe (also nest) but breeding pools usually smaller, more overgrown.

Slavonian Grebe *Podiceps auritus*

Identification: 33 cm. See PMH.

Status: winter visitor to S Caspian, perhaps a few Turkey. Vagrant NW Africa, Cyprus, Israel and S Iran.

Habitat: fresh and coastal waters.

Black-necked Grebe *Podiceps nigricollis*

Identification: 31 cm. See PMH.

Status: see map. Partial migrant. Winters south to coasts of Atlantic, Mediterranean, Gulf of Suez, Arabian Gulf; also on some inland waters mainly in or near breeding range, and in N Egypt and sparingly in Arabia.

Habitat: fresh-water throughout the year, also coastal in winter. Nests at water-level in shallow pools with good vegetation.

Black-browed Albatross *Diomedea melanophris*

Identification: 90 cm (wing-span 240 cm). See PMH.

Status: vagrant Morocco. Range southern oceans.

Habitat: maritime.

Shy Albatross, adults (left and centre), juvenile (right)

Shy Albatross (White-capped Mollymawk) *Diomedea cauta*

Identification: 91 cm (wing-span 230 cm). Sexes alike. Medium-sized albatross, about twice size of Cory's Shearwater. *Plumage white with blackish-brown upperwing and mantle, contrasting with white neck and white rump*; short tail blackish, underwing white narrowly edged black, with *characteristic dark mark at base of wing on leading edge*, visible at long range. Close views reveal *greyish wash on cheeks* forming mask through eye, and greyish bill with yellow tip. Juvenile similar but eye-mask smaller, bill tipped blackish and often has dark half-collar. Confusion possible with Grey-headed Albatross *D. chrysostoma* and Black-browed Albatross. Former slightly smaller, has grey head and neck, and black and yellow bill; Black-browed larger with yellow bill in adult plumage (greyish in juvenile) and has narrow dark streak through eye. Both have proportionally narrower wings than Shy, with prominent black border (especially on leading edge) to white underwing (narrow border in Shy); both lack characteristic dark mark on underwing base of Shy.
Status: vagrant Gulf of Aqaba. Range southern oceans.
Habitat: maritime.

Fulmar *Fulmarus glacialis*

Identification: 47 cm (wing-span 105 cm). See PMH.
Status: vagrant Morocco.
Habitat: maritime.

Schlegel's Petrel *Pterodroma incerta*   Illustration p. 16

Identification: 43 cm (wing-span 104 cm). Sexes alike. Almost as large as Cory's Shearwater or Fulmar. In fresh plumage has rich dark brown upper-parts; below, also dark brown except clean white underbody. In worn plumage throat and neck mottled whitish which may form pale collar, and upperparts generally greyer, especially on head. Ill-defined, long blackish eye-stripe. Juvenile in fresh plumage similar to adult but greyer on mantle. Legs flesh-pink. Virtual lack of face-pattern, and uniformly dark wings (above and below) contrasting with white underbody, are distinctive; see also Soft-plumaged Petrel.
Status: a probable, Gulf of Aqaba (summer). Range southern oceans, mainly S Atlantic.
Habitat: maritime.

15

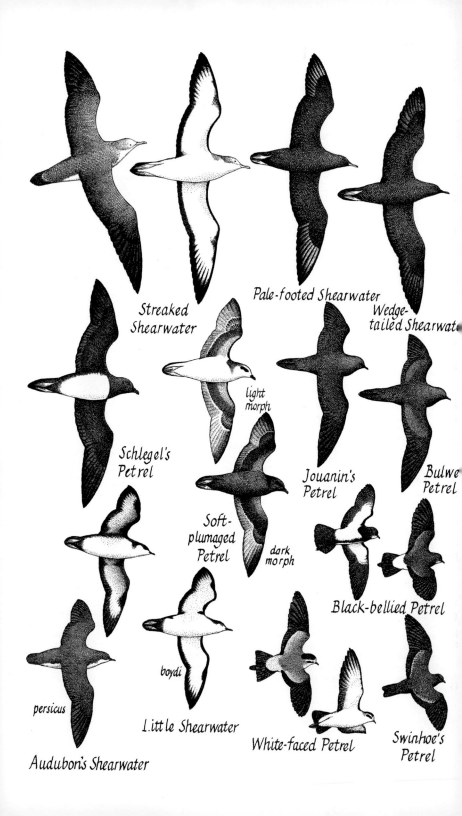

Streaked
Shearwater

Pale-footed Shearwater

Wedge-
tailed Shearwater

Schlegel's
Petrel

light
morph

Jouanin's
Petrel

Bulwer
Petrel

Soft-
plumaged
Petrel

dark
morph

Black-bellied Petrel

persicus

boydi

Little Shearwater

White-faced Petrel

Swinhoe's
Petrel

Audubon's Shearwater

Soft-plumaged Petrel *Pterodroma mollis*   Illustration p. 16

Identification: 35 cm (wing-span 90 cm). Sexes alike. Similar size to Manx Shearwater and even at a distance can be identified by greyish-brown upperparts, white underparts, dark underwing and diffuse greyish breast-band, though this is sometimes lacking. Close views reveal complicated pied pattern of *brownish upper head* and *mask through eye, dark band on upperwing-coverts* (forming 'M' shape) and pale grey tail; also *broad dark band through centre of underwing* and *whitish bases to inner primaries.* Juvenile similar to adult. Rare dark morph occurs; basically brownish-grey all over, but under- and upperwing markings similar to typical form. Fast flight with rapid wing-beats and much zig-zagging while gliding low over sea or towering above it.
Status: vagrant Israel (Dead Sea), presumably also occurs in Atlantic between Morocco and northern breeding quarters in Madeira; range also includes southern oceans.
Habitat: maritime.

Bulwer's Petrel *Bulweria bulwerii*   Illustration p. 16

Identification: 25 cm (wing-span 65 cm). Sexes alike. Noticeably larger than Storm Petrel. *Sooty brown all over with narrow diffuse paler panel on upperwing-coverts* and pale suffusion on underwing. Colour and rather narrow wings reminiscent of tiny Sooty Shearwater but with longish tail (wedge shape virtually impossible to see) and short stubby bill at closer range. Head protrudes; chest fairly deep. *Flight low over waves,* often lazy but quite fast: several leisurely Arctic Skua-like flaps, followed by short wavering glide on bowed wings. Usually seen singly though larger concentrations may occur, particularly near breeding grounds. See also Jouanin's Petrel and Wedge-tailed Shearwater; both similar in plumage but larger (especially Wedge-tailed) and generally do not overlap range of Bulwer's.
Status: recorded off W coast of Morocco, where it may occur regularly as it breeds Madeira and Canary Islands.
Habitat: maritime.

Jouanin's Petrel *Bulweria fallax*   Illustration p. 16

Identification: 30 cm (wing-span 75 cm). Sexes alike. *Slightly larger than Bulwer's Petrel* (which it closely resembles in shape and plumage, though distribution different) but has *heavier head and bill* (noticeable only at close range), lacks or shows less pronounced palish upperwing-bar on sooty-brown plumage and has *different flight.* Typically, in windy conditions flight is weaving though unhurried, rising well above waves before turning sharply to glide or swoop to troughs along which it progresses in banking sweeps. Noticeably more wing-beats in calmer conditions. Wedge-tailed Shearwater larger, and differences given under that species.
Status: see map. Widely dispersed in winter in Arabian Sea extending to Gulfs of Aden and Oman, vagrant Red Sea. In summer concentrates (for feeding?) near Kuria Muria Islands, also suggestion of breeding inland in neighbouring S Oman.
Habitat: maritime.

Cory's Shearwater *Calonectris diomedea*

Identification: 46 cm (wing-span 110 cm). See PMH.
Status: see map. Mainly summer visitor: in autumn most leave Mediterranean westwards, but some remain even in east. Also regularly N Red Sea. Vagrant Arabian Sea.
Habitat: maritime. Nests colonially among rocks and in hollows.

Streaked (White-faced) **Shearwater** *Calonectris leucomelas*
Illustration p. 16

Identification: 48 cm (wing-span 120 cm). Sexes alike. Similar size to Cory's Shearwater which it resembles in general colouration, but with longer, *distinctly pointed tail, thinner, grey bill* (yellow in Cory's), *whitish hind-crown and nape streaked blackish*, and *white face* (forehead and lores); this last feature identifying it from all other shearwaters. Upperparts medium-brown (slightly scaly when seen close) with darker tail and, usually, pale brown 'U' on uppertail-coverts. Underparts white with dark smudge at side of breast. Underwing greyish-white with dark brown border wider on trailing edge and (apparently on some birds) faint dark line up centre of underwing. Wing action relaxed and this, plus gliding on down-curved wings, causes further resemblance to Cory's. Legs and feet pink.
Status: unconfirmed record from Gulf of Aqaba. Range W Pacific.
Habitat: maritime.

Pale-footed (Flesh-footed) **Shearwater** *Puffinus carneipes*
Illustration p. 16

Identification: 43 cm (wing-span 100 cm). Sexes alike. Rather large, *blackish-brown shearwater* with *flesh-pink feet* and *thick, pale horn bill* with dark tip; very similar to Wedge-tailed and care needed to separate the two. Upperwing often shows slightly paler coverts and, with wear, pale tips to greater coverts; sides of head and neck can appear paler greyish-brown; in good light, even at a distance, can show *silvery flash at base of primaries below*. Flight lazy: series of slow, fairly heavy flaps followed by long glide on stiff wings; in windy conditions will rise well above waves. Separated from Wedge-tailed by more steady flight, straighter wings, whitish bases of primaries below (all-dark underwing in Wedge-tailed), and pale bill. From Sooty by broader wings, slower flight, restricted paleness on underwing (Sooty has silvery lining to whole underwing) and pale bill and feet (dark in Sooty).
Status: regular non-breeding visitor April-November to Arabian Sea, some coming close inshore; occasional Gulf of Oman. Vagrant Gulf of Aqaba.
Habitat: maritime.

Great Shearwater *Puffinus gravis*

Identification: 46 cm (wing-span 105 cm). See PMH.
Status: vagrant Lebanon, Algeria, Morocco (but no doubt regular in autumn in Atlantic west of Morocco).
Habitat: maritime.

Wedge-tailed Shearwater *Puffinus pacificus*
Illustration p. 16

Identification: 43 cm (wing-span 100 cm). Sexes alike. Fairly large, *sooty-brown* shearwater with *dark grey bill, pale flesh legs* and longish tail (though not obviously so) which shows wedge-shaped tip when seen well. Lacks pale panel on upperwing though pale bands may show across coverts in worn plumage. Compared to similar-sized and -plumaged Sooty, Wedge-tailed has longer tail, broader wings and more buoyant flight with wings curved down and held well forward when soaring. Typically, in windy conditions Wedge-tailed's *flight is erratic, almost dancing, often changing direction to circle back and soar up in low arcs* over waves with occasional bursts of wing-beats which are slower than those of Sooty. Differs from Jouanin's Petrel in noticeably larger size, longer grey bill (black in Jouanin's), and pale feet (dark in Jouanin's) and flight; from Sooty by longer tail, broader wings, flight, and all-dark underwing (pale lining in Sooty); from very similar Flesh-footed (which see) by broader-based wings, slightly longer tail, grey (not pale) bill, all-dark underwing and flight. Light phase (which has white underparts) occurring in Pacific never recorded in Arabian waters.
Status: vagrant or scarce (perhaps sometimes overlooked) Gulf of Oman, Arabian Sea and S Red Sea. Range includes Indian Ocean.
Habitat: maritime.

Sooty Shearwater *Puffinus griseus*

Identification: 41 cm (wing-span 100 cm). See PMH.
Status: autumn passage off Atlantic coast of Morocco; scarce but regular in spring N Red Sea and Gulf of Aqaba. Vagrant S and E Mediterranean and Oman.
Habitat: maritime.

Manx Shearwater *Puffinus puffinus*

Identification: 30–35 cm (wing-span 82 cm). See PMH.
Status: see map. Migrant or dispersive, occurring on passage or in winter in Atlantic off Morocco, Black Sea, widely in Mediterranean, and throughout the year in Bosphorus region. Vagrant Gulf of Suez.
Habitat: maritime. Nests colonially in burrows and holes or crevices under rocks, coastal or in mountains.

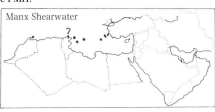

Little Shearwater *Puffinus assimilis*   Illustration p. 16

Identification: 27 cm (wing-span 62 cm). See PMH. Sexes alike. Superficially like a small Manx Shearwater, being black above and white below, but at once recognisable by shorter wings, more *rapid wing-beats, white sides of face* extending above eye (which can make whole head appear white, especially at a distance), and *white on undertail-coverts extending onto sides of rump*; these features give the bird a Puffin-like appearance. At close range upperwing of at least some birds in autumn shows silvery-grey secondaries and, when observed against strong sunlight, whole of upperwing may appear silvery. Flight varies according to conditions; in relatively *calm weather wing-beats are fairly shallow, rapid and fluttering*, interspersed with short, flat glides low over water with little banking. In strong winds periods of gliding are longer, with the bird rising and banking several metres above water, in typical shearwater manner. In characteristic feeding flight the bird patters over sea surface with wings outstretched.
Status: in winter in Atlantic off Morocco, occurring inshore as a vagrant. (Breeds on rocky coasts of the E Atlantic Islands).
Habitat: maritime.

Audubon's Shearwater *Puffinus lherminieri*   Illustration p. 16

Identification: 30 cm (wing-span 70 cm). Sexes alike. Text covers Persian race (*persicus*), the only one recorded in region. Small 'black and white' shearwater, very *similar in size and plumage to Little* (which see) from which separable with difficulty by *browner upperparts* (looking black at distance) *extending on head to just below eye* (thus lacking white sides of face of Little), *duskier white underwing with broad dark margins* (white underwing with narrow dark margins in Little) and *flesh-coloured legs* (grey in Little). Fast wing-beats interspersed with short banking glides, often rising in low arcs above waves, similar to Little but not so fast. Gregarious at fish-shoals, often with boobies, gulls and terns.
Status: see map. Breeding grounds recently discovered, more may yet be found. Recorded at most times of year in Arabian Gulf, Arabian Sea and S Red Sea. In Oman locally common in north in autumn and spring and concentrates off south coast in summer.
Habitat: maritime. Nests colonially in holes and crevices of rocks.

Wilson's Petrel *Oceanites oceanicus*

Identification: 18 cm (wing-span 40 cm). See PMH.
Status: an Antarctic species, 'wintering' (in our summer) in N Hemisphere. Rarely seen from land but recorded Atlantic off Morocco, W Mediterranean, S Red Sea (occasionally north to Egypt and Gulf of Aqaba), off coasts of S and E Arabia, S Iran.
Habitat: maritime.

Black-bellied Petrel *Fregetta tropica*   Illustration p. 16

Identification: 20 cm (wing-span 45 cm). Sexes alike. Small square-tailed sooty-black petrel with feet projecting beyond tail, white rump and *characteristic white markings to underwing and underbody*. Upper breast black with black line running down centre of belly to black undertail-coverts and separating *large white flank-patches* (but band is often difficult to observe and whole belly can look white.) *Underwing-coverts largely white and a noticeable field mark*; upperwing shows obscure pale band on coverts. Erratic flight, zig-zagging from side to side but generally close to water. *Similar to White-bellied Petrel, which see for differences.*
Status: regular in summer in central Arabian Sea, but only occasionally reaches coastal waters, e.g. off Oman.
Habitat: maritime.

White-bellied Petrel   Madeiran Petrel

White-bellied Petrel *Fregetta grallaria*

Identification: 19 cm (wing-span 46 cm). Sexes alike. Resembles Black-bellied Petrel, having sooty upperparts with broad white rump-patch above square tail, and wing-coverts rather paler than flight-feathers, the pale tips of primary coverts producing a diagonal wing-bar; underparts from breast forward normally all-black, as are undertail-coverts and tail, but *belly and flanks white, linking with white underwing-coverts*; underside of flight-feathers and narrow leading edge of underwing black. Thought to differ, usually, from Black-bellied in having *black chin* (not white); *white belly* (without Black-bellied's longitudinal black band running between legs and joining more extensive undertail-coverts to more extensive black breast); mantle slightly paler and *wing-bar more prominent* and, in the hand, tarsus measuring up to 37 mm (Black-bellied not less than 39 mm).

Note: the authors do not themselves know either White-bellied or Black-bellied Petrels and have read, confusedly, that they are surprisingly difficult to differentiate in life; that most may be safely separable at sea; that Black-bellied and White-bellied are 'sibling species' but that their 'taxonomy is complex'; that both birds may have two colour-phases but of uncertain validity, including (rarely) Black-bellied with wholly white bellies and White-bellied which are entirely black except on rump; and that exceptionally there are intermediates. So the authors feel unable to do more than offer the above notes without endorsement and with their good wishes to those making use of them.
Status: unconfirmed records from Oman. Range includes S Indian Ocean.
Habitat: maritime.

20

White-faced (Frigate) Petrel *Pelagodroma marina*   Illustration p. 16

Identification: 20 cm (wing-span 40 cm). Sexes alike. Highly pelagic, being rarely observed near land or boats. Unmistakable small petrel with patterned blackish-brown upperparts, *white underparts* and *underwing-coverts, white forehead and cheeks with dark patch through eye*. Closer views reveal that crown, nape and eye-patch are blackish, back and upperwing-coverts brownish (with paler rear-coverts) contrasting with blackish flight feathers, and *rump grey contrasting slightly with blackish tail*. Flight strong and erratic with much banking, though also fast and low over sea; long legs, which project slightly beyond tail, are occasionally dangled. Often in small parties.
Status: Atlantic off Morocco, presumably mainly in summer, but hardly seen in coastal waters. Also regular May-July off SE coast of Arabia.
Habitat: maritime.

Storm Petrel *Hydrobates pelagicus*

Identification: 15 cm (wing-span 38 cm). See PMH.
Status: see map. Probably resident in Mediterranean, dispersing from colonies in autumn; occurs then in E Mediterranean and stragglers enter Black Sea. Also passage/winter in Atlantic off Morocco where may also breed. Vagrant Red Sea.
Habitat: maritime, pelagic. Nests colonially under rocks, in stone walls, etc, on islands.

Leach's Petrel *Oceanodroma leucorhoa*

Identification: 20 cm (wing-span 46 cm). See PMH.
Status: passage in Atlantic off Morocco. Vagrant Morocco, Israel, Arabian Gulf.
Habitat: maritime, pelagic.

Swinhoe's Petrel *Oceanodroma monorhis*   Illustration p. 16

Identification: 20 cm (wing-span 45 cm). Sexes alike. A *dark-rumped* petrel, slightly smaller than Leach's. *Plumage all-sooty*, including underwing, with pale brownish panel along rear upperwing-coverts. Shallow fork in tail is usually difficult to see. As long-winged as Leach's and with distinctive bounding and swooping flight, at times somewhat resembling a small Black Tern.
Status: vagrant Gulf of Aqaba and Arabian Sea in summer. Regular N Indian Ocean.
Habitat: maritime.

Madeiran Petrel *Oceanodroma castro*

Identification: 20 cm (wing-span 45 cm). Sexes alike. Difficult to identify. Long-winged, slightly fork-tailed petrel, similar in size and shape to Leach's (see PMH) but with slightly shorter, broader wings. *Sooty above and below with clear-cut white rump* which extends onto lower flanks and sides of undertail-coverts, and indistinct brownish panel on the upperwing-coverts. Differs from Leach's in having *less distinct panel on wing-coverts, less forked tail* (very difficult to observe in the field), and *cleaner, more square-cut white rump* lacking central grey feathers of Leach's (though these are very difficult to observe in field). Storm and Wilson's Petrels smaller and plumper with shorter wings; they have square-ended (not forked) tails; Storm Petrel has white on underwing-coverts and Wilson's feet project beyond tail. Buoyant flight of Madeiran resembles Leach's but is *much steadier, with quick beats interspersed with shearwater-like glides*.
Status: occurs in Atlantic off Morocco though not recorded from mainland. Has been claimed Gulf of Aqaba.
Habitat: maritime.

Red-billed Tropicbird *Phaethon aethereus* Plate 1

Identification: 48 cm, with 50 cm tail (wing-span 105 cm). Sexes similar. Unmistakable, predominantly *white*, plump-bodied, seabird with *long white tail-streamers in adult* (those of male longer than female) *and conspicuous red bill*. White plumage is relieved by black stripe through eye, *narrow black barring on upperparts and coverts, and black on outer primaries* and inner secondaries. Juvenile similar to adult but tail, which is black-tipped, lacks streamers; it has denser barring on upperparts, yellow bill and black eye-stripe extending over hind-neck. Direct, fast, pigeon-like flight, interspersed with glides on horizontally-held wings, usually well above waves, is characteristic.

Voice: rapid, short, shrill rasping notes.

Status: see map. Resident (including Oman), with some dispersal in winter over Red Sea and seas surrounding S Arabia; has reached Gulf of Aqaba.

Habitat: maritime, mainly pelagic. Nests in rocky crevices, from shore level to cliffs well inland.

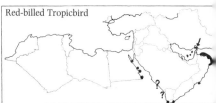

Red-billed Tropicbird

Red-footed Booby *Sula sula* Plate 1

Identification: 75 cm (wing-span 145 cm). Sexes alike. Rather slender booby, smaller than Masked. Adults have white and brown morphs; those most likely to be seen as vagrants in region are from Indian Ocean population which, in adult plumage, has *all white tail*; all other boobies likely to occur in the region, except adult Gannet, have black or blackish tails. White morph superficially resembles adult Masked Booby, being white with black trailing edge to wings; differs in *narrower black on secondaries and none on scapulars* (longest scapulars tipped black in Masked), *black carpal patch on underwing*, yellowish sheen on head and neck (no black mask), *red feet*, pale blue bill with rose-coloured base (yellow to dull green in adult Masked) and *all-white tail* (black in Masked). Brown morph is grey-brown, *including whole of underwing with* (in western Indian Ocean birds) *white tails*, and variably pale scapulars, head, neck and underparts. Bill and legs as white morph. Juvenile greyish-brown with darker primaries and head slightly darker than throat and upper breast, though juvenile of white morph has paler head, neck, rump and tail, sometimes distinctly so; bill blackish and legs yellowish-grey. Birds in intermediate/transitional plumages have patchy underwing without definite pattern, and tail only partially white. Great care needed with any bird that does not show a white tail.

Status: vagrant Arabian Sea and Red Sea. Range includes Indian Ocean.

Habitat: maritime.

Masked (Blue-faced) Booby *Sula dactylatra* Plate 1

Identification: 80 cm (wing-span 150 cm). Sexes alike. Slightly smaller than Gannet which adult superficially resembles. Adult is *all white with broad black trailing edge of wings* (above and below), *blackish tail, black 'face'* and stout orange-yellow to dull greenish bill; feet dark grey to olive or orange. (White morph of Red-footed Booby is smaller, lacks black face and black on longest scapulars, but has black carpal patch on underwing). Told from Gannet by black face-mask, black trailing edge to wing (secondaries white in adult Gannet), and *lack of any yellow on head*, and blackish, not white, tail. Juvenile has brown head and neck separated from paler brown back by variable *narrow white collar*. Upperwing brown with darker flight-feathers; underwing striped: white underwing-coverts with obvious black central band and black flight-feathers; bill yellowish-brown. As bird grows older, black band on underwing-coverts is reduced, white neck collar broadens and white starts to appear on upperwing-coverts, forming whitish mid-wing panel. Juvenile differs from Brown Booby, which it superficially resembles, by two-tone brown on upperwing (dark uniform brown in Brown Booby), *white neck collar, more restricted brown hood above pure white underparts and longer blackish band on white underwing-coverts*.

Status: see map. Mainly resident. Occasional visitor elsewhere off coasts of S and E Arabia including S Red Sea. Also reported from Morocco.
Habitat: maritime. Nests colonially on ground on sand or rocks.

Masked Booby

Brown Booby *Sula leucogaster* — Plate 1

Identification: 70 cm (wing-span 140 cm). Sexes alike. Similar in proportions to Gannet but smaller with proportionally longer tail. Recognised from that and other boobies by being entirely *uniform brown above* and brown and white below. Adult has *head, neck, upper breast and whole of upperparts dark brown*, whilst rest of underparts and underwing-coverts are conspicuously *white*, the latter bordered by brown flight-feathers and fore-coverts. The *pale greenish or greenish-yellow bill* can look silvery against dark head even at considerable range; feet green to yellow. Juvenile, like adult, entirely brown above (lacks white rump-crescent of young Gannet), brown on head, neck and clear-cut upper breast (though less sharply than in adult) while remainder of underparts mottled buffish-brown. The white on underwing-coverts appears at early age, though variable and scarcely visible in some birds. Flight similar to Gannet's but when gliding holds wing horizontally, with primaries slightly downward curved and nearly always lacks characteristic tilt from side to side of its larger relative. Catches fish by diving, with wings folded, from a height, often at a shallow angle. For separation of juvenile Brown from juvenile Masked, see latter species.
Voice: call raucous and high-pitched, usually heard only on breeding grounds.
Status: see map. Resident and dispersive, occurring widely in Red Sea and off S Arabia. Vagrant N Oman and Arabian Gulf.
Habitat: maritime, largely coastal. Nests, generally in colonies, on ground or rocks.

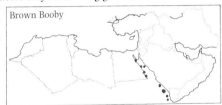
Brown Booby

Gannet *Sula bassana*

Identification: 92 cm (wing-span 170 cm). See PMH.
Status: passage or winter visitor off Atlantic coast of Morocco and W and central Mediterranean, often reaching E Mediterranean coasts.
Habitat: maritime.

Cormorant *Phalacrocorax carbo* — Plate 2

Identification: 90 cm. See PMH. Adult of the race *maroccanus* (of NW Africa) similar to European races but with snow-white, clean-cut underparts to mid-breast. Upperparts, lower breast and belly black, being glossy above and has white thigh-patch in breeding season. Juvenile off-white below, merging into dark on lower belly, the white cheeks extend above eye, and upperparts are dark greyish-black, often with pale grey on crown and hind-neck and paler on wing-coverts. On water or in flight the combination of white below and dark above creates diver-like appearance especially in juvenile.
Status: see map. Has bred Tunisia. Winters coasts of Atlantic, Mediterranean, N Red Sea, Arabian Gulf, Gulf and coasts of Oman, also Black and Caspian Seas. Occasionally inland in parts of Arabia. Vagrant Jordan, S Red Sea.
Habitat: mainly coastal but some inland on passage and inland breeding in tree colonies in Turkey.

Cormorant

23

Shag *Phalacrocorax aristotelis*   Plate 2

Identification: 70–80 cm. See PMH. In the region only the Mediterranean race *desmarestii* occurs, juvenile of which has whitish underparts. Separated from young Cormorant by more slender, less hooked bill, steeper forehead, slimmer neck, dark thigh patch and pale brownish upperwing-coverts contrasting with dark flight-feathers (juvenile Cormorant lacks contrasting thigh patches and has uniform dark upperwings).

Status: see map. Resident, with limited dispersal. Vagrant SE Mediterranean, Gulf of Suez and Iraq.

Habitat: maritime, frequenting rocky coasts and islands with steep cliffs and sea caves; in winter occasionally inland. Breeds colonially (sometimes singly) on rocky ledges and among boulders.

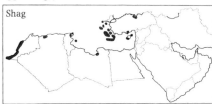

Socotra Cormorant *Phalacrocorax nigrogularis*   Plate 2

Identification: 76–84 cm. Sexes alike. Smaller than Cormorant, resembling Shag in behaviour and structure though confusion unlikely because geographically separated. Non-breeding plumage *all brownish-black with bronze-green wings and back.* Close views show that face and throat are brownish-black, thus *lacking white face and chin-patch of Cormorant in adult plumage.* Slim, Shag-like bill blackish-grey (greyish-yellow in Cormorant) with green at base of lower mandible. In more glossy breeding plumage has *white streak behind eye, fine white flecks on neck and whitish hair-like streaks on rump,* all features not shown by Cormorant which is further separated by white thigh-patch in breeding plumage. Immature grey-brown above, feathers fringed paler, paler brownish-white below with dark spotting on breast; in juvenile pale fringes to feathers on upperparts are reduced and dark spotting on breast absent or less obvious. Identification of juvenile Socotra from juvenile Cormorant can be difficult but *Socotra smaller and slimmer with finer grey bill, has white fringes on upper wing-coverts and dark spotting on underparts* (except in very young birds). Holds out wings to dry; often congregates in large flocks in and out of breeding season.

Status: see map. Resident and dispersive in Arabian Gulf and off SE coasts of Arabia to S Red Sea. Vagrant N Red Sea.

Habitat: maritime, largely coastal. Breed in large tightly packed colonies among boulders on rocky islands or on sand or gravel on level ground.

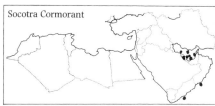

Pygmy Cormorant *Phalacrocorax pygmeus*   Plate 2

Identification: 48 cm. Sexes alike. *Small cormorant* (similar in body size to crow) with *short neck, rounded head, stubby bill and rather long tail.* In breeding season, body glossy black, spotted inconspicuously with white, with *bronze head and neck* and more evident greyish speckling on back and wing-coverts; dark bill. In winter white spots lost and throat becomes white. Juvenile has white chin, brown throat and breast, whitish belly and yellowish bill. Rather short neck, round head and long tail (appearing like protruding legs) give a Coot-like appearance in flight. Separated from Long-tailed by smaller size and *shorter, more stubby bill.*

Voice: grunts and quacks when in nesting colonies.

Status: see map. Partial migrant, dispersing locally in winter; rarely Israel. Vagrant Lebanon, Tunisia.

Habitat: large freshwater lakes and rivers with extensive reed marsh and often inundated trees. Nests in trees, bushes and reeds in marsh or water.

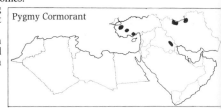

Long-tailed (Reed) **Cormorant** *Phalacrocorax africanus*   Plate 2

Identification: 50–55 cm. Sexes alike. Size between Shag and Pygmy Cormorant (closer to latter), but separated geographically. Adult in breeding plumage (unlikely in the region) blackish, with green gloss on head (which has short crest on forehead and fine white flecks on sides and a *silvery-grey gloss on upperparts and particularly on wing-coverts* (which look scaly at close range). *Bill orange-red,* facial skin yellowish and iris reddish. In non-breeding and immature plumage lacks crest, green gloss and whitish flecks on head; upperparts dull dark brown (adult winter) to brownish (immature), foreneck brownish-white, rest of underparts pale brownish to white, flanks blackish (underparts whitest in immature); *wing-coverts still silvery-grey with dark blotches* (less pronounced in immature) creating *pale patch in centre of upperwing-coverts in flight;* immature has yellowish bill, non-breeding adults usually with some orange-red. Separated from Cormorant by *much smaller size, distinctly longer tail* (which, in flight, *protrudes much more behind wings than in Cormorant*) and *pale patch on upperwing-coverts.* Long-tailed and Pygmy Cormorants are each long-tailed and size difference not very obvious; Long-tailed has pale upperwing-patch and longer, less stubby bill, often with some orange-red on it. (smaller Pygmy has dark bill in adult, brownish to yellowish in immature/non-breeding adult, and iris brown, never reddish as in adult Long-tailed).
Status: formerly bred Egypt but no records since 1900.
Habitat: creeks, rivers, lakes, sometimes far inland; also sea coasts.

Darter *Anhinga rufa*   Plate 2

Identification: 95 cm. Sexes alike. Similar to Cormorant but slimmer, *long-tailed and with incredibly thin, kinked, snake-like neck,* making it quite unmistakable. Head and neck chestnut-brown (male with black crown), paler, greyish on foreneck with pale line down side, more noticeable in male. Upperparts sooty brown, wings and tail black with *long, silvery feathers on coverts and scapulars,* making back (and wings, if held out) pale-streaked. Underparts black. Bill dagger-like, yellow-orange. Immature paler and browner, palest (buff) on neck and underparts. Swims, often with only thin neck showing; this is lowered forward when it sinks to dive. Often sits on bank or tree with wings outspread. In flight shows medium-broad wings, long slightly fanned tail, and slightly kinked neck held forward (very thin and pale neck can be difficult to see at a distance); wing-beats are interspered with short glides and at a glance can recall large *Accipiter.* Frequently soars, often high.
Voice: grunts or rattles at nest, otherwise mainly silent.
Status: see map. Formerly bred S Turkey and N Israel. Mainly resident but a few recent winter records SW Iran.
Habitat: large, biologically-rich lakes and swamps, usually with emergent vegetation and scattered trees. Nests colonially in low trees, bushes and sometimes reeds, often among cormorants and herons.

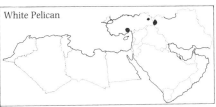

White Pelican *Pelecanus onocrotalus*

Identification: 140–175 cm. See PMH.
Status: see map. Partial migrant, some wintering from S Turkey east to Iran and south to Nile valley; scarce in W Arabia more irregular in east. Vagrant Jordan and NW Africa.
Habitat: large inland waters, marshes and shallow coastal lagoons. Nests colonially among reeds.

Pink-backed Pelican, breeding adult (left), non-breeding adult (centre), juvenile (right)

White Pelican, breeding adult (left), juvenile (right)

Dalmatian Pelican, breeding adult

Drawings by S. Christensen

Dalmatian Pelican *Pelecanus crispus*

Identification: 160–180 cm. See PMH.
Status: see map. Partial migrant, some wintering W & S Turkey, Iraq, S Caspian, S Iran, Egypt. Occasional Israel. Vagrant Gulf States, Cyprus.
Habitat: as White Pelican. Nest also similar though sometimes uses trees.

Pink-backed Pelican *Pelecanus rufescens*   Plate 2

Identification: 130 cm (wing-span 265–290 cm). Sexes alike. Adult smaller, duller and greyer than other pelicans, with darkish crest on nape. Face and underparts greyish-white, upperparts pale greyish; in flight *shows strong pink tinge to flanks, underwing-coverts, back and rump,* but pink usually lost when not breeding, these parts becoming whiter. From above, has dark brown primaries, paler secondaries, pale greyish wing-coverts and ash-grey tail. From below, flight-feathers *grey, bleaching paler, separated from whitish-grey or pink-rufous underwing-coverts by whitish translucent band along centre of wing.* Immature has pale grey-brown neck, brownish upperparts and tail, and whitish underparts. In flight, *broad white rump narrows into white band up centre of mantle,* almost to base of neck, framed by brownish shoulders and upperwing-coverts. From below underwing shows *paler, dull silvery-grey flight-feathers* (particularly primaries) than adult; forewing whitish-grey separated from flight-feathers by whitish band. Main points for distinguishing Pink-backed, White and Dalmatian in flight illustrated above. *Bill generally paler than White or Dalmatian's;* adult in breeding season has warm yellowish bill and orange-yellow pouch (White and Dalmatian adults have more or less dark bluish bill in contrast with orangy pouch); *out of breeding season and in younger birds bill whitish to greyish-flesh* and pouch pale fleshy-yellow. Legs fleshy, or whitish-pink, even rosy-pink during breeding, (White had fleshy or rufous-yellow, Dalmatian lead-grey legs). At close range shows dark eye, set in whitish surround of bare skin, with black spot in front of and often behind eye, the spot sometimes extending as blackish line to crest (White Pelican also has darkish eye but not whitish eye-ring or black spot in front of eye; Dalmatian has whitish eye, greyish eye-ring, but no black spot). Where feathers on forehead meet culmen they end in concave line (like Dalmatian, but pointed in White).

Voice: clacking guttural conversations; generally silent away from breeding colonies.

Status: see map. Resident augmented by summer visitors SW Arabia. Occurs regularly in area enclosed by dotted line. Regular S Egypt. Vagrant Israel.

Habitat: coasts, lagoons, rivers and inland lakes, resting on piers, reefs, sandbanks. Nests in mangroves and on sandy islands.

Pink-backed Pelican

Lesser Frigatebird *Fregata ariel*

(also Great Frigatebird *F. minor*)

Identification: 75 cm (wing-span 185 cm). Sexes differ, female larger. Frigatebirds have *long narrow wings, long deeply-forked tail* (often held closed, looking pointed), *short neck and long slim hooked bill*. Impressive soaring and gliding with manoeuvrable tail, and only occasional deep wing-beats. Very difficult to separate in juvenile and immature plumages (when most likely to occur in the region) from Great Frigatebird *Fregetta minor* which could also occur. However, at all ages, separated by *small white 'spur' on axillaries* (armpits), which is *absent in Great Frigatebird*. Adult male blackish with *narrow white breast-sides extending onto axillaries*; scarlet throat-patch inconspicuous except in courtship. Female blackish-brown above with narrow brownish-white collar and conspicuous pale bar across upperwing-coverts; underparts blackish, with *white breast which projects onto armpits and towards rear in prongs each side of belly*. Juvenile blackish-brown above with pale bar on wing-coverts; head, including chin and throat, tawny russet; white upper breast extends onto armpits; has complete or partial dark band across fore-neck; older juveniles have upper head greyish-white washed russet, chin and throat washed deeper russet, and belly mottled black and white; black band across fore-neck disappears. Immature male develops blackish head, and a dark longitudinal

Great Frigatebird, adult male (top), adult female (centre), juvenile (bottom)

Lesser Frigatebird, adult male (top), adult female (centre), juvenile (bottom)

stripe gradually appears on white upper breast dividing it into two triangular breast-side patches, extending onto armpits; later, upper breast becomes black-spotted. Immature female largely white-breasted and dark-bellied, later terminating in inverted V on lower breast; russet chin and throat slowly become darker.

Great Frigatebird characters: juvenile Great Frigatebird from Indian Ocean lacks white armpits, also differs from Lesser by having largely yellowish-white head and underparts, broken only by diffuse dark breast-band (Lesser has darker belly and russet throat); later, breast-band disappears and underparts, except flanks and ventral area, white. Immature male has white head (or some tawny on throat) and blackish mottling on white belly; with increasing age, head and throat become dusky, white breast spotted blackish and belly darker; sub-adult nearly all dark below except for mottled white horseshoe mark on belly (absent in Lesser). Adult male all-blackish below *without narrow white breast-side and axillary patch*, and usually with pronounced pale bar across wing-coverts. Immature female resembles older juvenile (*white from chin to dark ventral area*) but with increasing age develops blackish band across breast, dividing white upper breast from white belly (Lesser has brown-mottled throat, dark grey-brown later, and belly largely dark); sub-adult female like adult (white chin to breast, remaining underparts blackish) but still has a dark-mottled whitish belly-patch (Lesser *is dark-headed and dark-bellied*); adult female has pale bar across upperwing-coverts (like Lesser) but lacks brownish-white hind-neck collar.

Status: Lesser Frigatebird vagrant Oman. Range includes Indian Ocean. In addition unidentified frigatebirds (*Fregata* sp) have been seen off Sinai and Oman.

Habitat: maritime.

Bittern *Botaurus stellaris*

Identification: 76 cm. See PMH.

Status: see map. Partial migrant. In winter occurs in breeding areas, more widely in Turkey and Iran, south to Egypt, Iraq and Red Sea coast of Saudi Arabia; occasionally in Gulf States, Oman and Yemen. Vagrant Cyprus, Syria, Jordan.

Habitat: lowland swamps with dense reeds or other vegetation. Nests in reed-beds.

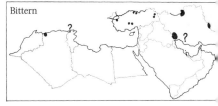

Little Bittern *Ixobrychus minutus*

Identification: 36 cm. See PMH.

Status: see map. Has bred Algeria, Tunisia. Mainly summer visitor; in winter in Nile valley, occasionally Oman. Passage includes SW Arabia.

Habitat: overgrown river banks, backwaters, ponds, wooded swamps, reed-beds, oases. Nests near water, occasionally in small scattered groups.

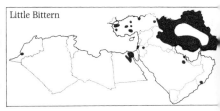

Night Heron *Nycticorax nycticorax*

Identification: 60 cm. See PMH.

Status: see map. Formerly bred Tunisia. Mainly summer visitor, with widespread passage and some wintering in many parts of area including Oman but few N Africa (except Nile) and S Arabia.

Habitat: dense tangled swamps, overgrown river banks, marshes with trees, feeding at dusk in more open marshes. Nests colonially, often with allied species in thickets, trees, locally also in reed-beds.

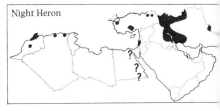

28

Green Heron *Butorides striatus*   Plate 4

Identification: 40–46 cm. Sexes alike. *Small, thick-set and hunch-backed dark heron with mouldy olive-washed appearance.* Size as Squacco Heron which it also recalls somewhat in mode of flight. Adult has black crown and elongated nape-plumes, *bluish-grey upperparts,* wings a little darker blue-grey *with buff fringes to coverts* and blackish tail; given good views upperparts show olive gloss. Underparts pale greyish, with dark central line on lower throat, dark moustachial streak and yellowish patch on lores giving marked facial pattern. Legs and feet rosy-red or pinkish, protruding just beyond tail in flight. Immature brownish above with whitish spots on tips of wing-coverts; neck and upperbreast distinctly streaked dark brown and white; legs yellowish-green. Small size and dark appearance (in flight with *dark upper-wings*) prevent confusion with other small herons in the region; streaked immature may recall young Night Heron but Green is distinctly smaller, and *mantle lacks white spots of most young Night Herons.* Solitary and furtive, often skulking during day; most active at dusk. If disturbed, creeps into inconspicuous horizontal crouching position; flight usually low with fast wing-beats.
Voice: normally silent. Alarm note 'chook-chook-chook'.
Status: see map. Mainly resident but apparently some passage Oman. Recorded regularly in S Nile valley.
Habitat: coastal mud-flats, especially with mangroves; also reefs and, inland, streams, lakes and swamps with dense cover. Nests in bush or tree.

Squacco Heron *Ardeola ralloides*

Identification: 46 cm. See PMH.
Status: see map. Has bred Tunisia. Mainly summer visitor. Some winter Nile delta and valley, SE Iraq to Oman; a few W Morocco. On passage widely, including Arabia.
Habitat: marshes, lagoons, swamps providing some cover. Nests colonially, often with allied species, in thickets, trees, also reeds.

Indian Pond Heron *Ardeola grayii*   Plate 4

Identification: 45 cm. Sexes alike. Closely resembles Squacco Heron, from which only safely separated in breeding plumage when adult has *unstreaked* yellow-white or buff-brown *head, hind-neck and elongated nape feathers* (streaked blackish in adult Squacco) and *much darker, maroon (but blackish-looking) long feathers on back* (paler, wine-red in adult Squacco). Breast buff (pale ochre in Squacco) and rest of plumage, including wings, white. Adult in winter lacks head plumes, and long feathers of neck and back much reduced; the back is dark earthy-brown or plumbeous buff-grey, but head (finely), neck and upper breast (boldly) streaked dark brown. Immature resembles adult in winter but outer primaries tipped dusky brownish. Legs dull greenish to yellow (some breeding birds have red legs). Immature and adult in winter very difficult to separate from similar Squacco; usually, Pond has clearly the darker back (but only apparent when the two are together). In flight shows strikingly white wings, rump and tail as Squacco, which it also resembles in behaviour.
Voice: sometimes a hard croak when flushed. At breeding colonies a conversational 'wa-koo', mixed with short croaks.
Status: see map. Apparently mainly resident; also regular visitor in very small numbers to Oman/E Arabia.
Habitat: frequents both fresh and saltwater especially with muddy margins and dense cover; rivers, lakes, small pools and man-grove swamps. Roosts and nests in trees.

Cattle Egret *Bubulcus ibis*

Identification: 50 cm. See PMH.

Status: see map. Mainly resident or dispersive but mostly summer visitor to S Caspian. Passage (with some wintering) Arabia, fewer in east and non-breeders may summer, eg, Tunisia and S Oman. Irregular Libya.

Habitat: less aquatic and less coastal than most herons. Commonly among feeding cattle in fields, marshes, or in dry open country. Nests colonially, often with allied species, in reedbeds, bushes or trees, over water or on dry land.

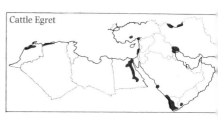

Western Reef Heron *Egretta gularis*   Plate 3

Identification: 55–66 cm. Sexes alike. Occurs in white, dark and rare intermediate phases. Slender egret, *slightly larger than Little, with longer, slightly thicker legs and bill. Dark phase is slate-grey* with *well-defined white chin and throat,* and sometimes a few white flight-feathers. In breeding season all phases have elongated plumes on head, breast and scapulars. West African race *gularis* has darkest bill and legs, ranging from brownish (non-breeding) to very dark brown (but black during courtship). Eastern race *schistacea* (Red Sea eastwards) has paler bill and legs; legs range from pale brown or greenish (non-breeding) to darker brown, flecked orange (during courtship); bill pale brown or yellowish (all seasons) but highly variable and usually flushed orange or red during courtship; toes green to dull yellow, flushed reddish or orange during courtship. Juvenile white phase Reef differs from adult in having a few or many grey flecks in plumage. Juvenile dark phase is paler grey than adult with white belly and patches on breast and forecrown; like adult can show some white feathers in wing. Separation of white phase from Little Egret sometimes difficult. Important features are *longer, slightly thicker bill with just perceptible droop* (straight in Little), *yellowish bill of eastern birds* (black in Little but rarely yellowish-horn in young birds), *paler brownish-green legs* (black in Little but rarely dark greenish-brown). Also Reef has *greenish-yellow or yellow facial skin* (more orange during courtship) while Little has blue-grey facial skin (reddish during courtship). See also Intermediate Egret. Less graceful than Little Egret; typical behaviour when searching for prey is quiet wading, with occasional sudden rushes, when may vigorously flap half-opened wings.

Voice: short throaty croak sometimes heard.

Status: see map. Resident or dispersive; some in non-breeding areas throughout year. The map does not distinguish between breeding and non-breeding range. Occasional Morocco, vagrant Tunisia.

Habitat: almost entirely confined to mangroves and reefs, rock pools and tidal mud-flats; rather coast-bound but can straggle far inland. Nests colonially in mangrove bushes or rocks.

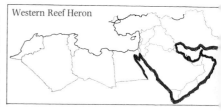

Little Egret *Egretta garzetta*

Identification: 56 cm. See PMH.

Status: see map. Summer visitor Turkey (except SW) and N Iran. Breeders elsewhere resident or partial migrants. Also winter visitor to W Morocco, N African coasts and some oases, Nile valley, Iraq marshes, S and SW Iran, Arabian Gulf, Oman and SW Arabian coast and highlands. Occurs widely on passage.

Habitat: marshes, lagoons, swamps. Nests in colonies, often with other herons, in bushes or trees, in wet marsh, swamps, dry open country, sea cliffs and woods.

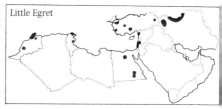

Intermediate Egret

Intermediate (Yellow-billed) **Egret** *Egretta intermedia*

Identification: 62–66 cm. Sexes alike. An all-white egret between Great White and Little in size, though closer to Little. Naked facial skin yellowish; bill yellow to orange-yellow, and in Asian race often with black tip which can be minute. Blackish legs have brownish to greenish-yellow joints and tibia but these colours often hard to see in the field. Not always easily distinguished from Great White without direct comparison though smaller size, less protruding legs (in flight) beyond tail, more s-curved, less kinked neck, and *shorter, rather stouter, bill* help distinguish it. Most conclusive feature is *thin black gape-line which does not extend behind eye* as does the **bold** line in Great White. Long breast-plumes of breeding plumage absent in Great White. From smaller Little Egret and Reef Heron (white phase) by black feet (usually yellowish in the other two), by *relatively shorter bill* which is generally even yellower than Reef Heron's (usually black in Little Egret), and Intermediate never has nape plumes. Much smaller Cattle Egret is far bulkier and lacks grace of *Egretta*-egrets, has heavier jowl, shorter thicker bill and usually entire legs paler.
Voice: generally silent; a loud croaking 'kwark' when alarmed.
Status: vagrant Oman, Jordan. Range includes Africa and India.
Habitat: marshes, mangroves, swamps and coastal flats.

Great White **Egret** *Egretta alba*

Identification: 90 cm. See PMH.
Status: see map. Mainly migratory. In winter in Tunisia and from W Turkey to N Egypt and eastwards to Iran, E Arabia and Oman; passage or vagrant elsewhere in Arabia and N Africa, also Cyprus.
Habitat: moist margins of lakes and rivers, open swamps, lagoons, estuaries. Nests usually in groups in reed-beds, rarely in bushes or trees.

Great White Egret

Black-headed **Heron** *Ardea melanocephala*

Identification: 85 cm. Sexes alike. Slightly smaller than Grey Heron which it recalls in shape. In adult, *crown and hind-neck black with contrasting white throat and upper fore-neck*; lower fore-neck has black and white vermiculations down centre. Wings and tail medium dark grey above with black primaries. Underparts pale grey. Legs blackish; bill pale with grey upper mandible (yellowish in Grey Heron). Juvenile has dark grey crown and hind-neck and whitish

31

Black-headed Heron, juvenile (left), adult (right and in flight)

underparts more or less tinged rusty on fore-neck. Separated from Grey Heron by contrasting black and white head pattern, and, in flight in all plumages, by *white underwing-coverts contrasting with blackish flight-feathers.* Frequents water less than Grey Heron, spending much time on dry ground.

Voice: loud nasal 'kuark'.

Status: vagrant Yemen, Oman. Range Africa.

Habitat: inland and coastal water margins also dry areas.

Grey Heron *Ardea cinerea*

Identification: 92 cm. See PMH.

Status: see map. Has bred Morocco, Tunisia and Egypt. Partial migrant. Widely scattered passage and winter on most coasts, and some inland waters, including Arabia.

Habitat: margins and shallows of a wide range of wetlands and waters including coastal. Nests in colonies in tall trees, reed-beds.

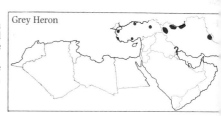

Purple Heron *Ardea purpurea*

Identification: 80 cm. See PMH.

Status: see map. Mainly summer visitor, few wintering Egypt, Iraq and S and E Arabia. Occurs widely on passage, including Arabia and N African oases.

Habitat: swamps, overgrown ditches, dense reed-beds, etc. Breeds in colonies, sometimes with other species, in reed-beds, occasionally in bushes.

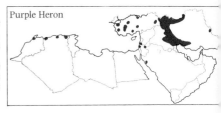

Goliath Heron *Ardea goliath*   Plate 3

Identification: 140–152 cm. Sexes alike. Very large, long-legged and heavy-billed heron, twice size of Purple Heron which it otherwise resembles. In adult, *head, including top, sides and back of neck rich chestnut*, throat whitish. Back, wings and tail medium bluish-grey. On foreneck, two black-spotted lines end in black and white streaked, elongated breast-plumes. Underparts and underwing-coverts deep chestnut-brown. *Young birds are paler rufous-orange on head* merging into grey neck and upperparts which have some rufous edgings to feathers; underparts white with dark streaks. Confuseable only with similar coloured Purple which is much smaller with thinner, snake-like neck; separated by *chestnut top of head* (black crown in adult Purple, black fore-crown in young), *absence of black line across cheeks* (unlike adult Purple, but vague in young Purple) and *bluish-grey bill* (dull yellowish in Purple), *dark legs* (yellow or greenish-yellow in Purple). On the wing, Goliath has entire upperwing even more uniform bluish-grey than in adult Purple (which had slight contrast between blackish flight-feathers and dark blue-grey coverts). Flight-silhouette like Grey or Purple Heron but legs protude more beyond tail, wing-beats are heavier and slower (almost Crane-like) and wings more bowed when gliding. Generally shy but seeks less concealment than Purple; nearly always solitary or in pairs.

Voice: a deep, loud 'arrk' usually uttered when flushed.

Status: see map. Resident and dispersive in Red Sea. Occasionally recorded Nile valley north to Suez. Vagrant Gulf of Aqaba, also reported Oman.

Habitat: reed-beds in rivers, lakes, swamps, and reefs or mud-flats on sea-coasts including small coastal islands. Nests in mangroves, reeds.

Goliath Heron

Hamerkop *Scopus umbretta*   Plate 4

Identification: 60 cm. Sexes alike. An *all-brown* Night Heron-sized bird but with shorter neck, *large 'hammer-shaped' head with backwards-projecting blunt crest on nape*; black bill is long and stout. In flight, plumage has slight orange hue with paler orange-brown bases to primaries and tail which has dark terminal band. Most often seen in small parties, though individuals or pairs not infrequent; may be seen sitting or standing at water's edge in hunched position with head held into shoulders, or feeding by running and jabbing at water with bill; often flicks wings on alighting. In flight almost resembles small eagle with slow wing-beats followed by a glide on very slightly bowed wings.

Voice: far-carrying, laughing cry with rising inflexion.

Status: see map. Resident. Some dispersal and flocking in winter.

Habitat: rivers and streams with stony and muddy banks and islands; shallow pools. In Yemen occurs up to c. 3,000 m, but usually much lower. Bulky roofed nest of sticks and straw in tree or on cliff.

Hamerkop

Yellow-billed Stork, adult (above), juvenile (below)

Yellow-billed Stork *Mycteria ibis*   Plate 4

Identification: 100 cm. Sexes alike. Adult unmistakable having long, *slightly drooping orange-yellow bill*, bare *red face*, white head and body and long orange-red legs; flight and *tail-feathers blackish at all ages*. In breeding plumage, mantle and tips of wing-coverts above and below have crimson-pink tinge. Sub-adults similar but largely sandy-buff with little crimson-pink on underwing-coverts, dirty yellowish bill and duller legs. First-winter, ashy-grey on mantle, head and on neck down to upper breast; rest of underparts dirty whitish; upperwing-coverts greyish with light edges, underwing-coverts brownish. Facial skin greyish to pale orange, bill pale yellowish-grey and legs greyish-brown. Adult resembles White Stork in flight but separated by colour and shape of bill and *black tail*.

Status: vagrant NW Africa, Egypt, Israel and S Turkey. Range Africa.

Habitat: swamps, river and lake margins, sandbanks, coastal mud-flats.

Abdim's Stork, adult (left), Black Stork, adult (right)   Drawings by S. Christensen

Black Stork *Ciconia nigra*

Identification: 97 cm. See PMH.

Status: see map. Summer visitor. Main passage Red Sea-Sinai-Near East, less Morocco, few Tunisia. Few winter SW Arabia, occasionally Egypt, Israel. Vagrant central and E Arabia.

Habitat: wild marshy tracts and damp meadows in forest. Nest in forest tree or on crag.

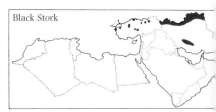

Black Stork

Abdim's Stork *Ciconia abdimii*   Plate 3

Identification: 81 cm. Sexes alike. Resembles small Black Stork but *lower back, rump and inner underwing-coverts white*. Head, neck, breast and rest of upperparts black glossed green, purple and violet. At rest, a *white line sometimes visible above bend of wing*. Bill, slightly shorter than Black Stork's, is greyish-green tipped reddish; dull olive-green legs, comparatively shorter than Black Stork's, have crimson joints and feet; bluish bare skin on cheeks, crimson round eye and on chin and small white spot on forehead. Juvenile resembles adult but browner without gloss, bill dirty flesh-pink, bare skin of cheeks whitish blue and legs fleshy-orange. Often in flocks circling or gliding high in air. Separated from Black Stork by slightly shorter neck, less protruding legs beyond tail, *larger white area on underwing-coverts* (in Black small white axillary-patch framed dark on leading edge of wing), and *conspicuous white lower back and rump* (upperparts all-black in Black Stork). Also in adult by greenish legs and bill.

Status: see map. Has bred S Yemen. Summer visitor. Irregular S Oman.

Habitat: dry plains and semi-deserts, also lower foothills. Nests in scattered colonies in trees and on straw roof-tops.

Woolly-necked Stork *Ciconia episcopus*

Identification: 86 cm. Sexes alike. Black-and-white, not unlike White Stork in size and shape. *Entirely black underwing, upperwing and breast, white woolly neck and small black cap* separate it from other storks. Black parts are glossed violet and blue; bill black merging into dull reddish tip; legs red. In flight, short forked black tail is covered by long stiff white undertail-coverts and bird appears white-tailed; together with white neck, this 'frames' black body and wings to produce characteristic flight-pattern. Immature duller, browner than adult with neck feathers longer and more fluffy. Often stands hunched with bill resting on puffed-out breast. Soars and glides at height like other storks, usually singly or in pairs.

Voice: usually silent away from breeding sites.

Status: vagrant Iran. Range includes Africa and India.

Habitat: flooded grasslands, shallow lakes, river margins, also coastal mud-flats, coral reefs.

Woolly-necked Stork

White Stork *Ciconia ciconia*

Identification: 102 cm. See PMH.

Status: see map. Mainly summer visitor to breeding areas. Conspicuous on passage at W end of Mediterranean, and at E end from Egypt to Turkey and east to Jordan but few Arabia and Libya. Winters S Iraq, SW Iran, SW Arabia, rarely in E Mediterranean countries north to Turkey.

Habitat: marshes, grassy plains, floodlands, arable. Nests on buildings and in trees.

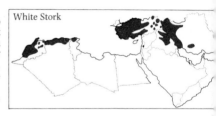

White Stork

Marabou

IW

Marabou *Leptoptilos crumeniferus*

Identification: 152 cm. Sexes alike. Very large stork with *long, conical fleshy bill* and long legs. In adult naked head, neck and inflatable chest pouch are pink-flesh, ruff white. Entire upperparts dark slate, at close range showing variable whitish streaks on greater coverts. *Blackish underwings, which have conspicuous white armpits,* contrast with rusty-white underparts. Juvenile has bare head and neck covered with hair-like down. In flight, looks thick-necked with neck sunk between shoulders, and pouch sometimes hangs down filled with air. Soars and glides, often at great height, like a vulture, on broad flattish wings with curved trailing edge and long deep fingers. Will feed on carcases in competition with vultures.

Voice: generally silent away from breeding colonies.

Status: vagrant Israel. Range Africa.

Habitat: dry savannas, also wetland margins.

Glossy Ibis *Plegadis falcinellus*

Identification: 56 cm. See PMH.

Status: see map. Mainly summer visitor. Widespread on passage, generally in small numbers. Winters in small numbers NW Africa, Iraq, few Arabia, S Nile valley, Israel.

Habitat: marshes, mud-flats. Breeds in colonies, frequently with herons or egrets, in large reed-beds among shallow water, occasionally in bushes or trees.

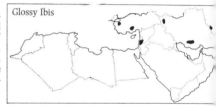

Glossy Ibis

Bald Ibis *Geronticus eremita*   Plate 3

Identification: 75 cm. Sexes alike. Similar in size to Glossy Ibis but *plumper with shorter legs and longer, more drooping tail*. Plumage black, exhibiting an oily green or bronze-green gloss with distinctive *purple-bronze forewing* at rest. Most characteristic features are the long, decurved, dull red bill and *bare reddish vulturine head, fringed by a shaggy mane of long black feathers*. Legs dull red. In flight, wing-beats rather slow, almost goose-like, and frequently interspersed with glides; *legs do not project behind tail* as in Glossy Ibis. First-winter, dull dark brown with glossy green tail and some green feathers in coverts; lacks purple-bronze forewing-patch of adult. Head, which is partly bald, dull pinkish-grey lacking adult's shaggy mane of long nape feathers; bill and legs pinkish-grey.
Voice: gutteral and harsh calls at nesting and roosting ledges.
Status: see map. In Morocco some winter; in Turkey summer visitor only (between about February and August). Vagrant elsewhere (Egypt, Israel, SW Saudi Arabia, S Yemen) except for N Yemen where has occurred on passage and through winter. Rare and declining.
Habitat: rocky, rather arid regions, feeding in flatter grassy or cultivated areas and near rivers. Nests colonially on ledges of inland or sea cliffs.

Sacred Ibis *Threskiornis aethiopicus*   Plate 3

Identification: 65 cm. Sexes alike. Unmistakable. Adult *white with blackish naked head, neck* and *long, decurved bill*, blackish inner secondaries and long scapulars which droop over tail. Relatively short dark legs. Juvenile has feathered head and neck mottled black and white, but throat and fore-neck white; lacks elongated scapulars. In flight, *black tips to all flight-feathers show as a diagnostic, clearly defined narrow band on rear edge of wing* and, at close range, narrow flesh-coloured bar across underwing-coverts. Laboured flight with longish neck out-stretched and legs protruding just beyond tail.
Voice: an occasional harsh croak.
Status: see map. Mainly resident Iraq; regular also in winter in neighbouring part of Iran where has been recorded in summer and might breed. Rare, but apparently regular N Yemen. Vagrant S Yemen, Oman, Bahrain and Kuwait.
Habitat: floodlands, cultivation, margins of wetlands, coastal marshes and mud-flats. Nests colonially in trees, in scrub on islands or on ground.

Spoonbill *Platalea leucorodia*

Identification: 86 cm. See PMH.
Status: see map. Partial migrant but race in Egypt resident. Passage and winter widely in coastal areas of N Africa, E Mediterranean north to SW Turkey (where very few winter); also Nile valley, Red Sea, S Iran; scarce E Arabia. Occasional passage Cyprus.
Habitat: shallow open water, reedy marshes, estuaries. Breeds in colonies in large reed-beds, on small bare islands, and in trees or bushes.

37

African Spoonbill

African Spoonbill *Platalea alba*

Identification: 91 cm. Sexes alike. Resembles Spoonbill in size, white plumage and characteristic spatulate bill, but lacks crest and orange-buff patch on breast of adult in breeding plumage. *Bare skin of face red* and, in adult, *bill grey, edged red* and *legs pink or red*. (Adult Spoonbill has black legs and bill, latter tipped yellow). Juvenile lacks (or has reduced) bare red skin on face, has blackish wing-tips (like young Spoonbill) and bill dusky yellow to horn, which overlaps in colour with pinkish to dirty yellow bill of juvenile Spoonbill; *feet and legs are blackish (legs becoming red with age), whereas young Spoonbill has generally dull fleshy legs*. At a distance, when bill-shape not evident, separated from white herons and egrets by more thick-set, less graceful appearance and *in flight by outstretched, not s-curved neck*, like Spoonbill.
Voice: usually silent but alarm note a double 'arrk-ark'.
Status: vagrant S Oman and S Yemen.
Habitat: shallow lakes, swamps and marshes, also coastal lagoons and estuaries.

Greater Flamingo *Phoenicopterus ruber*

Identification: 130 cm. See PMH.
Status: see map. Partial migrant. Winters in most countries bordering S and E Mediterranean, including Turkey, Cyprus and Syria, also coasts of Red Sea, and S Iraq, S Iran, E and S Arabia.
Habitat: saline shallow coastal lagoons, or flood waters, lakes, mud-flats, etc. Breeds colonially on mud banks, or in shallow water, building mud-heap nest, a few inches above water.

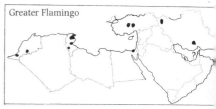

Greater Flamingo

Lesser Flamingo *Phoenicopterus minor*   Plate 3

Identification: 85 cm (standing 100 cm). Sexes almost alike. Adult generally *deeper and brighter rose-pink* than Greater Flamingo, often with deep rose-pink on face bordering the bill (where lacking in Greater) and on the long scapulars (pinkish-white or white in Greater); female and non-breeding birds often have paler colours, more like Greater; safest feature then is Lesser's largely *blackish bill (producing distinctive black-faced look)* with only some dark carmine-red near tip (in Greater, *most of bill much paler rosy-pink* with black confined to tip). At rest, rose-pink wing-coverts largely hidden (as in Greater); in flight shows rose-pink patch across centre of upperwing-coverts, bordered pinkish-white in front and at rear, while in Greater all secondary-coverts are rose-pink (but can bleach to nearly whitish); flight-feathers black. Iris red (lemon-yellow in Greater). Juvenile, greyish-brown with whitish rump and belly (like Greater) but has shorter darker bill (greyish in young Greater). Lesser Flamingo's clearly smaller size often difficult to establish for lone birds, and immatures of both species smaller

than adults. In flight, has shorter trailing legs and comparatively thicker neck than Greater. Highly gregarious.
Voice: similar to Greater's but rather higher.
Status: recorded S Yemen in all months, sometimes in numbers and nest building observed. Vagrant Morocco, Oman and possibly S Iran.
Habitat: brackish, mainly inland, lagoons or salt lakes.

Fulvous Whistling Duck *Dendrocygna bicolor*   Plate 4

Identification: 50 cm. Sexes alike. Fairly large *fulvous-brown* duck *with white rump*, long neck, long legs and upright stance. Head shape distinctive with steep forehead and wedge-shaped bill. In flight, shows *broad, rounded dark wing above and below, being fulvous-chestnut with black flight-feathers, and whitish band on upper-and undertail-coverts*. Black line from nape down hind-neck, whitish patch on lower neck-side streaked blackish, dark bars on brownish back and whitish streaks on flanks; bill grey. Juvenile (this plumage apparently only lasts a few weeks) differs from adult in *creamy-buff head and neck with dark cap*, paler wing and back markings, *dark grey* (not white) *uppertail-coverts* and pale fawn underparts with creamy flanks faintly barred grey. Not shy. Flight rather slow and laboured.
Voice: clear cackling whistle uttered in flight.
Status: vagrant Morocco. Range includes Africa and India.
Habitat: well-vegetated freshwater lakes and rivers, often in the vicinity of trees.

Mute Swan *Cygnus olor*

Identification: 155 cm. See PMH.
Status: see map. Partial migrant. Winters Turkey, N Iran and irregularly in Cyprus. Vagrant south to Egypt, Iraq, E Arabia.
Habitat: large remote lakes, marshes, deltas; in winter also on sheltered sea-coasts. Nests on ground near water, or in reeds etc. in water.

Bewick's Swan *Cygnus columbianus*

Identification: 122 cm. See PMH.
Status: winter visitor N Iran. Vagrant NW Africa, Libya, Israel, Iraq, NW Saudi Arabia and Oman.
Habitat: lowland or coastal wetlands.

Whooper Swan *Cygnus cygnus*

Identification: 155 cm. See PMH.
Status: winter visitor N Iran and Turkey. Vagrant Cyprus, Egypt, NW Africa.
Habitat: sea-coasts, tidal waters, lakes, large rivers.

Bean Goose *Anser fabalis*

Identification: 70–90 cm. See PMH.
Status: occasional in winter Turkey, Iran. Vagrant Cyprus, Egypt, NW Africa.
Habitat: grasslands near fresh water.

White-fronted Goose *Anser albifrons*

Identification: 65–75 cm. See PMH.
Status: winter visitor Turkey, N Syria, Iraq, N and W Iran, a few reaching Egypt, and sometimes Israel, Cyprus, Gulf States and Oman. Vagrant Saudi Arabia, Libya, Tunisia. Occasionally summers W Turkey.
Habitat: grasslands, marshes, estuaries.

Lesser White-fronted Goose *Anser erythropus*

Identification: 55–65 cm. See PMH.
Status: Winter visitor Iraq marshes, N and W Iran. Vagrant Turkey, Kuwait, Egypt.
Habitat: as White-fronted Goose.

Greylag Goose *Anser anser*

Identification: 75–90 cm. See PMH.
Status: see map. Resident and winter visitor, wintering Turkey, Iran, Iraq, south to Jordan, sometimes reaching NW and E Arabia, Israel. Also regular Tunisia and Algeria. Vagrant Libya, Egypt.
Habitat: grasslands, arable fields near coasts, marshes, estuaries. Breeds sociably in marshes, reed-beds, boggy thickets, islets.

Snow Goose *Anser caerulescens*

Identification: 60–70 cm. See PMH.
Status: vagrant Morocco.
Habitat: wetlands.

Barnacle Goose *Branta leucopsis*

Identification: 60–70 cm. See PMH.
Status: vagrant Morocco, Egypt.
Habitat: seldom far inland, preferring saltmarshes, grass fields near estuaries, tidal mud-flats.

Brent Goose *Branta bernicla*

Identification: 55–60 cm. See PMH.
Status: vagrant NW Africa, Egypt, Cyprus.
Habitat: maritime outside breeding season, frequenting coasts and estuaries.

Red-breasted Goose *Branta ruficollis*

Identification: 53–56 cm. See PMH.
Status: winter visitor to Iraq marshes, and very few Turkey. Occasional Iran. Vagrant Cyprus, Israel. (Not recorded Egypt this century.)
Habitat: normally winters on grassy steppes, roosting along sea coast.

Egyptian Goose *Alopochen aegyptiacus*   Plate 4

Identification: 63–73 cm. Sexes alike but male slightly larger; Shelduck-size with *pale stone-grey head, neck and breast* broken with *chestnut eye patches*, variable collar at base of neck, often rusty on hind-neck and crown. Upperparts rufous through to grey; underparts buffish-grey, tinged rusty, often with chestnut patch on breast. *Upper and underwing-coverts white* (but black line on upperwing-coverts) *contrasting with black primaries* and green speculum. Bill pink with black tip, cutting edge and base; longish legs pinkish. In flight, white wing-coverts cause resemblance to Ruddy Shelduck but readily distinguished by palish head and dark eye-patch (Ruddy Shelduck also has wholly orange-chestnut body). Juvenile and immature duller than adult and with darker head; they lack eye- and breast-patches, while bill and legs are yellowish-grey.
Voice: hoarse, rasping 'kraa-kraa-kraa'; can be noisy on wing or ground.
Status: see map. Resident and dispersive Egypt. Occasional in winter Algeria, Tunisia, Cyprus. Vagrant NW Saudi Arabia.

40

Habitat: freshwater marshes and near pools, lakes, rivers with grazing land available. Nests on ground in dense vegetation, hollow tree or sizeable old nest, or hole in bank or cliff-face.

Egyptian Goose

Ruddy Shelduck *Tadorna ferruginea*

Identification: 64 cm. See PMH.
Status: see map. Partial migrant. Winter concentrations in Morocco, Algeria, also Turkey, Iran, Iraq and E Saudi Arabia, some Egypt, scarce or irregular elsewhere in Middle East with stragglers reaching Oman and SW Arabia.
Habitat: much more terrestrial than Shelduck. In winter frequents sandy lake-shores, river banks, fields and even arid steppes. Breeds in holes in dunes, cliffs, old trees and walls.

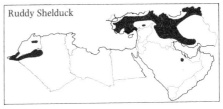

Ruddy Shelduck

Shelduck *Tadorna tadorna*

Identification: 61 cm. See PMH.
Status: see map. Breeding birds mainly resident. Migrants from further north winter widely NW Africa, Egypt, most countries in our Asian area, but in Arabia scarce or irregular south to S and N Yemen.
Habitat: sandy and muddy coasts, and salt lakes and marshes in steppes and semi-desert. Nests in hole in ground or tree or under thick cover.

Shelduck

Spur-winged Goose *Plectropterus gambensis*   Plate 4

Identification: 90 cm. Sexes differ. *Large, powerful, ungainly black and white goose with long legs which extend beyond tail in flight.* Upperparts blackish, glossed iridescent green and purple on head and neck; underparts, foreneck and face white. *In flight, conspicuous large red bill and legs;* bare red skin on forehead and crown with red knob in male. Obtains name from the 3 cm long spur projecting forward from carpal joint, but usually concealed by body feathers. Juvenile duller and browner than adult with head completely feathered; in flight shows less white than adult on leading edge of wing.
Voice: occasionally utters a whistle.
Status: vagrant Morocco, Egypt. Range Africa.
Habitat: tropical floodlands, lakes, river banks.

Cotton Teal *Nettapus coromandelianus*   Plate 4

Identification: 33 cm. Sexes differ. Smaller than Teal, gentle-looking with delicate black bill. Male unmistakable with white head and neck, small black cap, eye and back, the latter often showing greenish sheen; grey flanks and narrow black band across white breast (lost in autumn). In flight, looks white with green-tinged black wings with broad white trailing edge. Female like drab version of male with brown cap and back, buffish flanks and greyish-white head and neck, and dark marking through eye; dark bill can look flesh-coloured at base in sunlight. In flight female has brown wings with white restricted to tips of secondaries. A surface feeder, often dipping bill gently into water; not shy; flight fast.
Voice: usually silent but short sharp chuckling cackle may be given on the wing.
Status: vagrant Iran and E Arabia; almost annual in winter Oman. Range includes India.
Habitat: well-vegetated ponds and lakes.

41

Mandarin Duck *Aix galericulata*

Identification: 43 cm. See PMH.
Status: vagrant Morocco.
Habitat: usually on wooded inland waters.

Wigeon *Anas penelope*

Identification: 46 cm. See PMH.
Status: winter visitor to all countries in N Africa and most of the Asian area, even to parts of S and SE Arabia. Some passage evident in, eg, E Mediterranean, Egypt, slight in E Arabia.
Habitat: coastal mud-flats and salt marsh, and inland marshes, lakes.

American Wigeon *Anas americana*

Identification: 46–56 cm. See PMH.
Status: vagrant Morocco.
Habitat: similar to Wigeon's.

Falcated Duck *Anas falcata*   Plate 4

Identification: 50 cm. Sexes differ. A chunky, large-headed, surface-feeder, fractionally smaller than Mallard; distant males of both species can be confused because of plumage similarities. Male Falcated has *bottle-green head with bronzy-chestnut face and drooping crest on nape*; white chin and neck-ring often very difficult to see (as bird sits on water with head low). Back and flanks grey, finely vermiculated, breast slightly darker; *long, drooping, pale feathers* at *rear end* and black tail with Teal-like yellow patch at sides with *white strip in front*, a feature often aiding identification at distance. Female essentially brown with rather chunky, slightly crested head and black bill; often shows diffuse pale line on edge of wing at rest. In flight, *both sexes have greyish forewing* and black and green speculum. Female distinguished from other similar ducks (except Wigeon) by black bill, lack of dark eyestripe and lack of pale supercilium; from Wigeon by chunky head, usually held well into body and, in flight, pale coverts, which give it a rather Garganey-like appearance.
Voice: male has low whistle; female has Gadwall-like quack.
Status: vagrant Iraq, Jordan, perhaps Turkey, Iran. Range E Asia, India.
Habitat: large rivers, lakes, barrages, floodlands, also coastal.

Gadwall *Anas strepera*

Identification: 51 cm. See PMH.
Status: see map. Partial migrant. Winter visitor N Africa including Nile valley, and in Asia from Turkey and Iran southwards, but scarce in Arabia.
Habitat: like Mallard, but less cosmopolitan and seldom occurs on sea coasts. Nests in thick vegetation by water.

Teal *Anas crecca*

Identification: 36 cm. See PMH.
Status: see map. Almost entirely a winter, or passage, visitor occurring on coasts and inland (including Nile valley) in N Africa, also widely in Iran, Iraq, W half Turkey, parts of Near East (but few winter Israel), and fairly common Arabia in suitable places.
Habitat: wide range of quiet waters including shallow tidal, saltmarsh, lagoons, marsh ditches, reservoirs. Nests in thick ground-cover.

Blue-winged Teal *Anas discors*

Identification: 38 cm. See PMH.
Status: vagrant Morocco. Range America.
Habitat: marshes, pools and rice-fields.

Cape Teal *Anas capensis*   Plate 4

Identification: 40 cm. Sexes alike. *Pale brownish-grey* surface-feeder, slightly chunkier than Teal. *In strong light can appear extremely pale*, almost white. Upper parts brown with buffish feather-edgings, underparts marbled brown and white whilst head is pale buffish-grey finely speckled and with very *faint dark mask through eye and no dark cap*. Characteristic *rose-pink bill* (graduating to bluish tip) with black base; eye orange-red to light brown or occasionally yellow. In flight shows green *speculum with broad white borders giving appearance of double white wing-bar*. Immature similar but markings on under and upperparts less distinct; eye dark and bill sometimes without black base.
Voice: usually silent.
Status: see map. A south and central African species which makes some seasonal movements. Recorded more than once Kufra (Libya), possibly breeding there.
Habitat: fresh and brackish marshes and lakes. Nests on ground in vegetation.

Mallard *Anas platyrhynchos*

Identification: 58 cm. See PMH.
Status: see map. Possible feral origin for birds breeding in Arabia. Partial migrant. In winter leaves much of E Turkey and becomes widespread in Mediterranean basin, Iran, Iraq wetlands; generally rather scarce in Arabia but reaches most coasts, some inland.
Habitat: almost any water; in winter also on sea-coasts and estuaries. Nests on ground usually in thick cover or in hollow in tree.

Pintail *Anas acuta*

Identification: 56 cm. See PMH.
Status: see map. Mainly winter visitor and passage migrant, widespread in Mediterranean basin, Nile valley, W Iran, Iraq, also fairly common on passage and in winter in Arabia.
Habitat: chiefly sheltered, shallow coasts and estuaries in winter, also open, shallow inland waters. Nests on ground.

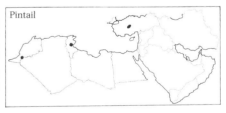

Garganey *Anas querquedula*

Identification: 38 cm. See PMH.
Status: see map. Summer visitor Turkey, NW Iran, otherwise mainly passage evident in Arabia, Egypt, to some extent Lebanon, Libya (more autumn than spring), and NW Africa. Some winter Arabia.
Habitat: as Teal, but seldom on salt water. Nests in long grass or rank vegetation near water.

43

Shoveler *Anas clypeata*

Identification: 51 cm. See PMH

Status: see map. Almost entirely winter visitor and passage migrant, wintering widely in Mediterranean basin plus W Morocco, and Nile valley route to E Africa; also Iran, Iraq, and coasts and inland Arabia; occasionally over-summers.

Habitat: less maritime than other surface-feeders; usually in marshes, floodlands and overgrown ponds. Nests on ground.

Shoveler

Cape Shoveler, adult males (rear), adult female (foreground)

Cape Shoveler *Anas smithii*

Identification: 51 cm. Sexes differ. Similar in size and shape to Shoveler (see PMH) but *smaller head further emphasises bill length*. Confusion possible with Shoveler in female or eclipse plumage. Male has *greyish-brown head and neck* streaked darker on crown, *paler than, and strongly contrasting with, russet flanks and breast*; breast and belly profusely spotted with blackish, and upper flanks with dark, crescent-shaped markings. Undertail coverts whitish, finely barred black and *tail brown with outer feathers edged cinnamon* (*edged white in Shoveler*). Upperparts blackish-brown edged buff with scapulars, rump and tail-coverts black with greenish-blue iridescence. In flight, upperwing-coverts pale bluish-grey separated from green speculum by a white bar. *Bill black* and spatulate. Female and eclipse male are paler than males, less russet and have more yellow or buff in basic ground-colour and more extensive dark centres to flank-feathers; they lack the male's iridescence on upperparts. Upperwing-coverts are duller and the bill dark grey. Iris pale yellow in male, dark brown in female and, at a distance, eyes of either sex can look dark against palish head. Differs from female Shoveler in *more russet or cinnamon and grey plumage and black or dark grey bill* (olive to yellowish-olive in Shoveler).

Voice: mainly silent but male has wooden note often uttered in series of four.

Status: vagrant Morocco (possibly escapes).

Habitat: wetlands.

Marbled Teal *Marmaronetta angustirostris*

Identification: 41 cm. See PMH.
Status: see map. Partial migrant; winter numbers and movements irregular. Winters NW Africa, (few in Egypt, Israel), S Turkey, SE Iraq, many SW Iran. Rare E and central Arabia. Vagrant Cyprus, Oman.
Habitat: fresh-water, especially well-vegetated. Nests near water, along stream banks, etc.

Red-crested Pochard *Netta rufina*

Identification: 56 cm. See PMH.
Status: see map. Partial migrant. Winters Turkey (many), Near East (few), Egypt, Iraq, Iran (many); also a few Morocco, Algeria. Irregular E and central Arabia. Vagrant Tunisia, Libya.
Habitat: large reedy freshwater lakes, or brackish lagoons, seldom on sea. Breeds among vegetation on islands in lagoons.

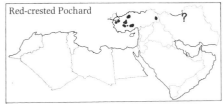

Pochard *Aythya ferina*

Identification: 46 cm. See PMH.
Status: see map. Partial migrant. Winters (and passage) in N Africa including parts of Nile valley, Near East, Cyprus, Turkey, Iran, Iraq; generally scarce or irregular coasts and inland Arabia.
Habitat: seldom on sea. Frequents large and small lakes, backwaters, etc. Breeds in dense reeds.

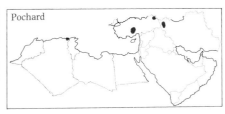

Ring-necked Duck *Aythya collaris*

Identification: 43 cm. See PMH.
Status: vagrant Morocco.
Habitat: mainly inland lakes, marshes, but can also occur on estuaries, etc.

Ferruginous Duck *Aythya nyroca*

Identification: 41 cm. See PMH.
Status: see map. Partial migrant. Nesting E Arabia follows recent creation of ponds. In winter scattered widely and occurs most countries in the area. Passage includes Nile valley, NW Africa, also Oman.
Habitat: fairly shallow, well-vegetated fresh waters, sometimes saline; in winter may occur on coasts, open lagoons. Nests on ground in dense reeds, etc.

45

Tufted Duck *Aythya fuligula*

Identification: 43 cm. See PMH.
Status: see map. Migrant from north, wintering in strength in Turkey, Iran, Iraq, also Near East, Egypt (and through to tropical East Africa), and scattered NW Africa, but rarely Libya; uncommon most parts of Arabia.
Habitat: seldom on open sea. Frequents large and small lakes. Nests on ground or in water, often in tussock.

Scaup *Aythya marila*

Identification: 48 cm. See PMH.
Status: winter visitor in small numbers to N and W Turkey, scarce in N Iran. Vagrant Cyprus, Israel, Iraq, NW Africa.
Habitat: maritime, usually in bays and estuaries.

Long-tailed Duck *Clangula hyemalis*

Identification: 53 cm. See PMH.
Status: vagrant N Iran, Gulf of Aqaba.
Habitat: mainly maritime.

Common Scoter *Melanitta nigra*

Identification: 48 cm. See PMH.
Status: regular autumn migrant and winter visitor on Atlantic coast of Morocco. Vagrant Libya, Cyprus, Turkey, Iran.
Habitat: mainly maritime.

Velvet Scoter *Melanitta fusca*

Identification: 56 cm. See PMH.
Status: see map. Summer visitor to Turkish breeding waters. Winters N and S coasts Turkey. Vagrant Israel, Egypt, NW Africa.
Habitat: mainly maritime in winter. Nests on ground in thick vegetation not far from freshwater lake-side.

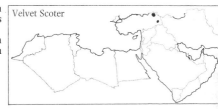

Goldeneye *Bucephala clangula*

Identification: 46 cm. See PMH.
Status: winter visitor to Iran (especially Caspian), and Turkey. Vagrant Iraq, Cyprus, Near East, NW Africa.
Habitat: coastal waters, often also on inland lakes.

Smew *Mergus albellus*

Identification: 41 cm. See PMH.
Status: winter visitor Iran (especially Caspian area), Iraq, Turkey. Vagrant most other countries in E Mediterranean area, also Libya, Algeria.
Habitat: lakes, reservoirs and rivers, occasionally on sheltered coasts.

Red-breasted Merganser *Mergus serrator*

Identification: 58 cm. See PMH.
Status: winter visitor in small numbers Tunisia and Libya, also south coasts of Black Sea and Caspian, a few regularly reaching S Turkey, S Iran and perhaps N Syria. Straggles southwards over much of E Mediterranean area and in Arabia recorded as vagrant in several places on Gulf coast, also Red Sea.
Habitat: chiefly maritime.

Goosander *Mergus merganser*

Identification: 66 cm. See PMH.
Status: winter visitor in small numbers to Turkey, Iran and Iraq. Vagrant Cyprus, Israel, NE Africa.
Habitat: large rivers, lakes, reservoirs.

White-headed Duck *Oxyura leucocephala*

Identification: 46 cm. See PMH.
Status: see map. Partial migrant, generally scarce. Winters NW Africa (especially Tunisia), Turkey, few Iran, Iraq, Syria, Israel and Egypt (rare). Vagrant Cyprus, Libya, Saudi Arabia.
Habitat: reedy, generally shallow, inland waters and brackish lagoons. Nests among reeds and aquatic vegetation in water.

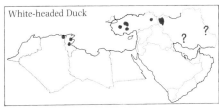

Honey Buzzard *Pernis apivorus*

Identification: 50–60 cm (wing-span 135–150 cm). See PMH.
Status: see map. Summer visitor. Considerable passage Morocco, Tunisia, E Mediterranean areas and NE Turkey but vagrant or rare in Libya and further east than Jordan though now recorded regularly in autumn in N Yemen.
Habitat: woodland when breeding. Nests in large tree.

Black-winged Kite *Elanus caeruleus*

Identification: 33 cm (wing-span 74 cm). See PMH.
Status: see map. Mainly resident, but some erratic movements. Vagrant in W Saudi Arabia, E Mediterranean north to Turkey, and Algerian Sahara.
Habitat: cultivated areas with scattered trees, or woodland glades, forest edges, etc. Nests fairly low in tree.

47

African Swallow-tailed Kite *Chelictinia riocourii*   Plate 5

Identification: 37 cm (wing-span 75–80 cm). Sexes alike. Small, tern-like, grey and white raptor with long pointed wings and, *in adult, deeply forked tail*. Adult has *entire upper-surface grey*, scapulars edged darker, upper back often washed sooty and flight-feathers edged whitish. Black patch around eye. Forehead and underparts white, *with long black patch on carpal joint of underwing*. Flight- and tail-feathers often look translucent. Juvenile has much less forked tail, is browner above with back, wing-coverts and inner secondaries edged rufous-brown; faint dark streaks on underparts; juvenile separated from Black-winged Kite *by absence of black on upperwing-coverts and by shallowly forked tail* (square-cut in juvenile Black-winged). Flight graceful and tern-like. Hovers repeatedly like Kestrel with great skill and grace, and very little wing-movement.
Status: vagrant S Yemen. Range tropical Africa.
Habitat: semi-desert plains or grasslands.

Black Kite *Milvus migrans*   Plate 5

Identification: 58 cm (wing-span 170 cm). Sexes alike. See PMH. The race *lineatus* (illustrated) from Siberia (wintering in Iran and S. Iraq) larger than European birds (size as Red Kite); adult more brown-headed and belly to undertail-coverts paler buffish-brown, less or no contrast with pale undertail (underparts uniform in European birds, with warm brown rear-body contrasting with paler undertail); larger whiter patch on under-surface of primaries generally less boldly barred darker (European Black Kites have smaller and duller greyish patch in primaries often bolder barred; sometimes no patch at all). In yellow-billed race, *aegyptius* (illustrated), of Egypt and Arabia, adult has entirely yellow bill (though some SW Arabian adults are black-billed), with brighter, rather uniform rufous underbody and underwing-coverts compared to European birds, and large whitish patch on under-surface of primaries inconspicuously barred darker (approaching Red Kite's); undertail also whiter but head less whitish, more greyish-brown. Juvenile 'yellow-billed' Black Kite has (at least in SW Arabia) black bill and generally paler, often patchy underbody.
Status: see map. Mainly resident in Egypt and SW Arabia. Elsewhere migratory, with noticeable passage W, C and E Mediterranean; some winter in various parts of area (the most northerly being S Caspian) but rare Libya.
Habitat: a wide variety of country from woodland to barren semi-desert, often showing preference for rivers and lowland lake margins, also frequenting villages up to 3,000 m (N Yemen) where garbage plentiful. Nests in tree, sometimes on cliff or building, often sociably.

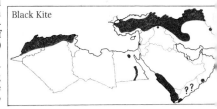

Red Kite *Milvus milvus*

Identification: 61 cm (wing-span 175–195 cm). See PMH.
Status: see map. Mainly resident; may still breed Algeria, Tunisia. Some winter immigration; scarce Turkey, infrequent N Iran, and more rarely in E Mediterranean countries between Iraq and Libya.
Habitat: woodland or groups of trees, hunting over more open country. Nests in tree.

African Fish Eagle *Haliaeetus vocifer*   Plate 6

Identification: 61–73 cm (wing-span 190–237 cm). Sexes alike, except female larger. Broad-winged and short-tailed eagle. Adult has *head, neck, breast, mantle and tail snow-white; rest of underparts, underwing-coverts and leading upperwing-coverts rich chestnut* (looking blackish at distance). Juvenile variable; upperparts blackish-brown with whitish mottling on back, and buffish bar across wing-coverts. Sides of head usually buffish, bordered below by *blackish-brown throat and upper-breast; lower breast creamy-white and upper belly mostly blackish-brown; all dark parts streaked and blotched creamy, and vice versa.* From below in flight, juvenile shows *white patch at base of primaries* and on axillaries, *brownish-white tail and narrow black terminal band*, and dark wing-coverts with whitish bar on median coverts. Immature shows increasing white feathering on head, neck, breast and mantle and reduced black band at tip of whiter tail; the whitish underwing markings remain well into sub-adult plumage when chestnut coverts start to appear. Soars with raised wings pressed forward and short tail well fanned; glides on more level, slightly kinked wings; juvenile slightly longer-tailed than adult and secondaries are pointed, giving saw-shaped trailing edge to wing. Juvenile stragglers require separation from similar Pallas's Fish Eagle (which see). African Fish identified by variegated whitish and dark underbody, whitish, narrowly black-tipped tail, much less whitish on rear underwing coverts and absence of dark patch on ear-coverts; both share whitish primary-patch, axillaries and bases of inner secondaries.

Voice: far-carrying yelping, like loud ringing Herring Gull.

Status: vagrant Egypt. Range Africa.

Habitat: large rivers, lakes, floodlands, also coasts including mangrove swamps.

Pallas's Fish Eagle *Haliaeetus leucoryphus*   Plate 6

Identification: 80 cm (wing-span 200–250 cm). Sexes alike. Large, well-proportioned, with narrower wings than White-tailed and relatively longer tail. Adult has distinctive *broad white band across centre of black tail* (but tail looks white with broad black terminal band), *pale creamy head and neck* and pale chestnut-brown breast and mantle; when seen well in flight shows slightly paler bases to flight-feathers above and below. Juvenile dark brown above, often with pale brown band across wing-coverts; brownish head has *blackish patch on ear-coverts*, sometimes continuing as dark band across lower neck, darker than *palish brown* underparts and yellowish throat (in juvenile White-tailed, head and neck blackish-brown and underparts darker); shares whitish axillary-patch and pale bases to inner secondaries with young White-tailed, but also shows *buffish or whitish band through centre of underwing* (young White-tailed has, at best, thin pale lines along central underwing-coverts). Often has large *white patch on primaries below* but in some only thin white streaks in inner feathers (no distinct white in primaries of young White-tailed); blackish tail may sometimes show narrow band of pale or whitish mottling at base of spread undertail (young White-tailed has blackish tail showing white centre to feathers when seen well). In immature, dark ear-patch and neck-band often emphasized by paler head and underparts, and narrow band of whitish mottling at base of undertail; underwing much as juvenile. Juvenile has slightly broader, more curved wings than adult with pointed tips of secondaries giving saw-shaped trailing edge. Immature separated from sometimes similar Golden Eagle by more parallel-edged wings, held flattish when soaring (usually lifted in Golden) and by longer, more protruding neck. When perched, bare tarsus and pale loral patch also separate it from *Aquila* eagles. See also African Fish Eagle.

Voice: in breeding season, loud Herring Gull-like yelping which lacks 'ring' of African Fish Eagle's call.

Status: vagrant Iran, E Arabia and Oman. Range Asia.

Habitat: chiefly inland lakes and rivers. Occasionally coastal in winter.

White-tailed Eagle *Haliaeetus albicilla*

Identification: 70–90 cm. (wing-span 200–240 cm). See PMH.

Status: see map. Adults resident; young often disperse in winter, rarely reaching Egypt, Israel, Iraq, S Iran.

Habitat: wetlands, rivers, lakes, coasts. Nests in trees or on cliff.

White-tailed Eagle

Lammergeier *Gypaetus barbatus*

Identification: 102–115 cm (wing-span 250–280 cm). See PMH.

Status: see map. Resident. Perhaps extinct Tunisia. Vagrant Cyprus.

Habitat: remote mountain ranges. Nests in cave on precipice.

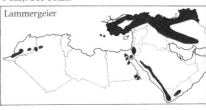

Egyptian Vulture *Neophron percnopterus*

Identification: 58–66 cm (wing-span 160–170 cm). See PMH.

Status: see map. May still breed NW Syria. Mainly migratory, withdrawing in autumn from most Mediterranean areas, N/central Iran, with passage most evident via Morocco, and through countries bordering E Mediterranean; some Tunisia. Winters S Sahara, S Egypt, Arabia and S Iran. Vagrant Cyprus.

Habitat: as Griffon, but also frequents village refuse dumps. Nests in recess on cliff.

Hooded Vulture, adult from below (left), from above (right) Drawings by S. Christensen

Hooded Vulture *Necrosyrtes monachus*

Identification: 65–70 cm (wing-span 169–176 cm). Sexes alike. Small, dark vulture, possibly confuseable with dark juvenile Egyptian. Size as Egyptian, with similar thin, slender bill but *wings broader*, less pointed (6 free 'fingers' compared to 5 in Egyptian), and *tail shorter, fuller and only slightly wedge-shaped* to almost square-cut (longer, sharply wedge-shaped in Egyptian). Adult has pinkish, bare head and neck with nape to hind-neck covered in creamy down and lacking lanceolate dark brown feathering of young Egyptian (which has darker-looking dull greyish head); juvenile has sparse blackish-brown down from crown to hind-neck. Small ruff at base of neck. Legs pale bluish but brownish in juvenile. Overhead, adult appears uniform dark brown (white on crop-patch and on 'trousers' often invisible); dark flight-feathers

50

become *gradually paler towards their bases* and *contrast with darker underwing-coverts* (juvenile Egyptian lacks this contrast, all blackish-brown flight-feathers being darker than underwing-coverts). Upperparts dark brown, bleaching paler, (*without* juvenile Egyptian's greyish hue on flight-feathers, and buffish-white wing-bars, lower back and rump). Tail dark brown (paler, buff-grey in juvenile Egyptian). Juvenile Hooded has upperwing-coverts edged buffish and lacks pale bases to flight-feathers below and white on crop-patch and thighs. Solitary, but congregates at carcases and rubbish dumps.

Status: vagrant Morocco. Range Africa.

Habitat: open areas, savanna, also towns.

Indian White-backed Vulture *Gyps bengalensis* Plate 6

Identification: 84–90 cm (wing-span 205–210 cm). Sexes alike. Smaller than Griffon which it resembles in silhouette (raised wings when soaring) but size difference not apparent unless both species together. Overhead adult has dark silvery-grey flight-feathers tipped blackish, but looks black at a distance. *Body, axillary-patch and narrow bar along leading forewing blackish-slate, contrasting with pure white underwing-coverts.* From above, mantle and wing-coverts *dark (oily) slate-grey with paler greyish black-tipped flight-feathers and conspicuous white patch on lower back and rump.* At close range, underparts thinly pale-streaked; ruff, crop-side patch and inner thighs white, but latter not seen in flight; head and neck dark grey. Juvenile, *which lacks white patch on lower back and white under-wing-coverts of adult,* darker than Griffon. In flight, body and underwing-coverts dark medium-brown or buff-brown, showing little contrast with dark flight- and tail-feathers; close view shows *thin well-defined white streak near leading edge of wing* (Griffon has paler underwing-coverts which contrast more with dark flight-feathers); also less contrast between warm dark brown back and wing-coverts and darker flight-feathers than in Griffon (but feathers do bleach to medium-brown). At close range, body and upper and underwing-coverts have broader whitish-buff streaks than Griffon; head and neck usually grey-to-whitish-buff (but can be darker), and pointed ruff-feathers are cinnamon-buff. Immature gradually develops creamy-buff bands on rear underwing-coverts, thus looking more like Griffon, but *white starting to appear on lower back* is diagnostic. Vulturine behaviour; gregarious, and will often allow close approach.

Voice: a series of hisses and squeals.

Status: see map. Resident.

Habitat: open regions, foothills, cultivation with villages and livestock. Nesting colonies in trees.

Indian White-backed Vulture

Griffon Vulture *Gyps fulvus*

Identification: 97–105 cm (wing-span 245–270 cm). See PMH.

Status: see map. Mainly resident but some passage occurs at both ends of Mediterranean. Probably extinct S Tunisia. Partial migrant Turkey. Irregular Oman, E Arabia. Vagrant Libya.

Habitat: ranges over all types of country, but normal habitat is mountainous. Breeds sociably in caves or on ledges.

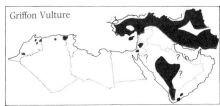

Griffon Vulture

51

Rüppell's Vulture *Gyps rueppellii*   Plate 6

Identification: 100 cm (wing-span 240 cm). Sexes alike. Slightly smaller than Griffon with 'chunkier' flight-silhouette, but proportions basically similar. Adult has *conspicuously scaly appearance on underparts* and on *upperwing-coverts*; at rest there are usually two conspicuous pale lines on rear upperwing-coverts, visible also in flight at close range. *Blackish underwing-coverts* have usual white 'vulture-streak' near leading edge of wing and two narrower whitish lines on rear coverts; at distance looks rather dark below (darker than Griffon) but with contrast above between blackish-brown flight- and tail-feathers and pale sandy or creamy-looking forewing (thus resembling Griffon). In the Ethiopian race (most likely race in Arabia), underparts almost creamy, variably spotted and blotched blackish, and *body appears paler than dark underwings*, sometimes conspicuously so. Blackish brown crop-patch bordered above by whitish ruff; head and neck usually whitish. Juvenile dark brown above and below with pale streaks; has white 'vulture-streak' near leading underwing, but lacks adult's scaly appearance and whitish lines on upperwing-coverts; ruff feathers pointed and fulvous. Juvenile and immature very similar to Griffon and hard to separate though upper- and underwing-coverts are darker in juvenile Rüppell's, accentuating underwing's white streak on leading edge. Soars and glides on flattish or slightly lifted wings (usually more lifted in Griffon). Vulturine behaviour; gregarious at carcases.
Status: vagrant Egypt, SW Arabia. Range Africa.
Habitat: arid mountains and surrounding open savanna.

Lappet-faced Vulture *Torgos tracheliotus*   Plate 6

Identification: 100 cm (wing-span 258–262 cm). Sexes alike. About size of Black Vulture which it superficially resembles in general colouration. Upperparts dull *grey-brown* (*bleaching paler*) *and generally little contrast with blackish flight- and tail-feathers* (usually much less contrast above than Griffon, but more than Black). Underwing at distance resembles Black Vulture but closer views reveal *contrast between black underwing-coverts and paler greyish flight-feathers with blackish wing-tip*; single narrow whitish bar near leading edge of underwing less distinct in juvenile birds, which also show irregular, scattered pale mottling in less black underwing-coverts than adults (Griffon has *paler* underwing-coverts which contrast with black flight-feathers). Dark brown breast has *whitish streaks and mottling and whitish patches at sides of breast and on thighs giving underparts a variegated appearance* (underparts uniform in Black and Griffon). When perched, heavy bill and pink parts of head (latter whitish at distance) and bare pink fore-neck aid identification. In flight, wings generally less parallel than Black, but not as curved as Griffon; tips of secondaries distinctly pointed, giving saw-shaped trailing edge (also a feature of Black but susceptible to wear). Soars on flattish wings, similar to Black (wings raised in Griffon); glides on flattish wings (more angled in Black with pronounced carpal bend and more lowered primaries; in Griffon flattish or raised). Usually solitary or in pairs, but several will congregate at carcases.
Voice: usually silent, but has growling sounds and series of grunts.
Status: see map. Mainly resident. Vagrant N and S Yemen, Libya, NW Africa.
Habitat: semi-desert steppes, savannas, rocky country with wadis containing acacias on top of which huge nest is built. A few pairs may nest in loose association.

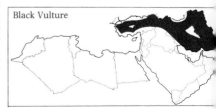

Lappet-faced Vulture

Black Vulture

Black Vulture *Aegypius monachus*

Identification: 98–107 cm (wing-span 250–295 cm). See PMH.
Status: see map. Adults resident; immatures dispersive, occasionally extending south (especially in winter) to many Middle East countries including Oman, also Egypt and Morocco, but always rare.
Habitat: ranges from semi-desert to grazed uplands and into mountains. Nests usually in tree, sometimes on cliff.

Short-toed Eagle *Circaetus gallicus*

Identification: 64–69 cm (wing-span 185–195 cm). See PMH.
Status: see map. Has bred Lebanon, Syria, Libya, perhaps Egypt, Saudi Arabia, Oman. Summer visitor to most breeding areas, but a few winter through Arabia. Passage concentration W and E ends of Mediterranean, also some central, fewer further east.
Habitat: arid stony foothills, semi-desert, open or lightly wooded plains. Nests in tree.

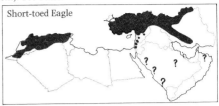

Bateleur *Terathopius ecaudatus*   Plate 5

Identification: 55 cm (wing-span 175 cm). Sexes differ. Unmistakable, *large-headed, tail-less flight-silhouette* and, in adult, striking colour pattern. *Male has black head, underbody and shoulders; tail and back deep chestnut;* upperwing-coverts brownish with black flight-feathers; underwing mainly white but with black secondaries and outer primaries. Female similar but *flight-feathers only tipped black, showing* on upperwing as *black trailing edge to whitish secondaries.* Bare orange-red face and cere; legs red. Juvenile dark brown above, paler rufous-brown below with creamy feather-tips to head and underparts; flight- and tail-feathers dark greyish but paler bases contrast with dark underwing-coverts; facial skin and cere greenish-blue. Immature mottled brown and blackish below while sub-adult is uniform sooty-blackish on upper- and under-surface, but flight-feathers of sub-adult female are a mixture of dark grey and whitish (all-dark in male); sub-adult also has underwing-coverts mottled white and brown, and first yellowish, later orange-red, facial skin and cere; legs pinkish, later red.
Unique flight silhouette *with deep s-curved trailing edge of wing and long outer primaries,* and *very short tail beyond which feet of adult project;* feet do not project beyond juvenile's slightly longer tail. Broad head and neck prominent. Generally seen on wing, gliding very fast in a 'tilting' manner with wings lifted in shallow V; only occasional wing-beats; if flushed from perch, wing-action rather fast and light.
Status: see map. Resident. Vagrant Israel, Iraq.
Habitat: open savanna and foothills, also thornbush and woodland. Nests in large tree.

Marsh Harrier *Circus aeruginosus*

Identification: 48–56 cm (wing-span 115–130 cm). See PMH.
Status: see map. Has bred Lebanon. Partial migrant but a summer visitor to E Turkey and parts of N Iran; otherwise occurs in winter and on passage widely but often thinly in much of Asian area, also N Africa.
Habitat: reedy swamps, marshes etc, also hunts over neighbouring farmland and mud-flats. Nests in reed-bed or other rank growth usually in water.

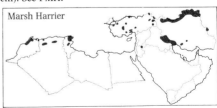

Hen Harrier *Circus cyaneus*

Identification: 43–50 cm (wing-span 100–120 cm). See PMH.
Status: winter visitor Turkey, Iran and Iraq. Scarcer further south being rare in Saudi Arabia (though regular in E Province) and vagrant to N Yemen; few winter in N Africa but seldom recorded in Algeria.
Habitat: rough grassland, marshes, sand-dunes, open farmland.

53

Pallid Harrier *Circus macrourus*

Identification: 43–48 cm (wing-span 100–115 cm). See PMH.

Status: may breed on N Iran steppes. Passage migrant throughout region west to Algeria, but most strongly in east. Winters Tunisia, Egypt, Near East and north parts of Asian area especially Iran; but few Cyprus and Arabia south to N Yemen and Oman. Vagrant Morocco.

Habitat: open natural grassland in plains and hill country, dry steppe.

Montagu's Harrier *Circus pygargus*

Identification: 40–46 cm (wing-span 95–115 cm). See PMH.

Status: see map. Mainly summer visitor. Also occurs on passage in countries where does not breed in N Africa, Near East, Cyprus, Iraq, more rarely Arabia including N Yemen and Oman where few also winter.

Habitat: marshes, or agricultural land. Nests on ground in wet vegetation, or on dry wild stretches with low shrubs, occasionally in growing crops.

Dark Chanting Goshawk *Melierax metabates*   Plate 7

Identification: 38–48 cm (wing-span 95–110 cm). Sexes alike. Medium-sized raptor, often perching upright in full view when *long yellow-orange to orange-red legs are conspicuous*. Adult grey (darkest on head) finely barred grey and white on lower breast, belly and thighs. Base of bill, *cere and skin on lores orange-red*. In flight, shows *black wing-tips and silvery blue-grey panel in upperwing*; graduated, white-tipped tail has distinct black and white bands on outer feathers, most evident from below; *white uppertail-coverts* inconspicuously barred grey. From below, finely barred underwing-coverts look whitish like flight-feathers, but wing-ends black. *Juvenile is brown*, where adult grey, *with coarsely streaked throat, neck and upper breast* with bold barring below; tail-feathers broadly banded; whitish underwing has rusty barring on coverts and grey secondaries, faintly barred darker; below at distance looks pale buffish with slightly darker secondaries; from above, brownish with paler warm buff bases to primaries, banded tail and white rump. Iris pale yellowish, cere greyish or yellowish, legs dull orange-yellow. In flight, shows medium-short rounded wings and fairly long, graduated tail; usually flies low with slow *Accipiter*-like wing-beats interspersed with glides on level or slightly raised wings, more raised when soaring; wing position and colour-pattern of adult reminiscent of male Marsh Harrier; can fly at speed with fast wing-beats.

Voice: series of melodious loud fluty whistles uttered from tree-top or post, 'kjiu-kjiu-kjiu-kjiu', etc, with upward inflexion on 'u'; also a high-pitched 'kleee-u'.

Status: see map. Resident with some dispersal. Vagrant Israel.

Habitat: open parkland or bushy country, often in semi-desert, grass or scrub. Nests in tree.

Gabar Goshawk *Micronisus gabar*   Plate 7

Identification: 28–33 cm (wing-span 60–65 cm). Sexes alike, but female larger. Slightly smaller than Sparrowhawk. Adult upperparts ash-grey with striking *white uppertail-coverts* which separate it from similar-sized hawks; brownish-grey broadly white-tipped uppertail has 3–4 bold dark bands and whitish undertail 4–5. *Throat and upper breast uniform pale ash-grey*, remainder of underparts and underwing-coverts white with fine dark grey bars, bolder on

54

flanks; under-surface of flight-feathers densely barred darker; *white trailing edge to secondaries most obvious from above* (and visible when perched unless very worn) and absent in other *Accipiters* in region. *Lacks blackish wing-tip below* of adult Shikra. Legs orange-red. *A melanistic phase (which has black uppertail-coverts)*, not yet recorded in region, could occur in SW Arabia; its flight- and tail-feathers are boldly barred above; white tips to secondaries and tail are absent. Juvenile has dark earth-brown upperparts with white-streaked hind-neck; cheeks, throat and breast boldly streaked rufous-brown while belly has rufous-brown bars. Like adult, has white uppertail-coverts, trailing edge to secondaries and tip of tail. In addition usually has distinct white edges to tertials which are conspicuous unless very worn. Flight silhouette resembles Sparrowhawk's but tail rounded with distinctly shorter outer feathers visible if soaring with spread tail (Sparrowhawk has square-cut tail with sharp corners). Active flight a series of flaps interspersed with glides on upcurved wings, also upcurved when soaring (as sometimes in Sparrowhawk). Habits recall Sparrowhawk.

Voice: during courtship a varied piping 'kew-ke, kew-ke, kew-ke'; also a high-pitched 'twee-twit-twee-twee-twit'.

Status: see map. Presumed resident in SW Saudi Arabia and probably N Yemen. Recorded S Yemen.

Habitat: savanna and bush country, preferably with acacias. Nests in tree.

Goshawk *Accipiter gentilis*

Identification: 48–60 cm (wing-span 95–125 cm). See PMH.

Status: see map. Mainly resident, with imma-tures dispersing. Winter visitor N Iran and some European birds reach Morocco; irregu-lar Cyprus. Vagrant elsewhere in N Africa, Near East, E Arabia and apparently SW Saudi Arabia.

Habitat: woods, especially coniferous, often near open country. Nests in large trees.

Sparrowhawk *Accipiter nisus*

Identification: 28–38 cm (wing-span 60–80 cm). See PMH.

Status: see map. Partial migrant, in winter expanding over most of Turkey, Iran, and reaching Cyprus, Near East, many parts of Arabia including Oman and Yemen, and N Africa.

Habitat: mainly conifer and mixed woods and copses, also hunting over more open country. Nests in tree.

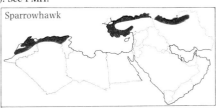

Shikra *Accipiter badius*   Plate 7

Identification: 30–36 cm (wing-span 60–70 cm). Sexes differ slightly; female larger. Resembles Levant Sparrowhawk in plumage but more like Sparrowhawk in flight-silhouette with *rounded wing-tip* when soaring (Levant has longer, more pointed wings); longish tail looks rather narrow when gliding, with rounded corners of tapering tip, recalling Levant (Sparrowhawk tail slightly longer, rather square-cut with sharp corners). Two races occur in region. In larger Iranian *cenchroides*, male pale dove-grey above with darker wing-tips, *uniform uppertail without bars* (except 4–5 on outer feathers when spread), *whitish throat with narrow dark central streak* and pinkish-buff barring on underparts, though *at distance looks creamy-white* *below with narrow black wing-tip.* Cheeks greyish; no white supercilium or nape-spot, but obscure buff collar on hind-neck (absent in Levant). Female pale brownish above, collar on hind-neck faint, and ashy-grey uppertail has blackish terminal band; underparts have bolder, browner barring and almost no black on wing-tip. Iris yellow to orange-yellow (reddish-brown in Levant). Separated from Levant by much less black on wing-tips, less pure white underwing (male), paler upperparts and wing-shape. In the smaller SW Arabian race *sphenurus*, both sexes *darker, soft blue-grey above* with *contrasting blackish wing-tips; under-surface whiter with much more extensive black wing-tips* in male; female less pure white on underparts with less black wing-tips; tail as Iranian birds but dark bars denser. Best separated from rather similar Levant by *blunter wing-tips* and, in male, absence of dark-tipped inner primaries below. Juvenile has dark throat-stripe, *longitudinally spotted underparts* (but often spot-barred flanks and sometimes belly), whitish nape-patch and 4–6 noticeable dark bars across uppertail; hardly any dark on wing-tips below. Best separated from juvenile Levant by shape of wing-tip. Sparrowhawk always lacks black wing-tip and is never white below as male Shikra; also has darker upperparts than Iranian Shikra and uppertail has 3–5 bold dark bars (central feathers plain in virtually all adult Shikras); Sparrowhawk often has white supercilium (particularly females) and nape-spot, features absent in adult Shikra. Juvenile Sparrowhawk is barred on most of underparts with streaks limited to fore-neck. Flight typical *Accipiter*, a series of shallow wing-beats, followed by a glide. Habits similar to Sparrowhawk. See also Gabar Goshawk.

Voice: unhurried 'ch-wick, ch-wich' like quiet Tawny Owl's call note; also fairly loud 'kik-kooi, kik-kooi', etc, repeated several times at nest site; in display also a whistling 'piu, piu, piu'.

Status: see map. Summer visitor N Iran; some winter SE Iran. Also probably resident N Yemen.

Habitat: lightly wooded regions, often near habitation; also savannas with wooded slopes. Nests in tree.

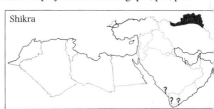

Levant Sparrowhawk *Accipiter brevipes* Plate 7

Identification: 32–39 cm (wing-span 65–75 cm). Sexes differ, and female larger. Shikra-like in plumage, but more slender in build, with longer, relatively narrower and *more pointed wings* (for further distinction, see Shikra). Adult male dull blue-grey above, female more brownish; *wing-tip blackish*, most pronounced in males, *in contrast with remainder of upperwing; central tail-feathers plain without bars*, outer feathers with numerous narrow blackish bars (seen when tail spread); female also has dark sub-terminal tail-band above. At a distance *entire underparts look stone-white with contrastingly blackish wing-tips, particularly in males*; at close range underparts narrowly but densely barred rufous (male), or bolder and brown (female); whitish throat has dark median streak; cheeks of male grey. Separated from Sparrowhawk by *longer, more pointed wings*, slightly shorter and more rounded tail, *contrasting dark wing-tips above and below, whiter under-surface* (male) and plain central tail-feathers above (boldly barred in Sparrowhawk); at close range, Sparrowhawk lacks dark median throat-streak and male has rufous cheeks, also both sexes have bolder barred underparts and undertail. Iris reddish-brown in Shikra (yellowish-orange in Sparrowhawk, even orange-red in some males). Juvenile rather dark grey-brown above with some whitish on hind-neck, barred uppertail and white underparts with dark throat-stripe and *longitudinally spotted underparts* (mainly barred in juvenile Sparrowhawk); extreme wing-tip below sometimes dark grey (never in Sparrowhawk); iris yellow-grey. Flight typical *Accipiter*, but more falcon-like outline when gliding; unlike Sparrowhawk, forms *dense flocks on migration*.

Voice: shrill 'keeveek' (unlike Sparrowhawk).

Status: see map. Summer visitor. Passage large numbers Turkey and Near East, also Iran, but rarely recorded south or west of Sinai. Vagrant Cyprus, Tunisia, Saudi Arabia, N Yemen where perhaps regular.

Habitat: much as Sparrowhawk, though more often in the open and in deciduous woods. Nests in trees.

White-eyed Buzzard *Butastur teesa*   Plate 5

Identification: 45 cm (wing-span 100 cm). Sexes alike. Size of small Buzzard; active flight reminiscent of large *Accipiter* but while soaring and gliding resembles cross between Honey Buzzard and harrier. Appears brownish when perched but in flight largely whitish below. Adult brown above with rusty tinge on lower back, rump and tail, and small white spot on hind-neck; wings dark with *buffish panel (bleaching paler) on upperwing-coverts*, grading into darker forewing; *warm brown dark-barred patch at base of black-tipped primaries*; cinnamon-rufous uppertail (either unbarred, or narrowly barred blackish) with black subterminal band. Underparts white with dark central streak on throat, prominent *dark lower moustachial streak and vinous to earth-brown on lower neck and breast, but at distance looks creamy-white below*; in some birds most underwing whitish, in others coverts are darkish brown; wing-tip blackish. Juvenile pale-headed with white underparts streaked dark brown, though streaking not seen at distance; cheek-streaks narrow or absent. In adult, iris white or pale yellow; brown in juvenile. Active flight fairly swift and direct, usually a few rapid wing-beats followed by short glide; soars and glides for periods without wing-beats, sailing slowly on relatively narrow wings held flat, slightly lifted or lowered (like Honey Buzzard); glides fast on angled wings, not unlike small harrier, except for flatter wings; tail relatively long and narrow, usually half-spread when soaring, when unbarred translucent outer tail-feathers evident. Perches erect for long periods.

Voice: plaintive, mewing 'pit-weer, pit-weer'.

Status: see map. Resident.

Habitat: scrub with occasional trees in dry open low country and open slightly wooded slopes of lower hills. Nests in tree.

Buzzard *Buteo buteo*

Identification: 50–56 cm (wing-span 115–125 cm). See PMH.

Status: see map. Partial migrant. In winter Turkey, N Iran, Near East, Arabia, occasionally including Oman, Egypt, NW Africa. Strong autumn passage NW and NE Turkey and SW Arabia; strong spring passage NE Egypt and Israel; regular elsewhere.

Habitat: wooded and cultivated regions, plains, mountain slopes. Nests in tree or on cliff.

Long-legged Buzzard *Buteo rufinus*

Identification: 60–66 cm (wing-span 125–150 cm). See PMH.

Status: see map. Has bred Sinai. Resident and partial migrant, more widespread in winter when reaches Nile valley, N Yemen.

Habitat: dry open plains and steppes, also cultivation and deciduous woodland; locally in mountains. Nests on rock ledge, occasionally in tree.

Upland Buzzard IW

Upland Buzzard *Buteo hemilasius*

Identification: 61–72 cm (wing-span 135–160 cm). Sexes alike but female larger. *Like a large Long-legged Buzzard* and very difficult to distinguish as size often not apparent and pattern basically similar apart from narrowly barred tail. Two phases occur: dark brown with barred tail, recalling dark phase of Long-legged; and a pale phase with creamy underparts, blackish-brown patches on throat, breast and belly, and brownish upperparts recalling Rough-legged (but latter has broad, black terminal tail-band). Both phases have blackish carpal patches and creamy-white patch on primaries above. *Uppertail often rather pale in contrast with dark rump; uppertail, however, can be browner and is always barred darker,* like young Long-legged (never completely unbarred as in many adult Long-legged, though may look so at a distance). *Upland less rufous in plumage than Long-legged Buzzard and, unlike that species, does not appear to have a rufous phase.* Some dark adults are coloured below much like adult Rough-legged Buzzard, with creamy U on breast of otherwise dark underparts (never in Long-legged where U absent in dark phase; dark throat and upper breast absent in pale phase). Long tarsus (longest of *Buteos*) is variably feathered, in extremes approaching Rough-legged Buzzard. Long wings raised when soaring, like Long-legged.
Status: old record from SE Iran. Range Asia.
Habitat: semi-desert or rather barren high plateaux or mountains.

Rough-legged Buzzard *Buteo lagopus*

Identification: 50–61 cm (wing-span 120–150 cm). See PMH.
Status: winter visitor N Turkey, N Iran. Vagrant Cyprus, Near East, N Africa.
Habitat: usually open country with rough cover, marshes, treeless hills, sand-dunes.

Lesser Spotted Eagle *Aquila pomarina*

Identification: 62–68 cm (wing-span 145–160 cm). See PMH. Sexes alike, but female larger. Medium to smallish eagle. Adult usually *pale brown on wing-coverts (both surfaces) and underbody, with darker flight-feathers,* shows contrast above between pale wing-coverts *and darker mantle; smallish but well-defined pale patch on primaries above and on uppertail-coverts is typical.* Juvenile warm dark to *medium-brown on underwing-coverts and body, either little paler than flight feathers, or of similar shade;* from above, *warm dark brown coverts contrast with darker mantle and flight-feathers;* primary-patch and uppertail-coverts like adult but generally whiter; small rusty-yellow nape patch often hard to see. Immature (and some adults) often with paler underwing-coverts than underbody (the contrast recalling that of many immature Steppe). Flight and tail-feathers generally unbarred, or dark bars less bold, more diffuse than in Steppe. Rarely, juvenile Lesser Spotted atypically coloured, eg mottled yellowish on dark medium-brown underbody and coverts. It is uncertain whether or not a *fulvescens* type (see Spotted Eagle) is found in this species. Relatively narrow-winged eagle with, generally, less long arm, less ample 'hand' (4th primary short or minute) than in larger species. Active flight less heavy than larger species, but hard to determine on lone birds. Soars and glides on slightly, to clearly, arched wings with primaries more or less lowered.

juvenile immature adult

immature immature

juvenile immature adult

Lesser Spotted Eagle Drawings by S. Christensen

Status: see map. Summer visitor. May occasionally winter E Mediterranean. Heavy passage between Turkey and NE Africa; few Tunisia and Cyprus. Vagrant Libya, Oman, possibly N Yemen.
Habitat: breeds in moist wooded lowlands and dry mountain woods. Nests in tree.

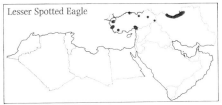

Lesser Spotted Eagle

59

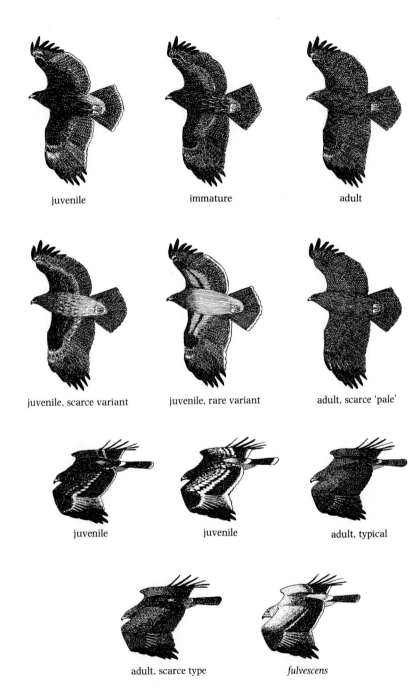

juvenile   immature   adult

juvenile, scarce variant   juvenile, rare variant   adult, scarce 'pale'

juvenile   juvenile   adult, typical

adult, scarce type   *fulvescens*

Spotted Eagle Drawings by S. Christensen

60

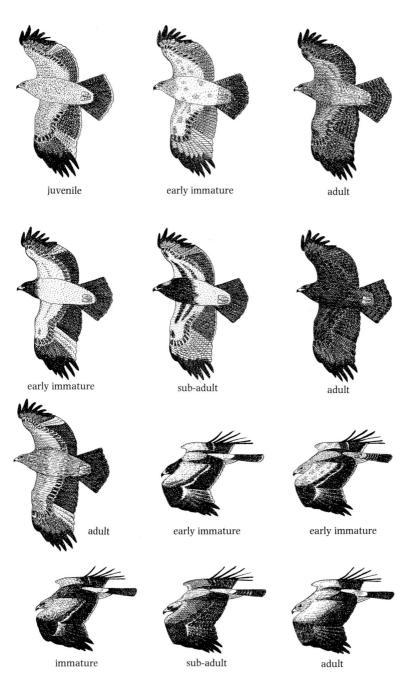

juvenile

early immature

adult

early immature

sub-adult

adult

adult

early immature

early immature

immature

sub-adult

adult

Tawny Eagle Drawings by S. Christensen

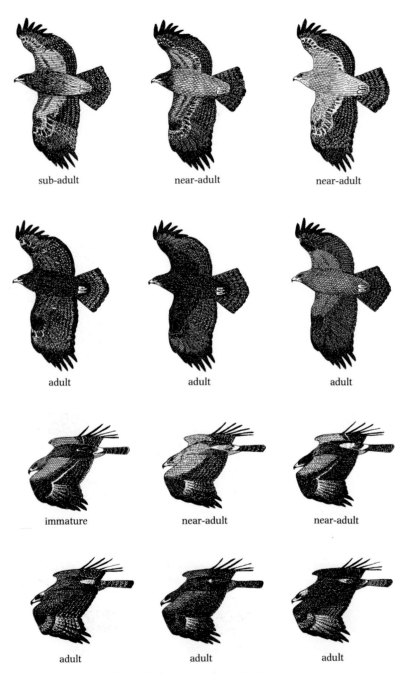

sub-adult   near-adult   near-adult

adult   adult   adult

immature   near-adult   near-adult

adult   adult   adult

Steppe Eagle Drawings by S. Christensen

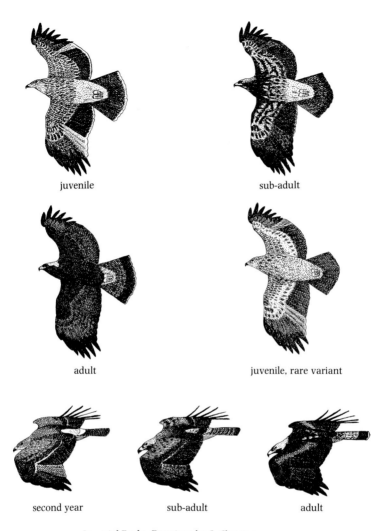

juvenile

sub-adult

adult

juvenile, rare variant

second year

sub-adult

adult

Imperial Eagle   Drawings by S. Christensen

63

Spotted Eagle *Aquila clanga*   Illustration p. 60

Identification: 65–73 cm (wing-span 150–180 cm). See PMH. Sexes alike, but female larger. Medium-sized eagle. Adult from below has *coverts either dark brown like flight-feathers, or blackish with paler contrasting flight-feathers*. Above, wing-coverts typically dark to mid-brown, like mantle, but mantle darker in some; *no conspicuous pale primary-patch above*. Thin diffuse bars sometimes shown on flight- and tail-feathers, but usually absent. Typically, juvenile below has *coverts clearly darker than flight-feathers*; above, wing-coverts with highly variable white spots, forming *up to 3 broad white bars which almost merge; leading forewing blackish-brown; large diffuse primary-patch* consists of whitish primary shafts. Rarely, juvenile Spotted abnormally coloured, eg, (1) *fulvescens*-type with creamy-white coverts and body (both surfaces); (2) yellow-brown coverts and body (both surfaces); (3) yellow-brown underwing-coverts and body, *but normal juvenile upper surface*; (4) yellow-brown upperwing-coverts and mantle, *but normal juvenile under-surface* and (5) dull dark grey secondary-coverts below, or pale-mottled blackish-brown underwing-coverts, with darker underbody; normal above. Relatively broad-winged eagle (adult) with less long arm, less ample 'hand' (shortish 4th primary) than larger species and active flight less heavy. Soars and glides on slightly, to clearly, arched wings with primaries more or less lowered.

Status: light passage in area between Egypt and Black/Caspian Seas. Winters Turkey, Iraq, Iran, Near East, Arabia including Oman and N Yemen. Vagrant elsewhere in N and NW Africa, Cyprus.

Habitat: usually near water, especially marshes with some trees.

Tawny Eagle *Aquila rapax*   Illustration p. 61 & Plate 8

Identification: 65–77 cm (wing-span 172–185 cm). Sexes generally alike, female larger. *Plumage highly variable.* In adult, body and underwing-coverts can be buffish-yellow, rusty-yellow, or *pale rufous to foxy,* some bleaching much paler; grey-brown or blackish-brown adult rare in the region (but not in tropical Africa). Upperwing-coverts rufous-yellow or paler (centred darker), contrasting well with dark flight-feathers, but can also be rufous or foxy. *Flight-feathers below vary from dark to pale grey,* mostly finely but densely barred darker, *or practically unbarred; sometimes a rather diffuse dark band* along trailing edge of wings and tail. Juvenile *pale rufous or foxy, gradually bleaching paler, to creamy-white.* Immature not well known; some resemble juvenile, others have foxy or *blackish-brown head and/or fore-body, contrasting with yellow-buff to creamy-white rear-body; underwing-coverts* pale rufous or creamy-white, in latter case *often with blackish-brown bands.* Pale birds of all ages generally have creamy-white back to uppertail-coverts, many also with *distinct yellow-grey wedge on inner primaries* below. Usually *very little, sometimes no pale primary-patch above* (except some juveniles). Fairly broad-winged eagle with ample 'hand' (long 4th primary) and well protruding head. Soars and glides on slightly, to clearly, arched wings and with primaries more or less lowered.

Voice: barking 'kowk-kowk' during courtship, otherwise silent.

Status: see map. Mainly resident in breeding areas. Vagrant Egypt, Tunisia.

Habitat: dry regions in mountains or plains often with trees. Nests on mound, ruin or small tree.

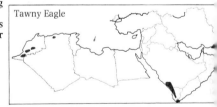

Tawny Eagle

64

Steppe Eagle *Aquila nipalensis*   Illustration p. 62 & Plate 8

Identification: 67–87 cm (wing-span 175–250 cm). Sexes alike, but female larger. Adult typically has medium to dark brown body and wing-coverts below, with slightly paler *dark-barred flight-feathers, blackish band along trailing edge of wing and dark carpal patches; tail also dark barred*. Dark brown upperparts often show paler coverts, *large pale, often dark-barred, primary-patch* and grey-brown uppertail *with dark terminal band. Frequently shows small rusty-yellow nape-patch*. Typical juvenile mid-brown below, with *broad white band through centre of underwings*, and white band on trailing edge of wings and tail; above shows white bar on greater coverts and white uppertail-coverts contrasting with dark rump. Typical immature has remains of juvenile white band on underwing and *darker body than underwing-coverts. Characteristic long gape-flange* can be seen at all ages. Long-winged eagle with ample 'hand' (long 4th primary), well protruding head, and heavy active flight. Soars and glides on slightly, to clearly, arched wings with primaries more or less lowered.

Status: Migrant, occurring on passage between Turkey/Iran and Egypt/Arabia, including Oman and Yemen. Winters in Iran, Iraq, Near East, widely in Arabia, rarely Turkey.

Habitat: open lowland steppe and semi-desert, also foothills, rubbish dumps in desert towns.

Imperial Eagle *Aquila heliaca*   Illustration p. 63

Identification: 72–83 cm (wing-span 190–210 cm). Sexes alike, but female larger. Adult below has *blackish-brown body and wing-coverts*, with paler, often poorly-barred flight- and tail-feathers, latter with broad blackish band. *Whitish-yellow rear-crown and hind-neck*; distinctly *silvery uppertail with broad black band at tip*; pale primary-patch, above, small or absent. White 'braces' on scapulars often hard to see but more distinct in Spanish Imperial, which also has narrow white leading lesser coverts above and below. Juvenile brownish-yellow on body and wing-coverts *with dark streaks on breast which form sharp contrast with unstreaked* rear-body; blackish flight-feathers with *distinct pale wedge on inner primaries below*; often shows two full wing-covert bars above and creamy-white patch on lower back. Pied immature mottled blackish-brown and yellowish on coverts and fore-body, latter contrasting with pale rear-body; adult hind-neck and tail-pattern appear gradually with age. Rather long-winged eagle with ample 'hand' (long 4th primary) and much-protruding head; adult relatively narrow-winged and long-tailed. Soars and glides mainly on flattish wings or wings slightly lifted; tail often (but not always) quite closed, looking narrow.

Status: see map. Partial migrant. Winters Turkey/Iran/Iraq, Egypt and Israel, also central and E Saudi Arabia, Oman, Yemen. Vagrant Syria, Libya, Morocco.

Habitat: park-like plains, steppes and marshes. Builds substantial nest in large tree.

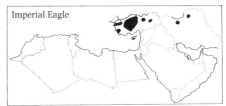

Imperial Eagle

Golden Eagle *Aquila chrysaetos*

Identification: 76–89 cm (wing-span 205–220 cm). See PMH.

Status: see map. Resident. Vagrant Cyprus and E Arabia.

Habitat: barren mountainsides, locally also upland and lowland forest, plains and semi-desert with trees. Nests on rocky ledge, sometimes in tree.

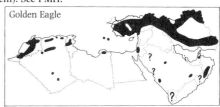

Golden Eagle

65

Verreaux's Eagle *Aquila verreauxii* Plate 8

Identification: 80–95 cm (wing-span 225–245 cm). Sexes alike but female larger. *Coal-black adult has strikingly white lower back to uppertail-coverts*, narrow white V along mantle edges (sometimes difficult to see) and *conspicuous white patch in primaries on both wing-surfaces* (looking translucent from below); cere, eye-lids and legs, yellow to orange-yellow. Juvenile from above shows large creamy-white patch on primaries, yellow-buff patch on centre of wing-coverts, rufous mantle and variably dark-spotted whitish lower back and rump; upper-tail-coverts whitish. White on trailing edge of flight- and tail-feathers and on tips of greater upperwing-coverts (all wear off). *Top of head yellowish-buff, contrasting with blackish-brown on rest of head, neck and upper breast* which again contrast with *buffish-white lower underparts*; large creamy-white primary-patch below and variably dark-spotted underwing-coverts. *At distance below shows dark wing-coverts and fore body with pale rear-body, flight- and tail-feathers, and paler primary-patch.* Characteristic flight-silhouette with oval wings: rather narrow at base, widest at outer secondaries, clearly shorter inner primaries and fairly pointed wing-tips. Slightly rounded tail medium long, but may look shorter when gliding on half-closed wings, when narrow wing-base 'disappears'. Glides, and in particular soars, on raised wings like Golden Eagle, but outer longest 'fingers' more upturned (recalling Bateleur); sails gracefully for long periods, without wing-beats. *Unique wing-shape distinguishes it at all ages from other eagles.*

Voice: calls rarely. Male has a 'chorr-chorr-chorr', female a high-pitched, thinner 'che-che-che', also tremulous ascending, clucking and ringing 'whace-whace-whace'.

Status: see map. Resident. Breeding at least attempted Sinai.

Habitat: wild, steep, mountainous country, relatively dry and without many trees. Nests on cliff, rarely in tree.

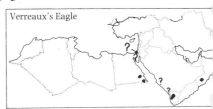

Booted Eagle *Hieraaetus pennatus*

Identification: 45–53 cm (wing-span 110–130 cm). See PMH.

Status: see map. Summer visitor to breeding areas. Passage mainly via Morocco or E Mediterranean countries; fewer Tunisia, Kuwait, Yemen, Oman; recorded only rarely elsewhere in Arabia, Iraq and Cyprus. Few winter N Yemen, occasionally E Arabia, E Mediterranean area and N Africa.

Habitat: deciduous and pine forests, with clearings; seldom far from trees. Nests usually in tree, but also on cliff.

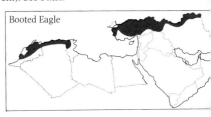

Bonelli's Eagle *Hieraaetus fasciatus*

Identification: 66–74 cm (wing-span 155–160 cm). See PMH.

Status: see map. Mainly resident; some dispersal. Occasional or vagrant several places E and NW Arabia.

Habitat: rocky mountainous country, but seldom at great altitudes; descends to plains and semi-deserts in winter. Nests on precipitous rock-face, occasionally in tree.

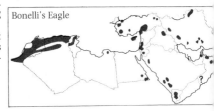

Osprey *Pandion haliaetus*

Identification: 50–60 cm (wing-span 150–170 cm). See PMH.
Status: see map. Resident and migrant, more
 widespread on passage including inland in
 Arabia. Winters coasts of NW Africa, Libya,
 Near East, Red Sea, Arabia, S Iran and
 marshes of Iraq.
Habitat: invariably near water; lakes, large
 rivers, or sea-coasts. Nests on small remote
 islands, rocky cliffs, trees, ruins, occasionally
 on sandy or rocky ground. Breeds in scattered groups in some localities.

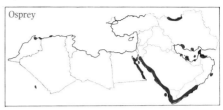

Lesser Kestrel *Falco naumanni*

Identification: 30 cm (wing-span 60–70 cm). See PMH.
Status: see map. May breed locally Syria.
 Mainly summer visitor, but a few winter N
 Africa (mainly in breeding areas), S Turkey,
 Oman. Widespread passage includes Arabia.
Habitat: old buildings, rocky gorges, etc, but
 usually hunts over open country. Breeds in
 colonies in holes in high walls, roofs, crevices
 in cliffs.

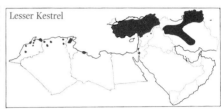

Kestrel *Falco tinnunculus*

Identification: 34 cm (wing-span 68–82 cm). See PMH.
Status: see map. Resident and partial migrant.
 More widespread in winter, reaching some
 Saharan oases, S Iraq, many parts of Arabia.
Habitat: open country with trees, cliffs, towns
 etc. Nests in hole or old nest in tree, cliff,
 ledge or hole in building.

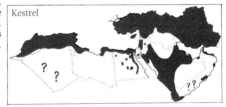

Red-headed Merlin *Falco chicquera*   Plate 9

Identification: 31–36 cm (wing-span 90 cm). Sexes similar but female larger. Merlin-like in
proportions but size similar to Hobby from which separated in silhouette by slightly longer
tail and wing-tips blunter (evident when soaring). Adult has *pale chestnut top of head, pale
bluish-grey upperparts with contrasting darker primaries* and broad black band near tip of blue-
grey uppertail (thus similar wing- and tail-pattern to male Merlin). White throat and
upperbreast, but rest of underparts and underwing-coverts *narrowly barred blackish and white*,
flight-feathers with dense dark grey bars and darker tips to primaries; at distance underwings
and underbody appear greyish. At close range there is a short, *pale chestnut moustache, white
patch on ear-coverts*, fine dark bars on upperwing-coverts and, usually, uppertail which is
tipped whitish; greyish-white undertail also barred black. Juvenile resembles distant adult
above but more buff to forehead and lower hind-neck (narrow blackish shaft-streaks difficult
to see), bolder blackish bars on upperwing-coverts (fine rufous fringes to feathers of upperparts
usually invisible in the field); underparts creamy-buff, with small blackish longitudinal spots
from lower breast to mid belly while *sides of body boldly barred black*; rest of underparts
unmarked; tail as adult. When perched, wing-tips fall well short of tip of tail, like Merlin
(unlike Hobby and Red-footed where wing-tips reach tip of tail). Bold, dashing with swift and
graceful flight, usually straight and low over ground. Usually hunts in pairs.

67

Voice: noisy at breeding grounds where shrill screaming calls are heard.
Status: see map. Resident.
Habitat: open country, bare open plains with some trees in which to nest.

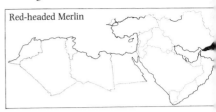

Red-headed Merlin

Red-footed Falcon *Falco vespertinus*

Identification: 30 cm (wing-span 60–70 cm). See PMH.
Status: passage migrant, mainly Turkey and E Mediterranean (uncommon Iraq, vagrant Iran, unconfirmed Arabia), more westerly bias in spring sometimes includes Morocco.
Habitat: open plains with trees, coppices, edges of woods and around farmsteads. Breeds colonially in old nests of Rooks, solitarily in nests of Magpie or Crow.

Manchurian (Eastern) Red-footed Falcon *Falco amurensis*   Plate 9

Identification: 26–32 cm (wing-span 65–75 cm). Sexes differ. Flight, silhouette and proportions as Red-footed. Adult male unmistakable, with *white underwing-coverts* contrasting with dark flight-feathers (but hard to see at dusk). Otherwise like male Red-footed, though darker slate on head and back, and paler slate on underparts and tail. Adult female differs from female Red-footed by *whitish cheeks contrasting with dark ashy-brown cap* and short moustache, clear *dark streaks or spots on breast, barred flanks*, sparsely *dark-spotted underwing-coverts* and, not least, by *rather whitish ground-colour on underwings and body* (where pale rufous-buff restricted mainly to thighs and ventral region); by contrast female Red-footed warm rufous-buff below, lacking any dark markings and without contrasting pattern on sides of head. Female Manchurian is also darker grey, less conspicuously barred above. Juvenile resembles female but has denser spotting on underwing-coverts and streaks on underparts, no flank bars, a buffish narrow band around nape and rufous-edged browner-grey upperparts with some contrast between coverts and flight-feathers. Unlike juvenile Red-footed, it has darker crown merging with short dark moustache, rather *contrasting whitish cheeks* and *whiter ground-colour on body and underwing coverts.* (Young Red-footed has buff ground-colour below, buff-brown crown, with isolated dark eye-patch, but in some, darker top of head merges with eye-patch recalling young Manchurian). Female and juvenile separated from young Hobby (sometimes with difficulty at distance) by *shorter moustache, whiter ground-colour* on body and *underwing* (which often has more conspicuous *dark band along trailing edge*) and by *barred uppertail*; at times, Manchurian's more dashing wing-beats and less powerful flight help separation; may hover, unlike Hobby. Immature male resembles immature male Red-footed, until white underwing-coverts appear at about one year of age. Hunts insects like Red-footed, often in loose flocks; gregarious, collecting in flocks at dusk at night-roosts, departing again shortly after dawn.
Status: scarce passage migrant Oman; vagrant flock SW Saudi Arabia. Breeds E Asia and winters SE Africa.
Habitat: open regions and cultivation near woods during migration.

Merlin *Falco columbarius*   Plate 9

Identification: 25–30 cm (wing-span 50–62 cm). See PMH. In the race *pallidus* (from W Siberia, wintering and passage Turkey eastwards) male distinctly paler blue-grey on upperparts, generally with more rusty crown, shoulders and mantle; underparts paler with generally thinner streaks than in European male. Female and juvenile clearly paler and warmer above than European female and juvenile, being gingery-rufous with blackish barring on back and upperwing-coverts. It thus recalls female Kestrel, but easily separated by underwing-coverts barred rufous and white, bars on primaries above, pale collar on hind-neck (streaked darker), about 4 buff bars across uppertail; dashing flight and compact shape with short wings.
Status: winter visitor Turkey and N Iran, less commonly further south in Iraq, Near East, Cyprus, Egypt, NW Africa. Vagrant Libya, Arabia including Yemen and Oman.
Habitat: open country, including low-lying coasts, marshes, farmland.

Hobby *Falco subbuteo*

Identification: 30–36 cm (wing-span 70–85 cm). See PMH.
Status: see map. Summer visitor. Has bred
Cyprus, Libya, perhaps Algeria. Widespread
on passage throughout area.
Habitat: agricultural and open country with
scattered clumps of trees, open woodland.
Breeds in tree, in old nest usually of Crow.

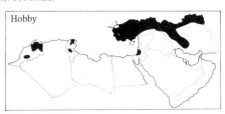

Eleonora's Falcon *Falco eleonorae*

Identification: 38 cm (wing-span 90 cm). See PMH.
Status: see map. Summer visitor. Regularly
seen in interior western Turkey well away
from known breeding areas, also mainland
Tunisia. Passage Near East. Vagrant Libya
and Bahrain.
Habitat: rocky islands and sea-cliffs, at times
hunting over wetlands. Nests colonially on
cliffs.

Sooty Falcon *Falco concolor*   Plate 9

Identification: 32–38 cm (wing-span 85–110 cm). Sexes almost alike; female larger and darker.
Slightly larger than Hobby with slender build, long wings and fairly long tail. Contrary to
previous statements in literature this species appears to have *only one colour phase*. Adult
*uniform slate-grey above with slightly darker head and clear contrast between blackish primaries
and slate (even silvery in certain lights) innerwing*. Entire underparts, except slightly paler chin,
uniform soft slate-grey; shade varies with light conditions and in strong light can appear soft
medium grey or even sandy-buffish, with darker wing-tips. Adult dark phase Eleonora's
Falcon has more uniform, darker upperwings and blackish underwing-coverts which contrast
with paler-based flight-feathers; adult male Red-footed Falcon has paler (silvery) primaries
than innerwing above, darker underwing and red thighs and ventral region. Sooty Falcon
has *conspicuous, yellow orbital-ring and cere; legs orange to reddish* in male (beware of confusion
with Red-footed), yellow or orange in female. *Juvenile has narrow yellowish bars on flight- and
tail-feathers* below, latter tipped yellowish; upperparts dark grey or sooty-brown with blackish
primaries; underparts buffish-yellow, usually with dense, dark slate streaks, or blotches, often
so dense that *breast looks almost uniformly dark* (juvenile Hobby and Eleonora's are paler,
more evenly streaked); dark grey underwing-coverts (finely flecked yellowish) only slightly
darker than flight-feathers (juvenile Hobby has paler even-coloured underwing; juvenile
Eleonora's has dark underwing-coverts contrasting with paler flight-feathers which have
dark band along trailing edge); small blackish moustache and buffish patch on cheeks close
to that of juvenile Eleonora's. Legs pale yellowish-green; cere bluish-green. Fast elastic flight
recalls Hobby, but slightly slower; has proportionally longer wings and longer, generally
more wedge-shaped tip of tail; larger Eleonora's has slightly longer tail and, when not
hunting, slower wing-beats. Soars on flat or very slightly raised wings. Crepuscular at times.
Voice: fairly slow 'kee-keee-keee-keee-keee-keee-keee', very like Hobby. Also querulous Kestrel-
type display call. Young call continuously in nest when parents near, a 'kwee-kwee-kwee-
kwee'.
Status: see map. Summer visitor. Scatter of
records in Arabia away from breeding areas.
Vagrant Cyprus, Iran.
Habitat: chiefly coral islands; also inland cliffs
in deserts. Nests in hole in coral or rock,
rarely under bush.

Lanner *Falco biarmicus*   Plate 10

Identification: 42–52 cm (wing-span 90–115 cm). Sexes alike but female larger. Size between Barbary and Saker. Long-winged and long-tailed falcon with broader, more ample 'hand' and blunter wing-tips than Barbary, most evident when soaring; tail also slightly longer. Very like Saker, but often not as large and heavy-chested. In adult, upper-head and nape *unstreaked creamy-buff* (in North African race *erlangeri* and Near East *tanypterus*) bordered by black forehead band and eye-stripes; but upper-head and nape more chestnut and forecrown dark-streaked in SW Arabian *abyssinicus*; hind-crown and nape paler chestnut in European *feldeggi*. Large white patch on cheeks (usually reaching eye), white lower forehead and long narrow black moustache. Barred upperparts and wing-coverts slaty brown-grey; rump and uppertail distinctly barred; little contrast between wing-coverts and flight-feathers above, except in *erlangeri*. Underparts buffish-white (washed golden-isabelline in *abyssinicus*), variably spotted black (but largely unmarked white in some), the spotting frequently confined to thighs and flanks (in Mediterranean birds). Underwing whitish with dark wing-tips, barred flight-feathers and dark-spotted wing-coverts; some show a dark band across rear underwing-coverts; sometimes primaries are translucent. Cere and legs yellow. Juvenile (bluish cere and legs) has darker, streaked crown (particularly forecrown), looking dark-headed (particularly *feldeggi*) with creamy or whitish supercilium (like Saker), rather dark brown upperparts with blacker primaries, and boldly dark-streaked underparts, appearing almost uniform below pale throat; *closed uppertail usually plain dark brown without barring.* Underwing-coverts heavily spotted blackish, particularly rear-coverts, forming *broad dark band in contrast with much paler flight-feathers* (like juvenile Saker but not like Barbary and Peregrine). Juvenile northern Peregrine *F. p. calidus* has more triangularly-shaped, more pointed wings, but can show head-pattern like cross between Lanner and Saker; it lacks underwing-contrast of Lanner and underparts are normally *thinly* streaked dark. See also Saker and Barbary Falcon.

Voice: screaming 'kirrr-kirrr' or 'shcreeee', often higher than Peregrine; also 'kazick'.

Status: see map. Resident and dispersive. Occurs additionally Syria, Gulf States and S Yemen; also (on passage) Oman. Vagrant Cyprus, Iraq.

Habitat: cliffs, ruins, rocky mountain slopes, extending to stony plains and semi-desert. Nests among rocks, sometimes in tree in nest of another species.

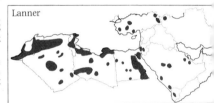

Saker *Falco cherrug*   Plate 10

Identification: 47–55 cm (wing-span 105–130 cm). Sexes alike but female larger. Like Lanner in silhouette but generally larger with broader-based wings and heavy chest, longer tail and, when soaring, broader 'hand' with blunter wing-tips. Most adults *separated from Lanner by rufous-brown to yellowish-brown upperparts and wing-coverts*, giving Kestrel-like contrast with *darker flight-feathers.* Less distinctive head-markings than Lanner, *moustachial streak faint or absent* (conspicuous in Lanner), and dark eye-stripe less well-defined. White crown streaked blackish, looking paler-headed than most Lanners and *some adults quite white-headed. Often shows pronounced whitish supercilium* (absent, or diffuse and creamy in Lanner), and crown evenly streaked, lacking darker fore-crown band, or streaking of adult Lanner. Closed uppertail usually has less distinct buff bars. Underparts whitish, variably spotted dark below throat, generally more than in Lanner; lacks dark bars on 'trousers' and flanks of some Lanners (but see comment below on eastern race of Saker). Whitish underwing with darker wing-tip as in Lanner; some show dark-spotted rear underwing-coverts, in contrast with very pale flight-feathers (such contrast absent in Peregrine and Barbary). Some Sakers (*saceroides*-type) are more uniform greyish above, including uppertail; these are separated by head-pattern and usually size. The eastern race *milvipes* (breeding in NE Iran) has dark bars on upperparts, pinky-rufous crown, boldly barred tail and bars on 'trousers' and flanks, thus resembling Lanner in these features. Juvenile (bluish cere and legs) generally darker brown above (less rufous), with denser streaking on underparts, *densely dark-spotted underwing-coverts, contrasting with pale flight-feathers* and denser streaking on crown. Difficult to separate from large juvenile Lanner, both showing whitish supercilium and more or less plain central tail-feathers but *crown more evenly streaked in juvenile Saker* (Lanner generally has darker fore-crown). Juvenile of pale tundra race of Peregrine *F. p. calidus* can be very pale-headed, with long thin moustachial streak; however it has large white cheek-patches, brownish-grey

upperparts and lacks contrast on underwing and dense streaks on underparts of juvenile
Saker. When perched Saker generally has heavier 'trousers' than Peregrine, and wing-tips
fall shorter than tip of tail.
Voice: calls like Peregrine, but harsher, also high thin querulous note like cross between Curlew
and Herring Gull.
Status: see map. Partial migrant. Winters
Turkey, Iran, Iraq, Near East, Arabia, Egypt.
Vagrant Libya, Morocco.
Habitat: wooded steppes, foothills; in east in
semi-desert plateaux and mountains. Breeds
in tree or on crag, usually in old nest.

Peregrine *Falco peregrinus*   Plate 10

Identification: 38–48 cm (wing-span 80–115 cm). See PMH; also Lanner and Saker.
Status: see map. Partial migrant. In winter
spreads to Iran, Iraq, Arabia, Egypt, Libya.
Habitat: open wild country, cliffs, mountains;
in winter also marshes and coasts. Breeds on
ledge on cliff, sometimes on building, or in
old nest in tree.

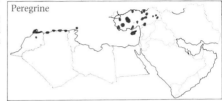

Barbary Falcon *Falco pelegrinoides*   Plate 10

Identification: 38–45 cm (wing-span 80–100 cm). Sexes alike but female larger. Resembles
Peregrine in outline but wings slightly narrower, giving somewhat longer-tailed impression.
Adult has dark top of head bordered by *rusty-red collar on nape* which, in some SW Arabian
birds, and particularly in eastern *babylonicus*, sometimes covers crown (but colour often
surprisingly hard to see); *dark moustachial streak usually narrow* and white patch on cheeks
usually large (almost reaching eye). Underparts whitish, pinkish-buff or even golden-buff,
according to race and sex (male warmest and more unmarked, particularly in eastern race)
with barring sometimes confined to flanks and thighs. Underwing whitish, with neat dark
wing-tips, but at close range faintly barred. Upperparts are pale blue-grey, palest on rump;
uppertail densely barred. Cere and legs yellow. Peregrine (notably the similar-sized Mediterranean race *brookei*), has blacker top of head, *much broader, blacker moustache* with cor-
respondingly *smaller white cheek patch*; underparts have more extensive, denser barring,
underwing is not as whitish looking and wing-tips not so dark as Barbary; the Peregrine
generally has *darker blue-grey upperparts* and *usually lacks rufous neck-collar* (overlap occurs
between NW African Peregrine race *brookei* and Barbary, and separation can be difficult).
Barbary sometimes confused with larger Lanner of NW Africa (*erlangeri*) and Near East
(*tanypterus*) as size can be difficult to estimate and both often appear pale blue-grey above;
Barbary is slimmer, generally with narrower more pointed wings evident when soaring; less
distinct head pattern with less clear-cut black eye stripe, no dark forecrown band and often
darker crown. Juvenile (bluish-grey cere and legs) warm dark brown above (paler grey-
brown in *babylonicus*), has narrow rusty-yellow nape collar (less so or absent in Peregrine)
and *thinly streaked underparts* (streaks usually much bolder in young Peregrine).
Voice: harsh 'keck-keck-keck', basically similar to Peregrine.
Status: see map. Resident and dispersive, or
partial migrant. In winter spreads to Iraq.
Occurs Libya (may breed).
Habitat: steppes and cliffs, inland and coastal,
semi-deserts and arid mountain regions.
Nests on cliff, occasionally on building.

Caucasian Black Grouse, female (above), male (below)

IW

Caucasian Black Grouse *Tetrao mlokosiewiczi* Plate 11

Identification: 40–48 cm. Sexes differ, male larger. Separated geographically from Black Grouse *T.tetrix* (see PMH) from which male differs in *absence of white speculum, vent and undertail-coverts* and by *longer tail with downwardly curved, shorter outer feathers* (lyre-shaped in Black Grouse). Plumage dull velvety-black, glossed deep blue-green; small white patch at carpal and red wattle above eye; axillaries and underwing-coverts white. Female resembles female Black Grouse, but tail longer and square-cut (shorter and slightly forked in female Black Grouse). Flight rapid, direct but short, with whistling wings. Lacks the vocal component of Black Grouse in display, and tail generally less manoeuvered; makes 'flutter-jumps' 1–1½ m up in air; displays in groups in morning and evening in spring.
Voice: male almost voiceless, apparently uttering only a guttural, barely audible 'chr-chr'. Female has cackle like female Black Grouse.
Status: see map. Resident.
Habitat: Alpine meadows with rich vegetation, rhododendron thickets and low birch; also subalpine meadows near tree-line; 1,500–3,000 m, occasionally higher. Highest ground abandoned in winter, descending to lower fir forest, down to 700–800 m in bad winters. Nests on ground in dense cover.

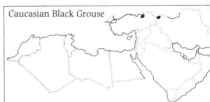

Caucasian Black Grouse

Caspian Snowcock

IW

Caspian Snowcock *Tetraogallus caspius* Plate 11

Identification: 55–58 cm. Sexes differ slightly. A very large game-bird; *male mainly buffish-grey above and below*, much darker on belly and thighs, *with dark moustachial streak and necklace on white cheeks and throat*. Ochre markings on back and rump, rufous spots on wing-coverts,

72

dense brown streaks on flanks and sparse black spots on breast. Tail dark brown, washed rufous at tip. *White flight-feathers (tipped darker) very conspicuous in flight,* but hidden at rest. Female rather smaller, duller, buffer on crown, neck and throat, and lacks spurs of male. Bill light horn, tinged bluish, tipped darker; legs yellowish-orange. Zagros race (SW Iran) is buffer, less grey, with moustachial stripe strongly flecked dark brown. Very wary, difficult to observe on ground; runs with agility, often uphill. Will adopt an upright posture when alerted.

Voice: two different, distinctive calls; a far-carrying Curlew-like ascending whistle, 'yyy, iii, iii, it' with final note very high-pitched and ending abruptly; also a Black Grouse-like bubbling, 'bob-bob-bob-bob-bobobobobao' of varying length which accelerates and ascends a little, and ends with downward curl. Alarm-call a cackling 'chok-chok-chok' on ground and in flight.

Status: see map. Resident.

Habitat: chiefly steep rocky slopes with meadows and bushes in alpine and subalpine zones 1,800–3,000 m or more. Slight altitudinal movements, apparently rarely descending to tree-limit. Nests on ground.

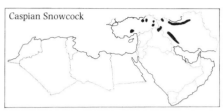
Caspian Snowcock

Chukar *Alectoris chukar*

Identification: 33 cm. See PMH. Sexes alike but male spurred. Medium-sized compact partridge, much resembling Rock Partridge of South Europe (see PMH). Black line from forehead, through eye to sides of neck, meeting on lower throat, *forms gorget encircling buffish-white throat* (the similar Arabian Red-legged Partridge has apparently non-overlapping distribution, broad white supercilium and blackish top of head); sides of tail rufous and flanks boldly barred black, white and chestnut. Rest of plumage varies with race, palest being *sinaica* of Sinai. Generally, upperparts are grey-brown, tinted sandy and more ashy on head, nape and rump, whilst breast greyish. Bill, eye-lids and legs vermillion red. Immature is smaller than adult, lacking clear pattern on head and throat and has greatly reduced barring on flanks. If disturbed, runs quickly or flies with whirring of wings and shrieking call.

Voice: song from prominent perch a far-carrying barnyard-fowl-like 'kakakakar-chuk, chuk, chuk', gathering speed and volume and often turning into 'chuk-or .... chuk-or' or 'chuk-uk-or'.

Status: see map. Resident.

Habitat: stony or rocky slopes with some vegetation, high mountains, barren plateaux, also semi-desert and wastelands with agriculture. Nests under a bush, rock, or in more exposed position.

Chuker

Barbary Partridge *Alectoris barbara*

Identification: 33 cm. See PMH.

Status: see map. Resident.

Habitat: scrub- and scree-covered hillsides, wadis, semi-deserts with a certain amount of water and cover. From lowlands to 3,000 m or more. Nests in ground cover or rocks.

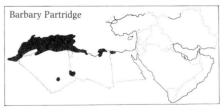
Barbary Partridge

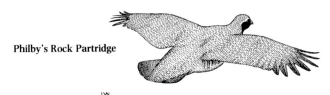

Philby's Rock Partridge

IW

Philby's Rock Partridge *Alectoris philbyi*   Plate 11

Identification: 33 cm. Sexes alike. Chukar-like but separated from it geographically; differs from Chukar (and Arabian Red-legged Partridge, which occurs in same areas) by *large black throat-patch* (whitish in Arabian), lower throat spotted cinnamon, *top of head ash-grey* (blackish in Arabian) and *greyish-white supercilium extending behind eye and bordering throat-patch.* Back and wings pale sandy-grey, with warm sandy-brown wash on mantle (in some extending onto wings). Underparts (below throat) grey merging into sandy-brown lower breast and cinnamon-buff belly, undertail-coverts rufous and flanks boldly barred black, chestnut and buffy white; rump and tail blue-grey with *chestnut distal half of outer feathers noticeable in flight* (blackish in Arabian). Tail appears longish at rest. Bill and eye-ring coral-red, legs pinkish-red. Juvenile brownish overall, finely barred above and with faintest shadow of adult's black chin and throat; rather pale pinkish-white legs.

Voice: song, delivered with bill raised and neck extended, a rapid 'chuk chuk chuk kar' or 'chuk chuk-a-chuk *kar*' with accent on last note, repeated regularly with rhythm of steam railway train. Most frequently heard at dawn and dusk. Alarm-note explosive 'chork chork chork' uttered in flight; also a squealing 'chuck-a-chuck-a-chuck' repeated few to many times. Young have a very soft 'chuk chuk-a-chuk' contact note.

Status: see map. Resident.

Habitat: barren rocky hillsides, also bush-clad slopes, sometimes near highland cultivation. From 1,500 m upwards, mainly above 2,400 m. Breeds under bush or rock cover. Endemic to SW Arabia.

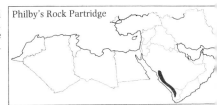

Philby's Rock Partridge

Arabian Red-legged Partridge

IW

Arabian Red-legged Partridge *Alectoris melanocephala*   Plate 11

Identification: 36 cm. Sexes alike, but male spurred. Chukar-type, distinguishable from Philby's by *broad white supercilium from bill to hind-neck* (where buffish), *white throat* (*black in Philby's*) *encircled by broad black gorget* which extends up through eye to bill, blackish crown (greyish in Philby's). Upperparts blue-grey, but in flight *distal half of outer tail-feathers blackish* (chestnut in Philby's); flanks narrowly but conspicuously barred black, blue-grey and buffish-white. Appears noticeably long-tailed in overhead flight. Bill bright red, eye-ring rose-red, legs dull rosy-red. Juvenile grey-brown with paler spots above, grey-buff below and with paler spots; crown gingery-rufous; lacks flank-barring and black gorget.

Voice: a series of rapidly repeated notes, 'qe-qe, qe-qe, qe-qe, qe-qe, qe-qe-qe-qeqeqeqe' or 'kok,kok,kok,kok,chok-chok-chok-chook'; begins as separate notes, then accelerates and descends. Also rapid 'chuk-chuk chuk chuk chuk'. Calls more frequently during day than Philby's.

Status: see map. Resident.
Habitat: rocky slopes with bushes and other vegetation, at times very steep but generally at lower altitudes (300–2,800 m) than Philby's. Nests on ground under bush. Endemic to S Arabia.

See-see Partridge *Ammoperdix griseogularis*   Plate 11

Identification: 23–26 cm. Sexes differ. Size between Grey Partridge and Quail. Male has *black forehead and long black supercilium*, bordered below by *white stripe from bill to behind eye*. Rest of head and neck grey, most noticeable on throat and cheeks; sides of neck speckled white. Upperparts and breast vinous-buff, flanks distinctly banded black, chestnut and white, sweeping up towards tail. Chestnut outer tail-feathers in both sexes visible in flight. Female and immature featureless, lacking grey throat and contrasting head-pattern and resembling female Sand Partridge (which see) although confusion unlikely due to different distribution. Bill, in male, bright orange; horn-coloured in female. Legs dirty greenish or wax-yellow. Often in small parties; active in early morning and at dusk. Can run fast and easily among rocks and up slopes. Flies little but if pressed goes off low and fast with whirr of wings.
Voice: a distinctive far-carrying, frequently repeated 'wuii-div' with stress on first syllable; also a Spotted Crake-like 'wuid-wuit'; flight call a fast 'bwuit-bwuit-bwuit'.
Status: see map. Resident. Recorded Syria.
Habitat: barren stony or gravelly hill-sides, open desolate tracts or broken ground, steep rocky banks. Avoids tall or thick vegetation but needs access to drinking water. Up to 2,000 m. Nests on ground.

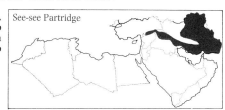

Sand Partridge *Ammoperdix heyi*   Plate 11

Identification: 24 cm. Sexes differ. Similar in size to See-see Partridge but sandier and more uniform. Male sandy pinkish-isabelline above with lower back greyer and finely barred. Head bluish-grey with *conspicuous oval white patch behind eye and on forehead; lacks black supercilium of See-see*. Underparts pinkish-isabelline, flanks heavily banded deep red-brown, blackish and buff, sweeping up towards tail; chestnut outer tail-feathers in both sexes visible in flight. Female and immature rather uniform sandy-grey, finely barred, lacking distinctive markings on head or flanks. Bill orange-yellow in male, yellowish-horn in female. The races *intermedia* (SW, S and NE Arabia) and *cholmleyi* (SE Egypt, illustrated) are much darker, being maroon or dark vinous red-brown; in Egyptian birds no whitish forehead spot. Behaviour much like See-see Partridge, which see.
Voice: male's call a quickly repeated, far-carrying 'qwei-qwei-qwei' or 'kuek-kuek-kuek'. Alarm-call an explosive 'wuit-wuit-wuit', uttered in flight; on ground a weak, soft 'ki-ru, ki-ru'.
Status: see map. Resident. Recorded Syria.
Habitat: desolate rocky and stony slopes and wadis, even cliffs, not far from water. Breeds on ground, under overhanging rock or bush.

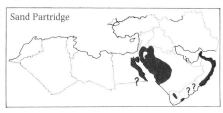

Black Francolin *Francolinus francolinus*   Plate 11

Identification: 31–34 cm. Sexes differ. A wary, plump, relatively large, stub-tailed game-bird, difficult to flush and more often heard than seen. Spurred male unmistakable, *jet black face and underparts, broken by white cheek-patch, chestnut collar* and vent, and conspicuous white spotting on black upper-mantle, sides of breast and flanks; back appears grey-brown (finely barred), wings spangled warm buff; in flight, chestnut collar not easily seen, flanks may appear whitish barred, and golden mottling on underwings contrasts with black underparts. Female dull brown; mantle and flanks strongly mottled with black arrow-shaped marks; belly paler, barred dark brown; *dull chestnut patch on hind-neck,* much buff on sides of face and buffish white throat. Hides in thickets, rarely seen in open; if disturbed, runs away with cocked tail (seldom noted in Grey Francolin, which see).

Voice: male's call, mainly heard morning and evening, is unexpectedly loud, penetrating, high-pitched, harsh, usually of 7–8 syllables uttered from ground or post, 'kvee, kveek-kveek-kveek-kveek, kvee-kvee' or 'ki-ki-ki-ki-ki, ki-ki', the 2nd and 5th note stressed (2nd ascending, 5th descending); also a rasping 'kar-kar, ke ke ke' (stress on second note), repeated at intervals of about 15 seconds.

Status: see map. Resident. A few records Hofuf (E Saudi Arabia) and UAE suggest possibility of feral breeding.

Habitat: densely scrub-covered lowlands and wadis, often not far from water, dunes with scattered vegetation, also reedy flood-plains. Nests on ground in thick cover.

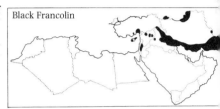

Grey Francolin *Francolinus pondicerianus*   Plate 11

Identification: 29 cm. Sexes alike but male spurred. Squat, stub-tailed, greyish-brown game-bird, slightly smaller than Black Francolin. Adult separated from female Black Francolin by *chestnut forehead,* rufous-buff cheeks and oval *pale throat-patch bordered by blackish flecks forming 'U' shape below.* Crown and ear-coverts grey-brown with buffish supercilium; *neck grey, finely barred black (chestnut patch in female Black Francolin).* Upperparts brownish-grey with *broad pale chestnut and narrow white and black barring.* Underparts whitish, finely vermiculated black. Flight-feathers grey-brown. Chestnut tail-feathers visible in flight. Bill dusky, paler at base, legs dull red. Immature has less chestnut on forehead and less obvious blackish 'U' on throat. In pairs or small parties, difficult to flush. When alarmed, runs off swiftly from bush to bush; if pressed rises with explosive whirr of wings, glides and runs again on landing. Roosts in trees or under dense bushes.

Voice: loud far-carrying yelping 'kiril-kiril-kiril-kiril-kiril-kiril' without change of pitch, each note repeated 7–10 times, or 'kiki ril, kiki ril, kiki ril' etc.

Status: see map. Resident.

Habitat: thorn scrub, edges of cultivation and semi-desert. Nests on ground under tuft or bush.

Double-spurred Francolin *Francolinus bicalcaratus*   Plate 11

Identification: 32 cm. Sexes alike but male spurred. *Striking head-pattern of black forehead, streak on side of rufous-brown crown and nape, white supercilium* and black loral streak separates this medium-sized game-bird. Underparts closely streaked black, bright rufous and white, heaviest on flanks and belly; chin and throat buffish, neck and upper mantle with narrow black, rufous and white streaks and spots; rest of upperparts brownish with thin brownish streaking on coverts and buff barring on brownish flight- and tail-feathers. Bill and legs greenish. Usually in small parties; sometimes perches in tree.

Voice: song, uttered from mound or post, mainly at dawn, a repeated deep-toned 'quair-quair' or 'koak-koak'.
Status: see map. Resident.
Habitat: open forest and clearings, dense scrub along streams, grasslands and cultivated country, also bushy wadis. Breeds on ground in vegetation, usually thick.

Grey Partridge *Perdix perdix*

Identification: 30 cm. See PMH.
Status: see map. Resident.
Habitat: farmland, pastures, wastelands, sand-dunes, etc. Nests on ground under bush or in long grass.

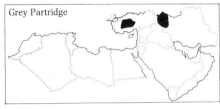

Harlequin Quail, female (left); **Quail** (above); **Andalusian Hemipode** (right)

Quail *Coturnix coturnix*

Identification: 18 cm. See PMH.
Status: see map. Mainly summer visitor. Passage widespread, but with concentration in N Africa and especially Egypt, Libya. Some winter Mediterranean basin (Turkey, Cyprus, N Africa), also Iraq, Iran, but apparently not Near East or Arabia (except Yemen).
Habitat: farmcrops, rough grassland, avoiding trees and bare ground. Nests on ground.

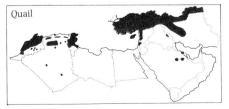

Harlequin Quail *Coturnix delegorguei*   Plate 11

Identification: 16–19 cm. Sexes differ. Slightly smaller *and, in flight, less narrow-winged than Quail* from which male separated by *broad black band down centre of breast* (absent in Quail), black-streaked *dark chestnut flanks and belly* and white cheeks and throat with blackish 'anchor' markings (dark chestnut-brown in Quail). Otherwise much like Quail, with similar head pattern but *long buffy-white stripes on back and rump are much less noticeable*. Female has *unmarked buff throat*, contrasting with *pale rufous underparts*, lightly mottled darker on upper-breast. Female Harlequin separated from male Quail by combination of unmarked throat and warmer colour of underparts; from female Quail by absence of distinct blackish spots across breast and by *warmer rufous lower breast and belly* (buffish in female Quail). Immature, which has blackish spots on breast, perhaps separable only by *uniform dark grey-brown flight-feathers* (barred buff in Quail). Rarely seen unless flushed. Flight fast as Quail. Separated from Andalusian Hemipode, which occurs in similar areas, by obviously larger size, longer, more pointed wings (short and rounded in the hemipode), uniform dark upperwing (pale fore-wing contrasting with darker flight-feathers in the hemipode); on ground by strongly patterned head and absence of golden-orange on underparts; Andalusian Hemipode lacks buffy-white back stripes of other two quails.

Voice: typically an explosive, whipping 'wit, wit-wit, wit-wit' (with gap of 1–2 seconds between each note/double note) and with rising inflexion; recalls Quail, but differs in being more 'whip'-like, rather similar to call of Spotted Crake.

Status: uncertain; possibly only an occasional visitor but may breed SW Saudi Arabia, N Yemen, also S Yemen where recorded in numbers a century ago; vagrant S Oman. Range Africa.

Habitat: open grassland and cultivated fields. Nests on ground.

Pheasant *Phasianus colchicus*

Identification: 55–90 cm. See PMH.
Status: see map. Resident.
Habitat: woodland borders and thickets, interspersed with farmland in lowland or rolling country, also reed-beds. Nests among thick ground cover.

Helmeted Guineafowl *Numida meleagris* Plate 11

Identification: 63 cm. Sexes alike. Large, plump game-bird with tiny head and drooping tail, closely resembling domesticated guinea-fowl. *Slate-grey plumage covered with profusion of white spots*, forming sweeping vermiculated lines on wings. Closer views reveal *bare bluish-white patch on side of head*, violet tinge on base of neck, *pale brown horny protuberance on crown*, red wattles at base of bill and below eye, yellowish-horn bill and dark greyish legs. Juvenile buffish-brown with buff or white spotting on body, especially wings and back. Older immature resembles adult but ornamentation on head less pronounced. Most active at dawn and dusk; gregarious and tame if undisturbed; when alarmed runs fast with head held high and is reluctant to fly; flight fairly rapid with occasional glides. Roosts in trees and thick bushes.

Voice: most common call is a loud repeated 'kek, kek, kek', heard especially at dawn and dusk.

Status: see map. Resident. Recent declines make it uncertain whether all the mapped areas in SW Arabia are still occupied; severely reduced Morocco.

Habitat: savanna, grassy plains, hills, wadis, often near cover. Nests on ground in thick cover.

Andalusian Hemipode (Little Button Quail) *Turnix sylvatica*

Identification: 15 cm. See PMH. Sexes differ slightly. Terrestrial but rarely seen, then usually only briefly in flight when identified by *tiny size, short tail, short rounded wings and buffish plumage (including underwing-coverts) with dark flight-feathers*. Quite unlike Quail or Harlequin Quail which are obviously larger and have longer, much narrower uniformly dark wings.

78

In flight could be likened to a tiny young partridge just able to fly but wings even shorter and more rounded. Generally grey-brown to buffish above with black spotting on sides of orange-rufous breast; in flight, can often show orange-rufous on upperparts, particularly wing-coverts. Female brighter than male with more chestnut tone to plumage. Flight short with whirring wing-beats, quickly settling in cover when becomes difficult to flush again.

Status: see map. Probably resident. Recent declines make it uncertain whether the mapped areas in NW Africa are still occupied. Formerly occurred in winter in S Yemen. Recent isolated records from N Yemen, SW Saudi Arabia and S Oman. Vagrant Iran.

Habitat: sandy plains with palmetto scrub, brush covered wastes, extensive low thickets, stubble and neglected cultivation. Nests in dense vegetation.

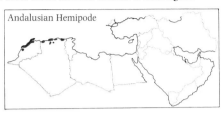
Andalusian Hemipode

Water Rail *Rallus aquaticus*

Identification: 28 cm. See PMH.

Status: see map. Partial migrant, but breeders mainly resident in our area. Also winter visitor occurring all parts Mediterranean basin, Iraq, Iran, Arabian Gulf and occasionally south to Oman, N Yemen.

Habitat: dense aquatic vegetation, reed- and osier-beds, overgrown ponds, ditches, riverbanks. Nests among reeds or sedges above shallow water.

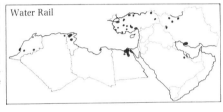
Water Rail

Spotted Crake *Porzana porzana*

Identification: 23 cm. See PMH.

Status: see map. Mainly migrant. Some winter Near East, Egypt, Oman, perhaps NW Africa and Saudi Arabia. On passage may occur almost anywhere in the region though vagrant Yemen.

Habitat: swamps and fens, overgrown ditches, outer margins of ponds, rivers, etc. Nests in thick vegetation by or in very shallow water.

Spotted Crake

Little Crake *Porzana parva*

Identification: 19 cm. See PMH.

Status: see map. Mainly migrant. Passage inconspicuous throughout area, wintering Egypt, Near East and perhaps Oman.

Habitat: as Spotted, but with fondness for high reeds in deeper water and lagoons with floating vegetation; accessible only by climbing or swimming. Nests in thick vegetation close to or in water.

Little Crake

Baillon's Crake *Porzana pusilla*

Identification: 18 cm. See PMH.

Status: see map. Mainly passage. May breed or has bred Algeria, Tunisia, Near East, Turkey. Inconspicuous passage through whole region, including Arabia though vagrant N Yemen. Winters Egypt, Near East, Iraq, Oman.

Habitat: usually prefers lower, denser vegetation (sedges, rushes) and smaller pools than Little Crake, in floodlands, fens, water margins, with abundant cover. Nests on ground or tussock in water.

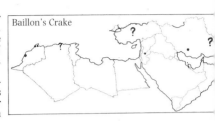

Baillon's Crake

Striped Crake, immature (left), adult male (right)

Striped Crake *Porzana marginalis*

Identification: 17 cm. Sexes differ slightly. *Small, size as Little Crake with short, heavy bill.* Adult male pale rufous-brown with darker crown, softly barred flanks, fading to whitish on belly; wings and back olivaceous-brown, with whitish edges to feathers giving striped appearance. Rump and tail blackish-brown with rufous edging; *vent and undertail-coverts unbarred deep cinnamon-buff. Culmen black, bill otherwise green with bluish-white lower mandible;* legs greenish. Female darker, duller and greyer with *grey not rufous on head, neck, chest and flanks;* back and wings as male. Juvenile similar to male but browner above, lacking streaks and with sides of face and body rufous; bill yellowish-horn.

Voice: 'tak-tak-tak', etc, rapidly repeated; also grunts and growls.

Status: vagrant Algeria, Libya. Range Africa.

Habitat: wet grasslands and marshes, shallow ditches.

Corncrake *Crex crex*

Identification: 27 cm. See PMH.

Status: has perhaps bred Turkey. Passage migrant, occurring chiefly in Mediterranean countries; scarce Iraq, Arabia though concentrations recorded in recent agricultural developments in E Saudi Arabia. May winter occasionally in Mediterranean area, but apparently not Egypt.

Habitat: meadows, lush vegetation, and crops. Avoids standing water.

White-breasted Waterhen *Amaurornis phoenicurus*

Identification: 32 cm. Sexes alike. Moorhen-sized bird with entire upperparts dark slate-grey; *forehead, face, front of neck and underparts white,* down to buff lower belly which merges into *deep rufous vent and undertail-coverts;* flanks dark slate as upperparts. The strong bill is swollen at base, greyish-green with yellower lower mandible and red spot at base of upper; legs and feet greenish-yellow or yellow-orange. Juvenile has white face obscured by slate-brown feathers and upperparts are more olive-brown. In laboured flight legs dangle and protrude

80

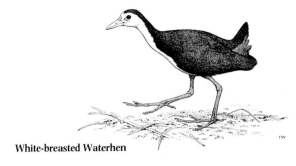

White-breasted Waterhen

behind tail like other rails; rufous sides of vent visible from side-view. Skulks, but will often come into the open, walking about with jerking tail, displaying its undertail-coverts.

oice: very vocal in spring or during monsoon, more often heard than seen; silent in dry season, thus often overlooked; calls loudly and continuously, a monotonous repeated 'kee-wak' or 'krr-kwaak-kwaak, krr-kwaak-kwaak', etc, preceded by loud croaks and roars.

tatus: vagrant Oman. Range includes Indian sub-continent.

abitat: swampy grass, water holes with dense vegetation, mangrove edges and reedy marshland.

Moorhen *Gallinula chloropus*

Identification: 33 cm. See PMH.

Status: see map. Resident and winter visitor. Range expanding in Arabia to occupy newly created waters.

Habitat: wetland and river margins, marshes, always requiring freshwater and nearby cover. Nests in aquatic vegetation or bushes near water.

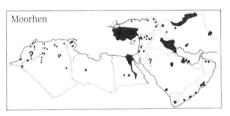

Allen's Gallinule *Porphyrula alleni*   Plate 12

Identification: 24 cm. Sexes alike. Slender, Moorhen-size; distinguished by *greenish back and wings*, dull *violet-blue underparts* with almost black head and rump, red bill and legs and *greenish-blue frontal shield*. (Much larger Purple Gallinule has very deep bill, red frontal shield and lacks green on wings in Egyptian birds). Juvenile brown above, mottled sandy, flight-feathers are washed greenish; underparts buff and frontal shield reddish-brown. Behaviour similar to other rails with tail jerked when moving; legs dangling in laboured flight. Swims well, climbs reeds with ease and walks on floating vegetation. Difficult to observe as often secretive.

oice: frog-like rolling 'gurr' and sharp 'chucking' alarm note.

tatus: vagrant Morocco, Tunisia, Egypt, Cyprus, Oman. Range Africa.

abitat: dense reed-beds, rank grass or thick bushes at edges of swamps.

Purple Gallinule *Porphyrio porphyrio*   Plate 12

Identification: 40–48 cm. Sexes alike. Large size (much larger than Coot). Adult easily distinguished by *bluish plumage* with striking *white undertail-coverts, very deep red bill*, frontal shield and long legs and toes. Western Mediterranean race *porphyrio* has bright turquoise sides of head, throat and upperbreast, back and wings purplish-blue; Egyptian race *madagascariensis* (Green-backed Gallinule) has bright deep bronze-green back; Middle East races, *caspius* and *seistanicus*, have greyer head and throat, and wings bluish-green. Juvenile duller, matt dark blue above and bright greyish or dirty-white below, *undertail-coverts conspicuously white*; bill and frontal shield lead-blue but becomes red during first autumn. Generally shy. Allen's

81

Gallinule is much smaller, has green wings and almost blackish head and neck; adults have greenish-blue frontal shield.

Voice: rich and variable, often deep and mooing; when feeding a 'tschak-tschak' etc., the first note longer than 2–3 following; call note longer and nasal; alarm note a mono-syllabic variant of call note. Flight call a metallic 'krr'. Song is a sequence of many nasal notes: 'quin quin krrkrr-quin quin krrkrr' lasting 8–15 seconds; male deeper, more sonorous, female higher-pitched and shriller.

Status: see map. Mainly resident, but some wandering. Vagrant Cyprus, Near East, Arabian Gulf and Oman.

Habitat: swamps with extensive reed-beds, borders of lakes and rivers fringed with dense tall aquatic cover, in which it nests in shallow water.

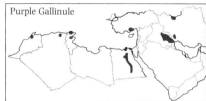

Coot *Fulica atra*

Identification: 38 cm. See PMH.

Status: see map. Range expanding in Arabia to occupy newly created waters. Partial migrant. In winter in most breeding areas, also reaches Cyprus, central Algeria, N Libya, Arabia south to Oman, also Yemen.

Habitat: prefers larger areas of open water than Moorhen. Packs occur on lakes, reservoirs and salt water in winter. Nests in aquatic vegetation in shallow water.

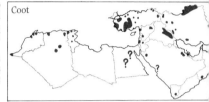

Crested Coot *Fulica cristata*

Identification: 41 cm. See PMH.

Status: see map. Mainly resident. May still breed Algeria.

Habitat: as Coot.

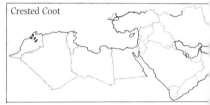

Crane *Grus grus*

Identification: 115 cm. See PMH.

Status: see map. Partial migrant. Passage mainly Near East and Egypt; few W Arabia and vagrant E and S Arabia including N Yemen. Winters Turkey, Iraq, Iran, Syria, Israel and NW Africa.

Habitat: bogs, lightly wooded swamps, reed-beds. In winter avoids wooded regions, occurring on river banks, lagoons, fields and steppes. Nests on ground, sometimes in shallow water.

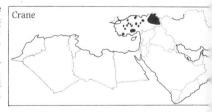

82

Siberian White Crane *Grus leucogeranus*   Plate 3

Identification: 130–140 cm. Sexes alike. Similar in size to Crane but with stork-like neck and bill. Adult *pure white* with scapulars and tertials elongated to cover wing-tips like a shaggy tail. *Primaries, which are visible only in flight, are black*; rather long *bill and naked skin on face reddish*, though bill frequently dark with red base. Legs dull reddish-pink; Juvenile/immature birds smaller, lack naked skin on face and have rusty-buff head and upper neck; rest of plumage whitish tinged patchily with rusty-buff, deepest on wing-coverts. In flight (which is stork-like), however, looks mainly white with black primaries; wing beats interspersed with occasional glides. Most frequently seen feeding or resting in shallow water. Usually wary.
Voice: call a rather musical, far-carrying Crane-like trumpeting 'broop broop' with rising inflection. Alarm note 'turr'.
Status: rare winter visitor N Iran. Range Asia.
Habitat: marshes, lagoons, and flooded meadows.

Demoiselle Crane *Anthropoides virgo*

Identification: 97 cm. See PMH.
Status: see map. Summer visitor. Breeding tenuous in Turkey; one or two pairs still occasionally seen Morocco; probably extinct Algeria. Passage over Cyprus and numerous W Saudi Arabia, seldom Egypt, Iran. Vagrant E and S Arabia, Near East, Tunisia.
Habitat: open or shrubby plains and high dry plateaux, with access to water; will feed on arable land. In winter fields, lake margins, sandbanks. Nests on ground.

Little Bustard *Tetrax tetrax*

Identification: 43 cm. See PMH.
Status: see map. Partial migrant. Resident Morocco and Iran, with winter immigration probable in both areas. May also winter Turkey, Libya, Egypt. Vagrant Cyprus, Near East, Iraq, Oman.
Habitat: rough grassy plains, large fields of corn or fodder crops. Nests on grounds.

Houbara *Chlamydotis undulata*   Plate 13

Identification: 66–73 cm. Sexes alike, male larger. Size between female Great and Little Bustard. In flight, *conspicuous white patch on upper surface of black-tipped outer primaries* (much less white on wings than Great and Little), and buffish bar across wing-coverts; whitish underwing has black secondaries and primary-tips. Striking wing-pattern concealed at rest when all upperparts appear sandy-buff with dark vermiculation; tail has three or four dark bars. Elongated black and white feathers on sides of grey neck puffed out during display; otherwise *broad black neck-streak*, often most conspicuous feature of bird at rest. Short crest on nape. Striking yellow eyes. Juvenile resembles adult but black neck-streak much less developed. In flight, long neck, tail, and fairly long narrow wings, distinctive; low flight considerably faster than it appears, with slow, deep, deliberate crane-like wing-beats, with accent on upward stroke, interspersed with glides on outstretched wings. Shy; will 'freeze' or run at speed if approached. See also Arabian Bustard.
Voice: silent; nestlings give piping notes.
Status: see map. Formerly widespread resident in Syria. Summer visitor to Iran breeding grounds; elsewhere mainly resident in declining numbers. Winter visitor coastal Iran, Iraq, Arabia excluding N Yemen. Vagrant Cyprus.

83

Habitat: stony or sandy steppes or semi-desert, open or with scattered shrubs and grass. Also occurs in marginal corn and other crops. Nests on ground.

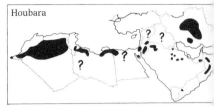

Arabian Bustard *Ardeotis arabs*   Plate 13

Identification: 74–90 cm. Sexes alike, but male noticeably larger and heavier. Huge, standing up to 1 metre, thus near size of Great Bustard. Grey crown *bordered by black feathers*, elongated at rear to form flat crest, *white supercilium* and narrow black malar-streak; throat and neck finely vermiculated grey and rest of upperparts dull gingery-brown with white tips to most wing-coverts. Moroccan race, *lynesi*, smaller and darker. The flight has heavy slow crane-like wing-beats with accent on upward stroke (but also recalling large vulture when taking off); *in flight broad whitish band across innerwing* (more conspicuous than Houbara's similar band) but whitish barring on inner primaries less conspicuous (smaller Houbara has unmarked pure white patch on outer-primaries). In male's display, neck thickens and balloons out, wings are drooped and tail raised and fanned. Usually seen alone or in pairs, but may display in loose association; relatively approachable where unmolested.

Voice: displaying male gives a liquid, hollow 'puk-puk' at intervals of about 30 seconds.

Status: see map. Probably extinct in SW Saudi Arabia. Resident.

Habitat: open savanna; in N Yemen largely confined to cereal fields in sandy plains. Nests on ground.

Great Bustard *Otis tarda*

Identification: 102 cm (male); 75 cm (female). See PMH.

Status: see map. Partial migrant in Turkey and Iran, mainly resident in Morocco. In winter occurs outside breeding areas in N Iran, N Iraq, N Syria, Turkey. Vagrant Cyprus, Near East, Tunisia, Algeria.

Habitat: open plains, grassy steppes, extensive cereal fields. Nests on ground.

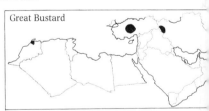

84

Pheasant-tailed Jacana, adult winter

Pheasant-tailed Jacana *Hydrophasianus chirurgus*   Plate 12

Identification: 57 cm (tail 27 cm). Sexes alike. Rail-like water-hen with very long toes adapted to walking on floating vegetation. In *breeding plumage, body dark chocolate* with black-tipped *white wings conspicuous in flight*; outer primaries elongated, pointing upwards when feeding, and very elongated blackish tail. Head and foreneck white, hind-neck golden-yellow, edged black. In non-breeding plumage (when tail and primaries short), upperparts paler grey-brown; flight-feathers remain white but inner central wing-coverts browner; crown and neck flecked brownish; underbody becomes white, but retains *dark gorget across breast*. Juvenile resembles non-breeding adult but gorget flecked white, top of head rufous-brown, neck grey-brown where adult is yellow, and upperparts paler. Legs and bill bluish in breeding plumage, otherwise greenish. Flight low and rapid with fast wing-beats, erratic and twisting, with large feet dangling. Normally not shy; gregarious in winter.
Voice: nasal mewing 'tewn-tewn'; also pleasant 'hoo-hoo-hoo'.
Status: winter visitor (from Indian sub-continent) Oman, where occasionally over-summers. Vagrant Yemen.
Habitat: swamps, ponds, creeks and marshes with patches of open water and floating vegetation.

Painted Snipe *Rostratula benghalensis*   Plate 12

Identification: 23–28 cm. Sexes differ. Separated from other snipes by *grey (male)* or *chestnut (female) foreparts, striking pale eye-ring and sharp division of black breast-band from white belly.* Male brownish above with buff stripe along edges of mantle forming V; buff crown stripe bordered blackish, prominent whitish buff eye-ring tapering backwards, and neck pale brownish-grey. Narrow blackish breast-band with whitish hind border running up to shoulder. Flight- and tail-feathers conspicuously spotted orange. Larger and brighter female has brilliant white eye-patch, rich chestnut cheeks and neck and black breast-band with hind border reaching shoulder; upperparts greeny-bronze with buff V. Juvenile similar to male but no black breast-band. Longish snipe-like bill slightly decurved at tip. Difficult to flush; rises suddenly with slow wing-beats and legs dangling like a rail; rather tail-less. White flank-feathers can give Ruff-like rump pattern and there is a small but conspicuous white patch in centre of *darkish grey underwing*. At rest bobs tail like sandpiper.
Voice: usually silent when flushed. Female's voice resembles sound of blowing into bottle.
Status: see map. Resident with some dispersal. Occasional Israel in winter. Vagrant Oman and S Yemen.
Habitat: well-vegetated swamps with muddy patches, reedbeds, and will feed on open fields. Nests on ground in thick marsh cover.

Painted Snipe

Oystercatcher *Haematopus ostralegus*

Identification: 43 cm. See PMH.

Status: see map. Mainly migrant in breeding areas. Winters coasts of N Africa (mainly Morocco, Tunisia, Egypt), Arabia, Iran, Iraq and a few S Turkey. Slight passage several parts E Mediterranean. Some non-breeders spend summer in wintering areas. Vagrant Jordan.

Habitat: margins of lakes and rivers; in winter mainly coastal. Nests on ground in open.

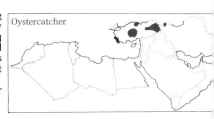

Black-winged Stilt *Himantopus himantopus*

Identification: 38 cm. See PMH.

Status: see map. Mainly summer visitor Turkey, N Iran, otherwise resident or partial migrant in breeding areas. Irregular breeder Cyprus. Widespread on passage, both coastal and inland. Winters NW Africa, Egypt, Near East, S Iran and Arabia.

Habitat: shallow freshwater or brackish wet marshes, lagoons, estuaries, without dense vegetation and with open margins. Nests on ground, usually in open.

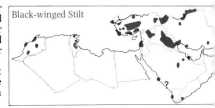

Avocet *Recurvirostra avosetta*

Identification: 43 cm. See PMH.

Status: see map. Partial migrant. Summer visitor central and E Turkey. Winters NW Africa, Egypt and most E Mediterranean countries, Iraq marshes, Iran, also on all coasts of Arabia with little inland passage. Some over-summer in S Arabia. Vagrant Libya.

Habitat: exposed, often saline, mud-flats, estuaries and sandbanks. Breeds colonially near shallow water.

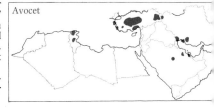

Crab Plover *Dromas ardeola* Plate 13

Identification: 41 cm. Sexes alike. Unmistakable *black and white stout wader with large head, heavy straight black bill with angled lower mandible*, and rather long whitish- or pale bluish-grey legs. At rest, largely white with black mantle, edge of wing and small spot around eye. In flight, neck is extended and legs protrude well beyond short white tail; primaries and their coverts dull greyish, grading into blackish wing-tip, secondaries and greater coverts are also blackish; black mantle and much elongated black inner scapulars cover sides of white lower back; underwing mainly whitish with darker wing-tip. Adult in winter, and immature, have dark streaks on pale grey crown and nape, in some extending down hind-neck in a narrow band; juvenile has mantle, shoulders and tail pale buffy grey-brown. Generally, horizontal carriage with neck tucked between shoulders; when alarmed, upright and with long neck fully extended. Has plover-like feeding-action; usually shy, partly crepuscular and often gregarious. Flocks fly in loose formation.

Voice: noisy; shrill 'tchuk-tchuk-chuk-chuk-chuk' near nest, and continuous 'tchuk-tchuk' at night. Alarm note loud sharp 'kjep' or 'kiep', repeated 4–5 times.

Status:see map. Partial migrant, or dispersive. Present all year in parts of Arabian Gulf (including Kuwait where may still breed on off-shore island), coasts of Gulf of Oman, Arabian Sea and S Red Sea, regularly reaching SE Egypt. Vagrant Turkey.

Habitat: sea-coasts, mud-flats, coral reefs; never inland. Nests in tunnel excavated in sandy ground; colonial.

Stone Curlew *Burhinus oedicnemus*   Plate 13

Identification: 41 cm. See PMH. Race *saharae*, which inhabits Mediterranean North Africa and Near East, is more sandy and rufous throughout and upperwing pattern generally more diffuse than in European birds. For distinction from Senegal and Spotted Thick-knee, see those species.

Status: see map. Partial migrant; mainly summer visitor in Turkey, Iran, N Iraq. Range expanded in winter in NW Africa. In Arabia uncommon or irregular passage and winter in all areas.

Habitat: stony, sandy, or dry mud, open plains or slopes with scant vegetation, including steppe, semi-desert and locally extensive arable; occasionally among scattered trees and light thorn scrub in hotter climates. Nests on ground.

Senegal Thick-knee *Burhinus senegalensis*   Plate 13

Identification: 37 cm. Sexes alike. Slightly smaller version of Stone Curlew, which it generally resembles (large yellow eye, stout bi-coloured bill and long greenish-yellow legs). Upperparts sandy brownish-grey with neat sharp dark streaks, underparts white with fine black streaks on sides and front of neck and breast. At rest and in flight, rather pale grey-buff upperwing-coverts framed by narrow dark forewing and black secondaries, *lacking the white bar along blackish band on lesser coverts* of Stone Curlew; pattern on primaries above resembles that of Stone Curlew (white spot near tip of outer primaries, white-tipped and white-based inner primaries). The *closed* uppertail is *plain* brownish-grey (lacks irregular buff and dark brown markings usually present in Stone Curlew). Juvenile resembles adult. Flight like Stone Curlew, with slow, deliberate wing-beats, interspersed with glides; behaviour much like Stone Curlew; more active from dusk. See also Spotted Thick-knee.

Voice: very different from Curlew-like whistle of Stone Curlew; a series of loud strong notes 'kvi-kvi-kvi-kvi-kvi,kvi,kvi,kvi,-kvi-kvi-kvi-kvi-', etc, starts slowly but accelerates and ascends in tone, recalling fast Oystercatcher, then descends in tone and speed towards end.

Status: see map. Resident, perhaps with some dispersal.

Habitat: rarely far from water; savannas, thorn-scrub, cultivation, margins of lakes, sandy beds of rivers where pools remain; occasionally on coast. Nests on sandbanks in rivers and on flat roofs of houses, even colonially.

87

Spotted Thick-knee *Burhinus capensis*   Plate 13

Identification: 37 cm. Sexes alike. Resembles Stone Curlew in shape and appearance (large yellow eye, stout bi-coloured bill and long lemon-yellow legs), but *more upright stance* and upperparts more rufous- or brown-buff and *spotted with black* (streaked in Stone Curlew and Senegal Thick-knee). Unlike other two thick-knees, *lacks bar on closed wing at rest*; tertials (which cover wing-tip) *barred buff and black* (plain with dark centre in other two). Closed upper-tail *barred buff and black* (usually irregularly blotched dark and buff in Stone Curlew, usually plain in Senegal Thick-knee). Underparts whitish with bold streaks on buffy breast and fore-neck. Juvenile has more streaked appearance than adult, especially on coverts, contrasting more with barred tail and tertials. *Flight pattern lacks the black and white lines on coverts* of Stone Curlew and Senegal Thick-knee (but greater coverts are uniformly greyish); pattern on primaries resembles that of the two other thick-knees (see Plate). Behaviour much like Stone Curlew, though preferring less open country; active from dusk.
Voice: loud, piping 'pi-pi-pi-pi-peo peo peo-pi pi', rising then fading away; also 'pi, pi, pee-pee-pee-pee', 'pip-i-pup, pip-i-pup' and Oystercatcher-like shrill whistles, usually at night.
Status: see map. Resident.
Habitat: savannas and scrub, rocky river beds, broken ground, more bushy than Stone Curlew frequents. Nests on ground.

Great Stone Plover *Esacus recurvirostris*   Plate 13

Identification: 51 cm. Sexes similar. Much larger than Stone Curlew; has similar nearly horizontal, hunched stance at rest, and more upright when alert. *Very heavy bill, twice as long as Stone Curlew's*, with lower mandible curved upwards, black with conspicuous yellow base. *Black patch on side of head behind eye conspicuous at distance* and white spectacle and stripe at rear of eye. Upperparts, unstreaked greyish-sandy, with long horizontal narrow dark band along closed wing. Underparts white, washed pale grey on neck and breast. *In flight heavily pied appearance of flight-feathers caused by large, double white patches on black primaries and small white mark on black primary-coverts*; sandy-grey coverts set off by black secondaries and dark fore-edge of wing. Large yellow eye; long legs greyish- or whitish-green. A fast runner and strong flier, but flight ungainly, like duck about to settle. Crepuscular, also at times active during day, but may stand still for long periods.
Voice: weak, high-pitched 'see' or 'see-ey', sometimes developing into trill.
Status: see map. Resident.
Habitat: rocky river beds and bars and their barren environs, also coastal reefs and rocky beaches, estuaries and salt-pans. Nests on ground, unsheltered.

Egyptian Plover *Pluvianus aegyptius*   Plate 13

Identification: 22 cm. Sexes alike. Distinctive short-billed wader. *Black crown and broad black eye stripe to sides of nape and distinct narrow black pectoral band across breast* (black glossed greenish-blue), all joining on mantle and running down to lower back in narrowing black band. *Long white supercilium extending to sides of nape.* Rest of upperparts, wing coverts and white-tipped tail, blue-grey. Underparts pale buff with undertail coverts almost chestnut. In flight, *black band diagonally across white primaries onto secondaries diagnostic.* Short blue-grey legs. Immature like adult but black markings washed brown, not glossed, and pectoral band narrower. Tame. Flies low over water with fast wing-beats.

Voice: short trill 'trrrt' or 'trrp'.
Status: formerly bred S Egypt on Nile. Vagrant Libya and Egypt. Range Africa.
Habitat: rivers and lakes with sandbanks and short vegetation.

Cream-coloured Courser *Cursorius cursor* Plate 13

Identification: 23 cm. Sexes alike. Slender, sandy-buff wader with shortish, tapering, decurved blackish bill and long, pale creamy legs. *Distinctive head-markings of black eye-streak and white supercilium,* curving from eye down around pale grey nape; *forehead and crown rufous.* Sandy-rufous tail has black band near white tip. The rapid flight has regular, almost Lapwing-like beats of rather rounded wings; legs protrude well beyond tail; *striking contrast between black primaries and sandy-buff upperwing-coverts,* and *all underwing is blackish* (except white line at tips of secondaries). Juvenile has slightly shorter, less curved bill, brownish mottled upperparts, buffer and much less distinctive supercilium bordered by much duller brownish eye-stripe and paler top of head than adult. Plover-like behaviour, runs quickly with sudden stops in erect position, or may crouch like Stone Curlew. Combination of distinctive head-pattern, decurved bill, pale plumage but black underwings, and short rounded tail, always distinguish it.
Voice: infrequently heard. On ground, a quiet 'wuk'; in flight, a short, loud 'pwit', or 'kwit-kwit', sometimes followed by deep 'nhark-nhark'.

Status: see map. Doubtless much more widespread in Arabia than mapped, but thought to be absent from Empty Quarter (SE Saudi Arabia). Partial migrant. In winter in N Africa occurs north in places almost to limit of breeding range and extends much deeper into Sahara, also S up Nile and to SE Egypt; in Asia breeding areas are vacated in Iran, N Iraq, N Syria and it becomes more widespread in Arabia, a few passage or wintering birds reaching Oman, Yemen. Passage E and SE Turkey. Vagrant Cyprus.

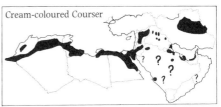

Habitat: sandy or stony semi-desert with thin, scanty vegetation, marginal cultivation, arid flat or rolling, but not broken, country. Nests on ground in open.

Collared Pratincole *Glareola pratincola*

Identification: 25 cm. See PMH.
Status: see map. Has bred Cyprus and Saudi Arabia. Summer visitor with few wintering N Africa. Passage outside breeding areas includes Libya, Cyprus, Syria, Arabia.
Habitat: sun-baked mud-flats and flat, firm plains with low vegetation, often near water. Breeds colonially on ground.

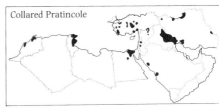

Black-winged Pratincole *Glareola nordmanni*

Identification: 25 cm. See PMH.
Status: may breed E Turkey. Passage migrant, occurring Egypt and most countries in Asiatic area, and generally scarce or irregular; rare in Arabia. Vagrant Libya.
Habitat: much as Collared Pratincole, but favours steppes.

Little Pratincole *Glareola lactea*   Plate 14

Identification: 17 cm. Sexes alike. Much smaller than Collared and Black-winged Pratincole, with short, *slightly* forked tail and diagnostic wing-pattern in flight. Pale sandy grey upperparts and wing-coverts, sandy- or yellow-buff throat and upper breast (*not encircled by black line* as in Collared Pratincoles) merging into pale grey lower breast which merges into whitish on rest of underparts. Black loral streak; forehead often darker and browner than rest of upperparts. Short blackish bill with red base of lower mandible and orange gape. Contrasting flight-pattern above with *black outer primaries, white inner primaries and secondaries, with black band near tips of latter; underwing has jet black coverts contrasting with white on flight-feathers* as on upperwing; in some there is also a small white spot at base of dark central primaries, larger on underwing. White rump and tail, latter with black band near tip. Juvenile has small roundish blackish spots scattered on whitish throat and breast, almost no black loral streak, and darker crown. Flight swift, graceful, bouncy and Swallow-like, wings narrow, long and pointed. Very active and gregarious, often hunting for prey over water around dusk when it can recall a bat.
Voice: curious low harsh note recalling marsh terns; Little Tern-like call and gecko-like 'tuck-tuck-tuck'.
Status: vagrant or rare winter visitor to S Arabian Gulf, Oman and S Yemen. Range includes Afghanistan and India.
Habitat: wide sandbanks of rivers, or mud-flats by lakes, hawking over wetlands.

Little Ringed Plover *Charadrius dubius*

Identification: 15 cm. See PMH.
Status: see map. Has bred Cyprus. Mainly migrant. Widely scattered throughout on passage. Winters in small numbers southwards from Turkey (rare), Mediterranean basin, Gulf of Oman.
Habitat: mainly freshwater localities, in particular gravelly river islands and sandy borders of lakes; also some brackish areas. In winter coastal as well as inland. Nests on ground.

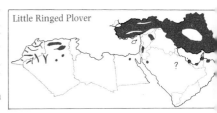

Ringed Plover *Charadrius hiaticula*

Identification: 19 cm. See PMH.
Status: widespread passage migrant, relatively uncommon inland. Winters on nearly all coasts in our area, more widely in Egypt and on some inland sites. A few remain in summer, for example Oman.
Habitat: sandy, muddy, and to some extent stony shores, coastal and inland.

Kittlitz's Plover *Charadrius pecuarius*   Plate 14

Identification: 14.5 cm. Sexes alike. Slightly smaller than Kentish Plover which, with its chunky head, it superficially resembles. Readily distinguished in all plumages by *darker upperparts with rufous-buff fringes to feathers, orange wash to breast* (though in immatures this can be obscure) and head pattern. Adult in summer plumage has *brown upperparts with narrow rusty fringes to feathers* and white underparts with a *soft orange-buff wash on the breast*; brown cap is bordered below by white supercilium and hind-neck, while black line from the bill extends through eye and down to a *black half-collar at base of white hind-neck; a black line traverses the forehead from eye to eye*. In winter more 'washed out', with less obvious fringes to feathers on upperparts, and very pale orangy-buff wash on breast; head markings reduced to dark eye-patch, and dark at base of *hind-neck which becomes buff as does the supercilium*; there is a diffuse brownish patch on sides of the breast. Some birds in winter can have quite deep rufous-buff supercilium, hind-neck and breast. In juveniles, rufous fringes to back feathers more obvious in fresh plumage, but can wear to very faint; otherwise as adult in winter but wash on breast only faint and eye-patch frequently just a blob before and behind eye. Bill black and legs greenish-grey. In flight, narrow white wing-bar and sides of tail; toes project beyond tail.

Actions similar to Kentish Plover. Often occurs in small, loose parties and tends, on being disturbed, to run initially rather than fly.
Voice: plaintive 'pipeep', usually uttered in flight.
Status: see map. Resident. Vagrant Israel.
Habitat: sandbanks of lakes and rivers, muddy margins, and flats with scanty vegetation, often dry but usually near freshwater. Rarely coastal in Egypt. Nests on open ground; eggs buried when parent disturbed.

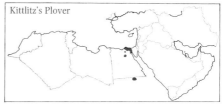

Kentish Plover *Charadrius alexandrinus*

Identification: 16 cm. See PMH.
Status: see map. Partial migrant or dispersive. In winter a large degree of overlap with breeding range, but it extends inland in Egypt, SW Saudi Arabia while vacating central Turkey, and inland N Iran.
Habitat: shingle, sandy and muddy beaches and dry mud-flats, mainly coastal but also inland, often by saline lagoons, and largely free of vegetation. Nests on ground.

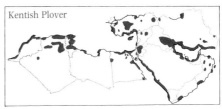

Greater (left) and **Lesser Sand Plover** in winter plumage

Lesser Sand Plover *Charadrius mongolus*   Plate 14

Identification: 19–20 cm. Sexes differ in breeding season. Slightly larger than Ringed Plover and longer legged. Resembles Greater Sand Plover (which is larger) and often best separated by relative proportions of bill and head, body bulk, leg length and, usually, leg colour. Two sub-species occur: *atrifons* (Central Asia), the race mainly occurring in the region, and *mongolus* (NE Siberia). Both are striking in breeding plumage; male of *atrifons* has *all-black forehead* and face mask (or with tiny white forehead-patches like some Greater Sand which, however, never shows completely black forehead); broad reddish-chestnut breast-band, sometimes extending onto flanks (Greater Sand usually with narrower breast-band); female has black of head reduced or replaced by rufous-brown; *mongolus* has mostly white forehead (like Greater Sand), and a narrow dark border to upper edge of chestnut breast-band. Bill and legs blackish. *In non-breeding and immature plumage very like Greater Sand*; upperparts greyish-brown or dull sandy-brown with darker, broad patch from bill to ear-coverts, variable whitish forehead, white underparts with dark grey-brown, often well-defined patches on sides of breast (sometimes joining). Best separated from Greater Sand by *slightly smaller size,* *less upright stance* (with less neck), *slightly smaller, more rounded head* (more angular in Greater Sand), *smaller, shorter, less bulbous bill* (but bill sizes can almost overlap), and proportionally slightly shorter legs which are generally *darker (often greyish) than the yellow-green legs of Greater Sand*. In flight, clear white wing-bar of fairly even width (slightly more prominent on primaries in Greater Sand) and dark tail with a little white at sides (Greater Sand has slightly more white at sides and more contrasting dark sub-terminal bar to tail); legs reach to or beyond tip of tail in flight (overlapping with some Greater Sands). Winter Kentish and immature Ringed Plover have shorter legs and white or whitish hind-neck.

Voice: quieter than Greater Sand; short sharp 'twip' or 'corrup'; short 'trr', 'trik', or 'tikit'; a 'kruit-kruit' or clear 'drriiiit'.

Status: winter and passage visitor to coasts of S Iran and Arabia; scarce Egyptian Red Sea coast. Also passage central Saudi Arabia. Some over-summer E Arabia. Vagrant Near East, Turkey.

Habitat: tidal mud-flats and sandy coasts.

Greater Sand Plover *Charadrius leschenaultii*   Plate 14

Identification: 22–23 cm. Sexes sometimes differ in breeding plumage. One-third larger than Kentish (with which it often associates) with proportionally much longer legs. *Resembles larger version of Lesser Sand Plover* (which see) and often difficult to separate the two species outside breeding season. Helpful to compare size with Kentish and Ringed Plover. Lesser Sand is same body-size or fractionally larger than Ringed; *Greater Sand is distinctly larger*. In addition, compared to Lesser Sand, Greater Sand has *proportionally larger, more angular head* (smaller, more rounded in Lesser Sand), *longer, stouter neck, longer, larger more bulbous bill* (but overlaps with Lesser), *larger eye and usually paler, more greenish-yellow, slightly longer legs* (however, colour can occasionally match Lesser's darker legs); stance also more upright. Male in breeding plumage basically like Lesser Sand, but forehead never solid black and breast-band often narrower, less extensive on flanks. Female sometimes with less black in mask through eye, and with narrower, less rufous breast-band. Non-breeding and immature plumages resemble Lesser Sand's and, for distinction, see that species. Birds breeding and wintering in Turkey and Near East are smallest race with shorter slenderer bills, and thus most easily confused with Lesser Sand Plover: their breeding plumages less colourful and, as nesting is early, birds in summer are often rather faded. Separated from Caspian Plover in non-breeding plumage by *bolder white wing-bar*, less delicate build, broader wings which, at rest, do not protrude much beyond tail, whiter underwing, less bold supercilium and lack of 'capped' appearance.

Voice: very vocal. When flushed, usual note Turnstone-like ripple, 'prrrirt'; also, in alarm, a 'prruit', or 'triep'. In song-flight, utters 'huit-huit-huit' or an ascending 'dui-dui-tui-dit', sometimes developing into longer series.

Status: see map. Summer visitor to breeding areas. Winter and passage on coasts of S Iran, Arabia, Egypt and Near East north to Cyprus; some remaining in summer. Also passage central Saudi Arabia. Vagrant Libya, NW Africa.

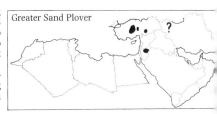

Greater Sand Plover

Habitat: in the region breeds on inland sand- and mud-flats, mainly near water, nesting on ground. Otherwise essentially coastal, on intertidal flats and dry foreshore.

Caspian Plover *Charadrius asiaticus*   Plate 14

Identification: 19 cm. Sexes differ in breeding season. Typical plover, resembling long-legged, slim-bodied Dotterel in shape but more tapering at rear, whereas fractionally smaller Greater Sand is a plumper, Ringed Plover type with heavier bill and shorter wings, not protruding beyond tail at rest. Adult male in summer has dark greyish-brown upperparts, *dark capped head* (no black mask as in Greater Sand) white forehead and *clear whitish supercilium*, particularly noticeable behind eye; white throat and *rich chestnut breast-band with narrow black border to lower edge*. Female has breast typically grey-brown (sometimes with very few white-tipped chestnut feathers admixed). Adult, in non-breeding, much like breeding female, but brown colours paler and white areas often sullied buff; well-defined grey-brown breast-band. Juvenile like non-breeding adult but pale-fringed feathers on upperparts and more diffuse breast-band. Bill, fine and tapering, is black; legs yellowish to dull green. In flight,

recalls Lesser Golden Plover with long, narrow wings showing only faint whitish wing-bar, greyish underwing, and greyish tail with white outer feathers (Greater Sand has bold white wing-bar, shorter, broader wings, whiter underwings and more white on outer tail feathers).
Voice: calls in flight short and sharp; single 'ptick', a 'ku-wit' or 'qiut', 'tiik', mostly repeated 3–4 times; rarely a 'ptrrwhet'.
Status: passage migrant Iran, Iraq, Arabia (scarce in south and east), few Egypt, Israel, perhaps regular E Turkey. Has occurred in winter Iraq, Gulf of Aqaba and N Yemen. Vagrant elsewhere in Near East, including Cyprus.
Habitat: fields, grassy plains, semi-desert; also coastal areas.

Dotterel *Charadrius morinellus*

Identification: 22 cm. See PMH.
Status: winter visitor across N Africa to Near East, Iraq, E Saudi Arabia and W Iran. Rare Gulf States and Cyprus. Vagrant Oman. Also passage Turkey.
Habitat: stony steppe, semi-desert and poor arable land often far from water.

Pacific Golden Plover *Pluvialis fulva*   Plate 14

Identification: 23–26 cm. Sexes alike. In non-breeding and immature plumage easily confused with similar Golden Plover, which it resembles in ground colour and general build, but Pacific separated by following characters: *underwing, and especially axillaries, dull greyish-brown* (mostly white in Golden); Pacific in abraded spring plumage has whiter underwings, but axillaries still greyish; *wings longer and narrower than Golden's in flight* and, at rest, often (but not always) *extending 1–2 cm beyond tail-tip*; at rest, *legs clearly longer, particularly the thighs*, (but often evident only on alert birds); in flight, *toes extend beyond tip of tail*, making tail appear more pointed when flying over (legs do not protrude in Golden). Slimmer and smaller than Golden, with *slimmer neck which, when alert, appears conspicuously long*; bill, proportionally, slightly stronger than in Golden. In non-breeding plumage has distinct yellow-buff supercilium (more indistinct in Golden); upperparts brown, spotted bright yellow (not unlike Golden), and breast buffish, spotted or mottled yellowish (in Golden, breast streaked darker, mottled yellowish). Juvenile similar to non-breeding adult but supercilium whiter, and flanks barred. In flight, wing-bar generally less pronounced than in Golden. The American Golden Plover, which has occurred in western part of the region, is slightly more bulky than Pacific with even more protruding wing-tips and more striking white supercilium. In non-breeding plumage it recalls winter Grey Plover; upperparts are greyer, spotted whitish and pale yellowish, and breast greyish, mottled off-white; juveniles are darker brown above than Pacific, spotted pale yellow or whitish; belly and flanks are barred; otherwise similar to Pacific with same underwing, but slightly shorter legs.
Voice: most typical call resembles softer edition of Spotted Redshank's, a clearly di-syllabic 'tu-ee' or 'chu-wit'; also a plaintive 'kl-ee' or 'ki-wee'; Golden Plover's call (a whistling 'tloo' or 'too-ee') is hardly di-syllabic, never recalling Spotted Redshank.
Status: winter or passage S and E Arabia including Yemen. Vagrant Iraq, Iran, Israel, Egypt, possibly Turkey.
Habitat: open grassland, cultivated fields, also mud-flats and coasts.

American Golden Plover *Pluvialis dominica*

Identification: 23–26 cm. See PMH and Pacific Golden Plover (above).
Status: vagrant NW Africa.
Habitat: as Pacific Golden Plover.

Golden Plover *Pluvialis apricaria*

Identification: 28 cm. See PMH.
Status: winter visitor to N Africa (mainly near Atlantic and Mediterranean coasts), most E Mediterranean countries especially Turkey, and N Iran; rare or vagrant Lebanon, Syria, Iraq, Saudi Arabia, Gulf States, Oman and S Yemen but perhaps some confusion with Pacific Golden Plover.
Habitat: dry and wet grassland, plough and stubble, and sometimes shores.

Grey Plover *Pluvialis squatarola*

Identification: 28 cm. See PMH.
Status: winter and passage visitor to coasts of N Africa, most E Mediterranean countries and coasts of Arabia and Iran. Some non-breeders remain through summer. Vagrant Syria.
Habitat: coastal, on intertidal flats and saltings; occasionally inland around shallow lakes.

Spur-winged Plover *Hoplopterus spinosus*   Plate 14

Identification: 26 cm. Sexes alike. Long-legged, upright plover distinguished by *conspicuous white sides of neck contrasting with black upper-head, flanks and underbody; black band down front from bill to breast.* Upperparts sandy grey-brown; tail white with broad black terminal band above and below. Shortish bill, eye and long legs black. In flight, above, sandy-brown coverts are separated from black flight-feathers by broad white band; underwing-coverts white; pattern thus similar to White-tailed Plover and Red-wattled Plover, but former species lacks black underparts and has all-white tail, whilst latter has white belly, red bill and red skin on face; both also have yellow legs (black in Spur-winged). Juvenile similar to adult. Lapwing-like flight action, rather jerky with emphasis on the downward wing-beat. Not very gregarious but can occur in small groups.
Voice: alarm call a loud 'treck, treck, treck', repeated very persistently on breeding grounds.
Status: see map. Summer visitor Turkey and Syria. Further south mainly resident or dispersive, with winter and breeding ranges very similar. Passage Cyprus (has bred), Sinai, less commonly Saudi Arabia. Vagrant Arabian Gulf, Oman, Iran.
Habitat: edges of fresh and saline marshes and irrigation, with short vegetation, nesting on dried-out mud or nearby sandy areas.

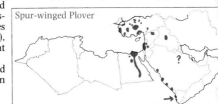

Black-headed Plover

Black-headed Plover *Hoplopterus tectus*   Plate 14

Identification: 25 cm. Sexes alike. Distinctive plover, slightly smaller than Spur-winged. Pale grey-brown upperparts and white underparts with *black head, line down middle of breast and long up-swept crest; white chin, forehead, line behind eye and nape.* Red wattle in front of eye, *red bill with black tip and long maroon-red legs.* In rather slow flight shows blackish flight-feathers, white outer wing-coverts and white tail with black sub-terminal band. Often active at dusk.
Voice: shrill, 'kervic kervic' flight note; also a high pitched rasping note usually uttered several times.
Status: old record from Jordan/Israel. Range Africa.
Habitat: dry thorn-bush country with open spaces.

94

Red-wattled Plover *Hoplopterus indicus*   Plate 14

Identification: 31 cm. Sexes alike. A large long-legged plover with *black breast, distinctive red wattles on face*, and *wing-pattern similar to Spur-winged*. Adult has head, neck and upperbreast black with *broad white band running from eye* down *side of nape to white underparts*. Upperparts brown with bronzy-green iridescence and light red tinge. Lower back, rump and tail-coverts white; tail also white with wide black subterminal band. Wings in flight show brownish coverts, black flight-feathers and a narrow white wing-bar (formed by the white-based secondaries together with white greater-coverts). Face pattern striking due to *red eye-ring and wattle* in front of eye and *red bill with black tip*. *Legs bright yellow.* Juvenile much as adult, but with narrow buff edgings to feathers of upperparts, off-white area on forehead, chin, throat and upper breast, and very poorly-developed wattle. A fairly tame, rather solitary plover which prefers to run rather than fly. On being flushed, flight is usually low with slow wing beats.
Voice: highly vocal; frequently-uttered alarm notes, loud and shrill, often rendered as 'did-he-do-it, pity-to-do-it', more stuttering when really excited.
Status: see map. Resident and dispersive with scattered records in Gulf States away from breeding areas. Vagrant central Saudi Arabia.
Habitat: open country, usually near fresh water, and showing preference for agricultural land. Nests on ground.

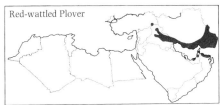
Red-wattled Plover

Sociable Plover *Chettusia gregaria*   Plate 14

Identification: 29 cm. Sexes alike. Similar in size to Lapwing but with the more upright stance of the typical plovers. Plump body with fairly small head and slim neck when alert. At a distance in winter can be overlooked as a large, rather plain, pale Golden Plover but with noticeable white forehead (its whitish supercilium being visible only when close). In this non-breeding plumage (when most likely to be seen in region) it is dun-brown above with *lightly mottled grey-brown breast*, and rest of underparts whitish; chin, throat and forehead white with *dark grey-brown crown and dark line behind eye, separated by long whitish supercilium meeting on nape*, the head pattern resembling that of much smaller Dotterel. Juvenile has buffish wash to forehead and supercilium, and buff edgings to feathers of upperparts. In breeding season much brighter with *more pronounced black and white head pattern, with black eye-stripe to bill, black crown, white supercilium*, creamy-buff sides of neck, grey wash to breast and upperparts and *chestnut-black patch on lower belly*. Fairly short bill, eye and *medium-long legs black*. Fairly rounded wing-tips in rather leisurely flight; conspicuous wing pattern above with brownish coverts contrasting with white secondaries and black primaries, whilst underwing is white with black primaries; thus almost similar to White-tailed Plover, but with *black band to white tail* and less protruding legs. Typical plover actions, making short runs with head tucked into body and stopping to peck at ground, or stand with head erect, motionless, blending with ground. In winter seen in small parties, sometimes in the company of Lapwings, Golden Plover and Cream-coloured Coursers.
Voice: on taking flight, a harsh 'chark-chark-chark' – rather Snipe-like.
Status: winter visitor Iraq, Israel, few Arabia including Oman. Passage Turkey, Near East, rare Egypt, Iran. Vagrant S Yemen, Morocco.
Habitat: rarely on coast, typically seeking semi-desert, steppes and ploughed or cultivated fields, often with winter cereals.

White-tailed Plover *Chettusia leucura*   Plate 14

Identification: 26–29 cm. Sexes differ slightly. Similar size to Spur-winged but longer neck and stouter bill. Apart from *long, conspicuously yellow legs, is rather featureless* on the ground, being sandy brownish-grey above with bronze-lilac sheen. Often appears white-faced with prominent eye and longish black bill. Upperbreast warm brown, merging into darker ashy-grey lower breast which has mauve wash; often has white mark up side of breast, like Common Sandpiper; female has breast paler grey. Plumage of both sexes becomes subdued

95

in winter. Juvenile paler on neck and breast, dark-mottled on upperparts with dark cap and faint brown tip to tail. In flight, *white tail and protruding yellow legs diagnostic*; black and white upperwing-pattern recalls Spur-winged but secondaries white above and below. Slender and graceful on ground, though often stands with neck retracted; when alert stands erect with long neck held vertically. When feeding, tips down so steeply that it almost stands on its head.

Voice: high-pitched 'kee-vee-ik' persistently repeated on breeding grounds; also short 'kit'.

Status: see map. Partial migrant; summer visitor N Iran, central Iraq, Turkey, and mainly resident further south. A few also winter sporadically E Arabia and probably Egypt, N Yemen. Scattered passage elsewhere Arabia, Israel. Vagrant Cyprus, Libya, Tunisia, Morocco.

Habitat: fresh or saline lagoons, marshy areas and wet plains. Nests on ground, sometimes colonially.

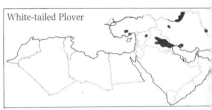

Lapwing *Vanellus vanellus*

Identification: 30 cm. See PMH.

Status: see map. Partial migrant. Winters N Africa (especially Morocco, Algeria, Egypt), also Turkey, Iran south to central Arabia, sometimes Oman.

Habitat: open grass or arable land, marshes, shallow freshwater margins and coastal flats. Nests on ground.

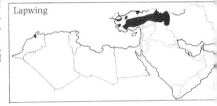

Great Knot, immature

Great Knot *Calidris tenuirostris*

Identification: 27 cm. Sexes alike. Redshank-sized, with *dark heavy-based bill, spotting on white underparts*, and *white rump contrasting with dark tail being the main distinguishing features from Knot*. Larger than Knot, with more elongated body, tapering at rear; deep-based bill longer than head and often very slightly decurved; longer legs than Knot, also longer neck when alert. Adult in breeding plumage has white underparts with dense blackish spots on breast and flanks, sometimes forming dark breast-band or solid black in centre. (Knot is unmarked reddish below in summer plumage.) Upperparts *blackish-brown with buffish-white tips, contrasting with chestnut spots on scapulars* (most upperparts fringed rufous in Knot); neck streaked blackish-brown. In winter plumage, upperparts greyish *with dark streaks on mantle, hind-neck and crown* (winter Knot plainer, practically unstreaked); whitish underparts with *fine streaks on breast*, occasionally with some *dark spots* (winter Knot is lightly marked on greyish breast). Juvenile has blackish-brown upperparts fringed buffish (juvenile Knot 'scaled' on upperparts); hind-neck and particularly foreneck and breast *streaked and spotted dark brown, usually contrasting well* with rest of largely unmarked white underparts (juvenile Knot has more diffuse streaking and lacks contrast below). Bill blackish, legs greenish-grey, paler greenish in juvenile, but generally darker than Knot's at all ages. In flight, appears longer-winged than Knot, with narrower, less obvious, whitish wing-bar.

Voice: rarely heard Knot-like 'knut-knut'; also a high trill 'prruu', not unlike call of Curlew Sandpiper.
Status: vagrant Morocco, Israel, Arabian Gulf, Gulf of Oman and Oman. Range Asia/Australia.
Habitat: tidal mud-flats and coastal creeks.

Knot *Calidris canutus*

Identification: 25 cm. See PMH.
Status: winter visitor NW Africa. Rare or vagrant most other countries in S and E Mediterranean including Turkey, also Iran. Vagrant Oman and Yemen.
Habitat: sandy and muddy shores, occasionally muddy freshwater margins.

Sanderling *Calidris alba*

Identification: 20 cm. See PMH.
Status: passage and winter visitor to most coasts throughout region, including Caspian and Atlantic. Some non-breeders remain during summer. Vagrant Syria, Jordan, Lebanon.
Habitat: sandy beaches, infrequently inland on passage.

Little Stint *Calidris minuta*

Identification: 13 cm. See PMH.
Status: passage and winter visitor on many coasts, and some inland, in most parts of the region including Arabia, but mainly passage only on Caspian and in Turkey. Often in large flocks. Few remain through summer.
Habitat: much as Dunlin.

Temminck's Stint *Calidris temminckii*

Identification: 14 cm. See PMH.
Status: passage across almost all the region. Winter includes N and NW Africa, Near East, Iraq, SW Iran, Arabia.
Habitat: well-vegetated inland water-margins and marshes, less often coastal.

Long-toed Stint *Calidris subminuta*

Identification: 14 cm. See PMH.
Status: scarce passage migrant and winter visitor Oman. Vagrant Arabian Gulf, central Saudi Arabia and Yemen. Range Asia/Australia.
Habitat: marshes, mud-flats and water-margins, both inland and coastal.

Pectoral Sandpiper *Calidris melanotos*

Identification: 19 cm. See PMH.
Status: vagrant Morocco, Israel, Arabian Gulf. Range America.
Habitat: grassy mud-flats and marshes, fresh or brackish, water-margins, occasionally on sea-shores.

Sharp-tailed Sandpiper *Calidris acuminata*

Identification: 22 cm. See PMH.
Status: vagrant N Yemen. Range Asia/Australia.
Habitat: as Pectoral Sandpiper.

Curlew Sandpiper *Calidris ferruginea*

Identification: 19 cm. See PMH.
Status: occurs mainly on passage in most of region, especially in Atlantic and Caspian/Arabian areas. Some winter from Israel and Iraq southwards around Arabian coast; few Tunisia. Some over-summer.
Habitat: much as Dunlin.

Purple Sandpiper *Calidris maritima*

Identification: 21 cm. See PMH.
Status: vagrant Morocco.
Habitat: rocky coasts, also breakwaters, etc.

Dunlin *Calidris alpina*

Identification: 18 cm. See PMH.
Status: passage and winter visitor (with occasional over-summering by non-breeders) to nearly all coasts of the region, and some inland.
Habitat: coastal and estuarine shores and muddy margins of inland waters, often in flocks.

Broad-billed Sandpiper *Limicola falcinellus*

Identification: 17 cm. See PMH.
Status: passage often sparse Iran, Black Sea, E Mediterranean, and Arabian coasts, also regular Egypt and Tunisia, petering out further west. Winters S Iran, E and S Arabia. Vagrant Cyprus, Jordan, Morocco.
Habitat: mainly salt-marshes, mud-flats, marshy water-margins.

Buff-breasted Sandpiper *Tryngites subruficollis*

Identification: 20 cm. See PMH.
Status: vagrant Tunisia, Egypt, Arabian Gulf. Range America.
Habitat: dry fields with very short grass, in preference to shores.

Ruff *Philomachus pugnax*

Identification: 23–29 cm. See PMH.
Status: passage and winter visitor to nearly all countries in the region, but not wintering Cyprus, N Turkey, N Iran. Some non-breeders over-summer. Often gregarious.
Habitat: inland marshes, lake shores, occasionally estuaries.

Jack Snipe *Lymnocryptes minimus*

Identification: 19 cm. See PMH.
Status: passage and winter visitor in very small numbers to most countries in the region, including Oman. Vagrant Syria, Yemen.
Habitat: much as Snipe.

nipe *Gallinago gallinago*   Plate 12

Identification: 27 cm. See PMH.
Status: passage and winter visitor to almost all parts of the region including S Arabia.
Habitat: wet grasslands, ricefields, marshy water-margins.

Great Snipe *Gallinago media*   Plate 12

Identification: 28 cm. See PMH.
Status: generally scarce passage migrant Turkey/Iran south to Egypt; perhaps only vagrant
further west in N Africa and rare in Arabia. Occasional winter records include Egypt, Cyprus,
N Yemen.
Habitat: drier localities than Snipe such as stubble fields, rough grassland; also marshes.

intail Snipe *Gallinago stenura*   Plate 12

Identification: 25 cm. Sexes alike. Resembles Snipe but heavier and plumper with slightly
shorter bill and slightly more rounded wings. Upperparts a little duller and greyer than Snipe,
with narrower and *less distinct stripes on back*; above, in flight, has *pale greyish-buff panel on
coverts and lacks white trailing-edge* of wing which is conspicuous in Snipe. From below,
underwing coverts completely barred, looking all dark (whitish with dark veins in Snipe); white
area on belly smaller than Snipe's, framed by bolder, more extensive flank-bars. Pin-shape
of outer 8–9 tail feathers invisible in the field, and lacks whitish tail corners of young Snipe.
Dark horn bill usually has grey-green base (usually paler brown in Snipe) and legs usually
greyish or brownish-green (usually paler yellowish-grey in Snipe). Great Snipe is larger with
more extensive barring on belly, has noticeable white bars outlining greater upperwing
coverts and much white on outer tail feathers. Pintail tends to sit 'close' and is difficult to
flush; in flight, has deeper body than Snipe, and bill more often held at downward angle; legs
may protrude a little beyond tail. Escape flight slightly slower, straighter and heavier than
Snipe's, often not towering, and dropping after short flight; flight not as heavy and low as
Great Snipe's.
Voice: flight call (uttered less repeatedly than Snipe's) is lower pitched, shorter and drier 'chat',
also rendered as 'kit' (not unlike Black Tern) or 'skarp'.
Status: vagrant (or rare passage/winter visitor) recorded E Iran, Arabian Gulf, Oman, N Yemen.
Range Asia.
Habitat: wet open fields, damp boggy areas, water-margins but more often on drier ground
than Snipe.

olitary Snipe *Gallinago solitaria*   Plate 12

Identification: 29–31 cm. Sexes alike. Largest snipe, patterned generally like others but size
precludes confusion except with slightly smaller Great Snipe. On ground separated from Great
Snipe by *warm brown (uniform or transversely patterned) gorget across foreneck and upperbreast*
(in Great Snipe underparts narrowly barred); face and head pattern more diffuse, with *white
median crown-stripe either flecked darker, appearing diffuse, or absent* (clear-cut in other snipes
in the region); whitish supercilium often flecked darker and appearing less broad and clear-
cut than in Great, and dark loral-streak broader. Mantle *often narrowly barred rufous-brown
and black* (but sometimes rather blackish like Great which is never barred rufous). Bill, usually
longer than Great Snipe's, is olive-brown with blackish terminal third; legs olive. Immature
resembles adult. In flight, *rump and tail coverts appear rather uniform warm brown* (spotted or
barred in Great); upperwing more uniform, the *greater coverts dark grey-brown, narrowly
framed by whitish tips* (Great Snipe has blackish coverts with broad white borders forming
bands); *no white trailing-edge to secondaries* like Pintail Snipe; *rufous-chestnut tail lacks white
corners* of Great Snipe and is more wedge-shaped. Underwing coverts densely barred (like
Great Snipe). Flight heavy and slow; usually sits tight but flies off zig-zagging when hard
pressed. Known for its solitary habits and choice of habitat.
Voice: harsher and louder than Snipe, which it otherwise resembles.
Status: may nest in NE Iran, and reported as migrant in small numbers E Iran. Vagrant central
Saudi Arabia.
Habitat: alpine and subalpine zone of high mountains; upper limit of moist forest and mountain
streams, mostly above 2,800 m. Descends in winter to lower levels, frequenting scrubby
upland bogs and paddy.

Long-billed Dowitcher *Limnodromus scolopaceus*

Identification: 29 cm. See PMH.
Status: vagrant Morocco. Oman. Range America.
Habitat: muddy freshwater pools with marginal vegetation.

Asiatic Dowitcher, adult winter (in flight) and juvenile

Asiatic Dowitcher *Limnodromus semipalmatus*

Identification: 32–35 cm. Sexes alike. Smaller than Bar-tailed Godwit with which it is most easily confused in the region, but *black bill broader based and straight*, and in flight, *white rump and wedge on lower back barred and spotted dark* (white in Bar-tailed); but beware, eastern race of Bar-tailed has dark back and rump and heavily barred uppertail-coverts, and then structural differences are important. In summer plumage, head and underparts chestnut with whitish ventral region; also white flanks barred greyish (wholly chestnut underparts and no barring on flanks in Bar-tailed). Upperparts blackish with feathers edged rufous and buff. In grey and white winter plumage, shows more finely streaked and spotted neck and breast, and bolder eye-stripe, than Bar-tailed. Colour and shape of bill always important: Asiatic black and straight with slightly swollen tip; Bar-tailed dark with pinkish base and slightly upturned. Juvenile similar to winter plumage but with buff wash to neck and breast, and buff edgings to grey feathers of upperparts; lower mandible may show some pinkish at extreme base. Flight wing-pattern similar to Bar-tailed, but feeding action (fairly rapid 'sewing-machine' probing) quite different. Differs from Long-billed Dowitcher in larger size, dark grey legs (yellowish-green in Long-billed), flight pattern (Long-billed has white oval on back and a narrow whitish trailing edge to wing) and in winter, finely spotted neck and breast (uniform greyish in Long-billed). Will often associate with Bar-tailed Godwits.
Voice: airy 'chaow' or 'aow', recalling distant human cry.
Status: reported S Yemen and UAE. Range Asia/Australia.
Habitat: mud-flats, sandbanks and estuaries.

Woodcock *Scolopax rusticola*
Identification: 34 cm. See PMH.
Status: winter visitor to most countries bordering Mediterranean, Black and Caspian seas. Vagrant Syria, Arabian Gulf and N Arabia.
Habitat: moist woodland, scrub, thick low cover.

Black-tailed Godwit *Limosa limosa*
Identification: 41 cm. See PMH.
Status: passage/winter visitor most countries of N Africa, E Mediterranean, Iran, Iraq, becoming scarcer Arabia but reaching Oman, Yemen. Some non-breeders over-summer. Passage heavy in Morocco.
Habitat: muddy freshwater margins, floodlands, marshes, also estuaries and tidal creeks.

Bar-tailed Godwit *Limosa lapponica*
Identification: 38 cm. See PMH.
Status: winter and passage NW Africa, scarcer to rare in centre of region (Turkey, Near East, Libya, Egypt), then locally common Arabian Gulf, Oman and S Red Sea.
Habitat: usually coastal, on mud-flats, sandy beaches or estuaries.

Whimbrel *Numenius phaeopus*
Identification: 41 cm. See PMH.
Status: winters Morocco, Arabian Gulf to E and SW Arabia, rarely elsewhere. More numerous and widespread on passage. Few remain summer. Vagrant Jordan, and barely regular Turkey and Lebanon.
Habitat: muddy and sandy beaches, creeks, rocky shores, coral reefs.

Slender-billed Curlew

Slender-billed Curlew *Numenius tenuirostris*
Identification: 41 cm. Sexes alike. Much smaller than Curlew, with which it can be confused, and more upright, with proportionately smaller head, neater, less angular appearance and shorter, finer and more tapering bill. Plumage similar to that of Curlew but *cleaner, whiter with less warm upperparts*; paler supercilium creates darker but finely-streaked crown. Underparts white with brown streaks on breast and *neat black spots on flank and side of belly* – the most important identification feature. In flight, has wing pattern similar to Curlew but with more contrast between dark primaries and paler inner wing; white on rump extends well down onto uppertail-coverts. White underwing (obvious in flight) of limited value for identification as eastern race of Curlew can look very white on underwing coverts. Bill dark (lacking extensive pale base of lower mandible shown by Curlew); legs dark grey, darker than the blue-grey legs of Curlew. Movements similar to Curlew's but quicker pace and less sedate.

101

Distinguished from Whimbrel by white underwing, black spots on white flanks and belly, lack of crown stripe, and by voice.

Voice: single 'cour-ee', shorter and higher than Curlew and lacking the liquid quality.

Status: becoming increasingly rare. Very few winter records NW Africa, mainly Morocco and Tunisia. Irregular passage records Turkey. Vagrant elsewhere in Mediterranean, also scattered records Jordan, Iraq, Kuwait, Oman and N Yemen.

Habitat: mud-flats, shores and margins of freshwater pools.

Curlew *Numenius arquata*

Identification: 53–59 cm. See PMH.

Status: winter and passage visitor; some non-breeders over-summer. Occurs on most coasts in the region, from Atlantic to Indian Ocean, and from Black and Caspian seas to Gulf of Aden, also some inland wetlands.

Habitat: mud-flats, tidal sands and rocks, coral reefs and mangrove swamps, creeks and drier flats; also to some extent inland on muddy or grassy margins of rivers and other waters.

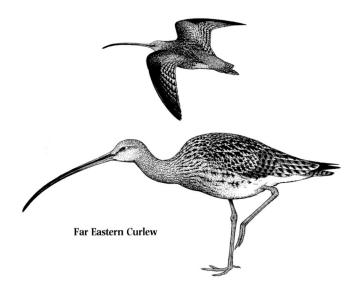

Far Eastern Curlew

Far Eastern Curlew *Numenius madagascariensis*

Identification: 56–63 cm. Sexes alike. Closely resembles Curlew, from which best separated by *brown lower back, rump and tail,* lacking white wedge up lower back of Curlew; *underwing-coverts densely barred dark* (whitish with few, scattered dark bars and spots in Curlew, though primary-coverts barred). Eastern race of Curlew (*N. a. orientalis*), which has longer bill than European birds – approaching and even overlapping bill length of Far Eastern Curlew – has practically unmarked whitish underwing-coverts and generally whiter underparts than Far Eastern, particularly on lower belly and vent.

Voice: call similar to Curlew's 'cour-li' but generally less pure and less melodious, typically 'krr-iii', more clearly two-syllabled than Curlew, the first note rather harsh and the second longer, higher in pitch and lacking rising intonation of Curlew call-note.

Status: may occasionally occur in E Iran, but no recent records. Range Asia/Australia.

Habitat: marshes, sea-coasts and mud-flats.

Spotted Redshank *Tringa erythropus*

Identification: 30 cm. See PMH.
Status: on passage widespread on most coasts, also inland marshes. Uncommon or scarce Arabia and a few coastal Iran. Scarcer in winter but range still wide. Occasional over-summering.
Habitat: as Redshank, but less coastal.

Redshank *Tringa totanus*

Identification: 28 cm. See PMH.
Status: see map. Widespread passage migrant and winter visitor throughout the region, occurring most coasts and some inland marshes; some over-summering.
Habitat: breeds inland in damp grassland or short sedges near open fresh or saline waters. Nests on ground. Winters mainly on coast on sheltered shores, mud-flats, creeks; also inland on muddy shallow watersides without much vegetation.

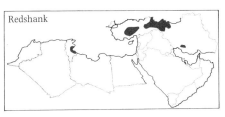
Redshank

Marsh Sandpiper *Tringa stagnatilis*

Identification: 23 cm. See PMH.
Status: widely scattered on passage, mainly in small numbers, but scarce Morocco. Fewer in winter generally, when rare north of Arabian Gulf and Iraq marshes.
Habitat: swampy freshwaters and marshes; also to lesser extent tidal creeks and flats.

Greenshank *Tringa nebularia*

Identification: 30 cm. See PMH.
Status: occurs throughout the region. Mainly passage in Mediterranean countries, also Iraq, Iran and Arabia; less common but still widespread in winter. Few non-breeders over-summer.
Habitat: much as Redshank.

Green Sandpiper *Tringa ochropus*

Identification: 23 cm. See PMH.
Status: broad-fronted passage, and winter visitor to freshwaters throughout the region. Seldom concentrated, but sometimes flocks Arabia in autumn.
Habitat: muddy banks of streams and channels, edges of floodlands, in marshes may use mud patches smaller than most waders tolerate, often with sheltering banks; sometimes brackish creeks. Rare on open shore.

Wood Sandpiper *Tringa glareola*

Identification: 20 cm. See PMH.
Status: widespread passage across the whole region. Small numbers winter, but only rarely in NE Mediterranean countries.
Habitat: freshwater marshy areas with muddy margins, less confined than sometimes chosen by Green Sandpiper; also at times saltmarsh.

Terek Sandpiper *Xenus cinereus*

Identification: 23 cm. See PMH.
Status: winters on coasts of S Iran and Arabia; common on passage there, occurring inland also. Passage declines westwards, becoming scarce at N end of Red Sea, but still regular Iraq and E Turkey, Israel and Egypt. Vagrant Cyprus, Syria, Libya, Tunisia. Some non-breeders oversummer.
Habitat: mainly coastal on tidal mud-flats, saltmarsh and mangrove creeks, coral reefs, estuaries. Scarce inland on passage.

Common Sandpiper *Actitis hypoleucos*

Identification: 20 cm. See PMH.
Status: see map. Passage through whole of the region. In winter widespread in small numbers in most of Mediterranean, commoner in Egypt and Arabia to S Iran but rare Turkey. Some over-summer in winter quarters.
Habitat: breeds along clear-running rivers, hillstreams and lakes, nesting on ground. Outside breeding season, water-margins of most kinds, running, standing or coastal, but seldom open shore or flats.

Turnstone *Arenaria interpres*

Identification: 23 cm. See PMH.
Status: passage and winter fairly widely coastal N Africa, especially Morocco; also Arabia and Iran. Passage includes Turkey, Cyprus, Israel. Occasional inland. Some over-summer.
Habitat: rocky or sandy coasts. Rarely inland lakes on passage.

Wilson's Phalarope *Phalaropus tricolor*

Identification: 23 cm. See PMH.
Status: vagrant Morocco, Turkey, Oman. Range America.
Habitat: margins of fresh and brackish waters.

Red-necked Phalarope *Phalaropus lobatus*

Identification: 18 cm. See PMH.
Status: winters at sea off coasts of Oman and S Yemen. On passage common in E Arabian Gulf and Oman, and heavy concentrations can occur on inland lakes in Iran, Iraq, and to lesser extent E Turkey; scarce SW Arabia, Near East, Egypt, vagrant in rest of Mediterranean area.
Habitat: maritime; inland lakes on passage.

Grey Phalarope *Phalaropus fulicarius*

Identification: 20 cm. See PMH.
Status: winters at sea off W Africa; scarce passage migrant Morocco. Elsewhere recorded occasionally in Iran, Egypt. Vagrant Saudi Arabia, S Yemen, Iraq, Israel, Libya, Tunisia.
Habitat: essentially maritime.

Pomarine Skua *Stercorarius pomarinus*

Identification: 51 cm. See PMH.
Status: winters at sea in Atlantic near Morocco, also probably Arabian Sea. Migrants occur sparingly off NW Africa (including Mediterranean); also E Mediterranean (including Lebanon), all coasts of Arabia, S Iran and probably S Caspian; at times many in N Red Sea. Vagrant Turkey.
Habitat: maritime, but must pass over land on migration.

Arctic Skua *Stercorarius parasiticus*

Identification: 46 cm. See PMH.
Status: some winter at sea off W Morocco, and off S and SE Arabia. Passage regular Arabian Gulf, Oman coast, Red Sea, especially north end and Gulf of Aqaba, also thin scattering of records in NW African and E Mediterranean countries and S Caspian.
Habitat: maritime, but must pass over land on migration.

Long-tailed Skua *Stercorarius longicaudus*

Identification: 51–56 cm. See PMH.
Status: scarce passage Gulf of Aqaba and Mediterranean Egypt. Vagrant Oman, Iran, Morocco, possibly Turkey.
Habitat: maritime, but passes over land on migration.

Great Skua *Stercorarius skua*

Identification: 58 cm. See PMH. *Note:* in dark plumages South Polar Skua very similar to Great Skua; palest birds quite different, with whitish head, underparts and neck-collar; intermediates differ in buffish underparts and neck-collar.
Status: passage with some wintering Atlantic off Morocco, where immatures remain in summer. Also occurs in W Mediterranean becoming a vagrant east to Egypt, Turkey. In Arabia uncommon summer and occasional winter records off Oman (and indeed Morocco) may refer to or include South Polar Skua *S. maccormicki*; the same may apply to Iranian vagrants in the Arabian Gulf; also vagrant in Gulf of Aqaba.
Habitat: maritime, but may pass over land on migration.

Sooty Gull *Larus hemprichii*   Plate 15

Identification: 43 cm. Sexes alike. A dark, long-billed, long-winged gull. Slightly larger, more robust and heavy-chested than White-eyed (but size hard to tell on lone birds). Separated from White-eyed in all ages by *stouter, thicker and straighter pale bill with clear-cut blackish tip* and *lack of bold white eye-ring* (though it does have short white crescent *above* eye, and occasionally below); White-eyed has slimmer, drooping all-dark bill and bolder white eye-crescents. Adult in breeding plumage has *sooty-brown head and bib* (black in similar White-eyed), separated from grey-brown upperbreast and upperparts by white half-collar from sides of bib round back of neck (like White-eyed). Dark underwings (coverts blackish) have white trailing edge above and below and blackish primaries, thus similar to White-eyed. *Bill yellow with black subterminal band* and orange-red tip; *legs yellow-green*. In winter, plumage duller and white half-collar less well-defined. Juvenile lacks sooty head and white half-collar of adult, has pale brownish-grey head; face and chin whiter, indistinct white crescent above eye. Upperparts brownish fringed buffish giving scaled appearance; brownish breast band extends onto flanks; tail mostly black with white at base. *Bill pale bluish-grey with clear-cut blackish tip* (all dark in juvenile White-eyed). Legs dark grey in first winter, becoming dull yellow-green later. In second-winter (much as non-breeding adult) has blackish subterminal band along narrower white-tipped secondaries; white tail has variable blackish subterminal band.
Voice: loud mewing 'kaarr' or 'keee-aaar', not unlike Common Tern; also high-pitched 'kee-kee-kee-kee-kee'.
Status: see map. Present throughout year in breeding areas. After nesting many leave to spread over much of Red Sea (few reaching Gulfs of Suez and Aqaba), also Iranian south coast but rarely into inner parts of Arabian Gulf.
Habitat: coastal; often near fishing ports and settlements. Nests on ground, close to edge of islands, sometimes under cover such as mangroves or suaeda.

Sooty Gull

White-eyed Gull *Larus leucophthalmus*   Plate 15

Identification: 41 cm. Sexes alike. Size as Common Gull, slightly smaller than Sooty Gull with wings narrower and chest less deep. Plumage superficially like Sooty. Adult in summer has *all-black hood and bib* (sooty-brown in Sooty), separated from *dark grey upperparts* (browner in Sooty) by white collar, most noticeable on sides of neck; *conspicuous white, broken eye-ring and long slim, dark red bill drooping towards ill-defined black tip, characteristic.* Flight-pattern like Sooty (which see). Pale grey breast band extends onto flanks; rest of underparts and tail white. Legs yellowish. In winter, hood and bib flecked whitish and half-collar less well-defined. Juvenile resembles similar Sooty, but upperparts less conspicuously pale-fringed, *bill all-dark* (distinctly bi-coloured in Sooty) and with broken white eye-ring (indistinct white crescent above eye in young Sooty). Tail blackish like young Sooty, with just some white at base; dark underwing as in young Sooty and legs washed-out greenish. Greyish feathers show through on mantle by first summer. In second-winter, brownish hood flecked and streaked paler on forehead-forecrown, while hind-neck collar imperfect; tail white with variable, blackish subterminal band. Frequently associates with Sooty Gull. At distance, low over sea, can be mistaken for a skua.

Voice: similar to Sooty but less harsh and deep.

Status: see map. Range practically confined to Red Sea and Gulf of Aden extending in summer to Gulf of Suez and Aqaba. Not all Saudi Arabian breeding sites regularly occupied. Vagrant Mediterranean coasts of Egypt and Israel, also Jordan, Iran, Oman.

Habitat: as Sooty Gull. Nests on open ground near shore of low-lying islands; colonial.

White-eyed Gull

Great Black-headed Gull *Larus ichthyaetus*   Plate 15

Identification: 66 cm. Sexes alike. Large, near Great Black-backed in size. Distinct in summer plumage with *black head,* pale grey back and powerful *yellow bill, with prominent black sub-terminal band and red tip.* In flight, mainly white primaries have ragged black sub-terminal crescent. In winter *black on head reduced to dark eye-mask and streaking on back of head.* Juvenile similar to juvenile Herring Gull, but larger with stronger bill, *brownish hind-neck extending into patches at sides of upper breast* (or sometimes breast band), scaly back pattern, *pale grey or grey-brown mid-wing panel,* and *sharply defined black tail-band; usually has dark mark around and behind eye with white crescents above and below at all ages* (lacking in Herring Gull). (Hind-neck and pectoral patches, wing-panel, dark mark behind eye and white eye-crescents, are also lacking in young Great Black-backed Gull). In first-winter, breast patch is reduced, mantle and most wing-coverts become pale greyish (pale mid-wing panel becoming more obvious) and the *bill yellowish-flesh with black tip* (bill more or less all-dark in similar-aged Herring, which also has brownish mantle and uniform wing-coverts). Other differences as for juvenile. First-winter more confusable with second-winter Herring Gull (both show greyish mantle, scapulars and some wing-coverts, and have similar coloured bills). Best distinguished by *eye-mask,* brown on hind-neck and breast sides, and *clear-cut band on tail.* Second-winter birds unmistakable since primary-pattern starts to resemble adult, and clear-cut black tail band remains through successive plumages to sub-adult. Structurally has deep chest (particularly noticeable in flight), 'mean-looking' gradually sloping forehead which accentuates length and size of bill, longish legs and fairly long wings with deep, almost heron-like wing-beat; also sits high on water. These features also assist in separation from immature Herring Gull.

Voice: a deep 'krah-ah'.

Status: winter visitor S Caspian (few non-breeders summer), Iranian Baluchistan, Arabian Gulf, coasts of Oman, Yemen and Red Sea (mainly passage Egypt); rare or accidental E Mediterranean from Egypt to Turkey and Jordan.

Habitat: low lying coasts and occasionally on inland lakes.

Mediterranean Gull *Larus melanocephalus*

Identification: 39 cm. See PMH.

Status: Summer visitor to Turkish breeding colonies. Autumn passage essentially westwards mainly to Mediterranean. Winters along N African coast including Atlantic; fewer in N and E Mediterranean; Gulfs of Suez and Aqaba reached regularly in small numbers. Many immatures summer in Mediterranean. Vagrant Syria, Iraq, inner Arabian Gulf.

Habitat: coastal; on inland lakes (usually salt) in breeding season. Nests on islands in lagoons.

Laughing Gull *Larus atricilla*

Identification: 42 cm. See PMH.
Status: vagrant Morocco. Range America.
Habitat: coastal waters.

Little Gull *Larus minutus*

Identification: 28 cm. See PMH.
Status: winters mainly offshore (but passage also inland) in Mediterranean, Black Sea, and S Caspian; few Atlantic coast of Morocco. Vagrant Arabian Gulf, Gulf of Aqaba, Gulf of Suez and N Red Sea.
Habitat: coastal and sometimes inland waters.

Sabine's Gull *Larus sabini*

Identification: 33 cm. See PMH.
Status: passage in Atlantic off Morocco. Vagrant Israel, Egypt. Range America, NE Asia.
Habitat: maritime, sometimes coastal waters.

Black-headed Gull *Larus ridibundus* Illustration p. 108

Identification: 38 cm. See PMH.
Status: see map. Widespread on passage and in winter all coasts and many inland wetlands (including in Arabia). Immatures often over-summer outside breeding range.
Habitat: coastal and inland waters. Nests colonially on edge of wetlands, shingle banks and lake islands.

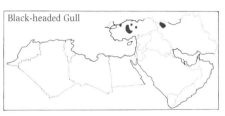

Black-headed Gull

Brown-headed Gull *Larus brunnicephalus*
Illustration p. 108 and Plate 15

Identification: 43 cm. Sexes alike. Similar in general appearance to Black-headed Gull but slightly larger, with slightly broader wings and *stouter bill*. Wing patterns differ – in Brown-headed, *outer-primaries white with broad black wing tip, which has small white mirror near tip* – Black-headed has white leading edge almost to tip of wing, and narrow black margin to trailing edge of outer-wing, lacking Brown-headed's substantial black at end of wing. In winter, head pattern similar to Black-headed; in summer, has brown head (paler than Black-headed) rimmed black round neck. Iris whitish (dark in Black-headed). Immature like Black-headed of similar age but differs in having *much bolder wing pattern with black on distal half of primaries contrasting with their whiter bases and primary coverts* (see line drawing, page 108). Red bill with black tip in adult; yellowish-orange with black tip in immature. Gregarious; actions similar to Black-headed Gull with which it often associates. See also Grey-headed Gull.
Voice: raucous 'keear', deeper than Black-headed.
Status: vagrant Iran, Gulf of Aqaba. Range Asia.
Habitat: coastal waters and large inland lakes.

Grey-headed Gull *Larus cirrocephalus* Illustration p. 108

Identification: 40 cm. Sexes alike. Slightly larger than Black-headed Gull, with broader wings, larger heavier bill, *sloping forehead* and longer legs, thus close to Brown-headed Gull (which has, however, rounder head without sloping forehead, and less strong bill). Adult in breeding plumage has *very pale grey hood, darker-rimmed around neck,* and whitish on forehead and chin. Upperparts grey with *black ends to wing with white mirrors and white flash on basal half*

Brown-headed Gull, adult winter (left), first-winter (right)

Grey-headed Gull, adult winter (left), first-winter (right)

Black-headed Gull, adult winter (left), first-winter (right)

Drawings by S. Christensen

of primaries, very like Brown-headed; *Underwing-coverts dusky* (white in Brown-headed and Black-headed) with blackish primaries and white mirrors. Winter adult (see line drawing) similar but hood even paler. Red bill, legs and eye-ring; whitish-yellow iris. Juvenile has greyish partial hood separated from brownish upperparts by white hind-collar; flight-feathers brownish with white bases of primaries forming patch in middle of outer wing; no white spot near wing-tip as in adult; grey band along wing above dark secondaries; *dusky underwing* with blackish ends to primaries. Bill yellowish to pink with darker tip; iris darker. First-winter (see line drawing) like first-winter Brown-headed Gull, but *darker greyish underwing-coverts,* much more diffuse dark spot on ear-coverts and distinctly narrower black sub-terminal tail-band. May show mottling on crown. During successive plumages to adult, pale grey hood appears and wing pattern becomes more like adult, but dusky secondaries, forming indistinct trailing ege to wing, remain through to second-summer. Gregarious.

Voice: long drawn-out, rather crow-like 'caw caw', also laughing cackling cry.

Status: vagrant E Saudi Arabia, and potentially Morocco as it breeds Mauritania and has occurred Spain.

Habitat: coastal and inland waters.

Slender-billed Gull *Larus genei*

Plate 15

Identification: 43 cm. See PMH.

Status: see map. Apparently breeds irregularly in Tunisia, perhaps Algeria and Morocco. Mainly summer visitor to breeding areas. Winters in central and E Mediterranean, and parts of all coasts (occasional inland) of Asiatic area, with some immatures over-summering. Sometimes reaches Atlantic coast of Morocco. Passage from Black Sea SW to Mediterranean and SE to Arabian coasts.

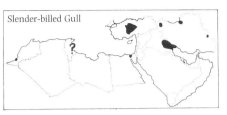

Habitat: coastal and inland waters. Nests in small colonies on edge of wetlands, marshes and islands in lakes.

Audouin's Gull *Larus audouinii*

Plate 15

Identification: 50 cm. See PMH.

Status: see map. Dispersive, or partial migrant, in winter reaching S Tunisia, W Libya and all Atlantic coast of Morocco where some immatures over-summer. Vagrant Egypt, Gulf of Aqaba, Near East.

Habitat: coastal. Nests colonially in vegetation among rocky cliffs.

Ring-billed Gull *Larus delawarensis*

Identification: 46–51 cm. See PMH.

Status: vagrant Morocco. Range America.

Habitat: coastal waters.

Common Gull *Larus canus*

Identification: 41 cm. See PMH.

Status: small numbers winter E Mediterranean and especially Black Sea coast of Turkey, Egypt, Iraq; commoner S Caspian; few S Iran and vagrant on S side of Arabian Gulf, NW Saudi Arabia, Syria and NW Africa.

Habitat: coastal and inland waters.

Lesser Black-backed Gull *Larus fuscus*

Identification: 53 cm. See PMH and Herring Gull (below).

Status: mainly passage and winter visitor but immatures present in some areas throughout year. Winter range includes all sea coasts within the region; rare in Nile valley. Passage heaviest on coasts, especially Atlantic.

Habitat: coastal and less frequently inland waters.

Herring Gull *Larus argentatus*

Identification: 55–65 cm. See PMH. Sexes alike. Subspeciation or variation of Herring Gull is considerable and several forms occur in region with distinct differences of plumage and bare parts from birds of NW Europe, which have pale grey upperparts and pinkish legs. For example, many Middle East forms have dark grey backs and yellow legs, thus similar to Lesser Black-backed Gulls. Herring Gull taxonomy and field characters are receiving renewed study, incomplete as yet, with immatures and their distribution no doubt presenting additional problems. Some workers regard Herring Gulls and Lesser Black-backed Gulls as belonging to same species; others recognise additional species such as Armenian Gull and Yellow-legged Herring Gull; others might wish to switch some intermediate birds from Herring Gull to Lesser Black-backed Gull and *vice versa*. Until the subject has been further developed we follow the general approach adopted by the editors of *The Birds of the Western Palearctic* and give below brief details for the separation of adults. For a fuller understanding of the problem, reference should be made to *Gulls: a guide to identification* by P. J. Grant, and *Handbuch der Vögel Mitteleuropas* Vol 8 by Bauer & Glutz.

heuglini (breeds NE Europe/NW Asia, winters south at least to S Arabia). Dark grey upperparts, as dark as some Lesser Black-backed Gulls; bold, but sparse streaking on head and neck in winter; yellow legs and red eye-ring.

taimyrensis (breeds N Asia, winters south at least to Arabia). Upperparts dark grey but paler than *heuglini* and head apparently less streaked; pink or yellow legs.

michahellis (breeds and winters around Mediterranean). Upperparts darker, more ash-grey than NW European Herring Gull with more black in wings; head only faintly streaked in winter, yellow legs and red eye-ring.

cachinnans (breeds S Russia and N Turkey and winters south to E Mediterranean, Suez and Oman). Similar to *michahellis* but upperparts slightly paler grey, yellow legs and red eye-ring.

armenicus (breeds Armenia, NE Turkey and NW Iran, winters south to E Mediterranean). Ash-grey upperparts (darker than NW European Herring Gull) with rounder head, shorter bill and more black on wing-tips; bill distinct: orange-yellow with red spot and black sub-terminal band; orange-yellow legs and red eye-ring.

Status: see map. Resident or dispersive in west. More migratory in east, producing passage and wintering through Black and Caspian seas and southwards to all coasts of Arabia. Some over-summer south to Oman.

Habitat: coastal and inland waters. Nests usually colonially on rocky coast edges or islands in inland lakes and occasionally roofs of buildings.

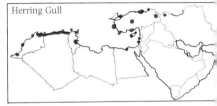

Herring Gull

Glaucous Gull *Larus hyperboreus*

Identification: 64–74 cm. See PMH.
Status: vagrant Morocco; also old record from Gulf of Aqaba.
Habitat: coastal waters.

Great Black-backed Gull *Larus marinus*

Identification: 64–78 cm. See PMH.
Status: vagrant NW Africa, Turkey, Iran, Israel; doubtfully elsewhere in E Mediterranean.
Habitat: coastal waters.

Kittiwake *Rissa tridactyla*

Identification: 41 cm. See PMH.
Status: uncommon NW Africa though recent large wreck. In E Mediterranean rare generally, though apparently regular Lebanon. Vagrant Gulf of Aqaba, Iran, Oman.
Habitat: coastal and offshore waters.

Gull-billed Tern *Gelochelidon nilotica*

Identification: 38 cm. See PMH.

Status: see map. Mainly migrant. Breeds irregularly Algeria; has bred Morocco. Passage includes NW Africa, Nile valley, E Mediterranean, Jordan and coastal Arabia where some over-summer. Winters Iran, Arabia, N Africa.

Habitat: salt marshes, sandy coasts and inland waters. Nests colonially on sandy shores and islets in saline lagoons.

Caspian Tern *Sterna caspia*   Plate 16

Identification: 53 cm. See also PMH. Sexes alike. Large tern, size almost of Herring Gull. Adult in summer separated by *very heavy and deep, bright coral-red bill*, black cap extending from forehead to slightly elongated nape-feathers and, in flight, by *blackish-grey under-surface of primaries* which contrasts with otherwise whitish underwing. Legs blackish. In winter, forehead white and crown streaked; bill tipped darker. Juvenile has similar head-pattern to winter adult but bill paler, more orange but tipped darker, and mantle and wing-coverts have variable dark scaling, not forming distinct blackish bands on innerwing (though sometimes diffuse dark carpal bar; secondaries show dark greyish band); primaries, above, blackish-grey, tail tipped dark, and legs yellowish but become blackish during first-winter. In powerful heavy flight, large bill, neck and head are set well forward of rather broad wings; tail short and only slightly forked. See Royal Tern for distinctions.

Voice: loud, deep and raucous Grey Heron-like 'kaak' or 'kraa-uh'; quite unlike call of other terns.

Status: see map. Partial migrant. Passage most coasts (but rare Algeria and much of E Mediterranean including Cyprus). Winter coasts of S Iran, Arabia, Egypt, fewer N Africa, very few SW Turkey. Some over-summer S and SE Arabia.

Habitat: chiefly coastal but also lakes and large rivers on migration. Nests on ground on sandy coasts or islands, singly or colonially.

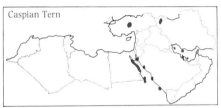

Royal Tern *Sterna maxima*   Plate 16

Identification: 46–53 cm. Sexes alike. Large, fairly heavy-billed tern, between Sandwich and Caspian in size. Resembles larger Caspian but wings more slender and tail more forked; *bill also more slender, more dagger-like, drooping and warm yellow-orange* (deeper and coral-red in Caspian), black cap frequently broken by white forehead (forehead black only in early breeding season) and, in flight, (all plumages) *primaries white below, tipped blackish* (see Caspian which has solid black wing-end). Pale grey upperparts and faint greyish tinge to centre of rump; rest of plumage white; legs blackish, shorter than Caspian's when standing together. In winter, bill yellower and black on head usually confined to narrow streak from eye to black nape, sharply demarcated from white forehead and crown; at times only nape black, leaving an isolated dark eye, like some winter Swift Terns; (winter Caspian more dark-streaked on forehead and crown). Juvenile has paler, yellowish bill (dull orange in young Caspian), becoming more orangy during first winter; legs orange-yellow becoming blackish during autumn. Greyish upperwing has weak darkening on fore wing; *blackish bar on coverts and secondaries* (compare with Caspian) and blackish outer wing; rump is tinged pale greyish and tail tipped darker. Separation from young and first-winter Lesser Crested often tricky, both having similar bill colour and upperwing pattern; larger size and longer legs of Royal are best features if comparison possible. Flight, less heavy than Caspian.

Voice: higher-pitched, less raucous than that of Caspian, 'chirrip', 'keer', 'krit, krit'.

Status: small numbers occur on Atlantic coast of Morocco north to Tangier (in northward dispersal from Banc d'Arguin), mainly autumn, very few mid-winter.

Habitat: coastal including harbours; rare inland.

111

Swift Tern *Sterna bergii*

Plate 16

Identification: 43–48 cm. Sexes alike. Large slender tern, approaching Caspian in size but slimmer body, narrower wings and more slender bill. Told from Lesser Crested by *larger size, longer wings, deeper, drooping, waxy-yellow bill* in summer (slimmer, less drooping, rich orange-yellow in Lesser Crested) and by *darker, ashy-grey upperparts*, including rump and tail; in some lights appears as dark as palest Lesser Black-backed Gull, with conspicuous white trailing edge to wings and silvery primaries while in other lights upperparts appear much paler. In summer, black crested cap always broken by white forehead band (never black as in some Lesser Crested); tail slightly longer and more forked; legs blackish. In winter, bill pale waxy greenish-yellow; top of head whiter, rear crown streaked blackish, solid black area confined to nape, extending forward to front of eye or, often, not reaching eye, which is then isolated from black rear cap. Upperparts as summer, or slightly darker, with rump and tail almost as dark as back; outer primaries and forewing sometimes darker. Juvenile has *greyish-white panel* in centre of innerwing, bordered in front by *blackish-brown carpal bar*, at rear by dark medium-grey greater coverts and blackish-grey secondaries; primaries blackish-brown. Head pattern much as winter adult (often with isolated eye). Loses pale mid-wing panel in first winter, inner wing then appearing dark medium-grey; in first spring, inner primaries become paler, contrasting with darker outers. Steady flight with rather shallow wing-beats, and neck often extended giving elongated appearance.

Voice: similar to Sandwich Tern, but deeper, rougher and less ringing 'kee-rit'; also a high-pitched scream 'kree-kree'.

Status: see map. Resident but dispersive within general area of breeding range. Vagrant Mediterranean coast of Egypt.

Habitat: coastal. Nests colonially on sandy or rocky shores and islands.

Swift Tern

Lesser Crested Tern *Sterna bengalensis*

Plate 16

Identification: 38–43 cm. Sexes alike. Fractionally larger than Sandwich Tern but plumage more like Swift Tern. Differs from Swift in smaller size, *more slender orange-yellow bill* (deeper, more drooping, drab waxy yellow in Swift Tern) and *pale ashy-grey back, wings, rump and tail* (rump and tail paler grey), clearly paler than Swift Tern but marginally darker than Sandwich. Legs blackish. Slightly crested nape black, as may be forehead for short period between April and August, but forehead otherwise white most of year, as always in Swift; eye rarely isolated from black nape (as often in Swift Tern). In *winter, bill is paler orange-yellow* (greenish yellow in Swift) and upperparts often darker grey than in summer; outer primaries also slightly darker. Juvenile has dark outer wing and pale grey inner wing, with dark bar on secondaries and greater coverts; it thus shows two dark bars on inner wing (virtually absent in young Sandwich). Head-pattern much as winter adult but shorter; much less forked tail has dark corners; bill dirtier, greyish-yellow. Dark on innerwing usually retained to first spring when inner primaries become paler, contrasting with dark outer. In fairly graceful flight, wings slightly more centrally placed than Sandwich Tern and bill often carried more horizontally; also tail and trailing-edge of wings do not appear translucent, as often in Sandwich in strong sunlight. Despite size difference, *can be difficult to separate from Royal Tern*, which see.

Voice: high-pitched, not very grating 'kreet-kreet' or 'krriik, krriik', similar to Sandwich Tern but less ringing and not so di-syllabic; also 'krr-eep' and 'kee-kee-kee'.

Status: see map. Has bred Tunisia. Present all year in some areas, mainly dispersing within general breeding range but local movements little understood. Some passage N African coasts, also over-summering Libya, rarely winter Morocco; mainly passage Oman. Vagrant Turkey.

Habitat: coastal. Nests colonially on sandy or rocky shores and islands.

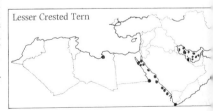

Lesser Crested Tern

112

Sandwich Tern *Sterna sandvicensis*

Identification: 41 cm. See PMH.
Status: has bred Tunisia. Passage on most coasts, but vagrant Cyprus. In winter Arabian and Iranian coasts, S Caspian, Black Sea, NW Africa, and E Mediterranean. Over-summers Egypt, Oman.
Habitat: coastal waters.

Roseate Tern *Sterna dougallii*

Identification: 38 cm. See PMH.
Status: see map. Passage Morocco. Vagrant Algeria, Tunisia, Libya, Egypt, Israel, Arabian Gulf.
Habitat: coastal, more maritime than Common Tern.

Common Tern *Sterna hirundo*

Identification: 36 cm. See PMH.
Status: see map. Has bred Libya. May nest Euphrates valley, Syria. Mainly summer visitor and widespread passage migrant, few winter Oman to N Yemen. Few over-summer S Arabia.
Habitat: coastal and inland wetlands. Nests colonially on beaches, sand dunes, islands and edge of lakes.

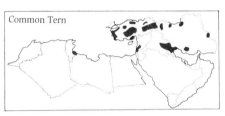

Arctic Tern *Sterna paradisaea*

Identification: 38 cm. See PMH.
Status: passage Morocco. Vagrant Algeria, Cyprus, Turkey, Israel.
Habitat: coastal and occasionally inland waters, more maritime than Common Tern.

White-cheeked Tern *Sterna repressa*   Plate 16

Identification: 32–37 cm. Sexes alike. Similar to Common Tern but slightly smaller with shorter wings. In breeding season, adult has *dark silvery-grey upperparts, rump and tail* (slightly paler than back), with *contrasting whitish-grey inner primaries*; underparts *dark vinous-grey with distinct whitish cheeks* bordering black cap; *greyish* underwings have *whitish area in centre* of secondary-coverts; black line at tips of primaries below is *long and broad at all ages* (shorter in Common, narrower in Arctic). Relatively long bill dark red with extensive black tip, but looks all dark at distance; orange-red legs slightly shorter than Common. In some lights White-cheeked looks fairly pale, approaching Common, while in others looks darker than Arctic. General darkness (including rump and tail), pattern on sides of head and on upper- and underwing, separate it from Common and Arctic (latter a vagrant within White-cheeked's breeding area). In winter, head-pattern much like Common; underparts white while upperparts *are greyish, clearly darker* than in winter Common (where rump and tail greyish-white) but primaries often paler. Some adults with white underparts in November show pattern on upper parts as in breeding plumage. First-winter shows *broader black band* on leading forewing than Common, and dark grey bar on secondaries like Common; *darker innerwing* creates less contrast with blackish forewing and secondary-bar (first-winter Common has paler centre to innerwing); rump and tail *clearly greyer* than in Common.
Voice: loud harsh 'kee-err', 'kerrit' or 'kee-leek' with accent on short variable second syllable (Common has accent on first; Arctic accent on second, usually more drawn out).

113

Status: see map. Mainly summer visitor; a few
winter records Arabian Gulf, Oman.
Habitat: coastal and maritime. Nests colonially
on small sandy islands and beaches,
occasionally among other terns.

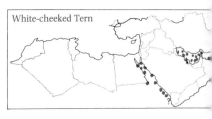

White-cheeked Tern

Bridled Tern *Sterna anaethetus*   Plate 16

Identification: 35–38 cm. Sexes alike. Medium-sized slender tern with deeply forked tail; separated from other terns, except Sooty, by *dark grey-brown upperparts, blackish wings and black
bill and legs*. Adult throughout year has white forehead band *extending behind eye as narrow
superciliary line* and whitish under-parts. Black crown and nape contrast with *whitish collar*
(often impossible to see on flying birds) and dark grey-brown back. White leading edge to
innerwing (as Sooty). Dark grey-brown upperwing-coverts contrast slightly with blackish
flight-feathers, but in some lights Bridled *can look all-black above*. Long outer tail-feathers show
broad white sides. Whitish underparts and underwing-coverts contrast with dark (silvery-
grey) flight- and central tail-feathers. Juvenile has crown and lores flecked whitish, without
distinct supercilium; paler brownish-grey back and wing-coverts, broadly edged buffish,
contrast with dark flight-feathers and shorter tail, which lacks white outer-feathers. Young
Sooty quite different, having sooty-brown underparts and underwing-coverts. Flight swifter,
more graceful, with quicker wing-beats than Sooty, but hard to detect unless both species
together. Does not dive, taking food from surface of water.
Voice: high-pitched 'kee-yharr', yelping 'wep-wep'; also harsh grating 'karr'.
Status: see map. Summer visitor to breeding
grounds. In winter a few remain SE and E
Arabia, but mainly dispersed or pelagic then.
Habitat: maritime. Breeds colonially on rocky
or sandy islands with crevices and low vegetation below which it nests.

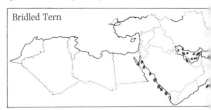

Bridled Tern

Sooty Tern *Sterna fuscata*   Plate 16

Identification: 43–45 cm. Sexes alike. *Darker and larger than Bridled* (which see), *with entire
upperparts blackish and broad white forehead with short white supercilium* (not extending behind
eye as in Bridled) and *black loral-streak broader*. Narrow white line on leading edge of
innerwing, and long outer tail-feathers white (narrower than in Bridled). Cheeks and entire
underparts white except black flight-feathers and tail (sometimes slightly greyish on
underwing, belly and undertail-coverts). Non-breeding plumage similar. Bill and legs blackish.
Juvenile *sooty-brown above and below* but has whitish leading edge to wing, *upperparts
flecked whitish*, pale whitish belly and undertail-coverts, and mottling on underwing-coverts
becoming more hoary with age. Differs from young Noddy in whitish vent and undertail-
coverts, pale underwing and forked tail. First-summer Sooty like adult but has blackish throat
and upper breast.
Voice: a high-pitched 'ker-wacki-wah', quite different from Bridled, is most characteristic call.
Status: see map. Summer visitor to breeding
grounds. Migratory/pelagic in Arabian Sea,
apparently absent in mid-winter. Vagrant
Gulf of Aqaba, SW Saudi Arabia.
Habitat: maritime. Nests colonially on sandy,
stony or rocky islands, often with vegetation.

Sooty Tern

ittle Tern *Sterna albifrons*

entification: 24 cm. See PMH.
atus: see map. Has bred Cyprus, Syria.
Summer visitor, also widespread passage
including smaller numbers Arabia. Does not
winter N Africa; position on coasts of Iran
and Arabia obscured by possible confusion
with Saunders' Little Tern.
abitat: coastal around the Mediterranean but
otherwise mainly inland waters, including
wide rivers. Nests on sand or shingle beaches
or sand bars in rivers.

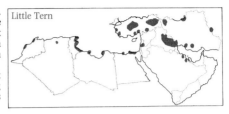

aunders' Little Tern *Sterna saundersi* Plate 16

entification: 23 cm. Sexes alike. *Very similar to Little Tern and not always separable from it.*
Adult is summer differs slightly in *reddish-brown or darker legs* (paler, more orangy in Little,
though yellower in European birds); *rump and uppertail generally greyer* than in Little, almost
same colour as back (varies, and can appear as white-rumped as Little, which in turn can
have pale grey rump in fresh plumage, paler than back, bleaching to white); *three outer
primaries blackish* (in Little this darkening confined to outer two which are usually, but not
always, suffused greyish). The *white forehead is more restricted than in Little*, its upper edge
running straight across forecrown between eyes, while in Little it tapers back narrowly on
side of head above eye. In winter Saunders' is darker grey on mantle, wing-coverts, rump
and tail, in some with little contrast between back and rump; leading upperwing-coverts
form broad blackish bar; winter Little Tern is paler throughout, notably on rump and tail.
Habits as Little Tern.
oice: thin strident 'kit-kit' or 'kit-ir-ik', recalling Little Tern but often lacking the chattering
quality of that species.
atus: see map. Mainly summer visitor but
recorded wintering E and S Arabia and in S
Iran.
abitat: coastal; occasionally inland. Nests on
beaches.

Vhiskered Tern *Chlidonias hybridus*

entification: 25 cm. See PMH.
atus: see map. Mainly summer visitor with
widespread passage through the region.
Winters Iraq, Iran, Egypt (large numbers in
Nile delta) and few in NW Africa, Israel, E
Saudi Arabia and Oman, occasionally
Turkey and probably Syria.
abitat: inland waters but also coastal areas
on passage and in winter. Nests colonially
building floating nest on vegetation (eg
water lilies) in lakes and marshes.

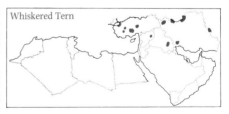

Black Tern *Chlidonias niger*

Identification: 24 cm. See PMH.

Status: see map. Summer visitor; rarely recorded in winter in N Africa. Passage in Mediterranean area, also few N Iran. Vagrant elsewhere in Asiatic area from Syria/Iraq to S Arabia.

Habitat: inland waters, but also coastal areas on passage. Nests in scattered colonies building floating nest in shallows of marshes and lagoons.

White-winged Black Tern *Chlidonias leucopterus*

Identification: 24 cm. See PMH.

Status: see map. Summer visitor to breeding areas. Widespread passage in most Asiatic countries and Nile valley, less common further west in N Africa, and rare Morocco. Few winter E and S Arabia and may over-summer there.

Habitat: inland waters and also some coastal areas on passage. Nests much as Black Tern.

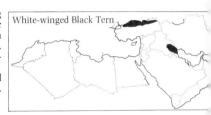

Common (Brown) Noddy *Anous stolidus*   Plate 16

Identification: 40–45 cm (wing-span 83 cm). Sexes alike. Size as Sandwich Tern; *dull chocolate-brown plumage and long wedge-shaped tail, (yet shallowly forked when spread)* distinguish it from other terns, except Lesser Noddy. In adult, top of head *pale ash-grey grading into white forehead, contrasting sharply with black lores* (which continue over base of bill as narrow band, visible on perched birds); in certain lights and in abraded birds, head appears white-capped. Brown upperwing-coverts contrast slightly with blackish-brown flight-feathers; on underwing the latter *contrast more strongly with pale brownish-grey underwing-coverts* (all-brown underwing in Lesser). Legs and relatively long robust bill black. Juvenile has top of head varying from brownish-grey to whitish; immature (up to about 3 years of age) becomes extremely abraded, appearing paler than adults. Separated from young Sooty Tern by *dark brown underwing-coverts* (can be whitish in Sooty) and tail shape. May recall small dark skua at distance over sea. Flight usually low over water; wing-beats slower than Lesser Noddy; does not feed by diving, but hovers above surface before swooping low to pick prey. For separation from Lesser Noddy, see that species.

Voice: at breeding sites deep and guttural, at times *Corvus*-like 'kwok kwok', 'karruk' or 'krao'.

Status: see map. Summer visitor breeding Oman, also SW Saudi Arabia and occasional records Yemen.

Habitat: maritime, rarely approaching land except to breed. Nests colonially on rocky islets and cliffs.

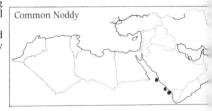

Lesser (Black) Noddy *Anous tenuirostris*   Plate 16

Identification: 30–34 cm (wing-span 60 cm). Sexes alike. Closely resembles a *smaller, shorter-tailed version of Common Noddy* (size as Common Tern) but *pale ash-grey* (not pure white) *of forehead and crown often extends below eye,* and lacks the sharp demarcation of Common Noddy; however some Lessers show black lores and are similar in head markings to Common

116

Noddy. *Bill proportionally longer, thinner* and less robust than in Common and also lacks narrow black forehead-band over bill. Body plumage more greyish, less brownish, particularly on sides of nape, mantle and underparts, *but wings darker without the contrast on underwings* of Common Noddy (but reflecting light can make underwing-coverts appear paler). Juvenile's crown varies from pale grey to brown, some having extremely restricted pale forehead. In flight, narrower wings and fast wing-beats give a lighter jizz than in Common Noddy (which is bulkier with heavier body); at distance over sea, size, ground-colour and head-pattern not easy to see and separation of a lone bird may be difficult. Behaviour at sea as Common Noddy.
Status: a non-breeding summer visitor in small numbers to Masirah Island, Oman (usually with Common Noddy).
Habitat: maritime, rarely approaching land except to breed. Nests colonially on islands or islets.

African Skimmer *Rynchops flavirostris* Plate 15

Identification: 36 cm. Sexes alike. Resembles large tern but distinguished by *black back and wings with white trailing-edge to secondaries,* and *huge, slightly decurved, orange-red bill with longer yellow and translucent-ended lower mandible.* Wings long and slim, stretching well beyond tail at rest. Smaller than Indian Skimmer (which see) but similar in structure, plumage and actions. Differs from Indian in lacking white collar – the black cap connecting with blackish mantle (though dusty-white collar in winter), and *broader black band on central tail with less white on side of tail.* Juvenile has black cap and upperwing-coverts of adult replaced by buff-edged dark brown feathers, the pale edges forming narrow line along rear-edge of wing coverts. Bill shorter than adults and black with yellow base. Lacks whitish collar of juvenile Indian. Often in groups which pack together and adopt 'follow-my-leader' in flight. Rather slow flight with *accent on upstroke of wing-beat.* 'Skims' by flying over water with bill open and long lower mandible breaking the surface.
Voice: harsh 'kreeep' and loud, harsh 'kip'.
Status: rare non-breeding summer visitor south Nile valley (Egypt). Vagrant N Yemen, Israel, Egyptian Red Sea coast.
Habitat: rivers with sandbanks and marshes with open water; rarely on coast.

Indian Skimmer *Rynchops albicollis* Plate 15

Identification: 42 cm. Sexes alike. Larger than African Skimmer (which see) but otherwise very similar. Adult differs in having *white collar, narrow dark central stripe on white tail* (tail usually looking all-white at distance) and paler orange bill. Juvenile differs from juvenile African in having white collar (hind-neck, nape and crown brown, mottled whitish, in African).
Voice: rarely, a nasal 'yap'.
Status: vagrant Oman; also old record from Iran.
Habitat: rivers with sandbanks and marshes with open water; rarely on coast.

Guillemot *Uria aalge*

Identification: 42 cm. See PMH.
Status: vagrant Morocco.
Habitat: maritime.

Razorbill *Alca torda*

Identification: 41 cm. See PMH.
Status: winters in Atlantic south to S Morocco, and in Mediterranean east to Algeria. Vagrant Egypt.
Habitat: maritime.

Puffin *Fratercula arctica*

Identification: 30 cm. See PMH.
Status: winters Morocco coast south to 28° and occurs within Mediterranean east to Tunisia.
Habitat: maritime.

Lichtenstein's Sandgrouse *Pterocles lichtensteinii* Plate 17

Identification: 25 cm. Sexes differ. Plump-chested, Turtle Dove-size with *short square-ended tail* and finely barred plumage. Male yellowish-buff, body *vermiculated with black and white* except for *two black bands across yellowish breast-patch*; broad *white supercilium and white forehead crossed by two black bars*, the foremost forming a solid band. *Orange bill* (duller in female). Female duller sandy-buff with even finer black vermiculations and no bold black markings on head or breast; *lacks yellow throat* of similar Crowned Sandgrouse. In flight, above, black flight-feathers with *broad pale panel on rear edge of coverts*; tail has narrow, pale terminal band; below, no distinctive markings except slightly darker flight-feathers and pale tip to tail. Usually seen singly or in small parties coming to drink in late dusk or before dawn; rarely flies in full daylight unless flushed, which is infrequent as it sits tight, often in shade of acacia.
Voice: fast gurgling, almost purring 'trrrr' or whirring, frog-like *'quark-quark-quark'*, not unlike call of female Mallard with chicks when alarmed. Call on coming in to drink, a quiet 'kwital'.
Status: see map. Resident. Vagrant Iraq.
Habitat: dry, rocky, semi-deserts, wadis and hillsides, with scrub usually acacia. Nests on ground.

Crowned Sandgrouse *Pterocles coronatus* Plate 17

Identification: 28 cm. Sexes differ. Somewhat featureless, subtly-plumaged, with *short, pointed tail*. More slender than Lichtenstein's but, like all sandgrouse, has horizontal stance, stretching neck upwards when nervous. Male has white forehead, narrowly bordered with black, and black chin forming *a black mask around bill, a feature shown by no other sandgrouse*. Head and neck warm yellowish-buff with russet-brown crown, flanked by a soft grey stripe joining at the nape. Orange-yellow neck merges into grey-buff, lightly spangled upperparts and ash grey upperbreast, which in turn merges into creamy underparts. Female *sandy-buff, finely vermiculated with black except for unmarked large, warm yellow throat and cheek-patch*, which immediately distinguishes it from very similar, but even more finely barred Lichtenstein's. Immature male lacks black face-pattern of adult, and can thus appear similar about the head to Spotted (which see). In flight, above, sandy-grey upperparts and wing-coverts (golden in some lights) *contrast with solid blackish primaries* and secondaries, the latter showing as narrow line along rear edge of wing; below, *pale with white underwing-coverts contrasting with black flight-feathers*. (Compare with Spotted Sandgrouse.) Pointed, short tail, which, when fanned on landing, shows white terminal band. Comes to water mainly in morning in small parties, though drinking congregations may build to several hundred.
Voice: call a frequently repeated guttural chattering, less clearly defined than Red Grouse, 'ch-chok-choker' or 'chuck-a-chuck-a-chuck', or 'ka-karak-karak'.
Status: see map. Breeding distribution in Arabia mapped very tentatively. Mainly resident, somewhat nomadic. In winter extends further north in Morocco/Algeria, and some records in UAE where may breed.
Habitat: stony and semi-deserts. Nests on ground.

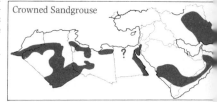

Spotted Sandgrouse *Pterocles senegallus* Plate 17

Identification: 33 cm. Sexes differ. Rather small sandgrouse with fairly long, slim wings and *pointed tail* (but long central feathers can be difficult to see). As with all of family, views on ground not easy to obtain for it blends perfectly with surroundings and when alarmed invariably remains quite still until flushed. Male has ashy-grey head and nape with orange-yellow throat and cheeks, and pale russet crown. Upper- and underparts spangled pale golden-vinous with some darker markings on the wings; *narrow black patch runs from belly to undertail-coverts* but this can be difficult to see. Female has mottled and spotted upperparts and breast; unmarked ochre-yellow on cheeks and throat. In flight, upperparts grey-buff with indistinct dark rear border to wing; *below pale with black-tipped primaries and prominent black secondaries.* Wing pattern best distinguishing character from Crowned which shows all blackish primaries and secondaries above and below in contrast to pale coverts; crowned also has tail white-tipped above and below.

Voice: frequently uttered flight note is a bubbling, guttural 'whit-oo' or 'kwut-al'; also a single 'whilp'.

Status: see map. Resident, with slight northward expansion in Morocco and Algeria in winter.

Habitat: mainly sandy deserts; also semi-deserts with sparse vegetation but sometimes fairly thick scrub. Nests on ground.

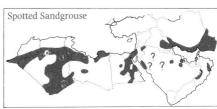
Spotted Sandgrouse

Chestnut-bellied Sandgrouse *Pterocles exustus*   Plate 17

Identification: 32 cm. Sexes differ. Small-bodied sandgrouse, in flight showing *blackish underwing and belly and elongated tail.* Male has warm buffish-yellow head merging into grey-buff breast, then (after narrow black band) into *dark chestnut lower breast and belly.* Upperparts greyish-buff with broad pale tips to feathers; more golden on wings with some scaly dark barring. Female above buffish, narrowly vermiculated blackish, and with broad, irregular pale stripes on the wing; face yellowish-buff with neck and upper breast streaked and spotted; *belly to undertail-coverts closely barred chestnut-black.* In flight, above, sandy-brown with black flight-feathers, narrow white trailing edge to outer wing and broad, pale band along coverts; *below, underwing all-dark and continuous with dark chestnut lower breast and belly.* Only other sandgrouse with extensive dark underparts is Black-bellied, which is larger, has short tail and white underwing with black primaries. May come to water in large flocks in early to mid-morning.

Voice: calls include a deep, short 'whit-gerut', 'whit-gerut', 'ke-rep, ke-rep' with stress on last syllable; also melodious 'gattar-gattar'.

Status: see map. Resident, and nomadic; has become very rare Egypt. Vagrant Israel.

Habitat: semi-deserts with sparse or moderate vegetation, though often near marginal agriculture. Nests on ground.

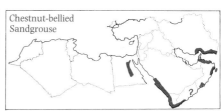
Chestnut-bellied Sandgrouse

Black-bellied Sandgrouse *Pterocles orientalis*   Plate 17

Identification: 34 cm. Sexes differ. Largest and most distinctly marked sandgrouse of region, being slightly larger than Rock Dove, with deep, plump chest, long, rather narrow wings and short tail. Male has soft pale grey head and breast with chestnut and black on throat and narrow *black pectoral line.* Rest of underparts whitish with *clearly demarcated black belly and flanks.* Upperparts golden buff with darker mottling. More soberly dressed female is sandy-buff, streaked and spotted darker on head and narrowly vermiculated with black on upperparts; breast spotted, with black line on lower edge; *black belly* as in male. In flight, above, mottled sandy with black flight-feathers (though secondaries show only as narrow black line along rear edge of wing) and broad tawny band along rear edge of coverts. Below, prominent *black primaries and narrow secondaries contrasting with white underwing-coverts,* large black belly-patch and, in male, black line on pale breast. More regularly seen on wing throughout day than other sandgrouse, in small to medium-sized parties.

Voice: deep, purring 'currru', or 'tschurr-rurr-rurr'; usually repeated 2 or 3 times.

119

Status: see map. Resident N Africa; partial migrant SW Asia, expanding in winter to E Iraq, Syria, Jordan, NE Egypt, Kuwait (now scarce), occasionally central Arabia. Passage S Turkey, Cyprus.

Habitat: dry regions with fairly sparse vegetation and at the edges of cultivation. Nests on ground.

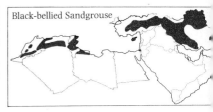

Black-bellied Sandgrouse

Pin-tailed Sandgrouse *Pterocles alchata*   Plate 17

Identification: 37 cm. Sexes differ. Combination of fast flight, long narrow wings, golden upperparts, and tendency to form large flocks, makes it even more reminiscent of in-flight Golden Plover than other sandgrouse. Male has spangled green and golden upperparts with chestnut on coverts, *orangy face, black throat and eyestripe*, and *broad chestnut-buff breast-band, bordered narrowly by black above and below*. In winter barred yellowish-buff and black on upperparts, black throat-patch is lost, face and upper neck change to a dull sandy-brown with dark spotting on sides of face. Female mottled and barred golden-buff on upperparts, with buff cheeks and *three dark bands on golden-yellow breast*. In flight upperparts golden-buff (with greenish sheen and chestnut on coverts of male if seen close) with greyish primaries. Underwing *white with black primaries and narrow black line along rear and fore-edge; prominent bands across breast*; tail-end always looks tapered, but quite long pin-tail rarely visible except when bird is directly overhead. Gregarious, frequently occurring in very large flocks, often in line formation and passing rapidly high overhead.

Voice: frequently-uttered 'kar' or 'kat-tar' when flighting to or from drinking holes; not deep and can be reminiscent of distant crows.

Status: see map. Resident and nomadic/partial migrant. In winter expands in Saudi Arabia, Morocco, Algeria and abundant in NE Iran. Irregular Kuwait, vagrant Egypt, Lebanon.

Habitat: dry plains and stony semi-deserts often near areas of cereal cultivation. Nests on ground.

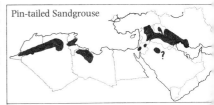

Pin-tailed Sandgrouse

Pallas's Sandgrouse *Syrrhaptes paradoxus*   Plate 17

Identification: 35–40 cm. Sexes differ. Large sandgrouse with *longest tail* and longest, narrowest, most curved wings of any resident in region. Male sandy-buff above with black mottling on back and wings, looking quite golden in strong light on back and inner wing. Head and neck soft grey with indistinct orange face and throat; neck terminates in *pectoral band of fine flecks*, below which the underparts are buffish-white with *a black belly-patch* (very much smaller than Black-bellied). Buff-coloured female shows more spotting above than male; readily identified from all other sandgrouse by *small distinct black belly-patch on virtually unmarked buffish-white underparts, and long central tail-feathers*. In flight above shows indistinct chestnut band on rear edge of coverts and *narrow dark trailing edge to secondaries and grey primaries*; thus at a distance appearing rather featureless. *From below, very pale*, with small but distinct belly-patch and small black spots on axillaries. Only sandgrouse in region with wholly *pale underwing, black belly-patch and elongated tail*.

Voice: bubbling flight calls include 'puk-puh-purr', 'puk', 'kicki' or 'garruak'.

Status: probably irregular winter visitor to Iran steppe east of Caspian; irruptions have reached Turkey.

Habitat: during irruptions from its E Asian breeding grounds can inhabit any open country such as semi-deserts, steppe, waste land and cultivated areas.

120

Rock Dove *Columba livia*

Identification: 33 cm. See PMH.

Status: see map. resident, with few local movements.

Habitat: typically, pure forms occur in rocky upland areas and around sea cliffs but ferally can occur almost anywhere. Nests in crevices or caves among rocks.

Rock Dove

Stock Dove, adult

Eastern Stock Dove, adult

Drawings by S. Christensen

Stock Dove *Columba oenas*

Identification: 33 cm. See PMH.

Status: see map. Resident/partial migrant, range in winter expanding across N Algeria, N Egypt, Israel, Cyprus, Iraq and NW half Iran. Vagrant Tunisia, Syria, Oman, Bahrain.

Habitat: wooded areas with old trees, but more widespread on passage including fields. Nests in hole in tree, rock or building.

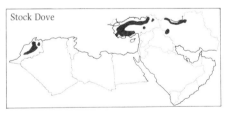

Stock Dove

Eastern (Yellow-eyed) Stock Dove *Columba eversmanni*   Plate 18

Identification: 29–30 cm. Sexes alike. Slightly smaller, slimmer and shorter-tailed than Stock Dove but with relatively longer and more pointed wings. Differs from Stock Dove in *whitish lower back* (like many Rock Doves) and *wing-pattern* (see sketch); upperwing medium grey with diffuse paler panel, pale-based primaries and *broad dark hind-border* (in Stock Dove dark wings with smaller well-defined pale panel); *top of head mauve-pink* like breast; underwing almost white with slightly darker hind-border (Stock Dove's underwing-coverts pale greyish with much darker flight-feathers). *Iris and broad eye-ring yellowish* (Stock Dove is dark-eyed). Otherwise resembles Stock Dove with metallic green patch on sides of neck, black tail with faint grey bar at base and 2–3 inconspicuous broken black bars on innerwing above. Rock Dove occurring in eastern part of region usually has lower back grey like rest of body, but sometimes has white patch as Eastern Stock. Rock Dove, however, is larger, has two bold

121

black bars across inner wing (broken and inconspicuous in Eastern Stock) and more sharply defined black terminal tail-band. Juvenile duller than adult and has fawn on breast.

Voice: song resembles Stock Dove's, a subdued 'oo-oo-oo'.

Status: partial migrant; a few present NE Iran all year (breeding not proved), but most apparently winter from Iranian Baluchistan eastwards.

Habitat: small groves, river banks, cliffs or ruins. Nests colonially in trees.

Woodpigeon *Columba palumbus*

Identification: 41 cm. See PMH.

Status: see map. Mainly resident, but in winter migrants mainly from north reach N Algeria, W Turkey, S Iran and Israel. Vagrant Kuwait.

Habitat: wooded areas, including coniferous, but more widespread on passage including fields. Nests in tree or hedge, sometimes using old nests.

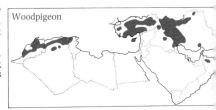
Woodpigeon

Olive Pigeon

IW

Olive Pigeon *Columba arquatrix*

Identification: 40 cm. Sexes similar. *Dark blue-grey* dove, slightly smaller than Woodpigeon with shorter tail, and fairly thick *bright yellow bill, eye-ring and legs; tips of wing-coverts have well-marked white rounded spots*, more diffuse on greater coverts; foreneck to upperbreast ashy-grey with paler scaling while rest of grey underparts have *transverse whitish spots*, but lower belly to undertail-coverts unmarked blue-grey. Maroon tinge to lower neck. Tail dark blue-grey with darkening at tip. Flight steady with leisurely wing-beats; flight-feathers dark slate, little darker than blue–grey upperparts; uppertail may show inconspicuous broad dark terminal band. Skulks in centres of large trees, where sits motionless in shade, reluctant to fly.

Voice: deep note, followed by brief succession of coos.

Status: recently recorded (status uncertain) SW Saudi Arabia and N Yemen. Range Africa.

Habitat: woodland and areas of tall trees (especially fruit) usually in highlands.

122

African Collared (Pink-headed) Dove *Streptopelia roseogrisea*

Plate 18

Identification: 29 cm. Sexes alike. Very similar to Collared Dove but confined to tropical Africa, reaching north to SE Egypt and SW Arabia. Separated from Collared by *white lower belly and undertail-coverts* (uniform pale grey underparts in Collared), slightly smaller size, and *shorter tail which is darker above than the vinous-grey upperparts* (in Collared tail is uniform with rest of upperparts), also cleaner vinous-grey head and black collar on hind-neck slightly broader with more noticeable white edgings. Upperwing-pattern (dark flight-feathers contrasting with paler coverts) and whitish-grey underwing resemble Collared Dove's. Tail pattern shows white tips to corners of uppertail and white distal half of whitish-grey undertail. Juvenile paler, almost whitish-grey on head and underparts (distinctly paler than Collared). Flight much like Collared and difficult to make distinction, though tail proportionally shorter and wings slightly more rounded. See also Red-eyed Dove.
Voice: song (which differs distinctly from Collared's tri-syllabic song) starts with high-pitched, drawn-out note, then short pause, then series of broken descending rolling cooing notes: 'croo–cro cococo' or 'cuu;-currrruuu'; at distance sounds di-syllabic, 'coo;-coorrr'.
Status: see map. Resident.
Habitat: semi-deserts and savannas with trees such as palms, acacias and tamarisks; also coastal mangroves and parks in towns. Nests in trees, sometimes colonially.

Collared Dove *Streptopelia decaocto*

Identification: 28 cm. See PMH.
Status: see map. Recently reached Morocco where now breeding. Largely resident, but in Iran mainly summer visitor, wintering only in SW and in major cities.
Habitat: towns, villages and neighbouring fields. Nest usually built in tree.

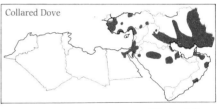

Red-eyed Dove *Streptopelia semitorquata*

Plate 18

Identification: 33 cm. Sexes alike. Rather large, plump, dark dove with collar on hind-neck. Larger and darker than Collared (from which geographically isolated) and African Collared and readily distinguished by *dark plumage and diagnostic black band across centre of tail, with distal* half of tail *buffish grey* or even buffish-rufous. Upperparts bronzy grey-brown with bluish slate on wing-coverts and blackish primaries; underwing grey; thus wings look nearly uniform dark in flight. *Fore-crown grey* shading into vinous nape and neck, the latter with black half-collar. Underparts deep vinous merging into grey belly and undertail-coverts. In flight, when neck markings not seen, may be confused with similarly dark Dusky Turtle Dove (which see), but Red-eyed's uppertail-pattern and generally slower, softer wing-beats help distinguish it. Juvenile lacks collar, is duller and browner than adult, with reddish-buff edges to mantle and coverts, and rufous wash to breast.
Voice: full song low, deep hoarse 'ko-koo, ko-ko, ko-ko', second note highest in pitch and often stressed, as sometimes is fourth note; also 'crooo-cro-cro', the first note stressed, and a far-carrying continuous deep 'ho-ho, ho-ho, ho-ho'. Alarm-call low, hoarse 'krraev'.
Status: see map. Resident.
Habitat: well-vegetated areas with tall trees and scrub, tree-lined agricultural regions; usually near wadis with running water; mainly 500–1,700 m. Nests in tree.

123

Red Turtle Dove

Red Turtle Dove *Streptopelia tranquebarica*

Identification: 23 cm. Sexes differ. Smaller than Palm Dove with relatively shorter tail than most other doves. Brightly coloured male has *unspotted red-brown upperback, ashy-grey head* and black collar on hind-neck; pale vinous brown underparts merge into whitish vent and undertail-coverts; lower back to tail-coverts, dark ash-grey. Tail-pattern recalls Collared Dove (distal half of undertail white), but closed uppertail considerably darker grey-brown. Unlikely to be confused with any other dove in the region. Female similar but less brightly coloured, more brownish above and below and head less pure grey. Juvenile resembles female. Female and juvenile separated from Collared Dove by *warm brown mantle and wing-coverts* (pale grey-brown in Collared), *much darker ashy-grey lower back*, darker uppertail, browner breast and whiter vent and undertail-coverts (in Collared, breast soft grey with pink flush, ventral region pale grey) and blackish, not red, legs. In flight, *dark underwings* (coverts ashy-grey) and shorter tail are further features (Collared has whitish underwing-coverts and longer tail). From Palm and Turtle Dove by black collar on hind-neck, greyer head and, in flight, by absence of bluish-grey panel on upperwing; also lacks blackish spots above of Turtle Dove.
Voice: dry, rattling, rhythmic, 'rak-a-tak-taaa', quickly repeated.
Status: vagrant Iran, Oman.
Habitat: open wooded country.

Turtle Dove *Streptopelia turtur*   Plate 18

Identification: 27 cm. See PMH. The race breeding throughout Nile Valley *isabellina* (illustrated) differs from European birds, *turtur*, in rather uniform pale upperparts, being pale buff-brown with black-spotted wing-coverts. The blue-grey panel on upperwing-coverts often absent; throat and breast lavender-buff. At close range (fresh plumage) has broad rufous fringes to wing-coverts, shoulders, rump and uppertail-coverts. The race *arenicola* (NW Africa, Near East to Iran) distinctly paler, more washed-out grey-brown on mantle and breast than European birds; *rufescens* (oases of W Egypt and perhaps in Libya) also lacks grey crown of European birds, is richly dark foxy-red above and violet-brown to vinaceous on breast, and pale buffish on belly; underwing-coverts darker slate than other races.

Status: see map. Summer visitor. Widespread passage, including SW Arabia. Winters south Nile valley, and perhaps occasionally N Yemen.
Habitat: open country with bushes, scrub, scattered trees or small woods. Nests in bushes, thickets, orchards etc.

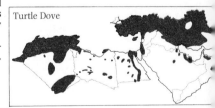

Turtle Dove

Dusky Turtle Dove *Streptopelia lugens*   Plate 18

Identification: 31 cm. Sexes alike. Larger, plumper and darker than Turtle Dove with more rounded wings and rather slow wing-beats. *Dark blue-grey plumage* with *unstreaked black patch on side of neck*, pinkish tinge to breast and *chestnut feather-edges on inner secondaries and greater coverts* while *scapulars and rest of coverts slate-grey, thinly edged whitish-grey*. In flight shows dark wings with *hardly any chestnut* (paler Turtle Dove has chestnut-brown inner-wing

Dusky Turtle Dove

Red-eyed Dove

Drawings by S. Christensen

contrasting with blue-grey wing-panel and dark flight feathers). Narrow whitish-grey terminal band to dark brownish-grey tail (in Turtle, pure white and more contrasting terminal band is broken on central pair). Juvenile paler and browner, lacks black neck-patches; distinguished from other juvenile doves by broad tawny edges to inner secondaries and wing-coverts. See also Red-eyed Dove which it resembles superficially.

Voice: deep, gruff, purring 'coorrrr-coorrr---coorrr-coorrr', first note most gruff, last two slightly higher but sometimes omitted.

Status: see map. Resident, with some dispersal in winter. Has been recorded in S Yemen.

Habitat: wooded areas, wadis with acacias, tree-lined agriculture from 1,000 to at least 2,800 m, sometimes lower in winter. Nests in tree, occasionally bush.

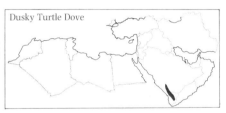

Dusky Turtle Dove

Rufous Turtle Dove *Streptopelia orientalis* Plate 18

Identification: 33 cm. Sexes alike. Slightly larger and more heavily built than Turtle Dove with slightly longer, broader wings and proportionately shorter tail. Flight slightly heavier, at times straighter with less jerky wing-beats. Plumage rather similar to Turtle Dove but separated by combination of the following characters. *Nape and hind-neck, cinnamon – or greyish-brown contrasting with ash-grey crown* (in Turtle Dove, blue-grey on both head and hind-neck), *neck-patch usually larger with 4–6 blackish streaks fringed blue-grey* (in Turtle 3–4 bolder black streaks fringed white), *breast darker and browner* more like mantle (in Turtle, breast paler mauve-grey); often shows double whitish wing-bars (lacking in Turtle, whose wing coverts are paler, more orange) and has *less broad pale grey or white tip to undertail* than Turtle. *Outer wing-coverts darker, contrasting less with innerwing* (in Turtle, form paler, brighter blue-grey patch). In addition has darker mantle, rump and central tail and *larger, more ill-defined dark centres to feathers of wing-coverts. Bare, rosy ring round eye is circular* (in Turtle more conspicuous, purer red and slightly elongated horizontally). Juvenile lacks neck-patches and is generally paler, more uniform brownish on body and wing-coverts; basically separated from juvenile Turtle in same way as adult but pale fringes on breast feathers (absent in adult) diffusely fringed orangy-rosy white (yellowish-brown in juvenile Turtle). Race occurring in region, *meena*, has whitish belly, undertail-coverts and distal part of undertail like Turtle Dove, but central Siberian race *orientalis*, which might straggle to the region, has these parts greyish.

Voice: mournful 'goor-gur-grugror', repeated slowly, phrased like Woodpigeon.

Status: scarce passage in E Iran and very few Oman; more irregular or vagrant elsewhere in Arabian Gulf area.

Habitat: wooded regions, light open forest near cultivation.

125

Palm (Laughing) Dove *Streptopelia senegalensis*   Plate 18

Identification: 26 cm. Sexes alike. Smallish rather dark, *reddish-brown* dove with *shorter more rounded wings and longer tail* than Turtle Dove; further separated from Turtle by *larger and bluer patch* on wing-coverts, *densely black- and copper-spotted upper breast* and *unspotted, bright reddish-brown* upperparts (Turtle has black spots above). Head and breast vinous-pink shading to whitish belly and undertail-coverts. Dark uppertail has less clear-cut white corners than in Turtle; *undertail white with extreme base black.* Juvenile pale dull brownish where adult red-brown, dull tawny-grey where adult pink, and lacks spotted upperbreast. Population in Istanbul is very dark. Flight slower, more laboured with less twists and turns than Turtle Dove. Tame. See Dusky Turtle Dove.

Voice: usually five-syllables, 'doo, doo, dooh, dooh, doo', third and fourth notes slightly longer and higher in tone.

Status: see map. Mainly resident, spreading in Saudi Arabia; rare Morocco where now perhaps breeding. Vagrant Cyprus, Iraq, E Saudi Arabia.

Habitat: towns, villages, gardens, palm groves, oases, agricultural areas, savanna with trees. Nests in trees, bushes or on houses.

Namaqua Dove *Oena capensis*   Plate 18

Identification: 29 cm (including 9 cm tail). Sexes differ. Unmistakable *small dove with long black central tail-feathers and chestnut patch in primaries visible in flight* (blackish when perched). Male has *black face and upper breast*, remaining underparts white; head, neck and shoulders pale blue-grey, merging to earth-brown on mantle; narrow white and black bars on lower back and iridiscent purple spot on secondaries. Bill orange with lilac base. Female has brownish-grey head and upper breast, sharply demarcated from white below, and black and buff bars across lower back. Bill greyish. Juvenile barred black and buff on crown, throat, wing-coverts and lower back, with ill-defined bar on latter. Flight very fast and direct, recalling small parakeet. Spends much time on ground.

Voice: song a mournful 'hu-hu, hu-hu'; also a mournful deep 'coo'.

Status: see map. Mainly resident (but apparently spreading), with some nomadic movements. Vagrant Morocco, Algeria, Gulf States.

Habitat: semi-desert and thorn-bush or scrub. Nests in low bush or tree.

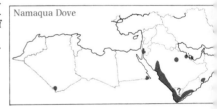

Bruce's Green (Yellow-bellied) Pigeon *Treron waalia*   Plate 18

Identification: 31 cm. Sexes similar. Distinctive dove with *head, neck and breast greyish-green*; *upperparts and scapulars yellowish olive-green* and *lower breast and belly bright yellow* bordered at sides by greyish-green; undertail-coverts chestnut with creamy tips. Dull purple patch on shoulder and pale yellow fringes to coverts; flight-feathers blackish. Tail dark greyish-green above, white below with blackish base. Juvenile lacks purple shoulder patch. Pale grey bill and sandy-orange legs. Wings make rattling sound in rapid flight. Can be surprisingly inconspicuous when perched in tree.

Voice: quarrelsome chatter and unmistakable rippling, crooning, whistle.

Status: see map. Proved and probable breeding areas (including Oman) apparently occupied in summer only.

Habitat: well-vegetated wadis, park-like open country and gardens; invariably with tall trees, especially fig; 700–2,400 m. Nests in tree.

Ring-necked Parakeet *Psittacula krameri*   Plate 18

Identification: 42 cm. Sexes differ. *Bright green parakeet*, with long, graduated, pointed tail (bluish-green above), pointed wings and short, heavy, *deeply-hooked red bill*. Male has black throat running into *narrow, rose, ring around neck* (attained in third year). Female and juvenile have green throat and lack neck-ring, but bill dull-coloured. Distinguished from Alexandrine Parakeet by *lack of red shoulder-patch, clearly smaller bill, smaller size and greenish-slate legs* (dirty yellow in Alexandrine). Flight swift, rapid and direct. Gregarious, very active when coming to roost at dusk. Enjoys fruit.

Voice: noisy, loud, shrill, screaming 'kee-ak'.

Status: see map. Mainly resident with some wandering; perhaps even passage in Oman; thought to have originated from escapes.

Habitat: gardens, cultivation and open deciduous areas. Nests, often colonially, in holes in trees, walls and ruined buildings.

Alexandrine Parakeet *Psittacula eupatria*   Plate 18

Identification: 53–58 cm. Sexes differ. *Considerably larger size, much heavier red bill and large red patch on shoulder* (often partly hidden) separate it from Ring-necked Parakeet which it otherwise resembles. Male has black throat running into rose ring around neck (broader than in Ring-necked). Smaller female and immature have green throat and lack neck-ring; both have red shoulder. Bill red (dull in immature), legs dull horny-yellow (greenish-slate in Ring-necked).

Voice: loud, hoarse, screaming note 'kii-e-rick', with stress on first syllable, usually repeated 2–3 times.

Status: see map. Feral resident; escapes also recorded Gulf States, Oman, N Yemen.

Habitat: plantations and gardens with trees. Nests in hole in tree.

Jacobin Cuckoo *Clamator jacobinus*   Plate 19

Identification: 33 cm. Sexes similar. Slender, crested, glossy *black and white cuckoo with long graduated tail*. Entire *upper-parts, including wings and tail, black with white patch at base of primaries*, and often with white tips to outer tail-feathers, conspicuous in flight and visible at rest. Underparts usually white but sometimes tinged greyish or fulvous, and some are even black below (thus all-black, with white in wings). Bill and legs horn-black. Juvenile has black replaced with sooty-brown, and white underparts washed fulvous or grey; crest less developed. The larger Great Spotted Cuckoo (see PMH) has white-spotted wing-coverts and flight-feathers and no white primary-patch, but juvenile Great Spotted has large chestnut primary-patch.

Voice: loud, metallic 'piu-piu-pee-pee-piu, pee-pee-piu'.

Status: see map. Also apparently breeds SE Iran. Summer visitor and/or passage migrant to Yemen and SW Saudi Arabia, thought to breed but not proved. Scarce passage Oman and formerly recorded Iran.

Habitat: well-wooded country, thorn scrub, cultivated areas and gardens usually below 1,000 m. Parasitises nests of passerines particularly bulbuls, shrikes and flycatchers.

Great Spotted Cuckoo *Clamator glandarius*

Identification: 40 cm. See PMH.

Status: see map. Mainly summer visitor; has bred Tunisia, Lebanon and formerly Syria and Iran. Winter visitor Morocco, S. Algeria, and has wintered N Saudi Arabia. Scarce passage Kuwait, W Arabia. Vagrant elsewhere in Arabia, also Libya.

Habitat: light woodland, olive groves, areas of cultivation with bushes and trees. Parasitises nests of crows, particularly Magpie and Hooded Crow.

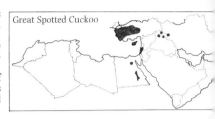
Great Spotted Cuckoo

Didric Cuckoo *Chrysococcyx caprius*   Plate 19

Identification: 18 cm. Sexes differ. Small bronzy-green cuckoo, about size of Wryneck and resembling Klaas' Cuckoo (which see). *Male bright metallic bronzy-green on back and wings, with white spotting on coverts and secondaries* (unspotted in Klaas' Cuckoo); head metallic-green, with white brow broken by eye, and white crown-streak (only small white mark behind eye in Klaas'). Dull green *tail has outer feathers barred white* (outers largely white in Klaas'); white underparts with black malar-streak and *bold, dark bronzy-green bars on flanks, vent and undertail-coverts* (unbarred or very faintly barred in Klaas'). Female duller, earth-brown on head and neck, with less contrasting head-pattern (slighter buffer eye-brow and median crown-streak); mantle and wing-coverts duller bronzy-green, white spotting in wings less extensive; tail-pattern as male but white partly replaced by chestnut; bars on underparts as male, but rufous on throat and breast sometimes with narrow streaks and larger spots; distinguished from female Klaas' in same way as male. Juvenile separated from juvenile Klaas' by *unmarked rufous-buff upperparts* (densely barred buff and dark-green in young Klaas'), *rufous-buff throat and upperbreast with fine dark streaks or, on breast, spots and boldly barred flanks* (Klaas' is *densely barred from chin to lower belly*) and tail-pattern (which resembles females). Appears long-necked and -tailed in flight.

Voice: plaintive loud 'dee-dee-dee-*dee*deric', with emphasis on start of last phrase.

Status: see map. Summer visitor. Passage N Yemen where may breed; also recorded S Yemen. Vagrant Cyprus.

Habitat: mainly dry thorn bush country and open woodland. Parasitises nests of passerines.

Didric Cuckoo

Klaas's Cuckoo *Chrysococcyx klaas*   Plate 19

Identification: 16 cm. Sexes differ. Slightly smaller than Didric Cuckoo, which see for difference between the two species. *Male bright metallic-green above* often with strong violet-bronze on back and inconspicuous white brow behind eye; *tail violet-green but three outermost feathers largely white* (few dark spots, also on central feathers). White underparts with large green patch at sides of breast (almost forming broken collar in some), *flanks unbarred* or only faintly so and *isolated dark green lower flank-spot*; *vent and undertail-coverts virtually unmarked white*. Female dull brown above with violet bronze-green on mantle which grades into bright green, narrowly barred bronze-brown on back and wings (thus lacking white wing spots of Didric); buffy underparts with grey-brown at side of breast and *narrow, well-spaced bars*, mostly across breast or breast-sides (much bolder flank bars in Didric); has dark isolated lower flank-spot (as male), and vent and undertail-coverts either unmarked whitish or with few narrow bars (bold dense bars in Didric), tail pattern resembles male's. Juvenile distinguished from juvenile Didric by upperparts *entirely barred with buff-brown and bright-green* (unmarked rufous-buff in juvenile Didric); *underparts distinctly and densely barred* dark green and white (juvenile Didric has fine dark throat-streaks, spots on breast and boldly spot-barred flanks, unmarked in centre of belly); tail-pattern resembles adults and thus quite different from Didric; appears long-necked and -tailed in flight.

oice: mournful 'whit-jeh', repeated 2–3 times with pauses of 5–10 seconds between phrases.
tatus: see map. Summer visitor. May breed N
Yemen; also recorded S Yemen.
abitat: bushy country and open woodland.
Parasitises nests of passerines.

uckoo *Cuculus canorus*

dentification: 33 cm. See PMH.
tatus: see map. May sometimes breed Syria,
Lebanon and Cyprus. Summer visitor. Widespread passage includes Oman, SW Arabia,
N Africa.
abitat: woodland edges, bushy open country
with or without trees; wetland edges. Parasitises nests of passerines.

'ellow-billed Cuckoo *Coccyzus americanus*

dentification: 30 cm. See PMH.
tatus: vagrant Morocco. Range America.
abitat: copses, thickets and woodlands.

enegal Coucal *Centropus senegalensis*   Plate 19

dentification: 35–42 cm. Sexes alike. Magpie-sized, with long graduated tail, short wings and
heavy black bill with curved culmen. *Head to hind-neck, and tail, black* glossed green, *contrasting
with chestnut wings*; lower mantle and shoulders warm brownish. Underparts creamy-white;
red eye conspicuous at close range. Lacks supercilium and streaks on hind-neck, throat and
breast of White-browed Coucal, and has different distribution. Juvenile has upperparts barred
dark brown and buff, browner head and nape than adult, with some white streaks on hind-
neck; tail-feathers thinly barred buff. Lacks buff supercilium and diffuse blackish streaks on
throat, sides of neck and breast of juvenile White-browed. Secretive, keeping to cover if
possible but will sit freely in open to sun itself. Flight heavy and low, with weak uncertain
wing-beats followed by glide, the bird going from cover to cover.
oice: song a series of 15–20 bubbling notes 'who-who-who', ... or 'bub-bub-bub', ... descending and accelerating in hollow deep sonorous sound.
tatus: see map. Resident.
abitat: thick bushes, scrub, dense tall grass
often near water. Nests low down in thick
cover.

White-browed Coucal *Centropus superciliosus*   Plate 19

Identification: 38–44 cm. Sexes alike. Size and build as in Senegal Coucal (which see). Head to mantle dark earth-brown with narrow whitish streaks from nape downwards; *whitish supercilium, from bill to well behind red eye*, separates dark crown from dark mask through eye; bright rufous-chestnut wings but lower mantle and shoulders warm brownish; lower back to uppertail-coverts finely barred greenish-black and buffish; long, broad graduated, finely white-tipped tail greenish-black. Underparts dirty white, finely vermiculated on flanks and vent; *thinly streaked blackish* on throat, breast and sides of neck. Juvenile has thin, well-spaced pale bars on most tail-feathers, barred dark brown and buff back, *buffish supercilium* and scattered thin whitish streaks on head and mantle and diffuse dark streaks on throat, neck and breast. Clumsy, keeping low in thick cover, and will sit on top of bush to sing or sun itself.

Voice: loud cackle of about 25 'kak' and 'hok' notes, increasing in pitch and speed to a crescendo and then trailing off. Also rapid series of 10–15 loud deep hollow 'hoo' notes, slowing down and becoming lower in pitch near end.

Status: see map. Resident.

Habitat: dense scrub usually in or near wadis, especially those with permanent water. Nests in thick cover.

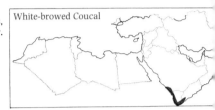

Koel *Eudynamys scolopacea*   Plate 19

Identification: 43 cm. Sexes differ. Large, heavy-bodied, long-tailed cuckoo-type with short wings, and thick bill with strongly curved tip of culmen. *Male all-black with bluish gloss; bright yellow bill. Female basically dark brown with top of head to hind-neck thinly white-streaked, mantle with small crake-like whitish spots; chin and throat heavily white-streaked;* rest of underparts densely barred dark brown and buffish-white; dark brown shoulder and uppertail with numerous thin whitish or buff bars; bill dark grey. Immature resembles female. Characteristic stance when undisturbed of long tail held downwards, hunched lower back, bulky breast and (in calling male) clearly uptilted head and bill. Elusive, unobtrusive with cuckoo-like direct flight.

Voice: male calls (often continuously) a loud hollow 'kooyl', with ascending curl on y-note. Female has shrill 'kik-kik-kik', etc. Both sexes also have various croaks.

Status: vagrant or scarce winter visitor Oman, Iran (from Indian region).

Habitat: open scrub, woods, gardens, cultivated areas, towns and villages; also coastal mangroves.

Barn Owl *Tyto alba*

Identification: 34 cm. See PMH.

Status: see map. Resident. Distribution in Arabia uncertain. May breed Libya, Saharan Algeria. Recorded Kuwait and SW Iran.

Habitat: open country (including semi-deserts) with trees, edges of woods, often near human habitation. Nests in holes in trees, buildings, ruins, etc.

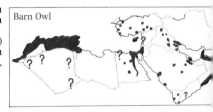

130

In SW Arabia and Iran (and elsewhere in Asia) the situation regarding scops owls (*Otus* sp) has been obscure largely because of great similarities in appearance. However, recent detailed work by T. J. Roberts and Ben King (following the thorough pioneering research of J. T. Marshall in SE Asia) appears to have established specific identification based mainly on voice. We are adopting this approach and it follows that a truer understanding of the identifications may lead to a re-appraisal of distribution and status; the maps, meanwhile, must be regarded as tentative.

ndian Scops Owl *Otus bakkamoena*   Plate 20

?ormerly called Collared Scops Owl, that name now given to *O. lempiji* of SE Asia.)

dentification: 23–25 cm. Sexes alike. Smallish 'eared' owl recalling Scops Owl, Striated Scops and Senegal Scops, but larger and paler; *best separated by voice*. Slight plumage differences are *broad, nearly unmarked pale yellow-buff or isabelline collar on hind-neck* (less obvious if head sunk between shoulders) and rather indistinctly patterned, *almost unstreaked whitish underparts* (longer, bolder pattern of streaks in the other three owls). Upperparts pale grey-brown with diffuse dark streaks broken by bars (unlike long crisp streaks of Striated Scops); otherwise, general pattern rather similar. *Iris yellow to brown* (always clear yellow in the other three scops in region). Crepuscular and nocturnal.

oice: mellow, frog-like, interrogative, rising, single 'wuk' or 'whut' or 'wak', repeated at irregular intervals, but most often 4–6 seconds. Not far-carrying. In breeding season male (?) calls at a higher pitch and is immediately answered by female (?), creating a two-note effect 'di-da-di-da-di-da'. See overleaf for voice of scops owls of region.

tatus: uncertain. May perhaps breed in SE Iran but confirmation required; old record Oman may be erroneous.

abitat: woodlands and plains, hills and lower slopes in mountains; gardens.

triated (Bruce's) Scops Owl *Otus brucei*   Plate 20

dentification: 20–22 cm. Sexes alike. Small, 'eared' owl, resembling Scops and difficult to separate from it in the field, *except by voice*. Usually paler and greyer than Scops, with *black streaks above and below more sharply demarcated*, giving neater, more precise pattern (in Scops, black streaks more broken by dark cross-markings, more submerged by darker ground-colour above, and more vermiculation and barring below). Hardly any rufous tint in plumage as in some Scops. Upperparts sandy-grey, underparts paler greyish; diffuse rufous-buff collar on hind-neck in some (hidden when head sunk between shoulders). Iris yellow. Nocturnal. In the hand wings more rounded than in Scops; longest primary 7th or 8th (Scops, 8th or 9th); length of 10th (outermost) primary falls between 4th–6th (Scops 5th–7th); length of 9th primary roughly equals 7th (Scops roughly equals 8th). Tarsus feathered to base of toes (not quite in Scops).

voice: two basic calls: territorial male call, a hollow resonant 'whoo' or 'whoop', rapidly repeated (about 8 times per 5 seconds); a similar hollow and resonant, but longer 'whooo', repeated irregularly, mostly at 3–5 seconds intervals; also 'ooo-ooo---ooo-ooo', sometimes uttered just once (all 4 notes), or can be repeated in continuous succession with gap of 5–10 seconds between each group; call soft and dove-like, not audible at long range unlike call of Scops. See overleaf for voices of scops owls in region.

tatus: see map. Partial migrant, said to be present all year Iran; summer visitor Iraq, Oman; vagrant Bahrain, Israel, Egypt.

abitat: arid foothills with preference for steep cliffs and gorges with small trees; also semi-deserts with cover; gardens in towns and palm groves. Nests in hole in tree.

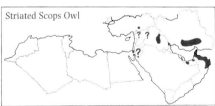

Striated Scops Owl

Scops Owl *Otus scops*

Identification: 19 cm. See PMH.

Status: see map. Resident Cyprus. Otherwise mainly summer visitor and passage migrant also occurring N Africa (where some winter) and much of Arabia but vagrant Yemen.

Habitat: trees near human habitation, plantations, oases, gardens, etc. Nests in hole in tree or building, occasionally in old nest of other bird.

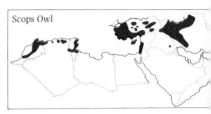

Senegal Scops Owl *Otus senegalensis*

(As *O. s. pamalae*, the breeding form in S. Arabia, is now regarded as a race of *O. senegalensis* (and not of *O. sunia* of India) we are not including Oriental/Asian Scops Owl as alternative English names).

Identification: 21 cm. Sexes alike. Resembles Scops Owl, but more uniform with rather obscure markings; lacks bright white scapular streaks of Scops, being generally more uniform pale greyish or dirty ochre. Slightly smaller than Striated Scops (which see) but without that species' feathering to base of toes. *Voice very important for identification.* In the hand, longest primary is 8th (Scops, 8th or 9th); length of 10th primary (outermost) shorter than 4th (Scops 10th between 5th and 7th) and length of 9th primary falls between 5th and 6th (Scops 9th roughly equals 8th).

Voice: single, less musical, rasping, 'awww' or 'wokk', lower-pitched than the pure whistled note of Scops Owl. See below for voices of scops owls in region.

Status: see map. Resident.

Habitat: hilly regions with trees. Nests in hole in tree.

SUMMARY OF MAIN CALLS OF SCOPS OWLS OF REGION

Scops Owl *O. scops*: single, clear, resonant and musical whistle 'tyuu', at intervals of about 2–3 seconds. Female's call similar but higher pitched. May duet.

Senegal Scops Owl *O. senegalensis*: single, less musical, rasping 'awww' or 'wokk', at intervals of about a second. Lower pitched than pure whistle of Scops;

Striated Scops Owl *O. brucei*: hollow, resonant 'who' or 'whoop', rapidly repeated (about 8 notes per 5 seconds). Similar, but longer 'whooo', at 3–5 second intervals. Also Stock Dove-like soft 'ooo-ooo---ooo-ooo' sometimes repeated at 5–10 second intervals.

Indian Scops Owl *O. bakkamoena*: single, mellow, frog-like, interrogative, rising 'whut' at 4–6 second intervals.

Eagle Owl *Bubo bubo*   Plate 20

Identification: 50–70 cm. Sexes alike. Eagle Owls similar to European birds (see PMH) occur in Turkey and Iran south to Near East; further south, in Arabia and throughout N Africa, the smaller, more desert-loving race *ascalaphus* occurs. Smallest examples only about 60% size of European; they are also paler and rustier, while extremes (sometimes called *desertorum*) can be very pale, almost whitish below, heavily suffused pinkish-yellow above and washed creamy-buff on sides of body; greyer and darker forms occur. The underparts-pattern variable,

132

and distinct streaks confined to upper breast, with most of lower underparts quite barred, often without clear dark shaft-streaks (recalling Spotted Eagle Owl, which see); whitish facial disk more distinctly bordered blackish at sides. 'Ear-tufts' when relaxed may droop, recalling those of Brown Fish Owl (which see).

tatus: see map. Resident, sometimes wandering in winter.
abitat: wild desert mountains and steppe regions, frequenting cliffs, crags and rocky outcrops. Nests on ledge or in crevice in rocks and down wells.

Eagle Owl

potted Eagle Owl *Bubo africanus*   Plate 20

lentification: 43–47 cm. Sexes alike. Medium-large owl with long 'ear-tufts'; sometimes confusable with small desert race of Eagle Owl. Arabian race has *dense dark brown bars on underwing-coverts and entire underparts*, below irregularly dark-blotched upperbreast; nape and hind-neck *with small white spots. Upperparts finely barred* dark brown and buffish with bold *pale and dark tail bands* of fairly even width. (Some desert forms of Eagle Owls have similarly barred underparts below boldly streaked upperbreast, though centre of belly often unbarred; others have dark shaft-streaks in the barring (absent in Spotted); top of head to hind-neck distinctly streaked continuing over upperparts, and dark bars in tail much thinner than in Spotted. Yellowish or orange iris, rarely brown (never brownish in Eagle Owl). Nocturnal.
oice: two-note song 'hu-hoo' by male synchronised in duet with female, whose call is lower in pitch (thus, their duetting often sounds like 4-syllabic call coming from one bird); dove-like, sleepy 'hoo doo doh dooh', second note higher in pitch than first, last two lowest; five-note call also heard, a descending, sleepy, hollow 'huw,huw,how,how,how'.
tatus: see map. Resident.
labitat: open woodland, rocky hills, ravines; sometimes in or near habitation. Nests on the ground under rock, cliff ledge or occasionally in tree.

Spotted Eagle Owl

rown Fish Owl *Ketupa zeylonensis*   Plate 20

lentification: 53–56 cm. Sexes alike. Large rufous-brown 'eared' owl, superficially resembling Eagle Owl, *but with flatter head (eyes level with top of bill), and ill-defined brownish facial disk* (lacking black or pale markings); *ear-tufts shaggier and often more drooping* (but may appear so in Eagle Owl, too, which see); *yellow-grey legs can look longish due to unfeathered tarsus.* Upperparts brownish mottled blackish; buff and brown patches on scapulars recall Tawny's pattern. *Underparts rufous with dark streaks* (Eagle Owl has broader streaks on breast often forming breast-band). Juvenile more rufous above with narrower dark streaks, and paler and duller below with narrow dark streaks. Iris more yellow, less orange than Eagle Owl's, but can look orange-red in spotlight at night.
oice: sequence of deep muttered hoots, rising at end in laugh and with distinct pause after first note, 'ku, ku-ku ku-ku ku-ku', etc, lasting about 4 seconds; soft muffled 'hup-hup-hu' audible only when close; also harsh scream 'we-aaah' rising and falling in tone.
tatus: see map. Resident. Some old records SW Iran; also from Adana (S Turkey) but latter from bird markets and thus origin unknown. Vagrant Lebanon.
labitat: lowland tree-lined streams or lakes. Nests in hole in cliff, dead tree or old raptor nest.

Brown Fish Owl

Snowy Owl *Nyctea scandiaca*

Identification: 53–66 cm. See PMH.
Status: rare winter visitor Turkoman steppes (NE Iran).
Habitat: rolling plains and open steppe.

Little Owl *Athene noctua* Plate 20

Identification: 22 cm. See PMH. The race in Sinai and neighbouring areas *lilith* is palest in region. Usually pale sandy with more noticeable white nape-spots, more whitish on back and wings than European birds; underparts much less streaked, soft sandy to warm brown; tail generally more regularly barred with buff; some individuals can be fairly dark.
Status: see map. Resident, southern limit uncertain in Libya.
Habitat: fairly open country with trees, stony wasteland, wadis, rocky semi-deserts, cultivated areas. Nests in hole in tree and in rocks, buildings and burrows.

Spotted Little Owl *Athene brama* Plate 20

Identification: 21 cm. Sexes alike. Recalls Little Owl but *underparts roughly and distinctly barred,* sometimes showing two dark pectoral patches (underparts streaked longitudinally in Little Owl). Upperparts colder, greyer, generally darker than Little with smaller, whiter and denser spots on back and shoulders; top of head and nape with small, white 'rice'-like dense speckles (larger buffish markings in Little). Darker uppertail has thinner and whiter cross-bars than Little. Juvenile more ginger than adult with diffuse barring below and prominent pectoral patches. Flight undulating like Little. Crepuscular but frequently seen during day.
Voice: double 'zi-gwet', also harsh screeching 'chirurr-chirurr-chirurr'.
Status: see map. Presumed resident. Apparently no overlap with Little Owl.
Habitat: gardens, villages, cultivated areas, semi-deserts and earth cliffs. Nests in hole in tree, wall, etc.

Tawny Owl *Strix aluco*

Identification: 38 cm. See PMH.
Status: see map. Resident.
Habitat: mature woods, parks, large gardens even in towns. Nests in hollow trees, old nests of large birds, also in buildings and sometimes on crags.

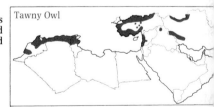

Hume's Tawny Owl *Strix butleri*   Plate 20

Identification: 35 cm. Sexes alike. Pale, *smaller than Tawny but with similar flight and proportions* (big round head, thick neck) though more 'leggy'.Upperparts brownish- or sandy-buff, head and neck more golden, but mottled back tinged greyish. Dark centre to forehead and ill-defined whitish-buff facial disk. Underparts, typically, whitish-buff with indistinct golden wavy scales. Separated from larger and darker Tawny Owl by *yellowish-orange iris in black surround* (iris dark in Tawny), *much paler underparts* without dark streaks, paler facial disk, and by *bolder barred uppertail with broad dark and buffish bands* and conspicuous pale terminal band (particularly obvious when seen in light of lamp). Also, distribution and habitat differences. Juvenile tends to be distinctly lighter in colour than adult. At dusk, when size-judgement difficult, can be confused with other pale owls with yellow-orange iris, such as pale sandy Little Owl (flatter, more angular head, fast undulating flight) and small male of pale desert race of Eagle Owl (ear-tufts not always visible; appears taller with broader chest than head, often dark border to facial disk and has richer orange iris; appears much bigger in flight). Barn Owl with white underparts has black eyes, characteristic heart-shaped face often dark-bordered facial disk, and long wings exceeding tip of tail, also flight- and especially tail-feathers are much less barred. Highly nocturnal.

Voice: territorial song typically consists of 5 rather even-pitched syllables with stress on first note which is drawn out and isolated 'whoo, woo-woo, who-who' or 'hoo, ho-hoo hoo, hoo'; not tremulous like Tawny's and has soft quality of Collared Dove. A single 'hooo' sometimes heard, again not tremulous like Tawny Owl's similar note; also a continuous 'hoo-hoo-hoo', sometimes broken by short throaty cough.

Status: see map. Isolated mapped spots in Egypt, N Yemen and Oman refer to records of single birds without proof of breeding. Range probably more extensive than shown and may include S Iran. Resident.

Habitat: rocky deserts with gorges, rocky wadis, desert earth banks; often near palm groves, acacias and sometimes near springs and settlements. Nests in hole or crevice in rocks or cliff-face.

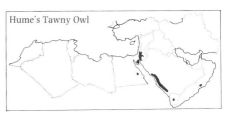

Long-eared Owl *Asio otus*

Identification: 36 cm. See PMH.

Status: see map. May breed Cyprus, occasionally Israel. Partial migrant. In winter reaches Iraq, Israel, Egypt, NW Africa. Vagrant Arabian Gulf, Oman, SW Saudi Arabia, Libya.

Habitat: Woods and stands of conifers; also deciduous woods and copses. Nests in old nest of raptor or crow, usually in a tree.

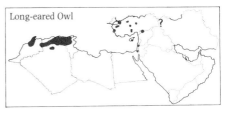

Short-eared Owl *Asio flammeus*

Identification: 38 cm. See PMH.

Status: has bred Turkey, Israel. Mainly winter visitor in NW and N Africa, most of the Asiatic countries south to central Saudi Arabia and Oman; vagrant further south.

Habitat: open, often marshy, country on coasts and inland. Nests on ground in vegetation near marsh.

Marsh Owl *Asio capensis*   Plate 20

Identification: 36–37 cm. Sexes alike. Resembles dark Short-eared Owl but has practically *unspotted, uniform dark brown back and wing-coverts* (greater coverts tipped whitish in Short-eared, back and wings paler brown with buff and whitish streaks and spots) and *unstreaked dark brown breast band*, which contrasts with buffish-white, indistinctly barred rest of underparts (in Short-eared, upperbreast boldly streaked contrasting with thinly streaked rest of underparts;

pale facial disk with *dark eyes each set in narrow black area* (in Short-eared, iris yellow and more dark-faced). Short ear-tufts seldom raised. Juvenile resembles adult. Crepuscular, but seen in daytime. Gregarious outside breeding season.

Voice: harsh, croaking 'quark', uttered singly or in rapid succession; also a snoring 'kor'.

Status: see map. Resident, with some dispersal.

Habitat: marshes and swamps. Nests in tussock.

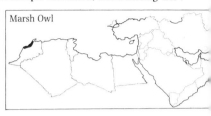

Marsh Owl

Tengmalm's Owl *Aegolius funereus*

Identification: 25 cm. See PMH.

Status: recently recorded from N and NW Turkey where heard calling.

Habitat: coniferous (occasionally mixed) forest in mountains. Nests in hole in tree.

Plain Nightjar *Caprimulgus inornatus*   Plate 30

Identification: 22 cm. Sexes differ. *Rather uniform, fairly short-tailed nightjar with variable ground-colour from rufous-brown through greyish to pinkish-grey,* finely vermiculated with sepia and showing *no obvious dark or whitish markings on head, shoulders or mantle; crown shows just a few fine black flecks.* Underparts slightly paler, finely barred. Flight-feathers above and below barred rufous-buff and black (resemblance to barring on a brown-phase Cuckoo); *shows no contrast between flight-feathers and wing-coverts, above or below.* Male has white spots near tips of outer primaries and white on distal half of two outer tail-feathers; female has white in wing replaced by tawny and lacks white in tail. Juvenile lacks white markings on wing and tail. Distinguished from Nightjar by uniform colour, smaller size, slim appearance, shorter tail, no grey central crown-stripe, less pronounced black streaking on crown and lack of obvious dark face or shoulder-patches. Male also has longer white tips to outer tail-feathers (half length in Plain, a third in Nightjar). Told from Egyptian Nightjar by smaller size, considerably darker ground-colour above, without Egyptian's strong contrast between coverts and flight-feathers; male differs further in having white in wing and tail which Egyptian lacks. Differs from Nubian Nightjar by having only faint black flecks in crown (more noticeable crown-flecking in Nubian, on fairly clear-cut greyish crown), absence of whitish spotting on wing-coverts, lack of contrast between underwing-coverts and flight-feathers and absence of chestnut patch at base of primaries.

Voice: sewing-machine-like 'tchurr-rr', similar to Nightjar.

Status: see map. Status uncertain; may be summer visitor from Africa in small numbers.

Habitat: poorly understood in Arabia but usually broken hilly country with scattered vegetation, to at least 1,400 m. Nests on ground.

Plain Nightjar

Nubian Nightjar *Caprimulgus nubicus*   Plate 30

Identification: 21 cm. Sexes differ slightly. Slightly smaller than Nightjar with shorter tail. More *rounded wings* and often *prominent chestnut primary-bases* with *conspicuous white patches on outerwing* and *outertail-feathers* (reduced in size in female), jointly separate it from region's other nightjars. Plumage greyish-brown to sandy grey with light streaking on crown, buff half-collar on hind-neck, irregular buff spots on scapulars and black-bordered wing-coverts; at close range may show narrow white bar on lower cheek, also white on either side of throat. Underparts pale sandy, finely barred. When disturbed in daylight flies short distance before re-settling. Becomes active after dark, thus less readily observed in dusk period than Nightjar. Fast wing-beats with accent on up-stroke, and wings seem momentarily held uplifted at top of stroke. If seen perched, short tail, protruding just beyond wing-tips, can be useful (longer tail in Nightjar); also, shows contrast between pale underwing-coverts and dark flight-feathers (virtually no contrast in Nightjar), especially noticeable if seen in artificial light (eg. headlights). For differences from Plain Nightjar, see that species.

Voice: double 'kwua-kwua', fairly liquid and steadily repeated at intervals of a few seconds, can recall distant barking poodle; sometimes becomes an excited triple note.

Status: see map. Perhaps mainly resident, but summer visitor Israel. Recorded autumn S Oman.

Habitat: deserts and semi-deserts frequently with shelter of dense low vegetation and tamarisk or palm clumps. Nests on ground.

Nubian Nightjar

Sykes' Nightjar *Caprimulgus mahrattensis* Plate 30

Identification: 22 cm. Sexes differ. Closest to Egyptian Nightjar but white or buff-white wing-patches – and white on ends of outertail-feathers of male – separate it (Egyptian lacks wing or tail markings except on undertail in male). Plumage also slightly darker with *fine blackish spotting on crown* and back (more uniform in paler Egyptian) *and slightly less contrast between flight-feathers and paler coverts in flight*; also small white spot on chin at base of bill and larger white spot on side of throat (much larger but less conspicuous in Egyptian). Female similar to male but lacks white in tail, and wing-flashes smaller and buffer. Plainer and sandier than Nightjar, with fine streaking on underparts (Nightjar is darker with grey crown, quite heavily streaked dark, and has dark throat and covert-band on closed wing). From Indian Nightjar (which see) by paler, plainer plumage.

Voice: long purr, after sunset and pre-dawn; also said to resemble frog. Soft 'cluck cluck' when flushed by day.

Status: see map. Resident; some dispersal in winter.

Habitat: deserts and semi-deserts, rocky wastes and abandoned cultivated areas particularly with tamarisks. Nests on ground.

Sykes' Nightjar

Indian Nightjar *Caprimulgus asiaticus* Plate 30

Identification: 24 cm. Sexes alike. Rather dark but brightly patterned nightjar, with relatively short tail and wings. Buffish grey above with black streaks on crown, *rufous-buff band on hind-neck* and black, rufous-buff markings on scapulars and coverts. Series of white flecks form line below ear-coverts and there is a conspicuous white streak encircled by brownish on the side of the throat. In flight shows white (sometimes pale buff) patch in wing and white ends to outer tail feathers. As with most nightjars, often settles on dusty roads. Easily confused with Nightjar but distinguished by rufous-buff collar, browner underparts (especially compared with *unwini*, the eastern race of Nightjar), almost unstreaked mantle, more uniform almost unmarked lower back and rump (rough irregular blackish shaft-spots in Nightjar) and less pronounced, more creamy spots on wing-coverts; also more reddish-buff underparts and underwing-coverts and rather greyish uppertail. In the hand the white patch on primaries includes the fourth outermost primary (7th), but does not in Nightjar.

Voice: song a far-carrying 'chak-chak-chak – charr-r-r-r' the notes slow at first, becoming faster and reminiscent of stone bouncing across ice on pond.

Status: status uncertain. May breed NE Iran. Vagrant SE Iran.

Habitat: plains, cultivated areas and gardens. Nests on ground.

137

Nightjar *Caprimulgus europaeus* Plate 30

Identification: 26 cm. See PMH. Race occurring in Iran *unwini* (illustrated) is distinctly paler grey than European birds (and those breeding elsewhere in region). Pale patches at sides of throat whiter and more obvious, and male shows larger white spots on outer primaries in flight. However, not easily separated from European birds.

Status: see map. Summer visitor to breeding areas. Broad front passage across most of the region, but infrequently noticed SW Arabia; regular Oman where some winter.

Habitat: open dry areas, edges of woods and heaths; also brush and stony steppe country with sparse vegetation; can occur in any open area on migration. Nests on ground.

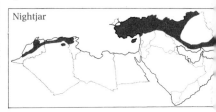

Red-necked Nightjar *Caprimulgus ruficollis*

Identification: 30 cm. See PMH.

Status: see map. Summer visitor. Vagrant Libya. Unknown further east.

Habitat: pine woods, bushy, semi-desert regions, pine and olive-clad hillsides. Nests on ground.

Egyptian Nightjar *Caprimulgus aegyptius* Plate 30

Identification: 25 cm. Sexes differ slightly. Slightly smaller than Nightjar. *Palest nightjar of region* and rather uniform on the ground. Upperparts *yellowish-sandy* to *sandy-grey, with minute blackish streaks on crown* and mantle (distinct in Nightjar); less bold blackish scapular band than Nightjar and *lacks its bold blackish forewing band*; large creamy spots on covert-tips inconspicuous due to pale ground-colour. Underparts sandy-buff to sandy-grey with faint barring; white patch on either side of throat less conspicuous than Nightjar's, again due to paler ground colour; *dark tail-bars distinctly narrower* than Nightjar's except on central pair. In flight *lacks white patches in wing or tail* but male has pale creamy-yellow spots on outer two tail-feathers visible from below; primaries have whitish and blackish saw-like bars on inner webs, which make *flight-feathers look pale below in flight* (underwing, including flight-feathers darkish in Nightjar); also, *above, pale coverts contrast with dark primaries*, a contrast shown to lesser extent by Sykes' which however shows white or whitish-buff wing-patches.

Voice: song a regular and rapidly repeated series 'kowrr' or 'purr', usually slowing towards end. Also a single, knocking 'tok, tok, tok'. Alarm-note a double 'klak-klak.'

Status: see map. Has bred Jordan. Mainly summer visitor; also passage N Iran, Arabia; winter records from Algeria, Egypt, Oman, Saudi Arabia, Yemen. Vagrant Libya, Israel, Syria.

Habitat: desert regions and other dry areas, often with palms and scrub. Nests on ground.

138

Plain Swift *Apus unicolor* Plate 25

Identification: 16 cm. Sexes alike. Easily confused with Swift and Pallid Swift, and ideally one
of these species needs to be present for comparison so that subtle differences can be observed.
Very slightly smaller and slimmer-winged than Swift. Dark matt brown in strong sunlight,
though slightly paler upperwing, paler still towards hind edge. In evening or dull weather
appears matt sooty all over, save for *semi-translucent flight-feathers below – a feature apparent
in all light conditions.* In sustained close views the *paler brown throat* can be seen, but beware
that in strong light the throat appears quite pale, suggesting Swift or Pallid Swift. (In all
lights Pallid shows white chin, pale forehead and paler brown-buff flight-feathers and greater-
coverts above, which contrast with dark brown body and forewing.) Flight rapid with fast
wing-beats, faster than Swift, though most apparent when direct comparison possible.
Voice: high-pitched scream (shorter and more wheezing than Swift's), 'zeeeeoo' or longer
'zeeeeee -zeeoo......zeeeeee-zeeoo', especially in screaming parties.
Status: vagrant (or perhaps winter visitor) Morocco. Breeds Canary Is.
Habitat: aerial.

Swift *Apus apus*

Identification: 16 cm. See PMH.
Status: see map. Summer visitor. Passage
throughout the region. Some winter records
in S Arabia.
Habitat: aerial; may occur anywhere but
especially in areas, including towns, with
suitable nesting sites or food abundance.
Nests in buildings, under eaves, occasionally
in cliffs.

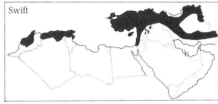

Pallid Swift *Apus pallidus*

Identification: 16 cm. See PMH.
Status: see map. Mainly summer visitor (can
arrive at southern sea-level breeding localities in January), but locally resident.
Habitat: as Swift, but greater preference for
cliffs in some areas. Nest as Swift.

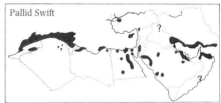

Alpine Swift *Apus melba*

Identification: 21 cm (wing-span 53 cm). See PMH.
Status: see map. Mainly summer visitor and
passage migrant, but considered resident in
W Arabia; winter records Egypt, Cyprus,
Iran, Yemen. Irregular passage Oman, E
Arabia.
Habitat: rocky mountain regions, also along
sea cliffs and in old towns. Nests (usually
colonially) in cleft rocks, natural crevices
and beneath rafters.

White-rumped Swift *Apus caffer* Plate 25

Identification: 14 cm. Sexes alike. Slightly larger and more slender than Little Swift (which see) which it resembles in having a white rump. Differs in *longer, forked tail* which often appears *rather long and pointed* (square-ended in Little) and *narrower white rump* (broader in Little, and extending onto sides of rump). Further differs from Little in narrower wings and darker, bluer plumage, though it often shows a greenish sheen to wings which can appear paler than body; throat white and often more sharply demarcated than in Little. White-rumped and Little Swift instantly distinguished from House Martin and Red-rumped Swallow (both of which show pale rumps) by all-dark underparts, and flight-action.
Voice: generally rather silent; screaming call, given in flight and at nest, has chattering quality.
Status: see map. Winter status in Morocco uncertain. Vagrant N Yemen.
Habitat: mountainous regions and gorges, also towns and villages. Nests under eaves, rock crevices and in old nests, for example of Red-rumped Swallow.

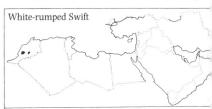

Little Swift *Apus affinis* Plate 25

Identification: 12 cm. Sexes alike. Gregarious, appearing *smaller, blunter and less rakish* than Swift, with *almost square-cut tail* but looking slightly rounded when spread. (White-rumped Swift (which see) has forked tail). Upper- and underparts dark blackish-brown with prominent *white rump extending onto sides* (not in White-rumped), whitish chin, throat and often pale forehead; rather translucent flight- and tail-feathers when seen against the light. Flight with rapid fluttering wing-beats and short glides, less dashing than Swift.
Voice: shrill, long, high-pitched fast trilling call 'kikikikikiki...', etc. and high-pitched 'tick'.
Status: see map. Partial migrant; few remain in north part of range in winter. Passage includes S Yemen, Libya, rare Egypt. Vagrant Iraq, E and central Arabia.
Habitat: varied from rocky ravines and cliffs to large towns; often near water. Nests are clustered below eaves, rocky overhang or ceiling of open building.

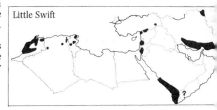

Palm Swift *Cypsiurus parvus* Plate 25

Identification: 13 cm. Sexes alike. Rather featureless swift in plumage. Slightly larger than Little but very different in appearance, being *much slimmer, much more elongated with long-forked tail* (*nearly always held closed and appearing pointed*) so that about two-thirds of total length is aft of long, *very thin wings*. Upperparts greyish-brown, slightly paler below, grading into slightly paler throat, but, unless seen close, overall impression against the sky is of a dark bird. Fast and direct flight with *rapid fluttery wing-beats;* often covers same area to-and-fro for several minutes; when gliding, wings are held in downward shallow V. Gregarious.
Voice: rapid, thin, chittering call 'ti-ti-ti-ti-ti-ti' not unlike Little Swift, most often heard from birds circling palms.
Status: see map. Resident. Vagrant Egypt.
Habitat: over open country, villages and towns, usually near palms in which it nests.

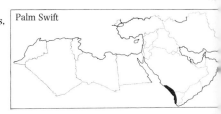

White-breasted Kingfisher *Halcyon smyrnensis*   Plate 21

Identification: 26 cm. Sexes alike. A large (Hoopoe-sized), noisy, brown and bright turquoise blue kingfisher with large white bib and very powerful red bill. *Head and underparts deep chestnut-brown with white chin, throat and centre of breast.* Upperparts, tail and wings turquoise (varying in tone with light), the latter showing chestnut and black coverts and *whitish panel at base of dark-tipped primaries in flight.* Juvenile similar to adult but duller and with crescent-shaped marks on breast.

Voice: noisy, call being a loud yelping whistle (like a referee's whistle continuously blown in bursts) 'kil,kil,kil,kil,kil'. Also tittering, descending song.

Status: see map. Recently recorded near Cairo where possibly breeds. Mainly resident, with some southward movement reaching Kuwait in winter. Vagrant or rare passage central and E Saudi Arabia; vagrant Lebanon, Cyprus.

Habitat: lakes and rivers with bordering trees and bushes; also palm and orange groves, gardens, sometimes well away from water; often near human habitation. Nests in hole in bank.

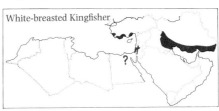

Grey-headed Kingfisher *Halcyon leucocephala*   Plate 21

Identification: 20 cm. Sexes alike. Slightly smaller than White-breasted Kingfisher. Unmistakable, *buffish-grey head and nape, deep blue-black back and coverts,* with conspicuous *ultramarine wings and tail.* Throat and upper breast buffish-white; remaining underparts chestnut. Large, deep red bill. In flight shows whitish panels on primary bases both above and below. Juvenile in autumn similar to adult but head slightly darker, underparts greyish-white with broad pectoral band of fine dark scalloping, orange-buff wash on ventral region and black tip to bill. Frequently sits on prominent perch on tree or telegraph pole. Does not eat fish; not dependent on water. Rather sluggish, with unhurried undulating flight.

Voice: weak chattering 'ji, ji, ji-jeee'.

Status: see map. Summer visitor.

Habitat: wet or dry wadis with trees, particularly palms and other sub-tropical vegetation; breeds mainly 250–1,500 m, occurring at lower altitudes on migration. Nests in hole in bank or cliff.

White-collared Kingfisher *Halcyon chloris*   Plate 21

Identification: 24 cm. Sexes alike. Slightly smaller than White-breasted Kingfisher and instantly recognised by *white underparts and greenish-turquoise upperparts with black-bordered white collar;* wings and tail blue; bill blackish. Juvenile similar to adult but has dusky barring on breast. Flight rather weak. Noisy, especially at dawn.

Voice: hoarse 'eatsch-eatsch-eatsch' in a long, fast series, each note ascending towards end.

Status: see map. Resident, probably dispersive.

Habitat: mangroves. Nests in hole in bank.

Kingfisher *Alcedo atthis*

Identification: 16 cm. See PMH.
Status: see map. Partial migrant. Some in breeding areas throughout year; others in winter reach all Mediterranean coasts, Nile valley, N and central Red Sea, Oman and Arabian Gulf; vagrant N Yemen.
Habitat: streams, rivers, canals and lakes; in winter also coastal areas. Nests in hole bored in bank.

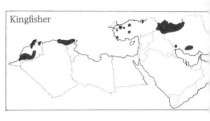

Malachite Kingfisher *Alcedo cristata*   Plate 21

Identification: 12 cm. Sexes alike. Smaller than Kingfisher, to which it has a general resemblance. *Upperparts are richer blue and chestnut of underparts runs unbroken up to eye.* (Kingfisher has long blue moustachial-stripe from bill to shoulder – lacking in Malachite – which separates chestnut cheeks and white neck-flashes from underparts.) When raised, *pale blue and black barred shaggy crest* characteristic. White throat and flash on side of neck; bill red. Juvenile has black mantle tipped greenish-blue, breast and sides of face dusky and bill black.
Voice: sharp but not very loud 'teep teep', usually uttered in flight.
Status: old record from S Yemen and recent claim for N Yemen. Range Africa.
Habitat: permanent water with fringe vegetation.

Pied Kingfisher *Ceryle rudis*   Plate 21

Identification: 28 cm. Sexes differ slightly. Conspicuous, *large, black and white kingfisher,* frequently seen in flight. Upperparts, wings and tail white, barred and streaked black; underparts white with *double breast-band in male* and *single* (often incomplete) *band in female.* Crown black with feathers elongated to form *short crest. Bill long and black.* Juvenile has greyish breast-band. Fishes from perch, or more often hovers several metres above water, before plunging headlong; frequently occurs in small loose congregations.
Voice: loud, querulous chattering 'chirrik, chirrik, chirrik', etc.
Status: see map. Mainly resident. Some dispersal in winter, along Nile, also Iran, Iraq; reaches Kuwait, but otherwise rare in south and east Arabian Gulf. Vagrant N and central Saudi Arabia.
Habitat: rivers, lakes, estuaries, salt pans and coasts. Nests in hole in bank.

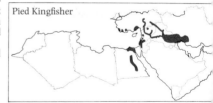

White-throated Bee-eater *Merops albicollis*   Plate 21

Identification: 30 cm. Sexes alike. Between Little Green and Bee-eater in body size with characteristic head pattern, *white with black crown and long black mask through eye. Upperparts blue-green with ochre on nape* and sides of neck, and *bronze wash on back.* Tail blue with very long central feathers. Underparts white with *black half-collar around throat* below which is greenish wash. In flight shows rich ochre upperwing, coppery underwing, both with black trailing edge.
Voice: softer, more gentle call than Bee-eater 'proo-proo-proo-proo'.
Status: see map. Summer visitor.
Habitat: gentle hills, plains and wadis with bushes and trees; often in agriculture; from sea level to 1,500 m though tends to be commoner at upper levels. Nests in hole in bank.

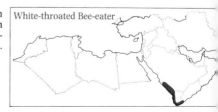

142

Little Green Bee-eater *Merops orientalis*   Plate 21

Identification: 25 cm. *Smallest bee-eater* of region; spends less time in the air than other bee-eaters, preferring to use a favourite perch from which to make fairly short, often low, foraging sallies. Predominantly green above and below with pale copper wash to entire underwing, elongated central tail feathers (in adult) and black stripe through eye. Usually in pairs; not colonial. Blue on face and neck varies according to race. Egyptian race *cleopatra* has black bar across upper breast, diffuse blue confined to just below black eye-stripe and very long central tail feathers; it is also paler, brighter green above and below, with more golden-orange wash on head and neck, and sometimes wings and mantle. In the W and S Arabian race (including Israel) *cyanophrys*, supercilium, throat and upper breast dark blue, dark breast-band rather diffuse and central tail-feathers relatively short. In the S Iranian race *beludschicus*, blue confined to chin and below eye stripe; black breast-band very narrow and central tail feathers long. All races *lack chestnut throat of larger Blue-cheeked Bee-eater* which is otherwise rather similar. Juvenile duller and more shabby than adult and lacks long central tail-feathers.

Voice: most frequent call a high-pitched 'tree-tree-tree', 'prrrit' or 'pyrriit-pyrrt'.

Status: see map. Mainly resident, but some seasonal movement. Vagrant elsewhere in Arabian Gulf.

Habitat: mainly lowland or open country with trees, cultivation. Nests in tunnel in bank.

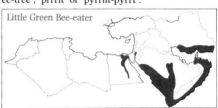

Little Green Bee-eater

Blue-cheeked Bee-eater *Merops superciliosus*   Plate 21

Identification: 30 cm. Sexes alike. Size as Bee-eater but with *longer central tail feathers*; plumage resembles that of Little Green Bee-eater. *Upperparts green* (in fresh plumage) quickly fading to dull turquoise blue, with, depending on race, golden hue in certain lights; black line through eye bordered above and below by pale blue, though this is often difficult to see unless close views obtained; forehead whitish-blue. *Yellow chin merges into chestnut throat* and extent of yellow varies between races and ages – in eastern birds can be quite conspicuous (depending on race, chin and throat are green or blue in Little Green which also has black throat-band). *Underparts green 'bleaching' to turquoise.* In flight, *copper underwing-coverts and flight-feathers, latter with dark terminal-edge.* Western birds paler, more golden above. Juvenile lacks long central tail-feathers, is duller and bluer than adults, with less obvious head markings. Green or turquoise plumage readily distinguishes it from Bee-eater, adult of which has blue underparts, yellow throat, chestnut crown and upperparts, yellow lower back, green tail and wings; however, in non-breeding plumage Bee-eaters have mainly green upperparts – then check throat colour: yellow chin and throat in Bee-eater; yellow chin merging into chestnut throat in Blue-cheeked.

Voice: 'pr-rip, pr-rip' flight-note, similar to Bee-eater but hoarser, less far-carrying and clearly di-syllabic; other calls identical to Bee-eater's.

Status: see map. Mainly summer visitor; also autumn visitor (in northward movement) to NW Africa. Passage Near East and Arabia; probably regular E Libya.

Habitat: dry sandy areas with scattered trees, often close to water. Nests colonially in holes in sandy bank.

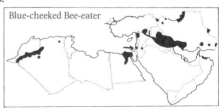

Blue-cheeked Bee-eater

Bee-eater *Merops apiaster*

Identification: 28 cm. See PMH.

Status: see map. Summer visitor. Broad front passage includes Egypt and all areas Arabia.

Habitat: open bushy country with scattered trees and telegraph poles, river banks also woodland glades. Nests colonially in holes in sand pits, river and roadside banks, etc.

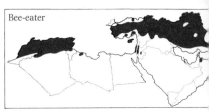

Roller, adult   Indian Roller, adult

Drawings by S. Christensen

Roller *Coracias garrulus*

Identification: 30 cm. See PMH.

Status: see map. Summer visitor. Passage includes Libya (common spring, scarce autumn), Egypt (scarce), Arabia.

Habitat: open woods or country with large trees; rarely up to 2,000 m. Overhead wires, etc, on migration. Nests in hole in tree, sometimes in rocks or building.

Abyssinian Roller *Coracias abyssinicus*   Plate 22

Identification: 45 cm (including very long tail streamers). Sexes alike. Very similar in structure to Roller but has slightly shorter, more rounded wings and, in adults, *very long outer tail feathers*. Colouration of adult generally resembles Roller having turquoise-blue head and underparts, brilliant ultramarine shoulder-patch and warm chestnut back, but Abyssinian is rather paler with *more extensive creamy-white on forehead and purple-blue (not black) flight feathers.* Juvenile and immature very difficult to identify from Roller, but shorter, more rounded wings and purple-blue primaries are of assistance.

Voice: usual call noisy, harsh grating 'krrrr krar krar'.

Status: see map. Formerly reported S Yemen. Mainly resident. Vagrant Libya, Egypt.

Habitat: savannas, semi-deserts and dry cultivated plains with scattered trees and other perching posts. Nests in hole in tree or building.

ndian Roller *Coracias benghalensis* Plate 22

lentification: 30 cm. Sexes alike. Similar size to Roller but duller when perched and with *characteristic wing and tail pattern.* Adult separated from Roller by *vinous-cinnamon neck, throat and breast* (streaked whitish), isolating *dark turquoise-green cap;* underparts, below vinous breast, turquoise blue-green (in Roller, head and underparts turquoise-blue). Mantle earth-brown (bright chestnut-brown in Roller), back dark bluish, and wing-coverts turquoise-green. Juvenile best distinguished in flight. Adult and juvenile have *large conspicuous, translucent, turquoise-blue patch on both surfaces of outer wing,* but tips of primaries dark (primaries all-blackish in Roller). Dark blue square-ended tail (slightly notched in adult Roller) has *broad pale turquoise-blue side panels, with clear-cut dark blue terminal band and tail-base* (Roller lacks clear-cut pale panels, dark terminal band and dark tail-base). Occurs singly or in pairs, often perching conspicuously on post. Like Roller has noisy, frequently observed, tumbling display flight.

oice: similar to Roller, but with more barking 'rak'.

tatus: see map. Mainly resident; immigration to Oman in autumn. Vagrant Kuwait.

abitat: open, often cultivated country and plains with palm plantations or scattered trees, rarely above 1,000 m. Nests in hole in tree or well.

Indian Roller

ilac-breasted Roller *Coracias caudata* Plate 22

lentification: 41 cm (with tail streamers). Similar to Abyssinian Roller but slightly darker with shorter tail streamers, rich lilac throat and breast, and whiter around face and forehead. Race most likely to occur in region is that from Somalia in which lilac is restricted to throat and sides of face. In juvenile, and adult in moult, lilac throat (and breast) become duller and browner, and ear-coverts can look quite brown. Often perches on telegraph poles and wires; typical Roller tumbling courtship flight.

oice: harsh, loud 'krack, krack', less raucous chattering 'kark'; in flight, sharper rasping 'kick-kick-kick'.

tatus: vagrant S Yemen. Range Africa.

abitat: woodland, open bush and plains with scattered trees or other perching posts.

ufous-crowned Roller *Coracias naevia* Plate 22

lentification: 35 cm. Sexes alike. Similar size to Roller but stockier and with stouter bill; lacks tail streamers. Plumage quite unlike other rollers of region, having *vinous chestnut head and underparts,* latter finely streaked white; *white forehead, supercilium and nape patch and dull olive upperparts.* In flight, wings show deep blue and purple coverts above with black-tipped flight-feathers; *below coverts are pinkish-white.* Deep blue rump and square-ended tail, latter with green central feathers. Actions similar to other rollers.

oice: similar to Abyssinian Roller but less vocal.

tatus: vagrant S Yemen. Range Africa.

abitat: similar to that of Abyssinian Roller but prefers more wooded areas.

oopoe *Upupa epops*

lentification: 28 cm. See PMH.

atus: see map. Egyptian breeders resident, but is mainly a partial migrant with small numbers present in most areas in winter but none Turkey, N and central Iran. Widespread passage.

abitat: open woodland, orchards, parkland, olive and palm groves, oases; more open bushy country in winter. Nests in hole in old tree or ruin.

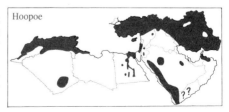

Hoopoe

145

Grey Hornbill

Drawings by S. Christensen

Grey Hornbill *Tockus nasutus*

Identification: 48 cm. Sexes similar (bill colour differs). Though predominantly brown, *quite unmistakable*, with *stout decurved bill, long tail, slow undulating flight and characteristic voice. Dark brown above with narrow white mantle band and buffish-white feather edgings to wings* giving mottled appearance; *head blackish-brown with long, broad, white supercilium*. Throat and upper breast brownish-grey, rest of underparts off-white; blackish-brown tail with white streaks and tips to feathers. Male has black bill and horn (barely noticeable – looking like part of bill) with ivory-yellow patch at base of upper mandible and 3–5 white lines on lower mandible; in female, ivory-yellow patch far more extensive and end of bill red. Flight unexpectedly slow, deeply undulating, with slow wing-beats interspersed with glides; fairly broad wings show conspicuous white trailing edge to blackish flight feathers, also white tip to tail. Rather unobtrusive, spending much time concealed on branches of trees, when more often heard than seen. Frequently occurs in small parties.

Voice: loud descending, plaintive mewing 'piiiuuu'; also loud, almost raptorial, 'kee-kee-kee-kee-kerra-kerra'. Song starts slowly 'coi, coi, coi etc' (or 'coi-coi-coi-coi-coi-coi' as continuous rising and falling trill) changing to 'trii-jip, trii-jip, trii-jip', etc, building to crescendo, with head thrown up and almost backwards.

Status: see map. Resident.

Habitat: acacia woodland, plains and hills (250–2,000 m) with mature trees, though commoner at lower altitude. Nests in hole in tree, where female is almost walled-in.

Grey Hornbill

Wryneck *Jynx torquilla*

Identification: 16 cm. See PMH.

Status: see map. May breed NW Iran. Mainly resident NW Africa. Summer visitor N Turkey otherwise widespread passage throughout the region, though generally uncommon. Has wintered SW Turkey, Cyprus, Egypt, Oman.

Habitat: gardens, orchards, parks and scrub with trees, can occur in any area with scrub or bushes on migration. Nests in natural holes in trees, masonry, etc.

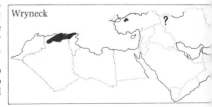

Wryneck

146

Grey-headed Woodpecker *Picus canus*

Identification: 25 cm. See PMH.
Status: Has been seen in N Turkey but no breeding records.
Habitat: As Green Woodpecker but also deciduous mountain forests up to tree line; occasionally in coniferous woods. Nest as Green Woodpecker.

Green Woodpecker *Picus viridis*

Identification: 32 cm. See PMH.
Status: see map. Resident.
Habitat: deciduous woods, parks, and open areas with scattered trees. Nests in hole bored in tree.

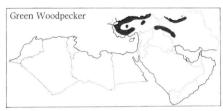

Levaillant's Green Woodpecker *Picus vaillantii*   Plate 22

Identification: 30 cm. Sexes differ. Very similar size and plumage to Green Woodpecker (from which geographically isolated) being green above with yellowish rump which contrasts with dark, barred tail (looks blackish in field) and pale grey-green below. Crown red in male, while in female red confined to nape. Grey cheeks with *black moustachial patch* (reduced in female) which *lacks red moustachial spot* typical of Green Woodpecker. Bill yellowish with darker upper mandible and tip. Juvenile like young Green Woodpecker, but less barred below.
Voice: similar laughing call to Green Woodpecker, sometimes higher and more musical – the notes rising and falling.
Status: see map. Resident.
Habitat: open deciduous woodland or areas with scattered trees in hilly country; also in evergreen oaks, larch and occasionally pine forests. Nests in hole bored in tree.

Scaly-bellied Woodpecker *Picus squamatus*   Plate 22

Identification: 33 cm. Similar in plumage to geographically separated Green Woodpecker and Levaillant's Green Woodpecker but very slightly larger. Upperparts yellowish-green, but duller than those of Green, and yellowish rump much less conspicuous; primaries and tail barred with yellowish-white. Underparts greyish-olive with *brownish scale-like markings* (in race occurring in the region) *from breast to undertail-coverts*. Crown red in male (black in female) narrowly bordered below by black line and *whitish supercilium*, pale greyish cheeks and black, flecked white. *Bill pale dull yellowish-ivory*; but greyish, tipped yellow in female (dark grey in Green) and eye dull red (yellowish-white in Green). Juvenile similar to adult but scale-like marks (which are duller) also on upper breast; black on hindneck and often rather grey-blotched on upperparts. Not shy and quite noisy; searches for food in trees and on ground.
Voice: short, fairly high-pitched 'kik'; also clear and melodic 'pi-coq' or far-carrying 'pirr'; an excited, rapid high-pitched 'kik-kik-kik eh', somewhat falcon-like. Laughing call similar to Green Woodpecker.
Status: see map. Status uncertain. No recent records though resident in breeding areas; may vary altitude in winter.
Habitat: mixed woodland and open country with scattered copses, orchards and junipers to 3,000 m. Nests in hole bored in tree.

147

Black Woodpecker *Dryocopus martius*

Identification: 46 cm. See PMH.
Status: see map. Resident.
Habitat: mature mountain forests particularly coniferous and beech. Nests in excavated hole often high in tree.

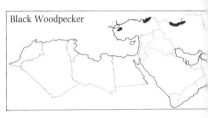

Great Spotted Woodpecker *Dendrocopos major* Plate 22

Identification: 23 cm. See PMH. Great Spotted occurring in Turkey resembles those in Europe, but race in S Caspian region of Iran, *poelzami*, (illustrated) is slightly smaller, longer-billed and has smoky-brown underparts. In Morocco birds show some tendency towards a red crescent across breast; in Algeria and Tunisia male of race *numidus* (illustrated) has distinctive red and black chequered gorget extending round breast from black shoulder mark. (Note that juvenile Syrian Woodpecker has variable red pectoral band, but is geographically isolated from this race of Great Spotted.)
Status: see map. Resident.
Habitat: deciduous and coniferous forests. Nests in hole bored in tree.

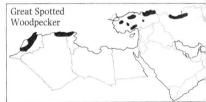

White-winged Woodpecker *Dendrocopos leucopterus* Plate 22

Identification: 23 cm. Sexes differ slightly. Geographically isolated black and white woodpecker, resembling Great Spotted in size and plumage, with similar black and white markings, red nape-patch in male (absent in female) and red undertail-coverts. White-winged differs in having *much larger area of white on scapulars, broader bands of white on secondaries and larger white neck-patch.* Juvenile browner-black above, sometimes with fine black bars in scapular-patch, buffish below with pinker undertail-coverts; young male has red patch on crown. Distinguished from Syrian Woodpecker by large white scapular-patch, smaller red nape-patch (in male) and black cross-bar on neck; from Sind Pied by large white scapular-patch, black cross-bar on neck, broader white bands on secondaries and, in male, red nape-patch (crown all-red in male Sind). Similar in behaviour to Syrian Woodpecker.
Voice: not fully known, but drumming and rattling calls.
Status: see map. Status uncertain; may occur in extreme NE Iran.
Habitat: sparsely wooded areas with deciduous trees particularly birch, poplars and willows in lowlands and lower slopes; also in gardens, orchards and oases in desert regions.

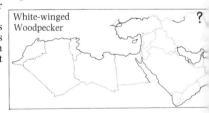

148

Syrian Woodpecker *Dendrocopos syriacus*

Identification: 23 cm. See PMH.
Status: see map. Resident.
Habitat: light woodland, gardens, olive groves often near villages or cultivation. Nests in hole excavated in tree.

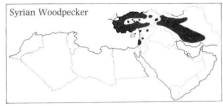

Sind Pied Woodpecker *Dendrocopos assimilis*　　　　Plate 22

Identification: 20 cm. Sexes differ slightly. Very like Syrian Woodpecker but slightly smaller, with finer bill, *all-red crown in adult male* (Syrian has black fore-crown and red hind-crown; but take care, juvenile Syrian has all-red crown), and *black moustachial-stripe extending less far down breast*. Hybridises with Syrian in Iranian Baluchistan and care is needed. Male Sind Pied has black upperparts with white scapular patches and bars on flight-feathers, white underparts with red undertail-coverts. Like Syrian, lacks cheek-bar, indeed cheek and sides of neck look noticeably white; forehead creamy-white. Female similar but has black crown.
Voice: call similar to Syrian, being a rather explosive 'ptik'.
Status: see map. Resident.
Habitat: trees, frequently palms and often in oases or gardens near water. Nest in hole bored in tree, with preference for tamarisk.

Middle Spotted Woodpecker *Dendrocopos medius*

Identification: 22 cm. See PMH.
Status: see map. Resident. Vagrant Iraq.
Habitat: deciduous woods (especially oak and oak/juniper), olive groves. Nests in hole bored in tree.

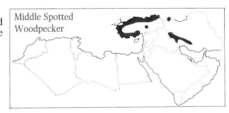

White-backed Woodpecker *Dendrocopos leucotos*

Identification: 25 cm. See PMH.
Status: see map. Resident. Probably more widespread in Turkey.
Habitat: mature deciduous woodland with rotting trees; also old coniferous forests. Nests in hole bored in dead tree.

Lesser Spotted Woodpecker *Dendrocopos minor*

Identification: 15 cm. See PMH.
Status: see map. Resident.
Habitat: fairly open woodland, old orchards, etc. Nests in hole bored in tree.

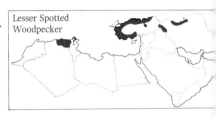

Lesser Spotted Woodpecker

Arabian Woodpecker *Dendrocopos dorae*   Plate 22

Identification: 18 cm. Sexes differ. Small woodpecker, slightly smaller than Middle Spotted. Male *olive-brown to olive grey-brown* (often quite deep and with golden tinge) with *crimson-red patch on nape* and five or six *white bars across blackish wings*; tail blackish but seen from below shows white spots forming bars. Underparts slightly paler olive-brown with a pale red patch down centre of belly; light barring on lower flanks and undertail-coverts not easily seen. Female, which lacks red on nape is duller, grey-brown above with slightly less prominent white wing-bars; underparts paler with very light smudgy barring on lower flanks and less distinct pale red patch on belly. Small bill slate to horn, legs greyish; eye usually dark but occasionally whitish. Typical woodpecker undulating flight, but undulations shorter than Great Spotted, at times almost straight. Perches freely on trunks but often feeds among small branches and outer twigs, as well as on the ground where it moves in Wryneck-like manner. The only woodpecker in SW Arabia.
Voice: does not always suggest woodpecker. 'Kik-kik-kik-kik', Kestrel-like but shorter; 'kek-kek-kek-ke-ke-kekekeke-ke-ke', accelerating, then descending; also a descending 'keck-keck-keck-keck-keck'.
Status: see map. Resident.
Habitat: scattered, open acacia woodland from near sea level to 2,400 m, but most frequently above 1,500 m; also in other trees including palms and often close to habitation. Nests in hole in tree.

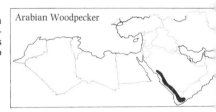

Arabian Woodpecker

Singing Bush Lark *Mirafra cantillans*   Plate 23

Identification: 15 cm. Sexes alike. Small, *broad-winged, relatively short-tailed lark* without crest, not unlike small Bimaculated Lark in flight. Upperparts warm brownish, streaked darker; underparts buffish-white with fine dark streaks or spots, in some birds forming dark smudge or spot at side of breast; *dull rufous tinge to flight-feathers above* (but not always pronounced) whilst underwing has pale rufous wash; dark brown tail has white outer feathers (tail invariably closed in flight, so outer-feathers difficult to observe). Whitish eye-surround and supercilium extends behind eye; buff-brown cheeks and ear-coverts flecked darker. Horn-coloured bill (yellower on lower mandible) fairly stout, longer than deep with *pronounced curved culmen*; long tertials reach tip of wing. Immature paler, sandy-buff above with more distinct blackish streaks, and streaks or spots on breast and dark breast-side smudge clearer than in adult; flight-feathers are fringed warm buffish rather than rufous, but long blackish tertials edged whitish. Movements on ground like Short-toed Lark. Flight weak, fluttering and undulating, often with *jerky wing-beats* and legs dangling, low over ground; after short flight will drop into grass and often vanish. Distinguished from other larks by combination of shape of bill, long tertials, rufous or buff flight-feathers and lack of crest; female Black-crowned Finch Lark is smaller, has dark underwing-coverts, less dark-streaked upperparts and shorter, stouter bill. In the hand Bush Lark's open nostril diagnostic.
Voice: song from ground, fence post or air where it flutters in Skylark-like manner, drifting back and forth at low level *with bat-like, jerky wing-beats*; chattering but quite musical song ends in Corn Bunting-like trill or jingle, 'ti-vit-tir-wit,che,che,che,che,' etc; accelerating and

descending. Call a quiet 'proop-proop'.
Status: see map. Apparently resident in N
Yemen but mainly summer visitor to Oman.
Habitat: dry grassy areas, undulating plains,
foothills and sparsely vegetated semi-desert;
often near or in cultivation and with scattered bushes. Nests in grass or near tuft.

Singing Bush Lark

Black-crowned Finch Lark *Eremopterix nigriceps*   Plate 23

Identification: 12 cm. Sexes differ. Small, short-tailed with *stout, deep-based whitish bill*. Male has *characteristic black, white and sandy plumage* but female and juvenile can be confused with other small larks. Female has *pale sandy unstreaked upperparts* with very *light streaking on crown and ear-coverts; white underparts with diffuse streaking on upperbreast and blackish underwing-coverts* (which separates Black-crowned from other larks of desert regions). Dark spots on median coverts and blackish tail with sandy-grey central feathers. Juvenile resembles female but spotted and scaled buff on upperparts and ear-coverts; has distinct dark streaks across breast, more streaking on crown and often a dark malar streak. Distinguished from Dunn's (which has similar tail-pattern) by smaller size, dark underwing-coverts, absence of whitish eye-surround, less streaked crown, whitish bill (yellowish in Dunn's), plumper build with shorter tail, wings and legs. Juvenile separated from Lesser Short-toed by heavier paler bill, tail and underwing colour, as well as unstreaked upperparts. Shuffling gait, fairly shy; undulating flight with short rounded wings and short tail. Male's display flight (can last 5 mins) circling on slow vibrating, lifted wings, interrupted by short glides.
Voice: song, persistent repetition of 2–4 loud, sweet and mellow notes (varying with individuals), 'chee, dee-vee' or 'pooo, pee-voo-pee', first note usually longest and isolated. Flight call a bubbling twitter and dry 'rrrrp'; also a soft 'tchep'.
Status: see map. In Arabia distribution outside
mapped areas uncertain but breeds erratically and probably opportunistically north
to dotted line. Partial migrant and wanderer.
Mainly summer visitor S Iran, NE and
central Arabia but present throughout year
in E Arabia from Bahrain southwards and
in Red Sea regions. Vagrant Egypt outside
breeding range, also Morocco, Algeria,
Israel.
Habitat: flat semi-desert and sandy savanna
often with scattered low acacia, sometimes
at edge of cultivation. Nests on ground.

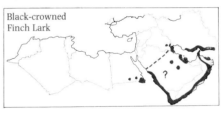

Black-crowned
Finch Lark

Dunn's Lark *Eremalauda dunni*   Plate 23

Identification: 14 cm. Sexes alike. Slightly smaller and less dumpy than Desert Lark, more elongated and with slightly more upright carriage of body and bill. Pale sandy or pinkish-grey with *dark-streaked mantle and particularly crown*, but in some birds streaks reduced to vague dark mottling. Underparts, off-white with faint streaks on breast, either confined to sides or forming well-marked gorget. At rest, sandy-brown central tail feathers conceal blackish tail with thin pale margin on outermost feathers (pattern recalling Black-crowned Finch Lark). Pale pinkish-orange or yellowish bill heavy and conical, *with deep base, thick near tip where culmen curves noticeably downward*, bluntly tapering. Typical facial pattern shows broad whitish eye-ring, short whitish eye-brow, pale ear-coverts and dark moustache and malar streak, but pattern sometimes less distinct. *Long tertials almost reach tip of wing* when not abraided. In flight, broad and round-winged like Desert Lark. Fairly tame and approachable. Desert Lark has less massive bill with more smoothly curved culmen; lacks distinct streaks on crown and mantle (but vague mottling in some, overlapping with some Dunn's); streaks on breast overlap with some Dunn's but shorter tertials reach only half way to wing-tip; also has quite different tail pattern. Bar-tailed has finer bill, distinct blackish wing-tips (not covered by shorter tertials) and bar on tail. *Calandrella* larks have white outer tail-feathers, smaller bills, much more contrasting pattern on upperwing-coverts; they appear

151

less dumpy, and in flight less broad-winged and longer-tailed.

Voice: song (mainly from ground but also air) scratchy warbling interspersed with short melancholy whistles. Flight-call 'ziup', 'tree-chup' 'two-weep'; also thin liquid 'prrrp'; alarm on rising 'chee-opp' 'tu-wep' or 'chup-chup-chup'.

Status: see map. Poorly known distribution. May breed occasionally Sinai. Mainly resident; some local, perhaps nomadic, movements. Vagrant Lebanon, Israel.

Habitat: sandy or stony deserts and semi-deserts with sparse scrub and grasses. Nests on ground in grass.

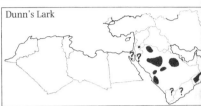
Dunn's Lark

Bar-tailed Desert Lark *Ammomanes cincturus*   Plate 23

Identification: 13 cm. Sexes alike. *Small sandy-coloured* short-tailed lark, *little smaller than Desert Lark,* with more upright stance, *rounded head* and *slightly shorter, finer bill.* Plumage pinkish-buff or sandy-buff above in *arenicola,* occuring in most of region (greyer, less pinkish in E Iranian race) with faint streaking on crown when seen close. *Black bar to end of orange-brown or brownish tail* more evident when tail spread but not seen in closed tail (in Desert, dark brownish tail-end gradually merges into paler brown base). Blackish wing-tip contrasts slightly with *wings which show orange wash, more noticeable in flight.* Underparts whitish with buff wash on breast. Bill yellowish-orange with darker culmen and tip, or just pinkish horn. For differences from Dunn's Lark see that species. Female Black-crowned Finch Lark has thicker pale bluish bill, dark underwing-coverts, fine streaks on crown and ear-coverts and different tail pattern.

Voice: song consists of 3 fine-quality notes 'cher-holf-hee', first 2 notes quick, quiet and low in pitch, the 3rd high, pure and drawn-out; repeated regularly at intervals of $1\frac{1}{2}$ seconds and often only last note heard; song also rendered as 'dee-dee-doo' with 2nd note higher in pitch and 3rd lower and drawn out. Flight call like Short-toed Lark's though shorter, more purring 'prrit'. Also short, rather soft 'see-oo'.

Status: see map. Mainly resident with local movements, but summer visitor to northern half of Iranian range. Irregular Kuwait. Vagrant Syria.

Habitat: deserts and semi-deserts, sometimes with scattered vegetation; preference for flat areas. Nests on ground.

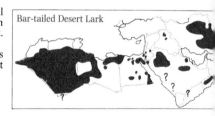
Bar-tailed Desert Lark

Desert Lark *Ammomanes deserti*   Plate 23

Identification: 15 cm. Sexes alike. Short-tailed, dumpy lark with *broad rounded wings and floppy, slow undulating flight.* Colour variable but *generally unstreaked sandy grey-brown above* (in some, vague dark mottling on crown and ill-defined streaks on mantle) with rufous tinge to rump, fringes of flight-feathers and underwing. *Uppertail shades darker brown towards tip* and lacks any white or black. Underparts buffish or greyish-white, often unmarked, but faintly spotted or streaked on sides of breast in some, in others a gorget of dark grey streaks. Variable whitish eye-ring and often dark malar streak. Rather featureless apart from *longish, stout yellowish-horn bill.* See also similar Bar-tailed (blackish bar at tip of tail), Dunn's Lark (deeper, blunt tapering bill, mostly black tail) and female Black-crowned Finch Lark (smaller, dark under-wing-coverts, stouter short bill). Most other larks eliminated by their obvious streaks on mantle, white or black in tail, or crests. Desert Larks tend to match colour of ground they frequent, giving rise to ten or more races. Most distinctive is dark sooty-grey *annae* (black lava desert of N Jordan) and palest race the whitish-isabelline *azizi* (whitish soil and rocks of E Arabia). More typical is *deserti* of Libya/Egypt, also illustrated.

Voice: melodious song includes phrases of call-note; sings chiefly from ground, sometimes in descending gliding flight. Call-notes variable, but typically short, soft and melodious 'dy-lyit'.

152

Status: see map. Recently discovered Turkey. Resident but locally slight dispersal in winter. Rare Lebanon, vagrant Cyprus.
Habitat: arid, broken hilly ground, stony and rocky slopes, wadis, semi-deserts and lava deserts; often with scattered vegetation and trees. Nests on ground beside stone or bush.

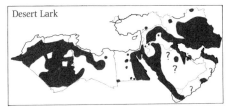

Hoopoe Lark *Alaemon alaudipes*　　　　　Plate 23

Identification: 18–19 cm. Sexes alike. Slender, upright lark with *long decurved bill, rather long creamy legs, long tail* and, in flight, *black and white wing-pattern. Upperparts unstreaked sandy-buff or brownish-grey* (depending on race). Underparts white, often with black spotting on breast. Black tail has brownish-grey central feathers and white outers; white supercilium and black malar streak. In low, undulating flight, *two broad white bands on black flight-feathers.* Juvenile spotted on mantle, almost no spots on breast, less decurved bill and vague head-markings. Runs with great speed, then suddenly stops, when head and bill often tilted upwards. In characteristic song-flight male ascends vertically for 2–5 m, twists over and spirals to ground with outstretched wings.
Voice: melodious and melancholy song starts slowly, accelerates and ascends in tone, then drops in speed and tone and slowly dies away; 'dee---dee---dee---dee---dee--dee--de-de-de-de-de--dee---dee---', etc.
Status: see map. Mainly resident, with some undefined seasonal movements. Vagrant Lebanon.
Habitat: flat deserts and semi-deserts, rolling dunes, with or without sparse low bushes; also on sandy shores. Nests under shelter of bush.

Dupont's Lark *Chersophilus duponti*　　　　　Plate 23

Identification: 17 cm. Sexes alike. Slender lark with *long, slightly decurved brown bill,* rounded head with whitish line in centre of crown, dark malar streak and whitish supercilium. Upperparts dark brown, streaked, with white fringes to blackish-centred wing-coverts; eastern race (Algeria to Egypt) much paler, more cinnamon-rufous, and more mottled than streaked. Underparts white with crisp streaks on throat and breast. Shortish tail with white outer feathers. Exceedingly skulking and reluctant to fly. Runs remarkably fast and stands slim and upright. Male soars to great height during song-flight, often at night; Hoopoe Lark is larger, longer-tailed and has black and white patterned wings in flight. No other lark has similar-shaped bill except NW African race of Crested, which during complete summer moult also lacks crest.
Voice: call, double ascending whistle 'hoo-hee' and nasal Greenfinch-like 'dweeje' also heard in rather nasal song. Alarm note shrill 'tsii'.
Status: see map. Resident.
Habitat: arid inland scrub and coastal regions, semi-deserts with low bushes and often plentiful concealing cover of grasses and herbs. Nests on ground at foot of bank or plant.

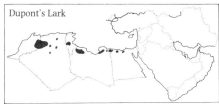

153

Thick-billed Lark *Ramphocoris clotbey*   Plate 23

Identification: 17 cm. Sexes differ. Large, heavy-headed lark with enormous *pale bill. Sides of face and neck blackish (mottled in winter) strongly patterned with white. Broad white band on trailing edge of wing*; otherwise flight feathers and underwing mainly black; tail has dark band near tip and white outer feathers. Upperparts greyish, wings warmer brown, underparts white, *boldly blotched with black spots or streaks*, which may concentrate to form broadish line down centre of breast. Female has less black on head and underparts. Juvenile fairly uniform without black on head, neck and underparts, resembling large Desert Lark in colour; upperparts warm pinkish-grey, underparts creamy-white with greyish tinge on breast and flanks; obscure dark mottling on mantle, wing-coverts and breast. Flight- and tail-feathers have broad pinkish-grey fringes but flight-pattern as in adult. In low, undulating flight, looks long-winged with large round head. Erect stance; can run at great speed.

Voice: flight-calls including quiet 'peep' or 'co-ep', soft 'blit-blit'; on landing 'shrreeep', on ground conversational 'woot-w-toot'. Jingling song with some quiet, sweet warbling notes given on ground and in flight.

Status: see map. Mainly resident, some dispersal in winter, at times occurring N Egypt, Kuwait, and south to about 25° in Saudi Arabia; vagrant S Yemen.

Habitat: stony deserts; outside breeding season also in less desert-like areas including grassy wadis, rocky slopes and marginal ploughed land. Nests in shallow depression on ground, ringed with small stones.

Calandra Lark *Melanocorypha calandra*   Plate 23

Identification: 19–20 cm. See PMH. Sexes alike. Large, short-tailed lark, larger than Skylark, with heavy head and stout longish yellowish-brown bill. Upperparts grey-brown streaked blackish, and supercilium white. Underparts whitish with dark streaks on breast and *distinct black neck-patches* (which occasionally meet on upperbreast); head pattern often less bold than Bimaculated Lark. In flight, triangular-shaped wings look *blackish from below with distinct white trailing edge* (in Bimaculated, underwing buffish grey without white trailing edge), and tail has white outer feathers (absent in Bimaculated). Wing-and tail-pattern also separates juvenile which may have barely visible neck-patches, and has scaly buff edges to feathers of upperparts. Female Black Lark (which see) also has black underwings, but lacks white trailing edge and white in tail. May flock outside breeding season.

Voice: flight-call harsh, dry rolling 'kleetra', at times not unlike Skylark. Song in high circling flight, but sometimes low or on ground, is stronger than Skylark's, more jangling with shorter phrases and often including characteristic flight-call.

Status: see map. Partial migrant, present all year in breeding range, extending in winter to Egypt, parts of Iraq, SW and central Iran. Vagrant E Arabia.

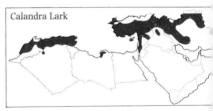

Habitat: open cultivated plains, grass and cereal fields, waste-land and steppe. Nests on ground.

Bimaculated Lark *Melanocorypha bimaculata*   Plate 23

Identification: 16 cm. Sexes alike. Resembles Calandra but dumpier, slightly smaller and with shorter tail. Readily separable in flight by *lack of white trailing edge to wing* (conspicuous in Calandra), *buffish-grey underwing* (blackish in Calandra), *buff-brown outer tail-feathers* (white in Calandra) and *white-tipped tail*. Upperparts brownish streaked darker; underparts white with variable black neck-patches which often join to form breast-band. Generally more contrasting head-pattern than Calandra with broader, whiter supercilium (giving Wood-lark-like appearance), blacker loral streak and more rufous ear-coverts. Stout yellowish-brown bill. Juvenile has wing- and tail-pattern as adult, but blackish neck-patches mainly confined to sides of neck, and breast more heavily spotted.

Voice: churring harsh 'klee-trra'; Calandra-like song from ground or air rich and varied with notes well separated, interspersed with call-notes.

Status: see map. Has bred Kuwait. Mainly summer visitor to breeding areas. Passage migrant and generally scarce or irregular winter visitor Egypt, Israel, Jordan, N Saudi Arabia, Arabian Gulf coasts, E Iran and Oman. Scarce passage Cyprus. Vagrant Yemen.

Habitat: thinly vegetated hill country or marginal rock-strewn cultivation, 1,200–2,400 m. Nests on ground under tuft.

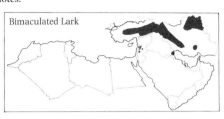

Bimaculated Lark

White-winged Lark *Melanocorypha leucoptera*　　　　　Plate 24

Identification: 18–19 cm. Sexes differ. Between Skylark and Calandra in size with stout bill, shortish tail and fairly long wings. Separated in flight from other larks *by large white patch on secondaries contrasting with blackish primaries* (both surfaces) and *rufous-chestnut forewing above; innerwing below whitish* (Calandra has all-blackish underwing with narrow white trailing edge). Male has head almost unstreaked with chestnut crown and ear-coverts, but rest mainly whitish including supercilium; large dark eye. When perched *white secondaries patch and rich chestnut markings on coverts.* Mainly unmarked whitish underparts with chestnut spot at sides of breast, sometimes faint with dark mottling on gorget and dark flank-streaks. Notched tail has white outer feathers. Female less rufous, more streaked crown, less chestnut on coverts and more pronounced streaking below. Juvenile lacks rufous in plumage; recalls similar Calandra but dark spot at sides of neck/breast rounder and smaller; has white in wing like adult. Snow Buntings that show white secondaries have white on wing-coverts; they are also much smaller with finer bill (culmen straight).

Voice: flight-call recalls Skylark, a repeated, slightly metallic 'wed' or 'wad', also Calandra Lark-like 'schirrl-schirrl-schirrl' but deeper and more steady in rhythm.

Status: winter visitor N Iran on Turkoman Steppes, less regular elsewhere on S Caspian lowlands; vagrant Turkey.

Habitat: dry grass steppe and fields.

Black Lark *Melanocorypha yeltoniensis*　　　　　Plate 24

Identification: 19–20 cm. Sexes differ. Large, near size of Starling with *stout yellowish bill* (dark-tipped when breeding), slate legs; short, slightly notched tail. *Male almost all-black in summer; in autumn black obscured by broad buffish feather-fringes* which are gradually lost through winter and spring. Tail and both wing-surfaces blackish without white margins (unlike Calandra, which see). Female superficially resembles Calandra; grey-brown above with dark feather-centres edged buff; *whitish margins obvious on edges of tail and tertials; underparts off-white with blackish feather-bases forming blotchy spots especially on lower breast and belly;* dark feather-centres sometimes join to form blackish patch on uppersides of breast (larger mark in Calandra). Pale feather-edges partly disappear in spring and summer when female more blackish-brown. *Underwing coverts dark grey-brown.* Juvenile similar to winter female, but pale feather-edges above more rusty-brown and tail and flight-feathers paler; slate-coloured legs identify it from all other larks. *Identification of female and juvenile best made on underwing-pattern, coverts being noticeably darker than dusky under-surfaces of flight-feathers which show no obvious pale trailing edge.* Other larks with dark underwings (notably Calandra) have underwing-coverts uniform with under-surfaces of flight-feathers, or have obvious white trailing edges.

Voice: flight-call Skylark-like. Song recalls Calandra with many imitations, though perhaps less melodious and with shorter phrases.

Status: very irregular sporadic winter visitor N Iran, but can be numerous. Vagrant Turkey, Lebanon.

Habitat: grassy steppes and agricultural regions.

155

Red-capped Lark *Calandrella cinerea*   Plate 24

Identification: 14 cm. Sexes alike. Closely resembles Short-toed Lark (may be conspecific), which
see. Occurs in SW Arabia where Short-toed Larks are grey-crowned; Red-capped separated
by chestnut-red crown, finely streaked blackish with tendency to dark streak on side of fore-
crown; also more horizontal dark patches on side of neck (comprising vertical streaks) which
can almost meet in centre below whitish throat. Behaviour as Short-toed Lark.

Voice: song, uttered in circular and slightly undulating flight, 'chee chew chew chew', mixed
with call-notes and fluid phrases. Flight-call 'drelit-drelit' like Short-toed; sometimes followed
by short twitter, 'pit-vit-pit', which may be uttered alone and appears to differ from Short-
toed. Other notes include intense, almost whistling 'peeeep', soft 'tsuru' and explosive Corn
Bunting-like 'pt' flight-note.

Status: see map. Mainly resident. Little dispersal in winter.

Habitat: open stony plateaux often with scattered bushes and near cultivation, mainly
1,800–2,500 m, but often lower in winter.
Nests on ground.

Red-capped Lark

IW

Short-toed Lark, (top) *hermonensis* resident Israel, Syria and Lebanon; (below) *dukhunensis*,
called **Rufous Short-toed Lark**, vagrant from Tibet, China

Short-toed Lark *Calandrella brachydactyla*   Plate 24

Identification: 14 cm. See PMH. Sexes alike. Small, usually pale lark with *white underparts lacking
any distinct streaking*, this being the main distinguishing feature from Lesser Short-toed (which
see). Short-toed however often shows *small blackish patch on side of neck*, or a few diffuse flecks
on breast or vague buffish breast-band. Dark-streaked upperparts, including crown, vary
from sandy-grey through brown to rufous-brown, depending on race. Short pale bill (usually
longer than in Lesser Short-toed), distinct white supercilium (often broader than Lesser's),
bold dark-centred median coverts and tertials almost reaching wing-tips (shorter in Lesser).
Crown washed rufous in most N African breeding birds. Juvenile has buffish edges and tips
to feathers of upperparts, and some streaks or blotches across breast, very like juvenile Lesser.
Flight undulating; foraging and migrating flocks pack densely and fly low. Told from desert

larks by heavily streaked back and white outertail-feathers. See also Hume's Short-toed and Red-capped Lark. An oriental race *dukhunensis*, with dark plumage and blackish legs, has occurred as a vagrant in Israel.

Voice: calls, sparrow-like 'tjirp' and Skylark-like hard 'drre-lit', also recalling House Martin. Song diagnostic (chiefly in flight high overhead), an unvaried repetition of a short burst, not unlike start of Corn Bunting's song, coinciding with an *abrupt undulation in circling flight* as wings momentarily closed.

Status: see map. Mainly summer visitor. Common on passage N Africa, especially Egypt, E Mediterranean countries and parts of Arabia; fairly common Oman. Some winter N Saudi Arabia, few Israel, N and NW Africa, occasionally Oman, very rarely S Iran.

Habitat: open country, waste-lands, dried salt marshes, steppes, semi-deserts and cultivated plains. Nests on ground.

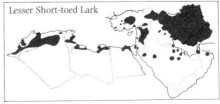
Short-toed Lark

Hume's Short-toed Lark *Calandrella acutirostris*   Plate 24

Identification: 13 cm. Sexes alike. Very closely resembles grey race of Short-toed Lark *longipennis*, and only separable at closest range or in hand. *White in outer tail-feather less extensive than in Short-toed*, confined to narrow outer web and tip of inner web near shaft and showing thin whitish edge in spread tail (in Short-toed outer tail-feather white, apart from dark brown basal half of inner web and closed undertail looks largely white). Slightly less brownish on upper-parts than *longipennis* race of Short-toed and rump and uppertail-coverts slightly more rufous; more pointed bill averages 10% longer, but all characters overlap with Short-toed. In the hand, *4 longest primaries equal in length* (in Short-toed 4th distinctly shorter).

Voice: call sharp 'trree' or Short-toed-like 'tre-lit'. Song poor and monotonous.
Status: status uncertain. Only recorded from NE Iran, but may be merely vagrant there.
Habitat: grassy steppes and rocky uplands.

Lesser Short-toed Lark *Calandrella rufescens*   Plate 24

Identification: 13 cm. See PMH. Sexes similar. Small with streaked sandy-grey upperparts (ground-colour more reddish, browner or yellower depending on race), white underparts with *fine streaks across breast* (absent in Short-toed, which see) and flanks often with few rufous-brown feathers streaked darker (lacking in Short-toed) and *tertials shorter* (do not reach wing-tip as, almost, in Short-toed). Short pale bill (generally smaller than in Short-toed) and whitish supercilium (generally less noticeable than in Short-toed) are additional features; tail has white outer feathers. Crown not tinged rufous as in some Short-toed; no crest but crown-feathers can be raised. Juvenile has streaks on breast and is very similar to juvenile Short-toed, but first-winter plumage (adult-like) attained August/September. Separated from other small larks by more streaked breast and upperparts, and white outertail-feathers. Desert, Dunn's and young Black-crowned Finch Lark can approach Lesser Short-toed in streaks on upperbreast, and former two species in streaks on upperparts. However all three have stouter bills, different tail-pattern and flight-silhouette; latter two also have longer tertials reaching almost to wing-tip. Often semi-colonial.

Voice: calls, Skylark-like 'drrie', clicking 'sik' and characteristic purring 'prrrit' or 'prrir-irr-irr'. Song, in spiralling flight with unbroken wing-beats (so lacking yo-yo undulations) much more varied, melodious and vivacious than Short-toed's, with some longer notes and imitations.

Status: see map. Mainly resident in breeding areas, but more widespread in winter, when common E Arabia, and reaching Cyprus (irregularly), central and SW Saudi Arabia, Oman.

Habitat: arid regions, dry steppes and salt plains, rather bare pastures, waste and cultivated land. Nests on ground.

Lesser Short-toed Lark

157

Indian Sand Lark *Calandrella raytal*   Plate 24

Identification: 12–13 cm. Sexes alike. Smaller and shorter-tailed than Short-toed Lark, with *greyer and whiter appearance. Upperparts pale or silvery-grey* with fine dark streaks on crown and mantle (streaks bolder in Short- and Lesser Short-toed). Underparts white with soft fine dark streaks at sides of breast (less distinct than Lesser Short-toed); proportionally longer relatively fine bill. On closed wing, tertials do not reach wing-tip (like Lesser Short-toed, unlike Short-toed); blackish tail has white outer feathers.

Voice: call dry or throaty rippling 'churrp', or dry 'che-chir'. Song and display flight more like Lesser Short-toed than Short-toed Lark; song a short rather disjointed throaty warbling, from ground or air.

Status: see map. Resident.

Habitat: dry open coastal and river sand banks, flood plains, salty mudflats and islets. Nests at base of small bush or tuft in the sand.

Indian Sand Lark

Dupont's Lark

Crested Lark *macrorhyncha* (S. Algeria)

Crested Lark *cristata* (N Morocco)

Thekla Lark *erlangeri* (N Morocco)

Crested Lark *Galerida cristata*

Identification: 17 cm. See PMH. Several races ocurring in region vary in colour tone from European birds. Generally races become paler and sandier in east and south of region. Some populations however can be quite reddish (especially in W Morocco), often reflecting soil type. Others from higher altitude can be quite grey and dark. Furthermore, bill shape and size can vary: birds in NW Africa generally having largest bills. See also Thekla and Dupont's Lark.

Status: see map. Resident. Some slight dispersal, and immigration from north in winter.

Habitat: generally flat grassy or arid country, cultivated plains and semi-deserts; often near habitation, dusty tracks and roadsides. Nests on ground.

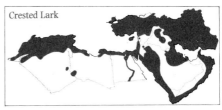

Thekla Lark *Galerida theklae*

Identification: 17 cm. Sexes alike. Almost identical to Crested and often very difficult to separate. Thekla is slightly smaller, with *crest slightly shorter and less spiky*; bill generally shorter, often looking broader-based and straighter (Crested slightly or more positively decurved, depending on bill-length of race concerned). Breast-spots bolder, more sharply defined, blackish against cleaner, whiter ground-colour; densest on side of neck, but sharp demarcation before reaching ear-coverts leaves *whitish half-collar*, accentuated by darkness of ear-coverts (see line-drawing). *Underwing-coverts are greyish* (Crested has all underwing rusty-buff). *Uppertail-coverts light rufous-grey, contrasting with grey-brown rump* (virtually no contrast in Crested). Thekla Larks in N Africa generally have longer bills and are paler sandy or warmer brown than European birds.

Voice: song basically similar to Crested Lark. Given from ground, in flight, and (more often than by Crested) from top of bush or tree-perch. Call usually 2–4 notes, with emphasis on last.

Status: see map. Resident.

Habitat: generally on more stony, often hillier ground than Crested, with some bushes or small trees. Nests on ground.

Woodlark *Lullula arborea*

Identification: 15 cm. See PMH.

Status: see map. Partial migrant, mainly resident in breeding areas. Winter immigrants reach Cyprus, Iraq, Near East, Egypt, occasionally Libya, NW Africa. Vagrant E Arabia south to Bahrain.

Habitat: open woodland edges, hillsides and heaths with scattered or occasional trees; in winter frequently in fields. Nests on ground.

Small Skylark *Alauda gulgula*   Plate 24

Identification: 16 cm. Sexes alike. Resembles small, short-tailed Skylark, with similar slight crest, streaked breast and upperparts, but dumpier with *comparatively longer bill*, longer, whiter and more clear-cut supercilium (but overlaps with Skylark). Often *small blackish spot at sides of neck* (where breast-streaks coalesce) and, especially in autumn and winter, *longer tertials almost reaching wing-tip* (like Short-toed Lark); in spring and summer worn tertials considerably shorter. Ear-coverts and particularly fringes of flight-feathers more rusty than Skylark but less pronounced or absent in spring; moustachial and malar streaks less distinct. In flight, plumper than Skylark, with broader-based, blunter wings and shorter tail; flight

159

more undulating, approaching Woodlark. Often *buffish trailing edge to wings* (more distinct white in Skylark, but in Small Skylark can bleach to whitish). In autumn, *sides of tail edged buffish*, less contrasting than the white in Skylark's tail; however, outer feathers bleach to whitish (spring and summer) and difference lost. May be confused with Short-toed Lark, but larger and bulkier, with shorter tail; at closer range streaked breast and usually buffish/whitish trailing edge to wings are important features.

Voice: song-flight recalls Crested Lark. Song recalls Skylark's but includes buzzing notes of flight-calls. Diagnostic flight-call soft 'pyup' or 'twip' recalling Ortolan Bunting; also hard buzzing 'pzeebz', 'shwerrrk' or 'baz-baz'; less frequently, also *Calandrella*-like 'trrp' and rather Skylark-like 'chirup'.

Status: see map. Partial migrant, with movements mainly short distance, nomadic or altitudinal. Occasional in winter Israel. Vagrant E Arabia.

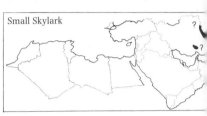

Habitat: open moist grassy and cultivated lowlands, but also in grassy hills. Nests on ground.

Skylark *Alauda arvensis*   Plate 24

Identification: 18 cm. See PMH.

Status: see map. Partial migrant and winter visitor. In most breeding areas regarded as resident, but summer visitor Iran. More numerous in winter, occurring in almost whole region but scarce Oman and absent SW Arabia.

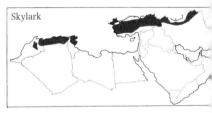

Habitat: high and low grasslands, cultivated fields; in winter more widely in open areas. Avoids deserts. Nests on ground.

Shore Lark *Eremophila alpestris*   Plate 24

Identification: 16 cm. See PMH. Within Europe, racial details unimportant but knowledge of various races in N Africa and W Asia helps separation from Temmink's Horned Lark. Shore Larks of this region have paler, sandier upperparts; moreover, forehead and throat yellow in Morocco (illustrated), white in E Iran, Levant and S Turkey (illustrated), and in fresh plumage is yellow-tinged in N Turkey to W Iran. (In all these areas Temminck's forehead and throat are always white). Also in Asia (but not Morocco) Shore Larks have black of cheeks joining black breast-band (unlike Temminck's, which see).

Status: see map. Mainly resident, dispersing to lower levels in winter when occasionally recorded SE Caspian.

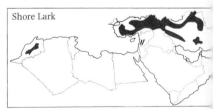

Habitat: mountains above tree level (often over 3,000 m, rarely below 2,000 m); in winter reaches plains. Nests on ground under a tuft.

PLATE 1

Red-footed Booby
white morph

d-billed Tropicbird   juvenile

Red-footed Booby
brown, white-tailed
morph

own Booby
venile
educed scale)

juvenile
white-morph

Masked Booby
juvenile
(to reduced scale)

adult
Masked Booby

adult
Brown Booby

PLATE 2

Pink-backed Pelican

juvenile

non-breeding
adult

juvenile

non-breed
adul

juvenile

Shag
desmarestii

adult
summer

juvenile

adult
summer

ju

Cormorar
marocc

Socotra
Cormorant

adult
non-breeding

juvenile

Darter

adu

juven

adult ♂
breeding

adult
summer

adult   winter   juvenile
Long-tailed Cormorant

adult
summer

adult
winter

juven

Pygmy Cormorant

PLATE 3

Abdim's Stork

juvenile

immature

Lesser Flamingo

Bald Ibis

juvenile

dark phase

Western Reef Heron

juvenile

light phase

Sacred Ibis

immature

adult

Goliath Heron

Siberian White Crane

IW

PLATE 4

Hamerkop

adult
non-breeding

juvenile

Green Heron

Yellow-billed Stork

juvenile

Fulvous
Whistling Duck

adult bre

juvenile

Indian Pond Heron

Spur-winged
Goose

♂ ♀

Cotton Teal

Egyptian Goose

juver

Cape Teal

juvenile (with all-pink
bill)

♂ ♀

Falcated Teal

PLATE 5

African Swallow-tailed Kite

juvenile

venile pale type
aegyptius

adult

Black Kite

adult lineatus

Bateleur

♂

juvenile

♀

Bateleur

adult

♀

juvenile

adult

White-eyed Buzzard

PLATE 6

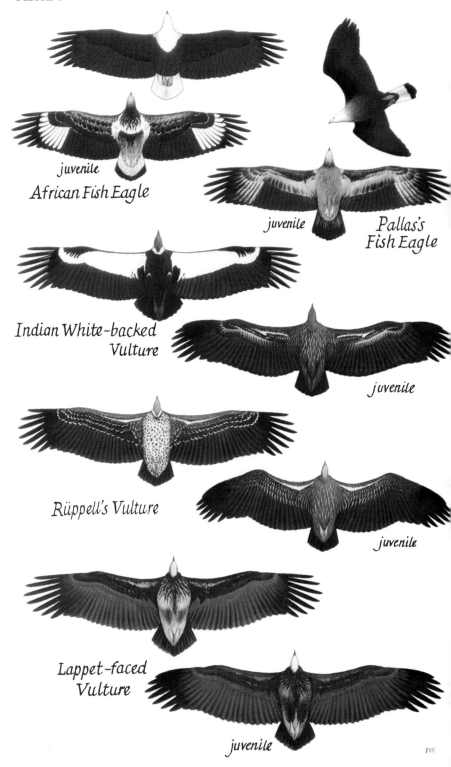

juvenile

African Fish Eagle

juvenile

Pallas's Fish Eagle

Indian White-backed Vulture

juvenile

Rüppell's Vulture

juvenile

Lappet-faced Vulture

juvenile

PLATE 7

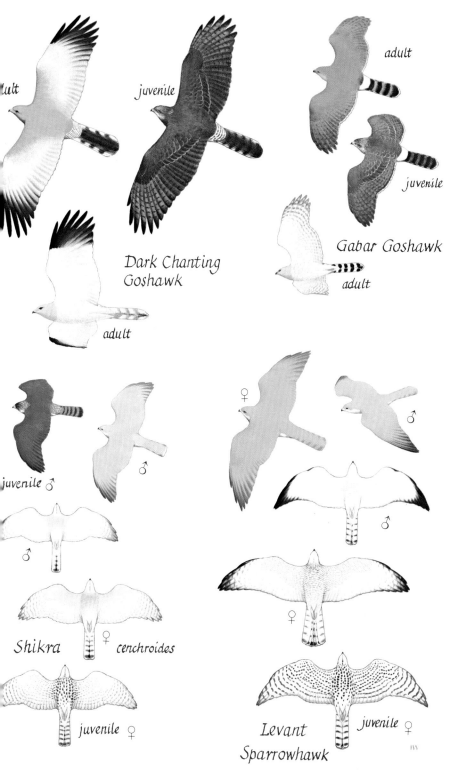

adult

juvenile

adult

juvenile

Gabar Goshawk

adult

Dark Chanting
Goshawk

adult

juvenile ♂

♂

♂

♀

Shikra

cenchroides

juvenile ♀

♀

♂

♀

juvenile ♀

Levant
Sparrowhawk

PLATE 8

juvenile

juvenile

Steppe
Eagle

sub-adult (pale form)

adult

Tawny
Eagle
belisarius (NW Africa)

juvenile (pale form)

adult (dark form)

juvenile

juvenile

adult

Verreaux's Eagle

IW

PLATE 9

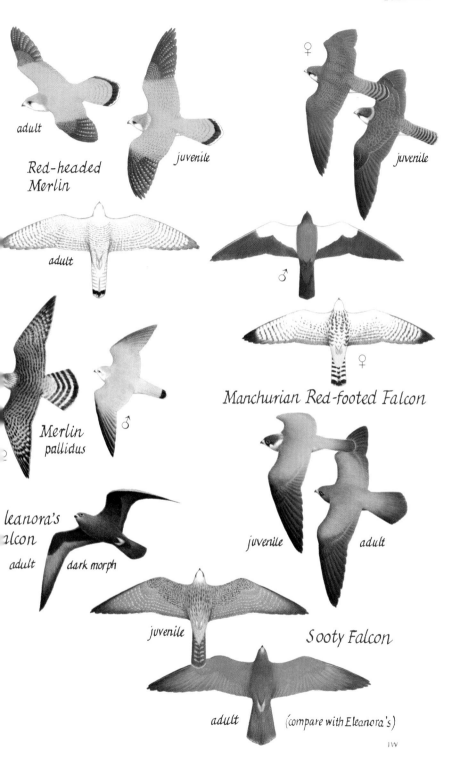

Red-headed Merlin

adult

juvenile

adult

♀

juvenile

♂

Merlin
pallidus

♂

Manchurian Red-footed Falcon

♀

leanora's
ılcon

adult   dark morph

juvenile   adult

juvenile

Sooty Falcon

adult   (compare with Eleanora's)

IW

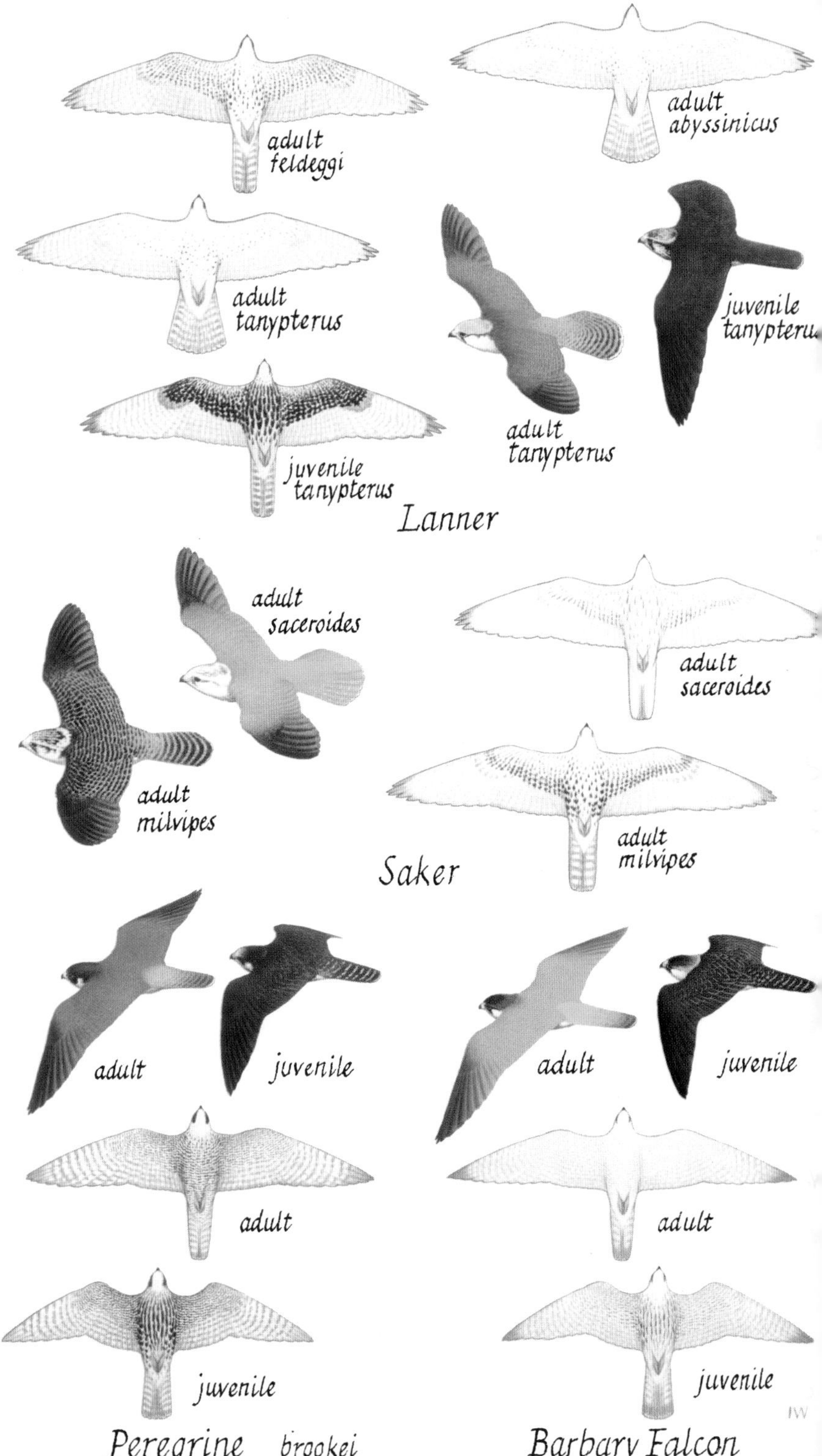

PLATE 10

adult
feldeggi

adult
abyssinicus

adult
tanypterus

juvenile
tanypteru

adult
tanypterus

juvenile
tanypterus

Lanner

adult
saceroides

adult
milvipes

adult
saceroides

adult
milvipes

Saker

adult

juvenile

adult

juvenile

adult

adult

juvenile

juvenile

Peregrine   brookei

Barbary Falcon

PLATE 11

Helmeted Guineafowl

Caucasian
Black Grouse

♂

♀

...ilby's
Rock Partridge

Arabian
Red-legged
Partridge

Caspian Snowcock

♂
...see
...tridge

♀

cholmleyi

Black Francolin

♂

♀

Sand
Partridge

...Near East)
heyi   ♀

♂

Grey Francolin

♂

Double-spurred
Francolin

♀

Harlequin Quail

JW

PLATE 12

immature caspius

adult madagascariensis

adult caspius

Purple Gallinule

♂

♀

Painted Snipe

Allen's Galli

juvenile

Snipe

Pheasant-tailed Jaçana

juvenile

adul winte

adult summer

Pintail Snipe

Solitary Snipe

Great Snipe

IW

PLATE 13

oubara

Arabian
Bustard

Stone
Curlew

Great Stone Plover

Cream-coloured Courser

juvenile

egal Thick-knee

Egyptian Plover

otted Thick-knee

Crab Plover

juvenile

IW

PLATE 14

Red-wattled Plover

White-tailed Plover

adult

juvenile

adult
summer

Sociable Plover

adult

adult
winter

adult
summer

juvenile

Black-headed
Plover

Spur-
winged
Plover

Kittlitz's Plover

juvenile

Caspian Plover

adult

winter

summer

juvenile

Pacific
Golden
Plover

summer

adult
winter

juvenile

Greater Sand Plover

adult
summer

adult
winter

summer

juvenile

Little Pratincole

Lesser Sand Plover

adult
summer

adult
winter

summer

juvenile

PLATE 15

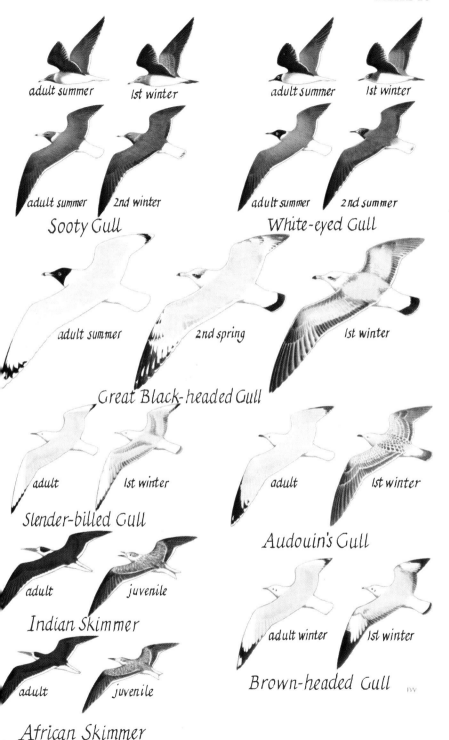

adult summer   1st winter

adult summer   2nd winter

Sooty Gull

adult summer   1st winter

adult summer   2nd summer

White-eyed Gull

adult summer

2nd spring

1st winter

Great Black-headed Gull

adult   1st winter

Slender-billed Gull

adult   1st winter

Audouin's Gull

adult   juvenile

Indian Skimmer

adult   juvenile

African Skimmer

adult winter   1st winter

Brown-headed Gull

PLATE 16

adult breeding

adult early breeding

adult non-breeding

adult most of y

juvenile

juven

Caspian Tern

Royal Tern

adult breeding

adult breeding

1st autumn

1st autu

Swift Tern

Lesser Crested Tern

adult breeding

adult breedi

adult non-breeding

1st autu

1st autumn

Sooty Tern

White-cheeked Tern

adult breedin

Lesser Noddy

1st autumn

Bridled Tern

adult

1st autumn

adult breeding

1st autumn

Common Noddy

Saunders' Little Tern

PLATE 17

Lichtenstein's Sandgrouse

Spotted Sandgrouse

coronatus

♂ coronatus

♀ coronatus

Crowned Sandgrouse

saturatus
S.E.Arabia

...tnut-
...llied
Sandgrouse

Black-bellied
Sandgrouse

♂ summer

♂ summer

Pin-tailed Sandgrouse

Pallas's Sandgrouse

PLATE 18

Ring-necked Parakeet ♂

Alexandrine Parakeet ♂

Namaqua Dove ♂ ♀

Bruce's Green Pigeon

Dusky Turtle Dove

Red-eyed Dove

Rufous Turtle Dove

turtur

Turtle Dove

isabellina

African Collared Dove

Eastern Stock Dove

typical

Palm Dove

dark morph

JW

PLATE 19

typical

ck morph

Jacobin Cuckoo

White-browed Coucal

Senegal Coucal

juvenile

♀

♂

Klaas's Cuckoo

♀

juvenile

♂

Didric Cuckoo

♀

♂

Indian Koel

JW

PLATE 20

ascalaphus

desertorum

Eagle Owl

Spotted Eagle

Hume's
Tawny
Owl

Brown Fish O

Marsh Owl

lilith

Little Owl

Striated Scops Owl

Spotted Little Owl

Indian Scops Owl

LW

PLATE 21

White-cheeked
Bulbul

Yellow-vented
Bulbul

Common Bulbul

Pied Kingfisher

♂

White-breasted
Kingfisher

Malachite
Kingfisher

White-collared
Kingfisher

Grey-headed Kingfisher

cyanophrys

Little Green Bee-eater

Blue-cheeked
Bee-eater

cleopatra

White-throated
Bee-eater

PLATE 22

Rufous-crowned Roller

Abyssin[ian] Roller

Indian Roller

Lilac-breasted Roller

♀
♂

♀
♂

Scaly-bellied Woodpecker

Levaillant's Green Woodpecker

♂

numidus
poelza[mi]
Great Spotted Woodpecker

♂

♂

Arabian Woodpecker

♀

♀

♀

Sind Pied Woodpecker

White-winged Woodpecker

IW

PLATE 23

Calandra Lark

Bimaculated Lark

poe Lark

Thick-billed Lark

juvenile

Dupont's Lark

arenicolor

Bar-tailed Desert Lark

Dunn's Lark

deserti

inging Bush Lark

♂

azizi

Black-crowned Finch Lark

♀

annae

Desert Lark   IW

PLATE 24

♂ winter

♀

Black Lark

♀ winter

White-winged L

♂

Small Skylark

bicornis

atlas

Shore Lark

Skylark

Temminck's Horned Lark

Lesser Short-toed Lark

Short-toed Lark

Red-capped Lark

Hume's Short-toed Lark

Indian Sand Lark

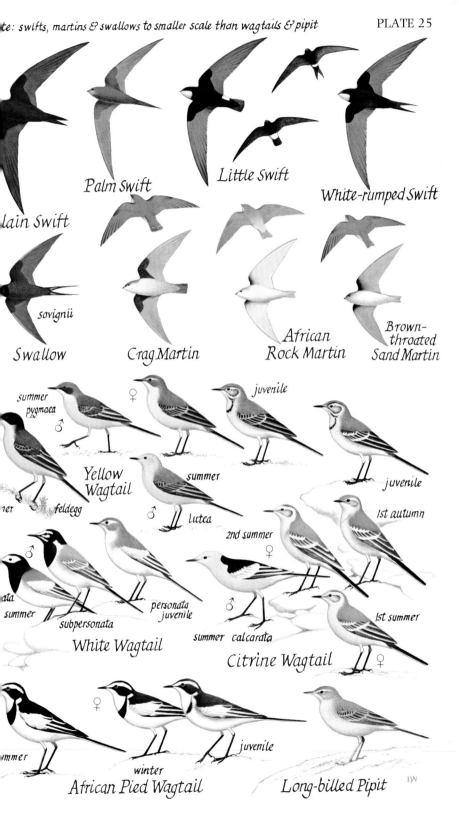

Palm Swift

Little Swift

White-rumped Swift

lain Swift

savignii

Swallow

Crag Martin

African
Rock Martin

Brown-
throated
Sand Martin

summer
pygmaea
♂

♀

juvenile

Yellow
Wagtail

summer
♂
lutea

juvenile

ner   feldegg

1st autumn

2nd summer
♀

♂
ata
summer   personata
juvenile

subpersonata

White Wagtail

summer   calcarata

Citrine Wagtail

1st summer
♀

♀

immer

♀

winter
African Pied Wagtail

juvenile

Long-billed Pipit

IW

PLATE 26

♀

♂

variegata
Stonechat

♂ Pied Stonechat ♀

♀

♂ Red-flanked Bluetail

♀

Black Bush Robin

White-throated Robin ♂

montana

Alpine Accentor

Arabian Accent

Radde's Accentor

winter

Black-throated Accentor

PLATE 27

Eversmann's Redstart

♂ summer

♂ winter

♀

Moussier's Redstart

♂

♀

oenicuroides ♂

♀ phoenicuroides

ochrurus ♂

Black Redstart

samamisicus ♀

samamisicus ♂

Redstart

Red-tailed Chat

♀

♂

Güldenstädt's Redstart

Blackstart

JW

PLATE 28

Pied Wheatear

♂

♀ spring/summer

Cyprus Pied Wheat

spring

capistrata ♂

picata ♂

opistholeuca ♂

picata

Eastern Pied Wheatear

South Arabian
Wheatear

♂

♀

lugens
(sexes alike)

halophila

Mourning Wheatear

Desert Wheatear

♀

♂

dark-
throated

pale-throated

♀

♀

seebohmi

Wheatear

JW

Finsch's Wheatear

PLATE 29

black-eared morph

♂

black-throated
morph
♂

♀

melanoleuca

Black-eared Wheatear

Hume's
Wheatear

♂

♀

Isabelline
Wheatear

Hooded
Wheatear

♂

♀

Black
Wheatear

Red-breasted
Wheatear

juvenile

♂

♀

White-crowned
Black Wheatear

Red-rumped Wheatear

adult

♂

xanthoprymna

chrysopygia

Red-tailed Wheatear

PLATE 30

Little
Rock Thrush

Yemen Thrush

Fulvous
Babbler

winter
♂

adult
summer

♀

♂
1st year

Arabian Babbler

Black-throated Thrush

Common Babbler

♂

Plain Nightjar

Nubian Nightjar

Iraq Babbler

Egyptian Nightjar

Indian Nightjar

♂

♂

Sykes' Nightjar

unwini
Nightjar

PLATE 31

Blyth's Reed Warbler

brunnescens
spring

Clamorous
Reed Warbler

Great
Reed Warbler

Paddyfield Warbler

Upcher's Warbler

Olivaceous Warbler

adult
yellow type

Booted Warbler

1st winter
or grey adult

Olive-tree Warbler

Icterine Warbler

Graceful Warbler

inquieta

adult   yellow type

Scrub Warbler

1st winter
or grey adult

Melodious Warbler

saharae

buryi

PLATE 32

Tristram's Warbler

♂
♀

Yemen Warbler

♂
♀

Ménétries' Warbler

♂

Cyprus Warbler

♀

Arabian Warbler

♂

nana

desert

Desert Warbler

Lesser
Whitethroat

Plain Leaf Warbler

Hume's Lesser Whitethroat

Brown Woodland Warbler

humei   winter

Yellow-browed Warbler

Arctic Warb

Desert Lesser Warbler

Green Warbler

Mountain Chiffc

Greenish Warbler

IV

PLATE 33

♀

♂

summer

Semi-collared Flycatcher

Gambage
Dusky Flycatcher

African
Paradise
Flycatcher

passekii

tephronotus
Long-tailed Tit

atlas

cypriotus

ledouci

Coal Tit

Turkestan Tit

intermedius

persicus

Great Tit

rruthersi

Azure Tit

juvenile
nigricans

macronyx   adult

coronatus
adult

Penduline Tit

ultramarinus

Blue Tit

White-breasted White-eye

PLATE 34

Palestine Sunbird ♀ ♂

Purple Sunbird ♂ ♀

eclipse ♂

Nile Valley Sunbird ♂ ♀

Shining Sunbird ♀ ♂

juvenile ♂

♂

Algerian Nuthatch

juvenile

Krüper's Nuthatch

tschitscherini

persica

Nuthatch

plumbea

Rock Nuthatch

Eastern Rock Nuthatch

PLATE 35

pallidirostris

elegans

algeriensis

Great Grey Shrike

Black-headed
Bush Shrike

♀

♂

Grey Hypocolius

♂

♀

juvenile

Masked Shrike

juvenile

♂

Isabelline
Shrike

phoenicuroides

1st winter

♂

Bay-backed Shrike

♀

juvenile

♂

Black-headed Shrike

♀
juvenile

♀

♂

Rosy-patched Shrike

IW

PLATE 36

Amethyst Starling

Black Drongo

Magpie

mauritanica

Common Mynah

Bank Mynah

non-breeding

Tristr
Grackle

♂ non-breeding

♂ non-breeding

breeding ♂

immature

adult

Wattled Starling

Pleske's Ground Jay

IW

PLATE 37

♀ ♂

Rüppell's Weaver

♂ yattii

♂ moabiticus

♀

Dead Sea Sparrow

♂

Rock Sparrow

Pale
Rock Sparrow

♂ summer
juvenile

♂ summer

♂

♀

Sind Jungle Sparrow

♂ summer

Yellow-throated Sparrow

♂

♀

♀

♀

Lesser
Rock
Sparrow

♂

♂

Desert Sparrow

♂

Sudan Golden Sparrow

♂

Arabian
Golden Sparrow

adult
alpicola

alpicola
summer ♂

♀

♂

Snow Finch

Saxaul Sparrow

IW

PLATE 38

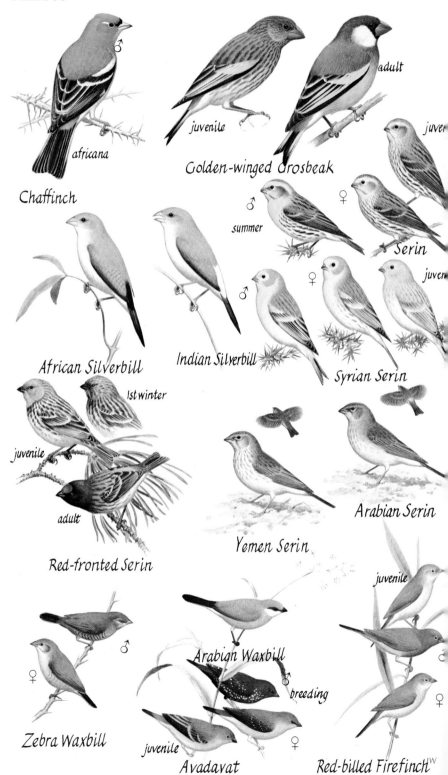

Chaffinch

africana

♂

Golden-winged Grosbeak

juvenile

adult

Serin

juver

♂ summer

♀

juver

African Silverbill

Indian Silverbill

♂

♀

Syrian Serin

Red-fronted Serin

juvenile

1st winter

adult

Yemen Serin

Arabian Serin

Zebra Waxbill

♂

♀

Arabian Waxbill

breeding

Avadavat

juvenile

♀

juvenile

♀

Red-billed Firefinch

PLATE 39

paropanisi

oldfinch

♀

♂

Yemen Linnet

♀

♂

Desert Finch

♀

♂

e-winged Grosbeak

♀

♂

♂

aliena

sanguinea

Crimson-winged Finch

♀

♂
brevirastris
summer

Twite

eat Rosefinch

♂

summer

♀

Mongolian Trumpeter Finch

juvenile

♂

♀

Sinai Rosefinch

♀

♂

summer

Trumpeter Finch

PLATE 40

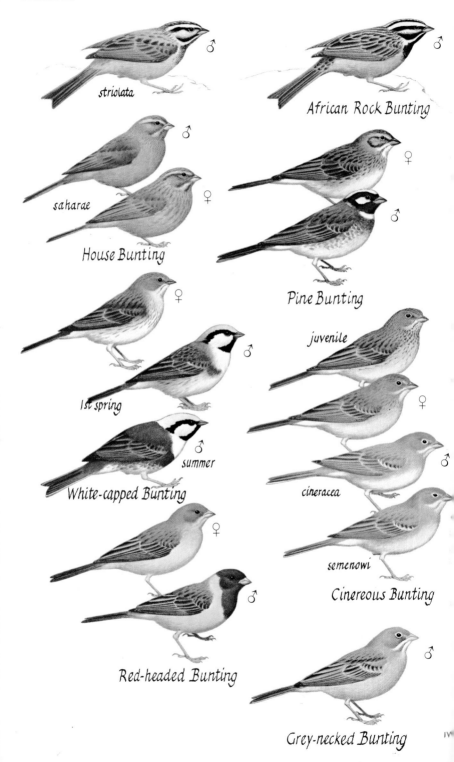

striolata

♂

African Rock Bunting

♂

♂

House Bunting

saharae

♀

♀

Pine Bunting

♂

♀

1st spring

juvenile

♂

♀

White-capped Bunting

summer

♂

cineracea

♂

Red-headed Bunting

♀

♂

semenowi

Cinereous Bunting

Grey-necked Bunting

♂

IV

Temminck's Horned Lark *Eremophila bilopha*

Plate 24

Identification: 14 cm. Sexes differ slightly. Closely resembles Shore Lark but smaller (smaller than Meadow Pipit). Distinguished from Shore Lark by *pale sandy-pink or warm sandy-buff upperparts*, often with diffuse rufous patch on lower hind-neck and upper mantle; *black on cheeks and throat never joining* (though can appear so when head sunk between shoulders) and always white, lacking yellow, on head and throat (Shore Lark variable yellow or white). Otherwise, much like Shore Lark with white underparts, black tail with sandy brown central feathers and white outers; in flight overhead white underbody contrasts with fairly long blackish tail. Female has less distinct head-markings. Juvenile lacks head pattern and upperparts have feathers indistinctly tipped whitish, quite unlike those of adult. Quick movements on ground and usually very approachable.

Voice: song very similar to Shore Lark; call also similar, a thin metallic 'see-oo', 'tsee-tsoo' or 'tsoo'.

Status: see map. Mainly resident; some dispersal in non-breeding season, occasionally in flocks. Vagrant Lebanon.

Habitat: open flat stony or sandy desert with or without sparse grassy vegetation, usually below 1,500 m. Nests on ground.

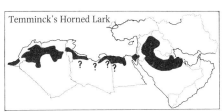

Brown-throated Sand Martin *Riparia paludicola*

Plate 25

Identification: 12 cm. Sexes alike. Typical martin shape with slightly shorter tail (which appears to lack fork) and broader-based wings than Sand Martin; rather like a slim Crag Martin. Plumage featureless with little contrast between mouse-brown upperparts and *greyish-white underparts, which deepen on upperbreast to merge into darker throat*. Lacks breast-band of Sand Martin and white tail-spots of Crag Martin. Unobtrusive; behaviour similar to Sand Martin.

Voice: weak, high-pitched twittering, harsher when bickering; also dry trill, shorter than Sand Martin, with more sonorous ending.

Status: see map. Resident. Vagrant NW and E Saudi Arabia, Oman.

Habitat: sandy river banks and their environs. Nests colonially in excavated holes.

Sand Martin *Riparia riparia*

Identification: 12 cm. See PMH.

Status: see map. Summer visitor to breeding areas, but present Egypt throughout year. Passage throughout the region. Isolated winter records in Arabia, Iran.

Habitat: open country with lakes, rivers, etc., more widespread on migration though usually over water. Nests colonially in tunnels bored in banks, sandy cliffs, etc.

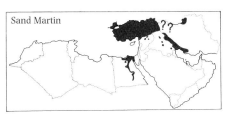

161

Banded Martins

Banded Martin *Riparia cincta*

Identification: 16.5 cm. Sexes alike. A chunky martin, *noticeably larger than Sand Martin* which it superficially resembles, though can sometimes also suggest short-winged Alpine Swift; *tail, however, is square or only slightly forked.* Upperparts dark brown with *short white streak on side of forehead. Underparts, including underwing-coverts, white* with prominent dark brown breast-band. Flight fast with occasional Crag Martin-like glides; wing-beats soft and slow.
Voice: occasional brief twitter.
Status: vagrant N Yemen. Range Africa.
Habitat: over open grassland and bush country, often near water.

African Rock Martin *Ptyonoprogne fuligula*   Plate 25

(Pale Crag Martin now regarded by some authorities as a race of African Rock Martin; others consider it is a separate species *Hirundo obsoleta*)

Identification: 12.5 cm. Sexes alike. Often difficult to distinguish from Crag Martin but *smaller and slightly slimmer, also paler, greyer above* (difficult to determine in strong sunlight) *and whiter below.* Upperparts smooth grey with darker brownish-grey wings and even darker wing-tips and tail. *Underparts, including chin, white shading to pale mouse-grey on undertail-coverts*; often a narrow diffuse dark mask through eye which is accentuated by pale plumage, and *chin lacks dark spotting* of Crag Martin. Underwing pale grey with dark brownish underwing-coverts; white spots in tail-feathers (noticeable when spread) common to both species. E Arabian race *perpallida* distinctly paler, french grey above and almost pure white below.
Voice: quiet, dry, martin-like twittering.

Status: see map. Summer visitor central and E Iran, with wintering/passage Oman, but resident in S Iran and apparently all other breeding areas in our region. Vagrant Kuwait.
Habitat: desert regions and dry hilly country with gorges and ravines often near human habitation. Nests, like Crag Martin, in caves, on rock faces or buildings.

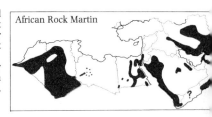

African Rock Martin

Crag Martin *Ptyonoprogne rupestris*   Plate 25

Identification: 15 cm. See PMH.
Status: see map. May breed N Yemen highlands. Northern populations, including Turkey and all Iran, migratory; otherwise resident, or perhaps moving lower in winter as in Cyprus. Uncommon passage or winter visitor most other parts including NW Africa, Egypt, Arabia.
Habitat: mountain gorges and rocky inland and coastal cliffs. Builds open half-cup shaped nest in cleft rocks or caves in cliff face or occasionally under eaves of building.

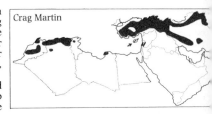

Crag Martin

Swallow *Hirundo rustica*   Plate 25

Identification: 19 cm. See PMH. Resident race in Egypt, *savignii*, differs from European birds in having underparts, including underwing-coverts, rich deep brick-red, as dark as forehead: it thus appears rather dark below in most lights. Migratory Palestinian race, *transitiva*, which occurs in Sinai and Egypt in winter, has paler, reddish-buff underparts; both races retain blue breast-band.

Status: see map. Has bred Bahrain and Musandam region of Oman; old breeding record for S Yemen. Resident Egypt and Israel, otherwise summer visitor with scattered winter records NW and N Africa, Arabia and SW, SE Iran. Passage throughout whole region.
Habitat: open cultivated country with settlements, but can occur over any area on migration. Nests on ledge in building or shed.

Swallow

Wire-tailed Swallows

Wire-tailed Swallow *Hirundo smithii*

Identification: 15 cm (including long outer tail-feathers). Sexes alike. Similar shape and size to Swallow but tail may look shorter and square-ended as *wire-like outer tail feathers are so fine they can be very difficult to see.* Upperparts iridescent ultramarine, bluer than Swallow, with dark blue eye-patch and *rufous crown. Underparts and underwing-coverts white*; white spots in tail visible only when tail spread. Readily separated from other swallows and martins (even if tail feathers not observed) by combination of entirely white underparts and rufous crown. Very fast flight. Ethiopian Swallow *H. aethiopica*, common in northern Sudan, a possible confusion species, has shorter and less fine outer tail-feathers (being more like those of short-tailed Swallow), and rufous on head confined to forehead; otherwise very similar plumage.
Voice: soft warbling twitter.
Status: unconfirmed records from Oman of a species which could conceivably occur in the region.
Habitat: near human habitation, bridges and along rivers and lakes.

Red-rumped Swallow *Hirundo daurica*

Identification: 18 cm. See PMH.
Status: see map. Summer visitor, but occasional winter records in SW Arabia. Light passage most parts of region.
Habitat: inland and sea cliffs; less partial to cultivated areas than Swallow, but in flat country frequents bridges and buildings. Flask-shaped nest with spout-shaped entrance is constructed from mud in caves, under rocky overhangs, bridges or buildings.

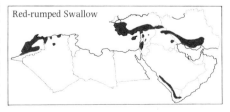

Red-rumped Swallow

163

House Martin *Delichon urbica*

Identification: 13 cm. See PMH.
Status: see map. Summer visitor; also passage most areas but irregular in Oman. Winter records NW Africa, Libya, Egypt, Arabian Gulf, N Yemen.
Habitat: like Swallow but more often near human habitation. Cup-shaped mud nest is built under eaves of house, sometimes on cliff.

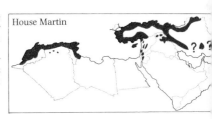

House Martin

Golden Pipit, male (above), female (below)

Golden Pipit *Tmetothylacus tenellus*

Identification: 15 cm. Sexes differ. Large yellowish-green pipit, similar in size to Tawny. Male olive-green above with slight streaks on crown and back; *broad, brilliant yellow fringes on wing and tail-feathers*; supercilium off-white. Underparts *bright yellow with black chest-band*. In flight, when extent of yellow in wings and tail fully displayed, strikingly yellow. Female and juvenile like much duller versions of male, and lacking chest-band and yellow on greater coverts and uppertail-coverts; throat and upperbreast whitish-buff with breast buff, mottled darker especially on sides. Typical pipit-like movements.
Voice: series of thin, sibilant whistles.
Status: vagrant S Oman. Range Africa.
Habitat: dry bush country; perches freely on trees.

Richard's Pipit *Anthus novaeseelandiae*

Identification: 18 cm. See PMH.
Status: see map. Thought to be rare resident in SW Arabia. Outside breeding season scattered records from most countries, African and Asiatic, within the region.
Habitat: in supposed breeding area occurs in mountains with open grassy slopes, 1,500–2,400 m. On migration, in any open, often grassy area. Nests on ground in cover of vegetation.

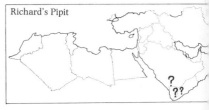

Richard's Pipit

164

Tawny Pipit *Anthus campestris*

Identification: 16 cm. See PMH.

Status: see map. Summer visitor; passage migrant through much of the region; also winters widely, but only occasionally Oman, Cyprus, Egypt, perhaps Iran and apparently not Libya.

Habitat: barely vegetated wastelands, edges of cultivated land, mountain plateaux. Nests on ground in shelter of vegetation.

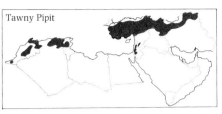

Tawny Pipit

Long-billed Pipit *Anthus similis*   Plate 25

Identification: 17–18 cm. Sexes similar. Fractionally larger than Tawny which it can closely resemble, with slightly more upright stance and *relatively shorter legs without conspicuously visible thighs*. Upperparts greyish-brown, finely streaked; earth-brown wings and *dark brown tail with buffish outer feathers*, though these can vary from non-contrasting cinnamon-grey (Arabia) to almost white when bleached (outer tail-feathers always whitish or buffish-cream in Tawny). Quite distinct off-white supercilium. Underparts buffish-white to grey-buff with faint grey streaking (somewhat blurred) on sides of breast, and generally *deep buff or buff-orange on lower underparts*. Bill, palish with darker tip, *typically longer than Tawny's, also stouter, almost to drooping tip* (Tawny's bill tapers gradually, culmen curving more smoothly). Legs flesh-red to flesh-orange. At distance generally looks dark sandy above, buffish (often deep) below, with contrasting dark brown tail. Long-billed can sometimes be separated from Tawny by more olive hue above (never in Tawny), narrower supercilium, darker forehead than rest of head and duller pattern of median coverts (distinctly dark-centred in Tawny). Juvenile, compared to adult, shows bolder streaking on crown and upperparts, darker centres to median coverts, blackish spots on breast and creamy-buff lower underparts; unlike juvenile Tawny Pipit it lacks moustachial streak. *When perched, tail often flicked upwards and fanned outwards.*

Voice: call a fairly loud 'cheree', not unlike Tawny Pipit; also rich 'tchup'. Song, from perch or in long, undulating song-flight, ending in tail-up parachute descent, is far-carrying, repeated, often disjointed, deliberately uttered series of 3 or 4 notes, some harsh, some more musical 'chrep, shreep, chew-ee', given in randomly varying sequence; sometimes rhythm of (1) 2 (or 3) syllables 'viuv-tryyit', more like Tawny Pipit.

Status: see map. Summer visitor to Iran breeding area otherwise mainly resident; some winter coasts of S Iran; vagrant Kuwait, Iraq, Cyprus.

Habitat: mountain slopes, often rocky and with scattered vegetation up to 3,000 m, descending to plains in winter. Nests on ground under rock or tuft.

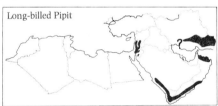

Long-billed Pipit

Olive-backed Pipit *Anthus hodgsoni*

Identification: 15 cm. See PMH.

Status: vagrant E Saudi Arabia, UAE, Israel.

Habitat: any area with trees.

165

Tree Pipit *Anthus trivialis*

Identification: 15 cm. See PMH.
Status: see map. Summer visitor. Very wide-spread on passage; few winter N Yemen and Oman.
Habitat: hillsides and fields with scattered trees and bushes, open woodland; on migration and in winter any open areas with trees. Nests on ground under vegetation.

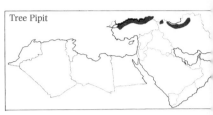

Tree Pipit

Meadow Pipit *Anthus pratensis*

Identification: 15 cm. See PMH.
Status: winter visitor to Mediterranean countries, eastwards to mid Iran and fewer southwards in Arabia to NW Saudi Arabia and down Arabian Gulf to Oman.
Habitat: open country including cultivated land, rough grassland, sea coasts, marshes, etc.

Red-throated Pipit *Anthus cervinus*

Identification: 15 cm. See PMH.
Status: mainly passage migrant, occurring in most parts of the region. Small numbers also winter from Turkey and Iran southwards to Oman, and more numerously in parts of Egypt and NW Africa.
Habitat: Moist open areas, marshes, cultivated land, grassland etc. nearly always near water.

Water Pipit *Anthus spinoletta*

Identification: 16 cm. See PMH.
Status: see map. Resident, with some winter movement, in Turkey, Iran. Winter visitor from Morocco east through Mediterranean countries and south to central and NW Saudi Arabia and Oman (few).
Habitat: mountains above the tree line; in winter in marshy lowlands, edges of lakes, etc. Nests in crevice in rocks.

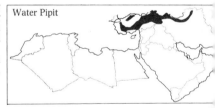

Water Pipit

Yellow Wagtail *Motacilla flava*　　　　·　　　　Plate 25

Identification: 16.5 cm. See PMH. Yellow Wagtail group is complex and at least 11 races have been recorded in region. All European birds migrate through region and males of other races that occur are similar in their yellow underparts and olive to yellow-olive upperparts, but, like European birds, vary in their head pattern; moreover hybrids/variants occur. Females and juveniles of all races very similar to each other and guidance on racial separation has not been attempted. For differences from Citrine Wagtail see that species. Some eastern forms have sharper calls than races in Europe, approaching call of Citrine.

M. f. lutea: illustrated, (Russia; migrating through Arabia and adjacent parts of Middle East) yellow head with olive streaks on crown and olive tinge to ear-coverts; yellow on head merges with yellow-olive upperparts; entire underparts yellow. Resembles *flavissima* race.

M. f. beema: (Russia; migrating through Arabia and adjacent parts of Middle East) pale blue-grey (often very pale) crown, nape and ear coverts with whitish supercilium.

M. f. feldegg: illustrated, (Balkans, Turkey, Cyprus, Near East and Iran; migrating through Middle East, Arabia, Libya, Algeria, Egypt) has glossy black head extending onto mantle, and entirely yellow underparts.

166

M. f. pygmaea: illustrated, (resident Egypt) small, with greenish-grey crown and nape, blackish (or dark greeny-grey) ear-coverts and white chin and often throat. Occasionally shows faint white supercilium, and dark blotches on sides of breast, which can form V-shaped breast-band.

M. f. melanogrisea: (S Russia; migrating through east Iran) black head, paler olive on back than *feldegg* and paler yellow below; white chin and white border below ear-coverts.

M. f. leucocephala: (Mongolian area; vagrant to NE Iran) white head with light grey shadow on ear-coverts and hind crown.

M. f. flavissima (Britain and adjacent Europe; migrating through NW Africa) olive crown, yellow supercilium and entire underparts. Illustrated in PMH.

M. f. flava (Continental Europe; migrating through N Africa and Middle East) blue-grey crown, white supercilium, chin usually white. Illustrated in PMH.

M. f. iberiae (SW Europe and NW Africa; migrating southwards) grey crown, darker than *flava*, white supercilium mainly behind eye, chin and throat white. Illustrated in PMH.

M. f. cinereocapilla (south central Europe; migrating mainly through N Africa) similar to *iberiae* but white supercilium either lacking or restricted, and less white on throat. Illustrated in PMH.

M. f. thunbergi (N Europe; migrating through N Africa and Middle East) dark grey crown, blackish ear-coverts, white supercilium absent in most birds, chin and throat usually yellow.

Status: see map. Resident Egypt; otherwise summer visitor to breeding areas. Passage throughout. A few winter in E and S Arabia and occasionally Iran, Cyprus and NW Africa.

Habitat: Flat open areas especially grasslands, almost invariably near water. Nests on ground amongst rank vegetation.

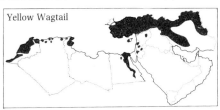

Yellow Wagtail

Citrine Wagtail *Motacilla citreola* Plate 25

Identification: 16.5 cm. See PMH. Sexes differ. Shape similar to Yellow Wagtail but slightly longer bill, legs and tail. Adult male in breeding plumage unmistakable with *head and underparts rich yellow*, with *blackish upper-mantle to rump* (southern Central Asian *calcarata*), or black upper mantle with rest of upperparts grey (N Russia and Central Asian *citreola*), or all grey usually without black on top mantle (western Central Asia *werae*); the last two races also less rich yellow with vent and undertail-coverts yellowish-white. *Two broad white wing-bars* and broad white edges to tertials much more prominent than in most Yellow Wagtails. Adult female has olive-slate crown merging into greyish mantle and greyish-brown cheeks surrounded by yellow supercilium; forehead often yellow; wings like male. Some adult female *calcarata* can be similar to male; in this race both sexes have, in first summer, washed out pale buffish-yellow (or even whitish) underparts; female's forehead can be buff, crown to rump darker brownish-grey; supercilium pale buff in front of eye, very broad and yellow behind (sometimes bordered dark above); ear-coverts often with pale centre and dark margins. Adult in winter like adult female in breeding plumage. Juvenile resembles juvenile Yellow Wagtail (greyish-brown above, blackish stripe above supercilium, blackish gorget) and best separated by *more prominent pale supercilium behind eye, often surrounding dark-margined pale ear-coverts*; also broader and whiter, more clear-cut wing-bars than usual in juvenile Yellow. First winter birds have *greyer, White Wagtail-like mantle to rump* (similar-aged Yellow has olive-brown tinge, normally) *greyish black uppertail-coverts* (normally olive-brown in Yellow); supercilium broader behind eye, usually surrounding dark ear-coverts which often have paler centre; (Yellow has narrower supercilium, not surrounding darker ear-coverts); some have brownish-tinged forehead (not in Yellow); underparts greyish-white with some beige-brown on breast, and *flanks greyish* (not in Yellow); *vent and undertail-coverts white* (usually pale yellowish in Yellow); two broad clear-cut pure white wing-bars, so typical in first winter Citrine, seen very occasionally in Yellow which normally has narrower yellow-buff bars.

Voice: monosyllabic flight call, harsher than in many Yellow Wagtails, with more pronounced r-sound (slightly recalling note of Richard's Pipit), 'tsreip' or 'screip'; however, some eastern Yellow Wagtails utter very similar note. Song comprises phrases of notes similar to call but with varied emphasis.

167

Status: see map. Resident and winter visitor Iran. Occurs annually E Turkey where recently proved to breed. Outside breeding season extends to SE and SW Arabia, Gulf of Aqaba (Israel) and recorded occasionally NW Arabia and most E Mediterranean countries including Cyprus.

Habitat: in breeding season near water, from swift flowing streams to open, swampy alpine meadows, 1,500–2,250 m; can occur anywhere near water on migration or in winter. Nests, often in loose colonies, in hollow in ground or bank overhung by bush or stone.

Grey Wagtail *Motacilla cinerea*

Identification: 18 cm. See PMH.

Status: see map. Has bred Lebanon. Partial resident in breeding areas. Occurs as passage or winter visitor throughout the region.

Habitat: streams in hilly country; also masonry by running water and cultivated areas on passage and in winter. Nests in hole in wall, bridge or bank.

White Wagtail *Motacilla alba*   Plate 25

Identification: 17.5 cm. See PMH. Of 8 races resident or migrant in region, 2 are distinct and illustrated: *personata* (NE Iran, wintering south to Iraq) has head and breast black with *white forehead and mask surrounding eye*, also in all plumages has white line behind eye; sexes similar; *subpersonata* (resident SW Morocco) is similar to *personata* but white on face broken by black line in front of eye, and larger white area behind eye. All other races similar to White Wagtail of European race *alba*, varying only in extent of black on crown and nape, size of black bib and white in wing.

Status: see map. Has bred Cyprus. Some present all year in breeding areas, widespread on passage, and winters, often commonly, throughout the region.

Habitat: any open flattish area with or without scattered vegetation, sometimes near water and often close to habitation. Nests in hole in wall or rock.

African Pied Wagtail *Motacilla aguimp*   Plate 25

Identification: 20 cm. Sexes alike. Longer-tailed than White. Entire upperparts, including fore-head black with *long white supercilium* and patch on side of neck; underparts white with *broad black gorget*. Conspicuous white on coverts and bases to flight-feathers forming *large white patch in folded wing, which in flight shows as broad translucent band* widening on secondaries and noticeable also from below (much more than Grey Wagtail). In winter black above, sullied greyish. Juvenile has greyish-brown upperparts and breast-band, and brownish wash on underparts.

Voice: flight-call single mono-syllabic 'tvirp' or 'tvuip' like cross between Yellow Wagtail and Tawny Pipit. Song consists of 'tviuip' note repeated about 4 times.

Status: see map. Resident. A record from last century in Jordan valley.

Habitat: edges of rivers and lakes, sometimes near habitation. Nests in hole in wall or rock.

African Pied Wagtail

White-cheeked Bulbul *Pycnonotus leucogenys*   Plate 21

Identification: 18 cm. Sexes alike. Similar in size and shape to Yellow-vented Bulbul. Race *leucotis*, which occurs in region, can show very slight crest (pronounced in Himalayan *leucogenys*). Immediately identified by black head (with greyer crown) and throat, with *large white patch fanning out behind and below eye*. Upperparts grey-brown, underparts paler grey with yellow undertail-coverts. Tail blackish with distinct white tips to tail feathers. Juvenile has browner head than adult. Behaviour as Yellow-vented Bulbul.

Voice: similar to Yellow-vented Bulbul.

Status: see map. Has bred Oman. Resident. Apparently introduced Riyadh, Qatar and UAE. Recently recorded Syria.

Habitat: as Yellow-vented Bulbul. Nests in bush, sometimes in occupied buildings, in verandahs, under eaves, etc.

White-cheeked Bulbul

Yellow-vented Bulbul *Pycnonotus xanthopygos*   Plate 21

Identification: 19 cm. Sexes alike. Tree-dwelling and reminiscent of small thrush with fairly long tail and rather floppy actions; often raises crown feathers. Sooty black head and throat shading into grey upperparts and paler greyish underparts; tail dark brown. *Conspicuous white eye-ring and yellow undertail-coverts* (absent in Common Bulbul). Usually in pairs or groups. Mobile, active, fairly tame and vocal; rather weak flight. Can be very abundant.

Voice: rather unvaried song has Golden Oriole-like quality: short, staccato, fluty and far-carrying 'bly-bly-bly-bly' or 'buli-buli-buli-buli' etc. Alarm-note 'trratsch'; also Nuthatch-like 'pwitch'.

Status: see map. Resident.

Habitat: most places with trees, bushes and scrub, including gardens, orchards and palm groves, wadis and semi-deserts; will inhabit centres of large towns. Nests in bush or palm tree.

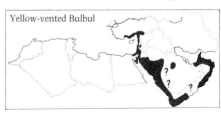

Yellow-vented Bulbul

Common Bulbul *Pycnonotus barbatus*   Plate 21

Identification: 19 cm. Sexes alike. The drabbest bulbul, with shape, structure and actions as Yellow-vented Bulbul. Upperparts grey-brown and underparts dirty buff shading into sooty brown face, occasionally with a warm hue. *Lacks the yellow undertail-coverts and white eye-ring of Yellow-vented Bulbul.*
Voice: as Yellow-vented Bulbul.
Status: see map. Resident.
Habitat: nest and habitat as Yellow-vented Bulbul.

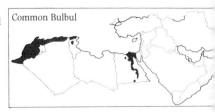

Common Bulbul

Red-whiskered Bulbul

Red-vented Bulbul

Red-whiskered Bulbul *Pycnonotus jocosus*

Identification: 20 cm. Sexes alike. Unmistakable with sooty-black crown and *erect pointed crest, white lower cheek-patch encircled below by black line,* red undertail-coverts, *sooty half-collar on sides of breast* and, when close, *small red patch (whiskers) behind eye.* Otherwise, upperparts hair-brown, *underparts whitish* and tail blackish with conspicuous white tips to undertail feathers. Juvenile lacks red whiskers; undertail-coverts orange-rufous. Similar in behaviour to other bulbuls.
Voice: noisy with variety of notes, more musical than notes of Red-vented Bulbul.
Status: recently recorded in E Saudi Arabia, Gulf States, and has bred UAE. Assumed to be escapes.
Habitat: gardens, orchards and cultivated areas, prefering deciduous. Nests in low bush or creeper.

Red-vented Bulbul *Pycnonotus cafer*

Identification: 22.5 cm. Sexes alike. A *sooty-coloured bulbul* with black, slightly crested, head and *red undertail-coverts.* Upperparts and *breast grey-brown to blackish grey, with fine pale scalloping* when seen close; wings brown with two pale bars. In some lights ear-coverts look brown or dirty pale greyish. In flight, shows white to *off-white rump* and white tip to blackish tail. Gregarious.
Voice: noisy: fairly deep and rich squabbling notes, similar to White-cheeked Bulbul.

Status: see map. Resident presumed to have originated from escaped birds. Occasionally recorded elsewhere in Gulf States.
Habitat: gardens, orchards and cultivated areas, prefering evergreen. Nests in shrubs, hedges, sometimes buildings.

Waxwing *Bombycilla garrulus*

Identification: 18 cm. See PMH.
Status: rare winter visitor Turkey, Iran. Vagrant Cyprus, Israel and Algeria.
Habitat: hedges and gardens with berry-bearing trees or shrubs.

Grey Hypocolius *Hypocolius ampelinus*   Plate 35

Identification: 23 cm. Sexes differ. Male reminiscent of a sleek Great Grey Shrike, but proportionately much longer and narrower *grey tail, tipped black,* and shorter wings. Male is soft pale blue-grey with conspicuous *black mask through eye broadening on side of neck to join across nape;* forecrown and underparts pale isabelline or whitish. Black primaries with pure white tips prominent in flight; feet straw-coloured to pinkish and noticeably pale. Female and immature rather featureless: upper and underparts uniform pale (even creamy) mouse-brown with creamy throat, *sharply demarcated from darker lower cheeks,* inconspicuous dark tip to tawny tail and whitish fringes to primaries. Often occurs in small groups feeding on berries, dates, etc, with deliberate balancing movements, particularly of tail. Can be very tame and easily overlooked sitting quietly in bush. Wide-ranging flight direct, with whirring wing-beats, well above tree-top level with silhouette like large Budgerigar; in winter small parties will fly up and circle round for several minutes.
Voice: mellow, liquid, Bee-eater-like 'tre-tur-tur', syllables short and run close together, the last 2 notes lower pitched than first. Also, when perched, descending 'whee-oo' with Wigeon-like intonation.
Status: see map. Endemic; summer and winter range confined to Middle East. Summer visitor to Iran, Iraq, wintering N and central Arabia, in Gulf area rarely south of Bahrain and in W Arabia south to Hejaz. Vagrant Oman, Yemen, Egypt.
Habitat: bushes, scrub, date gardens, etc. Untidy bulky nest is built in large bush or small tree.

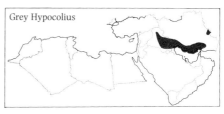

Dipper *Cinclus cinclus*

Identification: 18 cm. See PMH.
Status: see map. Formerly bred Cyprus. Resident with some dispersal to lower levels in winter. Vagrant Tunisia, Iraq.
Habitat: swift hill streams. Large domed nest built in crevice under waterfall, bridge, bank; invariably beside running water.

Wren *Troglodytes troglodytes*

Identification: 10 cm. See PMH.
Status: see map. Mainly resident, with expansion in winter reaching SW Iran, central Iraq and most of Turkey.
Habitat: low shaded cover in gardens, thickets or woods. Builds domed nest in hedge, hole in tree, bank, building, etc.

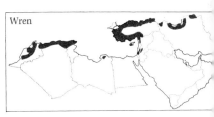

Dunnock *Prunella modularis*

Identification: 15 cm. See PMH.
Status: see map. Mainly resident. As winter visitor extends to N and W Iran. N Iraq, Cyprus and Israel; regular Tunisia, Egypt, but vagrant in rest of N African countries.
Habitat: scrub and wooded areas on low and high ground.

Siberian Accentor

Siberian Accentor *Prunella montanella*

Identification: 15–16 cm. Sexes alike, but female's head-pattern slightly duller. Dunnock-size and shape, rather similar to other accentors with dark heads and whitish supercilia that occur in region: Black-throated, Radde's and Arabian. *Mantle chestnut-rufous with diffuse brownish-grey streaking,* whitish tips to rufous-chestnut median and greater coverts; lower back and rump slate-grey; top of head dark brown with black lower border; noticeably long *warm ochre or even orange-buff supercilium* to sides of nape; blackish-brown ear-coverts clearly demarcated from *much warmer and more extensive ochre, or orange-buff, underparts of other accentors* in region; light rufous inconspicuous streaking on flanks and often dark mottling on lower breast; sides of neck greyish. Bill blackish with pale base to lower mandible and legs pinkish-flesh. First-winter bird similar to adult. Differs from Black-throated, Radde's and Arabian Accentors in chestnut tinge to diffusely streaked upperparts, inconspicuous rufous streaks on flanks and warmer (orange) buff supercilium and underparts. Similar in behaviour to other accentors.
Voice: call similar to Dunnock's but fuller, more ringing.
Status: vagrant Lebanon. Range Asia.

Radde's Accentor *Prunella ocularis*   Plate 26

Identification: 14.5 cm. Sexes alike. Skulking mountain accentor, similar in shape and movements to Dunnock; most noticeable feature slaty-black to *blackish-brown crown and cheeks separated by conspicuous long, white supercilium*. Rest of upperparts sandy grey-brown neatly streaked blackish-brown. Chin and throat off-white with faint moustache and necklace of very fine streaks; underparts warm yellowish-buff with *peach wash on unstreaked breast*; rear flanks and belly with short, brown, Dunnock-like streaks. Eye dark with narrow white eye-ring, bill dark, legs dull pink. Juvenile similar to adult but crown brownish streaked darker, supercilium with some dark streaking, paler (buff-white) underparts with streaking on side of throat, breast and flanks. Shy and secretive, moving with wing-flicking action mostly on ground among boulders and under low shrubs, both in breeding and wintering areas. For differences from Siberian, Arabian and Black-throated Accentor, see those species.
Voice: contact-call slurred, Dunnock-like chatter. Weak, brief song also has Dunnock-like quality but has fewer, less rapid notes 'di-diii-diii-diii-diii', somewhat trembling, the notes rising and falling; may be repeated 10 times per minute from top of low bush or rock.
Status: see map. Summer visitor to breeding grounds; winters usually nearby at lower levels; also regularly in small numbers N Israel.
Habitat: low scrub in mountains 2,500–3,500 m; in winter down to 1,000 m. Nests low in thick bush.

Arabian Accentor *Prunella fagani*   Plate 26

Identification: 15 cm. Sexes alike. Very similar to Radde's Accentor from which geographically isolated, as from all other accentors. Adult grey-brown above, streaked darker with warmer tone to coverts and pale tips to greater coverts. Crown dark grey-brown streaked darker (but looks dark grey) with blacker lower border adding to contrast with off-white supercilium; cheeks dark brownish-grey with whitish half eye-ring below eye. Chin and throat off-white with dark malar streak and border below throat of fine dark streaks (more obvious in some birds). Rest of underparts warm buff with diffused fine dark streaks on lower breast and belly and more noticeable streaks on flanks. Bill dark with yellowish base to lower mandible; legs flesh-orange. Differs from Radde's in *streaked, less blackish-looking, crown* with darker lower border, *fine streaking on lower breast and belly, warmer brown upperparts*, more noticeable streaking on moustache and lower throat, narrower supercilium and yellowish at base of lower mandible. Juvenile has less bright, greyish-white to grey-buff supercilium, more heavy streaks below without warm buff on breast, less clean throat and indistinct moustachial streak. Some (in moult?) can look quite mealy grey-brown above.
Voice: call note very similar to Dunnock. Song (uttered from top of rock, vegetation or low tree) short, fast 'drsi-drsi-drsi-dy-dy', of 6 to 9 notes often with scratchy end. Shorter than song of Dunnock, more staccato and notes more clearly separated. Also more trilling, slightly Wren-like 'dri-drrriii-tyi'driivivivi'.
Status: see map. Resident; also recorded S Yemen.
Habitat: bushy areas in rocky mountains often above 2,500 m; may straggle lower in winter. Nests in low vegitation.

Black-throated Accentor *Prunella atrogularis*   Plate 26

Identification: 14.5 cm. Sexes alike. Very similar in structure and plumage to Radde's, but main difference in all seasons is *black throat-patch* which, however, at least in winter, *can be mottled by palish tips to feathers*. In winter (only time likely to be seen in region) other differences are

173

pale brown crown with fine dark streaks (uniform dark grey in Radde's), broader, blackish cheeks and pale yellowish wash to breast (more orange in Radde's); also dark-streaked upperparts perhaps fractionally warmer brown than Radde's. In winter, supercilium, which turns up at rear, white, but yellowish-buff in summer. Juvenile similar to adult but supercilium less clear-cut, throat mottled dark and upper breast with gorget of streaks, a combination that produces rather patchy, pipit-like appearance. Typical Dunnock-like shuffling movements on ground, nervously flicking wings.

Voice: call a soft 'trrt' at least in winter quarters. Song which can be heard in winter is weak and thin, rather Dunnock-like.

Status: scarce winter visitor E Iran. Vagrant, perhaps annual Israel.

Habitat: in winter could occur in any area with cover including trees.

Alpine Accentor *Prunella collaris*   Plate 26

Identification: 17.5 cm. See PMH. The race *montana*, illustrated, similar to European birds but paler above and less streaked. Breeds in Turkey and Iran, some moving a little south in winter. All other populations in region similar to European birds.

Status: see map. Mainly resident with some altitudinal movements, and dispersal in winter reaching Iraq, Israel and Tunisia.

Habitat: mountains, above tree-line amongst boulders and rocks, stony alpine meadows, barren slopes, occasionally with scrub. Nests in holes among rock or vegetation.

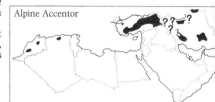

Rufous Bush Robin *Cercotrichas galactotes*

Identification: 15 cm. See PMH.

Status: see map. Summer visitor, scattered widely on passage.

Habitat: a variety of habitats with low cover from semi-desert scrub to gardens, palm groves and vineyards. Nests in prickly pear hedges, palm bushes and thickets.

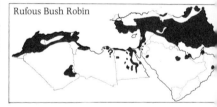

Black Bush Robin *Cercotrichas podobe*   Plate 26

Identification: 19 cm. Sexes alike. Unmistakable, small thrush-sized bird with long legs and very long graduated tail. *Plumage dull black with browner wings*, looking more rufous when fully spread, and *broad white tips to undertail-coverts* and outer few tail-feathers, though latter can be lost through wear. Though fairly tame, if alarmed will quickly 'disappear' into middle of bush. Often perches in open, when long tail frequently swept upwards over back and slightly fanned, particularly on alighting. Frequently in pairs.

Voice: song a long or short series of melodious thrush-like whistles occasionally interspersed with variations of 'tew-to-wheat' notes rising in pitch; often sings with slow upward sweeps of tail, from prominent perch. Call hoarse squeak or liquid chatter.

Status: see map. Resident, but extending range north and east. Vagrant Israel, Algeria.

Habitat: rolling or flat sandy plains with bushes, dry scrub and acacia wadis; also gardens. Nests in low bush.

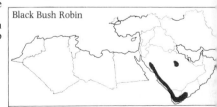

174

Robin *Erithacus rubecula*

Identification: 14 cm. See PMH.
Status: see map. Resident. Also winter visitor throughout the Mediterranean area, eastwards to central Iran, Kuwait, rare E Saudi Arabia and vagrant Bahrain to Oman, also Jordan.
Habitat: shady gardens, hedges, coppices, woods with undergrowth. Nests in holes or crannies in banks, trees, hedge-bottoms, etc.

Thrush Nightingale *Luscinia luscinia*

Identification: 16 cm. See PMH.
Status: passage migrant in eastern part of the region from Turkey and Egypt eastwards to Iran; uncommon or rare Arabia; vagrant Libya.
Habitat: on passage in thickets, swampy undergrowth and edges of reed-beds.

Nightingale *Luscinia megarhynchos*

Identification: 16 cm. See PMH.
Status: see map. Formerly bred Syria. Summer visitor. Occurs on passage in most countries south of breeding range although generally scarce, especially in Arabia though common S Oman (in monsoon vegetation).
Habitat: deciduous woods, gardens, thickets, sometimes on edge of wadi; on passage as Thrush Nightingale. Nests near ground in well hidden brambles, nettles, etc.

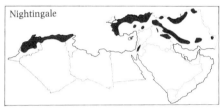

Bluethroat *Luscinia svecica*

Identification: 14 cm. See PMH.
Status: see map. Extent of breeding in E Turkey uncertain. Winters NW Africa, Egypt, widely scattered Arabia, Near East, Iran, Turkey, Cyprus. Also occurs widely on passage.
Habitat: swampy thickets in mountains; in winter also in reed-beds and dense vegetation bordering swamps. Nests near ground within cover.

Red-flanked Bluetail *Tarsiger cyanurus*   Plate 26

Identification: 14 cm. Sexes differ. Robin-sized. Male unmistakable, being *greyish-blue above* and on sides of throat and upper breast with slightly paler blue tail and uppertail-coverts; iridescent blue supercilia joining across forehead where sometimes whitish. *Underparts off-white with orange flanks* (not always immediately obvious). Less distinctive female and immature have *greyish-olive upperparts* (warmer olive-brown in immature) with very slightly paler supercilium, whitish eye-ring, rich ochrous wash in wing forming obscure panel, and *dull blue tail* which often looks dark; underparts smoky-buff with *white throat* (usually *bordered grey at sides*) and *orange-buff wash on flanks*. Often on or near ground, skulking and rarely staying in open for long, though may be observed briefly on roadside wire fences; quivers tail like Redstart or flicks it downwards.
Voice: grating Robin-like 'tik-tik'.
Status: vagrant Cyprus, Lebanon.
Habitat: usually in thick woodland undergrowth.

175

White-throated Robin *Irania gutturalis*   Plate 26

Identification: 17 cm. Brightly coloured, Nightingale-sized and similar in actions with tail frequently cocked, especially when alarmed or on alighting. Male has *black lower half of head with white throat (which can be just a narrow streak) and white supercilium*; upperparts slate blue-grey with dark brown wings and longish black tail. *Underparts buffish-orange* of varying intensity, with white ventral region. Female brown above with *black tail* and buffish below with grey wash on breast and sides of throat (recalling female Red-flanked Bluetail), orangy sides of breast with white centre of belly. Spends much time on ground, usually seeking out densest cover.

Voice: call a loud 'tji-thyt'; alarm-call a dry chatter recalling Thrush Nightingale. Song (from bush, tree or song-flight) loud, clear and persistent, with some harsh notes.

Status: see map. Occasionally breeds Lebanon. Summer visitor. Passage migrant Iraq, scarce or rare Arabia though commoner N Yemen. Vagrant Cyprus, Jordan and Egypt.

Habitat: stony hillsides and valleys with scrub, occasionally with taller trees, usually 1,000–2,200 m. On passage also dense scrub (recorded up to 2,800 m). Nests in bush.

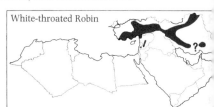

White-throated Robin

Eversmann's Redstart *Phoenicurus erythronotus*   Plate 27

Identification: 15 cm. Sexes differ. Redstart-size. Male distinctive with *rusty-red back, tail*, throat and breast with pale grey crown and hind-neck, *broad black* cheek-patch running back to shoulder and prominent *white longitudinal patch on black wing-coverts*. In autumn and winter, top of head browner and rusty-red feathers on underparts have whitish fringes. Female and first-winter, upperparts brownish-grey, underparts pale greyish grading into whitish-grey belly with slight rufous-buff tinge on throat, upper breast and flanks; wings dark grey-brown with *two narrow whitish wing-bars and clear whitish fringes to tertials, recalling pattern of Spotted Flycatcher* (thus differing from female Redstart and Black Redstart); rump and tail paler rufous than male. Further differs from female Redstart in being less rufous-buff on throat, breast and flanks (rufous-buff on Redstart contrasting with whitish centre of belly) and having creamy underwing-coverts (rufous-buff in Redstart). First-winter male resembles adult male in winter. Does not shiver tail like Redstart, but jerks it up and down. See also Güldenstädt's Redstart.

Voice: alarm-note a croaking 'gre-er'; call a softer, slurred version of alarm.

Status: winter visitor thinly but widely distributed Iran except NW, and rare scatter from central Iraq, along Arabian side of Gulf to Oman. Vagrant Turkey, NW Saudi Arabia.

Habitat: on passage/winter in wetlands, desert oases, juniper woodland, groves and coastal dunes.

Black Redstart *Phoenicurus ochruros*   Plate 27

Identification: 14 cm. See PMH. Three races occurring in region can differ markedly from European birds. The race *ochrurus* (illustrated) from Caucasus and N Iran is the most variable; some males grey below as in European birds; others like *phoenicuroides* (see below) but, usually, *black of breast diffuses into rufous lower belly*; upperparts generally blacker. Male *phoenicuroides* (illustrated) from NE Iran has *reddish-chestnut underparts below sharply demarcated black breast*; distinguished from male Redstart by more extensive black on breast, deeper coloured belly, darker upperparts (though upperparts also rather dark in near-eastern Redstart *samamisicus*), and by pale grey, not white on forehead. For separation in SW Arabia between wintering *phoenicuroides* and Little Rock Thrush see latter species. Male *semirufus* (not illustrated), from Near East, also resembles *phoenicuroides* but upperparts usually blacker than in all other races. Females of the three races variable, but look much like European female Black Redstart, although female *phoenicuroides* can closely resemble female Redstart.

176

tatus: see map. Largely summer visitor to mountain breeding localities. Winters in vicinity but also extends across N Africa and Arabia.
Habitat: mountainous regions, 2,500–5,000 m, in rocks, cliffs and stony slopes. In winter at lower altitudes, down to sea-level, in open rocky stony country, wastelands, dumps, etc, sometimes near scattered trees. Nests in hole or crevice in rock or stone wall.

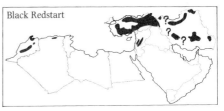

Redstart *Phoenicurus phoenicurus*   Plate 27

Identification: 14 cm. See PMH. In race *samamisicus* (from Turkey eastwards), male has white triangular patch on secondaries (rarely onto primaries) and often darker mantle. Female paler than European female, slightly greyer above and often with pale panel on secondaries.
Status: see map. Summer visitor; also passage throughout region. Some winter E and SW Arabia (not Oman), perhaps Iraq, also Libya.
Habitat: woodlands and parks with old trees, orchards, oak and cedar forest. On passage wherever bushes and trees exist. Nests in hole in tree or stone wall, etc.

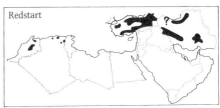

Moussier's Redstart *Phoenicurus moussieri*   Plate 27

Identification: 12 cm. Sexes differ. Behaviour and shape more like Stonechat than Redstart, with shortish tail (quivered like redstart); perches conspicuously in open. Male differs from Redstart and Black Redstart by *bright rufous-orange underparts from chin to belly*, and rump; tail as Redstart; most of *upperparts black* with conspicuous white patch in wing, and *white band across forehead, over eyes and down sides of nape*. Female plump and shorter-tailed than Redstart, noticeably so in flight; orange-buff below, pale buff-grey sides of neck, cheeks and ear-coverts; head slightly paler than grey-brown upperparts; *orange-rufous tail and rump*.
Voice: call 'psew'; also 'wheet' or 'hiip-hiip', sometimes followed by rasping note or short dry rattle, recalling Sardinian Warbler. Song, short scratchy warble, rather Dunnock-like, but not so musical.
Status: see map. Endemic NW Africa. Breeding suspected Libya. Resident or partial migrant with short-range dispersal.
Habitat: dry, bushy, stony or grassy hillsides and mountains up to 3,000 m; also in drier coastal forest and thickets. In winter reaches desert south of its range. Nests typically on ground, occasionally in hole in tree, or low down in dense bush.

Güldenstädt's Redstart *Phoenicurus erythrogaster*   Plate 27

Identification: 18 cm. Sexes differ. The largest redstart. Male has *creamy-white crown and hind-neck*, black throat, upper breast, neck, mantle and wings, latter with *large white patch across flight-feathers* (also on under-wing in flight); rest of plumage deep rusty-red, including tail (central feathers only slightly browner). In winter, white on head and black areas fringed ashy. Large size, extent of white on head and wings, and uniform deep red tail, prevent confusion with Redstart and Black Redstart. Female resembles large female Redstart; upperparts and wings are slightly paler and sandier, underparts greyish with slight fulvous tinge, buffer on flanks, centre of belly slightly paler (female Redstart more rufous-brown on breast

177

and flanks and more buffy-white on centre of belly). Rump and tail less bright than male's, with grey-brown central tail-feathers (in females of other redstarts in region, central tail-feathers are dark brown and contrast more with rufous-brown remaining tail-feathers). Large size, absence of clear whitish wing-bars and tertial-fringes also separate it from female Eversmann's, which see. Often moves its tail while sitting on low shrub. Usually solitary.
Status: vagrant Kuwait (earlier records from Iran now thought to be erroneous). Range Asia.
Habitat: rocky slopes, highland cultivation, also gardens.

Blackstart *Cercomela melanura*   Plate 27

Identification: 15 cm. Sexes alike. Resembles *ash-grey* female Black Redstart, but with broad-looking *black tail* which is *manoeuvred slowly downward and spread*, closed and raised again, *often half-spreading wings slowly at the same time.* Upperparts dull ash-grey, underparts paler greyish, more dirty on sides of breast in some; forehead and ear-coverts sometimes washed brownish; flight-feathers blackish with pale greyish fringes to secondaries and tertials. Juvenile recalls adult but browner. SE Egypt race greyish-brown above, that of SW Arabia considerably darker grey. Fairly long-legged, slender, perching freely on rocks or lower branches of tree. Black tail prevents confusion with any other chat.
Voice: subdued mellow song an often repeated 'chee-yu-chee-yu' or 'cheee-yu-chee', etc. Sometimes sings in flight. Alarm-call short deep 'tzeetch-eetch'.
Status: see map. Resident, but spreads into SW Syria/NE Israel in winter. Vagrant Kuwait.
Habitat: wild, rocky areas in semi-deserts, slopes, ravines and wadis with scattered, often thorny dry bushes; can approach agriculture. Nests in crevice in or under rocks or under large stone.

Red-tailed Chat *Cercomela familiaris*   Plate 27

Identification: 15 cm. Sexes alike. Blackstart-sized *grey-brown* chat *with bright rufous rump and tail,* latter concealed at rest by blackish central feathers; *tips of all tail-feathers blackish, forming clear-cut terminal band.* Upperparts dark grey-brown, wings dark brown, underparts grey-brown, belly, *flanks and ventral region tinged rufous*; rufous wash to ear-coverts. Juvenile mottled blackish below and spotted above with dusky and dull buff. Habits much like Redstart, active, catching insects in air or on ground; frequently flicks tail and wings. Usually tame.
Voice: 3-note scolding alarm 'whee-chuck-chuck'; contact-notes include whistling 'sweep-sweep-sweep' and creaking calls.
Status: vagrant S Yemen. Range Africa.
Habitat: rocky ground and cultivated or lightly wooded areas.

Whinchat *Saxicola rubetra*

Identification: 13 cm. See PMH.
Status: see map. Summer visitor. Widespread on passage through region, but in Arabia uncommon; scarce in winter Oman.
Habitat: wasteland, marshes, open country with few bushes and tall herb vegetation. On passage in cultivated fields and bushy country. Nests in coarse grass, often at foot of small bush, or large plant.

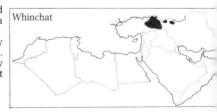

178

Stonechat *Saxicola torquata* — Plate 26

Identification: 12.5 cm. See PMH. Considerable racial variation in region. Birds of NW Africa and W Turkey (partial migrants) similar to European birds. Males of races *variegata* and *armenica* (which migrate through Middle East to winter in NE Africa) have prominent white area on rump, shoulders and sides of neck and, particularly in *variegata* (palest race in the region), much white at base of tail; tail-pattern at times resembles Wheatear. In the small race *maura* (breeding in NE Iran and wintering Iran and Arabia) male has white rump and trace of white at tail-base. First-winter *maura* paler sandy-buff above, lightly streaked darker, underparts pale sandy-orange; it further resembles Whinchat in having buffish-white throat and supercilium, but tail is all-dark and *rump is unstreaked* pale chestnut-buff. Rump may soon become white through wear, which together with *buff on white-edged secondaries* can strongly suggest female Desert Wheatear, but Stonechat has more conical bill than Wheatear, continually flicks and spreads tail when perched, and frequently makes hovering sallies. Male of resident race *felix* of SW Arabia has narrow band of white on uppertail-coverts; white at sides of neck purer and more extensive than in European birds.

Status: see map. Resident and partial migrant; in winter some high ground deserted (e.g. in E Turkey, NW Iran). Passage migrant and winter visitor to W Iran (rare in E), Near East, Arabia (where more evident on passage), also across N Africa especially coastal belt and northern oases.

Habitat: semi-cultivated open regions from sea-level to 3,000 m; also scrub covered slopes. Nests on ground amongst vegetation.

Pied Stonechat *Saxicola caprata* — Plate 26

Identification: 13 cm. Sexes differ. Slimmer and longer-tailed than Stonechat. Male predominantly *glossy black with white on lower belly and undertail-coverts* often not obvious. In flight reveals white rump and wing-patches which usually show as white line on edge of wing when perched. In autumn often has rusty feather-edgings. Female, which superficially resembles female Black Redstart, is more difficult to identify being grey-brown with faint *orange wash to breast* and belly, off-white undertail-coverts, dark brown tail and *orange-buff rump*; brown wings show buff edgings to secondaries and tertials. Plumage paler in autumn due to wide greyish feather margins. Juvenile resembles female but has rusty-buff spots on upperparts and broken buff spotting on breast; juvenile male has small white wing-patch. Perches in less upright position than Stonechat and longer tail less constantly and nervously flicked.

Voice: song a short, rich warble; alarm a curt 'chuk'.

Status: see map. Summer visitor (from India). Vagrant Oman, Iraq.

Habitat: cultivated lowlands and uplands with open fields and scattered bushes; near boggy ground. Nests in holes in walls, etc.

Isabelline Wheatear *Oenanthe isabellina* — Plate 29

Identification: 16 cm. Sexes alike. *Larger, paler, more uniform than female* Wheatear with rounder head, fuller neck and proportionally shorter, broader tail; also more *upright stance, longer legs*, longer bill (often held at slight upward angle), much broader black band to tail (sometimes with hardly any T-shape) and narrower white rump. Sandy wings have broader pale feather-edges, and *pale wing contrasts with isolated black bastard-wing*. In flight, fuller *wings show semi-translucent flight-feathers* (Wheatear looks dark-winged) also wing-beats shallower, more fluttering than those of Wheatear; underwing-coverts whitish (greyish in Wheatear) but difficult to see. General colour buffish sandy-grey above, pale sandy-buff below with breast and flanks often washed beige or pink. Lores blackish but creamy in some (particularly

179

immatures) and supercilium whitish, often broadest above lores (in Wheatear supercilium usually buff above lores, broader and whiter behind). Eye frequently more prominent than Wheatear's. Can run fast and *on alighting frequently wags tail several times* (normally only once or twice in Wheatear). Birds with much black in tail separated from Desert Wheatear by larger size, upright stance, longer legs, white rump and paler flight-feathers.

Voice: characteristic loud 'huit' or 'weet', likened to call of Wigeon. Song longer than Wheatear's, more powerful and variable, frequently imitating other birds.

Status: see map. Summer visitor to breeding areas. Passage and winters S coast Iran (also Seistan), Iraq, Syria, southwards over Arabia (fewer Oman) and Egypt; in Libya almost exclusively passage, which becomes thinner in Tunisia, Algeria; vagrant Morocco.

Habitat: steppes, stony deserts, barren arid plains and plateaux; on passage/winter also in cultivation. Nests in hole in bank or in burrow.

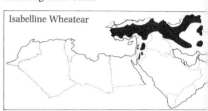

Isabelline Wheatear

Red-breasted Wheatear *Oenanthe bottae*   Plate 29

Identification: 17–18 cm. Sexes alike. Resembles earth-brown Isabelline Wheatear with even more upright stance, slightly longer bill and legs, and pronounced downward tail-wag. Distinguished by *sooty-brown forecrown, which often drops to eye, breaking clear-cut white supercilium and giving distinctive head-pattern*. (Isabelline lacks this distinct head-pattern, having buffish crown, whitish supercilium and dark eye-stripe distinctly shorter behind eye). Upperparts earth-brown, faintly streaked darker on mantle (unmarked in Isabelline); wings dark brown but greater coverts and secondaries fringed warm buffish; white rump-patch narrower than Isabelline's and sometimes tinged buffish. Underparts whitish, *breast and flanks delicate rufous or orange-buff* which sometimes extends onto white sides of neck. Juvenile slightly paler, lightly spotted pale buff above, with dark scaling below, especially on breast; has traces of adult head-pattern. Frequently in pairs. Runs at speed. In low flight tail usually held closed and rounded wings appear semi-translucent.

Voice: song has fluty and hard scratchy notes, often uttered in low flight; alarm-call 'tjeet'.

Status: see map. Resident.

Habitat: high plateaux and open hillsides with or without sparse vegetation, cultivated terraces, usually from 1,600 m upwards. Nests in earth-bank or stone wall.

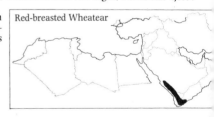

Red-breasted Wheatear

Wheatear *Oenanthe oenanthe*   Plate 28

Identification: 15 cm. See PMH. The race *seebohmi* (highlands of Morocco and Algeria) resembles European race of Wheatear, but underparts generally whiter, and male has *black throat*, cheeks and ear-coverts *sometimes narrowly connecting with black of wings* (recalling male Desert, which has all-black tail and whitish shoulder markings). In autumn, black throat partly or wholly obscured by pale fringes. Female paler, more sandy-bluish above than European females, with usually wider, more pronounced supercilium and, occasionally, slightly dark on sides of throat. Male distinguished from black-throated form of Black-eared by *pale blue-grey upperparts*, no black on shoulders, and by tail-pattern.

Status: see map. NW African population partial migrant or resident; elsewhere summer visitor, occurring widely throughout region on passage but scarce SE and SW Arabia, SE Iran. Occasionally recorded in winter.

Habitat: open highlands, high rocky slopes with bushes. On passage also in cultivation, etc., down to sea-level. Nests in hole in rock or stones.

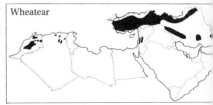

Wheatear

180

Pied Wheatear *Oenanthe pleschanka*   Plate 28

Identification: 15 cm. Sexes differ. Slender, relatively long-tailed wheatear. Male in summer has *jet-black mantle and upper back*, distinguishing it from male Black-eared and Finsch's; *black of throat and sides of neck connects with black of wing in shoulder-area* (is separate in Black-eared); upper head and hind-neck white but crown often tinged grey. Rest of body white with underparts tinged buffish below black bib; *tail-pattern resembles Black-eared's (terminal band of uneven width)*. In flight, *dark flight-feathers above* separate it from Mourning and South Arabian which show white or whitish panel. Easily confused with male Eastern Pied of race *capistrata*, which see. In autumn male has dark grey top of head, buffish-white supercilium and deeper buff underparts; black of mantle almost obscured by buff fringes, black on throat fringed whitish. Female in spring and summer is dull brownish-grey; throat buff-grey but browner on lower throat/upper breast (wearing to almost blackish in some midsummer females); rusty-brown breast-band sometimes confined to sides (female Black-eared warmer brownish or sandy above). Autumn female and immature difficult to separate from similar Black-eared (eastern race) but typically have *colder brownish-grey upperparts with scalloped effect* (typical autumn Black-eared warmer brownish, virtually without pale fringes; if present, ordered erratically, not in rows); throat dark greyish with rusty-brown breast-band which is sometimes confined to sides (Black-eared has warm buff, orange or sandy throat). See also female Eastern Pied (race *capistrata*). Rare male 'vittata' form of Pied (which lacks black on throat) has black mask from bill to ear-coverts connected in some with black on wings. Typically feeds from perch, swooping down, then back again to same or different perch, in shrike-like manner.

Voice: song highly imitative and musical, often with phrases resembling lark or wagtail. Sings on ground and in flight. Call a harsh 'tsak' and dry 'trrrlt'.

Status: see map. May have bred Turkey. Summer visitor, hybridizing extensively with Black-eared Wheatear in Elburz Mts (N Iran). Occurs on passage Egypt, Arabia north to central and E Iran, and in very small numbers to Turkey. Perhaps only vagrant Libya. Winters Yemen, few Gulf States.

Habitat: stony, barren and rocky hill-sides with scattered bushes. On passage/winter also towns, bare fields, wastelands and wadis with trees and bushes. Nests in hole, often in bank.

Pied Wheatear

Cyprus Pied Wheatear *Oenanthe cypriaca*   Plate 28

Identification: 13–14 cm. Sexes almost alike. Rather similar to male Pied but smaller. In summer, male differs slightly in generally warmer buff breast and slightly broader black tail-band. In autumn, crown and to hind-neck blackish-grey with buffish supercilium and *deep rusty-buff underparts, at times almost Redstart-like* (autumn Pied generally less rufous); black mantle and throat partly obscured by buffish-grey fringes. *Female in spring differs from male only by darker, blackish-grey crown and dull blackish-brown mantle*; by mid-summer, some females virtually indistinguishable from males as mantle becomes black, and crown pale grey on otherwise white upper head; in autumn resembles male closely. Juvenile like autumn adult, but broader pale fringes on blackish parts, partly obscuring black throat. Spring females separated from male Pied by combination of blacker crown and hind-neck, more rufous-buff lower breast and smaller size.

Voice: song distinctive, differing considerably from Pied's, recalls cicada, though less harsh, a purring 'bizz-bizz-bizz'; often ending in high-pitched, drawn-out piping note; call a hard 'tsak'.

Status: see map. Summer visitor to Cyprus where endemic breeder; winter range unclear, passage Israel.

Habitat: as Pied Wheatear.

Cyprus Pied Wheatear

181

Black-eared Wheatear *Oenanthe hispanica*　　　Plate 29

Identification: 15 cm. Sexes differ. Males dimorphic, either with *black mask through eye* or with addition of *wholly black throat, but latter never connected to black on wings.* Generally warm buff above or even warm brown (western race), or buffish-white, wearing whiter (eastern *melanoleuca*). Underparts buffish-white. *Tail-pattern resembles Pied Wheatear's, with much black on outermost feather, and terminal band of uneven width.* In autumn, upperparts buffish or rich golden-brown (mainly western race) or buffy grey-brown (eastern race), underparts pale buff, richer on breast. Told from autumn male Pied (which is pale-backed) by absence of blackish mottling in buff- or creamy-brown mantle. If head sunk between shoulders (and buffy-white sides of neck invisible), confusion of black-throated birds possible with male Finsch's (which has larger black 'bib' broadly joined to black of wings and black tail-band of even width; confusion also possible with male Seebohm's race of Wheatear (*O. o. seebohmi*). Typical western female pale sandy-brown above; typical eastern female browner; underparts buffish-white, warmer on breast while throat whitish, but some females of both races can be dark-throated; wings and shoulders dark brown; tail as male but white less extensive. Eastern female very difficult to separate from female Pied, which see for details; from Wheatear in autumn by more contrast between darker wings and shoulder and pale upperparts (more evident in spring), uneven width of terminal tail-band (even width in Wheatear) and by proportionately longer tail; also more slender and agile. See Finsch's Wheatear. Behaviour much like Pied, perching freely on bushes and trees.

Voice: song (frequently in flight) rapid, high-pitched 'schwer-schwee-schwee-oo'; call a hard 'tsak' followed by piping note; alarm-call soft 'krlll'.

Status: see map. Summer visitor, hybridizing with Pied Wheatear in Elburz Mts (Iran). Occurs on passage through almost all of region but uncommon or rare in Arabia especially SE and SW.

Habitat: open or lightly wooded arid country or stony slopes with scattered bushes, dry river banks. On passage also in cultivated areas, wastelands, coastal scrub and semi-deserts. Nests in hole in bank or wall.

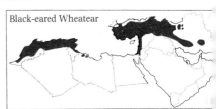

Black-eared Wheatear

Desert Wheatear *Oenanthe deserti*　　　Plate 28

Identification: 14.5 cm. See PMH. Sexes differ. Both sexes separated from other wheatears (except larger Red-rumped male and Isabelline) by having *tail black almost to base.* Male otherwise resembles black-throated form of Black-eared Wheatear but *rump tinged buffish,* wings not so jet-black, and *narrow whitish-buff area* on *scapulars and inner wing-coverts; black of throat also narrowly joined to black of wings.* (Black-eared, which has much white in tail, has white rump, and jet-black scapulars and inner wing-coverts, and black of throat does not connect with black wings, but may look so if head sunk between shoulders). Upperparts sandy greyish-buff, pinkish-isabelline or brownish-buff (depending on race); underparts buffish-white. Autumn male has whitish fringes on black throat, pale buff edges to wings and darker top of head with pale supercilium. Female pale sandy-buff or buffish grey-brown on upperparts, underparts buffish-white (but throat can be blackish). Dark brown flight-feathers edged sandy-buff and rump more buffish than male's. See also Wheatear (*seebohmi* race) and Isabelline. Often perches on low vegetation; rather shy.

Voice: song a brief piping phrase with downward plaintive inflection; occasionally some rattling notes; call a soft whistle.

Status: see map. May breed N Saudi Arabia. Summer visitor to breeding areas in Iran, Iraq, parts of Tunisia, Morocco. Mainly resident elsewhere in NW and N Africa and perhaps Near East. Also winters, and passage, Iran (S coast, Seistan), Iraq, all Arabia, and N Africa. Occasional Cyprus. Vagrant Turkey.

Habitat: bushy desert plains and semi-deserts with vegetation, flat stony ground, barren wastes and dry wadis; in winter also near cultivation. Nests in hole or burrow, in ruins or among rock.

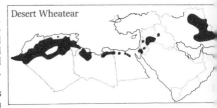

Desert Wheatear

Finsch's Wheatear *Oenanthe finschii* Plate 28

Identification: 15 cm. Sexes differ. Stocky in build, perching in fairly upright position. Male distinguished from all black and white wheatears by *continuous black from throat to wings, all-white or buffish nape and back (no black mantle)*, white rump and creamy-white underparts, tinged buffish in autumn (care needed with Black-eared Wheatear in which black of throat may appear continuous with wings, but when it stretches or turns neck a white gap will be seen). Black on throat also extends further onto breast and neck than in Black-eared and *silvery-grey undersurface of flight-feathers contrasts strongly with black underwing-coverts*, more than in Black-eared or Pied which have darker flight-feathers below. Fairly narrow black tail-band of almost even width (unlike Black-eared and Pied). Female dimorphic, some having blackish or part-blackish throat and ear-coverts (especially Iran, less so Turkey); underparts otherwise buffish white with underwing similar to that of male. Upperparts plain sandy brownish-grey, wings darker brown. Forehead and ear-coverts often tinged rufous; also diffused pale line above eye. Female and juvenile separated from similar Pied by greater contrast between paler mantle and dark wings, and tail-bar of more even width. From Black-eared by less warm plumage tones on upperparts and by pale scapulars, like mantle (in Black-eared scapulars often dark like wings, though less apparent in autumn); also eastern Black-eared quite brownish on upperparts in autumn). Dark-throated females recall female Mourning Wheatear (N African race) but that species has generally less sandy, more grey-brown upperparts, whiter eye-brow and a buffer ventral region. Both may occur in Egypt in winter. More ground-dwelling than Black-eared or Pied, perching less frequently in trees or vegetation. Has habit of frequently cocking tail (especially when landing) then spreading and lowering it slowly; this may aid identification of females.

Voice: song short, rich warble, at times scratchy and with clear whistles; phrases intermittent and include musical 'ctsi-tsi-tseeoo'; has descending zig-zag song-flight. Alarm-note, 'tsak'.

Status: see map. Breeds occasionally in Lebanon. Summer visitor to uplands, descending to lower levels in winter when it also reaches south to N Arabia and Gulf coasts, Egypt and occasionally Cyprus. Vagrant Libya.

Habitat: dry, rocky and stony areas, foothills and rocky valleys and semi-desert regions often with scattered vegetation. Nests in hole or fissure in rock or bank.

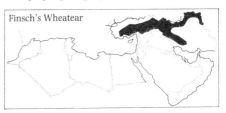

Finsch's Wheatear

Red-rumped Wheatear *Oenanthe moesta* Plate 29

Identification: 17 cm. Sexes differ. Large wheatear, with long legs and quite stout bill (often held uptilted). Male has dull *black throat, sides of face and neck joined to dull black of wings* which have *much white on coverts and fringes of flight-feathers*; in spring and summer, mantle dull black (sometimes with greyish cast), crown and hind-neck white with centre of crown mottled greyish, *rump whitish- or rufous-buff*; autumn male greyish on crown and hind-neck (with whitish supercilium), almost merging with *mealy-looking slate-grey mantle*; darker and richer rufous-buff lower back and rump. *Tail blackish-brown with rufous on base of outer feathers.* Pale-winged in flight, emphasised by silvery flight-feathers below, which contrast with blackish underwing-coverts. Female grey-brown or buffish-grey above, buffish-white below, in some washed rufous-buff on breast; *rump rufous-buff or whitish-cream* (richest in autumn), tail as male but generally with less black and larger area of rufous at sides; noticeable *golden-buff or cinnamon top and sides of head* and *buffish wing-panel*, in otherwise brown wings, separate it from smaller female Red-tailed; immature often has dirty white rump paler than adult's. See also autumn female Hooded. Active, bobbing and flirting wings and tail. Flight buoyant and tail more widely fanned than in many other wheatears.

Voice: musical short song, rather liquid with rusty intonation; when singing, tail frequently cocked and spread between slightly drooped wings.

Status: see map. May breed N Saudi Arabia. Resident. An old breeding record from N Sinai. Vagrant Israel, Turkey.

Habitat: flat saline regions or bush-clad desert-fringes. Nests in rodent-burrow in earth-bank.

Red-rumped Wheatear

183

Red-tailed Wheatear *Oenanthe xanthoprymna* Plate 29

Identification: 15 cm. Smaller and more slender than Red-rumped. Two races occur in region and are considered by some to be separate species. In *xanthoprymna* (E Turkey and parts of Iran) *male has black throat* and *sides of head, narrow whitish supercilium;* upperparts sandy, greyer in spring; *wings blackish-brown, not connecting with black of throat* as in Red-rumped (which has much white in wings). Underparts dirty creamy-white tinged rufous on vent and undertail-coverts. *Rump reddish-chestnut* (separating it from other wheatears, including Red-rumped); sides of tail *white,* sometimes orange-rufous (like Red-rumped) and *tail has much less black* than in Red-rumped, with narrow dark terminal band and central feathers. Underwing-coverts blackish with contrasting pale greyish flight-feathers. Female normally lacks black face and throat, has slightly paler upperparts, pale cinnamon-brown rump and tail-coverts; tail as male. Race *chrysopygia* (Iran, except W. Sexes alike) is *drab, greyish and featureless* with *orange-rufous rump and outer tail-feathers* and typical wheatear T shape tail-end. In spring underparts greyish-white with warm buffish flanks and rufous-buff undertail-coverts. Upperparts dull brownish-grey, ear-coverts warm brown and flight-feathers dark grey-brown. In autumn differs mainly in broadly fringed creamy-buff greater coverts and tertials, generally greyer plumage, slightly richer orange rump and end of tail conspicuously tipped buffy-orange; underwing-coverts whitish, flight-feathers pale greyish giving pale underwing. Intermediates occur as black-throated birds with orange sides of tail, or *chrysopygia*-like birds with white sides of tail. Juveniles of both races resemble adult of *chrysopygia* race. Birds lacking black throat but with orange sides to tail separated from larger female Red-rumped by absence of gingery golden-buff on top and sides of head, lack of buffish panel on flight-feathers and by less black in tail; also in autumn by broad orange tip of tail. Usually solitary; has bounding hops on ground; will perch in bushes. See also Hooded Wheatear (female).

Voice: song a brief rather slow throaty warble 'see, wat-chew, eeper' or short tuneful 'wee, chu, chree'; powerful and clear when echoing out from rocks. Calls include swearing 'steu-steu-steu-steu' and short, dry 'zuk' or 'zvee-tuk' alarm-note.

Status: see map. Summer visitor. Winters S Iran, Oman, UAE, generally uncommon elsewhere throughout Arabia (rarer in SW), Egypt. Scarce passage Iraq. Vagrant Syria, Israel, Libya.

Habitat: stony or barren hillsides with scree, scattered boulders and low scrubby vegetation, in winter also on agriculture, or even in deserts. Nests in hole in bank.

Red-tailed Wheatear

Eastern Pied Wheatear *Oenanthe picata* Plate 28

Identification: 15 cm. Sexes differ. Size and general build close to Pied. Three races occur in region but *picata* (which breeds in Iran) is the one most likely seen. Male resembles Hume's but smaller and lacks gloss, *upperparts, head and breast being dull black* with rest of underparts white, occasionally with buffish undertail-coverts. White runs less far up back between wings than Hume's (which see) and bib different shape; also flight-feathers paler below, contrasting strongly with black underwing-coverts. Female generally like male but brown, not black and bib less extensive; also underparts dull whitish, sometimes tinged rusty; may also show buffish tinge to head and throat. Male of race *opistholeuca* (occurs infrequently E Iran) resembles Black Wheatear in plumage: upperparts *to lower back, and underparts to vent black* with brownish flight-feathers; rump white; tail-pattern similar to Black Wheatear *but slightly more white* up *lower back.* Distinguished from black-crowned types of White-crowned Black by tail-pattern (no black terminal band in White-crowned). Female *opistholeuca* resembles male but is sooty-brown where male black. Male *capistrata* (may occur in E Iran) closely resembles male Pied but *top of head often uniform white* in spring or pale grey or grey-buff in autumn (Pied often has darker crown with whiter hind-neck); usually has less extensive black on outermost tail-feather with terminal band of more even width. Spring males are usually white below black upper breast (tinged buffish in Pied), but autumn males are rusty on lower breast and ventral region (latter usually whitish in autumn Pied). In autumn, whitish fringes on black throat and mantle *much less extensive* than in autumn Pied; also *paler flight-feathers, particularly below,* contrast more *with black coverts*; white rump-patch slightly less extensive than in Pied. Somewhat similar Asian race of Mourning Wheatear shows large whitish panel on wings in flight, less extensive black throat and more white up

Hume's Wheatear

Eastern Pied Wheatear, *picata* (centre), *capistrata* (right)

Pied Wheatear

Mourning Wheatear, *lugens* (left), *melophila* (right)

Finsch's Wheatear   **South Arabian Wheatear**

Drawings by S. Christensen

back between wings. Female *capistrata warm brown above*, buff-brown on throat and upper breast, with rest of underparts buffish-white but some spring females difficult to separate from female Pied, both sharing dull grey-brown upperparts, rufous-brown ear-coverts, almost similar tail-pattern and underwing-contrast (note: female Pied has considerably paler flight-feathers below than male Pied). Generally shy, difficult to approach.
Voice: rather scratchy song, far less pleasant than Hume's.
Status: see map. Summer visitor. Common winter visitor S Iran, including Mekran coast but apparently unrecorded anywhere in Arabia (a population of black and white wheatears breeding in basalt area of N Jordan/S Syria, and formerly thought to be this species, was in 1985 shown to be a form of Mourning Wheatear).
Habitat: barren or open boulder-strewn country with vegetation, steep river-banks; in winter also on cultivation. Nests in hole in rocks or bank.

Eastern Pied Wheatear

185

Mourning Wheatear *Oenanthe lugens* Plate 28

Identification: 13.5 cm. Sexes alike in Near and Middle East, but differ in N Africa. Smallish, stocky, black and white wheatear, resembling male Pied but *black below confined to throat* (extends to upper breast in Pied), white confined to top of head (extends further down onto nape in Pied) and white lower back extends further up between wings; *underparts usually pure white but ventral region pale orange-buff*; (in male Pied, underbody tinged buff while ventral region normally white, except sometimes in autumn); black tail-band of almost even width (unlike Pied). Near and Middle East birds (races *lugens* and *persica*) show *white panel in wing in flight* which distinguishes them from all other wheatears except S Arabian. See also Eastern Pied (*capistrata* race). N African male (race *halophila*) resembles those of Near and Middle East, but has greyish inconspicuous wing-panel. Female differs having pale greyish buff-brown upperparts sometimes with warm brown cheeks; wings dark brown without any obvious pale patch in flight; chin and throat normally blackish (sometimes extending to upper breast) but some have paler throat; remaining underparts buffish-white to white but *ventral region buff to orange-buff*. Though normally separated geographically from Finsch's, care should be taken in N Egypt in winter where black-throated female Finsch's may also occur; Finsch's is paler and greyer above and lacks orange-buff on ventral region. Autumn male Mourning differs from autumn Pied in lacking pronounced whitish fringes on black throat and buff-brown fringes on black mantle; also top of head and hind-neck are usually uniform medium grey (darker top in Pied, with white supercilium). Juvenile lacks black mantle and throat but has black mask through eye to ear-coverts, and blackish-brown wings have pronounced whitish bar on greater coverts and sometimes large white spot on primary-coverts.

Voice: song a vivid twitter; call-note 'check-check' and alarm-note 'pyt-pyt'.

Status: see map. Resident and dispersive NW and N Africa and Near East. Summer visitor Iran. Also winters Egypt and widely but in small numbers Arabia. Occasional passage S Iran. Vagrant Lebanon.

Habitat: broken, desolate rocky wadis and gorges in mountains, barren lava-plains, rocky desert and sandy semi-desert with scant vegetation, dry river beds. Nests in crack or hollow in rock, in a hole or burrow.

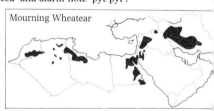
Mourning Wheatear

South Arabian Wheatear *Oenanthe lugentoides* Plate 28

Identification: 13.5 cm. Sexes differ. Resembles Mourning Wheatear (with which often considered conspecific) but slightly more thick-set; black of throat slightly more extensive reaching upper breast and broadly connected at sides of neck with black wings. *Black of upperparts more extensive, with narrower white patch on rump* than in Mourning; also white nape usually less extensive and *crown often distinctly streaked blackish* (not infrequently, however, crown greyish with whiter brow region). Underparts, below black 'bib', white, vent and undertail-coverts orange-buff, often more so than in Mourning. Tail-pattern as Mourning but often with rather more upward extension on outer feathers of the black terminal tail-band. In flight, *white fringes of primaries make smaller patch* than in Asian race of Mourning Wheatears (but still conspicuous; in Mourning, white approaches tips of primaries). Other black and white wheatears lack white patch in spread wing. Female has grey-brown upperparts (bleaching slightly paler) with darker flight-feathers and warm brown or even orangy-buff on ear-coverts (whole head sometimes washed this colour; *underparts off-white or dirty white* with variable *diffuse greyish streaks on breast*, though occasionally absent. Vent and undertail-coverts orange-buff, sometimes conspicuously so. Lacks white in primaries though these appear semi-translucent silvery-grey on base; rump and tail as in male.

Voice: typical wheatear song, with short loud bubbling musical phrases, also a musical 'to too-too'. Calls include 'chuck-a-doo' (like stones knocked together), rasping 'kaak', often repeated and interspersed with high-pitched 'seek'.

Status: see map. Resident. (Widely regarded until recently as a race of Mourning Wheatear).

Habitat: rocky hillsides and mountains with sparse vegetation; sometimes in areas with bushes and trees; also thick juniper scrub; often near cultivation; usually 1,000–2,500 m. Nests in hole in rocks, wall or bank.

South Arabian Wheatear

186

Hooded Wheatear *Oenanthe monacha* Plate 29

Identification: 17 cm. Sexes differ. Large, slim with fairly long tail and long bill; male has black sides of head and neck, chin to centre of breast, mantle and wings; with white crown and nape, lower back to uppertail-coverts and rest of underparts. *Tail white apart from black central feathers and corners of outer feathers, thus lacking black band at tip* which distinguishes it from other wheatears except White-crowned Black (in which underparts are black down to legs, rest white); underwing-coverts black, contrasting with pale greyish flight-feathers. Autumn and juvenile male have feathers fringed whitish on black breast and wing-coverts, broadly fringed greyish on mantle, looking almost grey-backed, and all white parts tinged buffish. Female sandy brownish-grey above merging into creamy-buff rump and tail-coverts; wings dark grey-brown, ear-coverts rusty-brown and underparts whitish-grey washed buffish on sides of breast, flanks and undertail-coverts; tail-pattern as male but black replaced by darkish brown and creamy-buff on distal half. Autumn female and juvenile can be reddish-buff on rump and underparts and almost reddish-brown on sides of tail, but *lack of band at tip of tail prevents confusion* with female Red-rumped and Red-tailed Wheatear. Flight buoyant, almost butterfly-like; recalls Spotted Flycatcher when catching prey, sometimes in long sallies. Tail invariably held closed in flight accentuating length; looks blackish, but characteristic tail-pattern revealed on landing when tail spread.

Voice: typical wheatear song with short melodious phrases, interspersed with some 'stone-clicking' notes; brief throaty thrush-like warble, lasting about 2 seconds, heard infrequently. Female utters a 'whit-whit'; also 'wit-a-wheat-wheet-wheet' or 'whee-whee-whee-wheeoo'.

Status: see map. Resident, probably with some dispersal. Vagrant Cyprus, Iraq, Gulf States.

Habitat: desolate, barren rocky ravines, slopes, gorges and desert-regions, usually without vegetation. Nests in hole in rock.

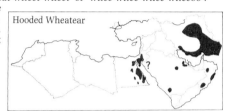

Hooded Wheatear

Hume's Wheatear *Oenanthe alboniger* Plate 29

Identification: 16.5 cm. Sexes alike. Very similar to *picata* race of Eastern Pied and great care should be taken. Hume's, however, is larger, with *noticeably 'bull-headed' appearance*, slightly longer bill and rather *more upright stance*. Black is more glossy and white crisper; black on throat confined to smaller area (and less bib-shaped) than in Eastern Pied, and *white extends further up back between wings, where border to black is rounded* (not square-cut like Eastern Pied). Undertail-coverts white, not buffish as in some Eastern Pied; tail-markings of the two species very similar; underwing-coverts black but grey flight feathers give less contrast than in Eastern Pied. Juvenile like adult but black replaced by matt blackish-brown.

Voice: loud, melodious song, short and not very varied. Call-note sharp, short and high-pitched whistle, uttered 3–4 times. Alarm-note harsh and grating.

Status: see map. Resident. Vagrant Gulf States.

Habitat: boulders at foot of barren hills with scanty vegetation. Nests in hole in rock.

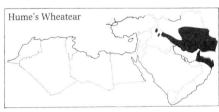

Hume's Wheatear

White-crowned Black Wheatear *Oenanthe leucopyga* Plate 29

Identification: 17 cm. Sexes often differ. Large black wheatear, with white crown, lower back to uppertail-coverts, lowermost belly and undertail-coverts; *tail largely white*, but central feathers black, *lacking black terminal tail-band* which, together with *more extensive white on lower belly* separate it from Black Wheatear. Female often, apparently, lacks white crown. Juvenile male less glossy and with black crown, but before adult male plumage attained every intergradation from fully black to white-crowned birds seen; juveniles of both sexes also have black terminal tail-band, thus closely resembling Black, but latter has much more restricted area of white on belly. Hooded Wheatear has tail-pattern similar to adult White-crowned but, in male Hooded, white on underparts extends to mid-breast and white on top of head more extensive (and no black crown at any age). Black-crowned birds separated from Eastern Pied by tail-pattern, much larger size and longer bill.

Voice: song consists of whistling and tuneful notes, sometimes scratchy, often with imitations of other desert birds; common phrase 'viet-viet-dreeit-deit', slightly descending. Call 'peeh-peeh'.

Status: see map. Resident, with some dispersal. Vagrant Gulf States, Oman, N Yemen, Cyprus.

Habitat: rocky deserts, ravines in rocky mountains, usually without vegetation and often around human settlements. Nests in hole, sometimes in building.

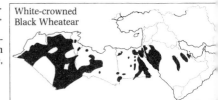

White-crowned
Black Wheatear

Black Wheatear *Oenanthe leucura*   Plate 29

Identification: 17 cm. Sexes almost alike. Large plump and large-headed with *black plumage* (slightly glossed above) and *white confined to rump, vent, undertail-coverts and sides of tail*; the latter has *broad black band at tip, the tail-pattern recalling Wheatear*. The tail-pattern also provides separation from White-crowned Black Wheatear, which even when head is all-black has almost entirely white tail, except for black central feathers, and white on vent extending up lower belly to black thighs. Black Wheatear's folded wings often paler, more brownish, than rest of bird. Female usually dull sooty-brown where male black; juvenile resembles female but is even duller. Relatively slow, almost laboured flight; solitary and usually shy.

Voice: song a brief mellow warble, comparable to Blue Rock Thrush, often introduced with churring note. Call 'chach-chach-chach' and 'pee-pee-pee'.

Status: see map. Resident.

Habitat: rocky edges of deserts, mountain regions and arid stony plateaux, typically at rather high altitudes; also near ruins or deserted houses, locally near coast. Nests in hole among rocks or under stone.

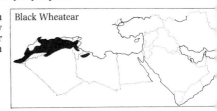

Black Wheatear

Little Rock Thrush *Monticola rufocinerea*   Plate 30

Identification: 15 cm. Sexes similar. Small rock thrush slightly larger than Black Redstart with which it can be confused but *tail shorter and bill longer*. Upperparts, head and *rounded breast-bib smoky-grey* with darker wings, which lack any pale feather edgings, except perhaps in younger birds; in dull light these colours can look sooty and sometimes show a trace of brownish. Rest of underparts chestnut-orange, as is lower back, rump and tail, which *has wheatear-like black terminal 'T' above and black terminal band below*. Bill and legs black. Female very slightly duller than male. Juvenile brown above with narrow white edgings to feathers producing fine white spotting, off-white below with fine shrike-like scalloping, palish panel on secondaries and dull red tail. Quivers tail in redstart-like manner when perched. Adult can be confused at a quick glance with one of eastern races of Black Redstart but Little Rock Thrush stouter with shorter tail, longer bill, and has *characteristic tail pattern*.

Voice: song a series of scratchy notes interspersed with fluty notes of varying (high and low) pitch; can also be short and melodious with fluty whistling 'tryyh-rrr-tvi-rirp-tschak-tshak', not unlike tone of Blue Rock Thrush. Alarm-call 'tyyt'.

188

Status: see map. Resident.
Habitat: highland regions, 1,600–2,500 m, often with steep rocky slopes, cliffs and gorges, always with some trees and bushes; also near agriculture, orchards and banks of wadis. Little information on nesting, but one nest was in cleft of large tree 1.3 m from ground.

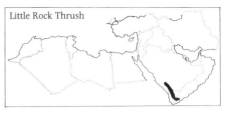

Little Rock Thrush

Rock Thrush *Monticola saxatilis*

Identification: 19 cm. See PMH.
Status: see map. Summer visitor; also on passage all Mediterranean countries, and less commonly Jordan, Iraq, and much of Arabia. Few winter records Algeria, Arabian Gulf coasts, Oman, N Yemen.
Habitat: breeds in open rocky regions, ruins, 1,000–2,600 m.

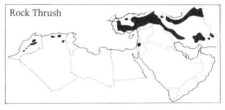

Rock Thrush

Blue Rock Thrush *Monticola solitarius*

Identification: 20 cm. See PMH.
Status: see map. Partial migrant. Summer visitor to mountainous breeding areas in Turkey, Iran; mainly resident Cyprus, Near East, NW Africa. In winter more widespread Morocco, Cyprus, but mainly limited to W in Turkey, and to S in Iran; also winters and on passage, Iraq, most parts Arabia, Egypt, Libya.
Habitat: rocky desert regions and bare mountain sides down to sea-level, on cliff-faces and ruins; in winter also edges of acacia wadis, olive-groves or other cultivation. Nests in crevice or hole in rock, cliff or building.

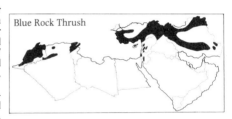

Blue Rock Thrush

Siberian Thrush *Turdus sibirica*

Identification: 23 cm. See PMH.
Status: vagrant Israel.

Yemen Thrush *Turdus menachensis*   Plate 30

Identification: 23 cm. Sexes alike. *Brown thrush* resembling Blackbird in build but shorter wings can give long-tailed appearance. upperparts dark brown with oily slate wash to wings and tail; throat and breast greyish, throat distinctly streaked blackish; more diffuse, less dark, spotting on breast; lower breast, belly and ventral region whitish, the latter with dark grey arrow-shaped markings – like Barred Warbler. In spring, generally less streaked below and underparts can appear quite brownish. *Bright orange to rufous underwing-coverts* seen in flight; at rest, dirty olive-orange flanks usually hidden by folded wing. *Stout bill warm yellow; legs greyish-flesh or fleshy-yellow;* iris chestnut. Juvenile has dark bill. Rather skulking and often difficult to observe, frequently feeds on ground.
Voice: calls Blackbird-like: quiet 'chuk, chuck', and thin, high 'seep' or 'psiii'; also explosive Ring Ousel-like 'chck, chuk' and quiet Fieldfare-like 'chuck chuck chuck'. Song, musical series of soft and high-pitched phrases, eg, fruity 'treep-treep' followed by insipid 'tsik-tsik'.

189

Status: see map. Mainly resident; reported absent from SW Saudi Arabia September–February, but present then in N Yemen.

Habitat: rocky hillsides with trees and bushes, especially acacia, juniper scrub, tree-lined terraces and cultivated wadis, 1,700–3,100 m. Nests in tree.

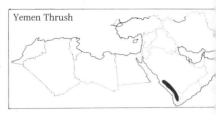

Ring Ouzel *Turdus torquatus*

Identification: 24 cm. See PMH.

Status: see map. Resident Algeria; summer visitor to breeding areas in Turkey and Iran. Winters W Iran, S Turkey, Cyprus, also NW Africa; less commonly Near East. Rare Libya, Egypt, Gulf States and Oman. Not recorded elsewhere in Arabia.

Habitat: mountains with alpine meadows and moorland, also upper limit of open forest, notably juniper. In winter also any area with trees and bushes. Nests in low vegetation or among rocks.

Blackbird *Turdus merula*

Identification: 25 cm. See PMH.

Status: see map. Resident most breeding range. Winter visitors reach same general areas, also Libya, Iraq. Rare or irregular, N Saudi Arabia and Gulf States.

Habitat: woodlands, often deciduous, gardens, thickets, plantations, often near cultivation. Nests in dense bush or tree.

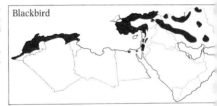

Eye-browed Thrush *Turdus obscurus*

Identification: 19 cm. See PMH.
Status: vagrant Oman.

Dusky (Naumann's) Thrush *Turdus naumanni*

Identification: 23 cm. See PMH.
Status: vagrant Israel, Cyprus, Kuwait.

Black-throated Thrush *Turdus ruficollis* Plate 30

Identification: 23.5 cm. Sexes differ. Rather heavy and at times clumsy thrush about size of Blackbird. Uniform grey-brown upperparts and pale buffish underparts *with throat and upper breast black* or with variable black spotting depending on age and sex. Adult male has *fairly solid black chin, throat and upper breast* (feathers faintly fringed whitish in winter) clearly demarcated from clean pale buff below. Female has whitish throat with few or no dark flecks and narrow band of dense streaks on upper breast. Juvenile and first-winter male have dark spotting on pale throat and upper breast with spotting often forming moustachial streak. At one extreme, markings on upper breast light; at the other, dense, but in *most cases clearly*

190

defined from rest of underparts. Underwing-coverts tinged rufous. Bill dull yellow with dark tip, often held at upward angle; greyish-flesh legs. Rather shy, often occurring in small parties; on being flushed from ground flies to branches of tree where it stands motionless, half-hidden and difficult to see. Flight in open fairly direct, like Song Thrush.

Voice: soft squawk 'chork-chork', sometimes of three notes, resembling quiet Fieldfare, but harsher; also repeated Blackbird-like chacking, quiet 'sip' like Song Thrush, and squeaky harsh 'tscheeik', not so regularly repeated as Fieldfare.

Status: Winter visitor, in Iran widespread except in NW, reaching Gulf and Mekran coasts, but scarce or irregular on Arabian side from Iraq through Kuwait to Oman and central Saudi Arabia. Vagrant Yemen, Israel, Egypt.

Habitat: winters in open country and sheltered areas near cultivation, in trees and neighbouring grassy areas.

Fieldfare *Turdus pilaris*

Identification: 25 cm. See PMH.

Status: winter visitor, moderately common NW Iran, Turkey, Cyprus, Lebanon, becoming scarcer further south to Egypt; irregular NW and Gulf coast of Arabia. Vagrant Morocco, Algeria, Tunisia, Libya.

Habitat: open country, in fields with groups of trees.

Song Thrush *Turdus philomelos*

Identification: 23 cm. See PMH.

Status: see map. Mainly resident in breeding areas. Winter visitor to all Mediterranean countries, also Iran, Iraq, E Saudi Arabia and Gulf States, few Oman; less regular elsewhere in Arabia south to Yemen.

Habitat: woodland, often deciduous, shrubberies, plantations, etc. Nests in bush or tree.

Redwing *Turdus iliacus*

Identification: 21 cm. See PMH.

Status: winter visitor. Regular NW Africa but few Tunisia, and vagrant Libya. Scarce Egypt and Near East, but can be common N Turkey and N Iran. In Arabia very irregular in east, Kuwait to Bahrain; not recorded elsewhere.

Habitat: winters in open country and light woods, cultivation.

Mistle Thrush *Turdus viscivorus*

Identification: 26 cm. See PMH.

Status: see map. Resident and dispersive, winter visitors reaching Cyprus, Syria, Lebanon, Israel, irregularly Libya, Egypt. Vagrant Jordan, Gulf States and N Saudi Arabia.

Habitat: wooded regions. In winter in open country and fields with trees nearby. Nests in tree.

Cetti's Warbler *Cettia cetti*

Identification: 14 cm. See PMH.
Status: see map. Resident, perhaps with some winter immigration in at least Tunisia and Iran and probably elsewhere. Vagrant Egypt, Jordan and Kuwait.
Habitat: low, dense tangled vegetation, bushy thickets, often near swamps, streams, ditches, reed-beds, locally up to 2,000 m. Nest well hidden in low vegetation.

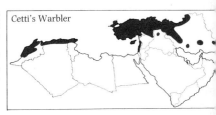

Yemen Warbler *Parisoma buryi*   Plate 32

Identification: 15 cm. Sexes alike. Large *Sylvia*-type warbler, rather attenuated with long rounded tail, short rounded wings, and at times rather tit-like actions. *Upperparts dark sooty grey-brown* (with touch of warm brown in crown), *darkest on lores and region around and behind eye* contrasting with whitish throat which merges into grey-white breast; rest of underparts pale greyish, with *rufous-buff or dull apricot patch between legs* often hard to see. Tail sooty with white fringes to underside of outer feathers. Bill bluish-black with curved culmen; *iris pale bluish-white*; legs dark bluish-grey. Secretive but active, often foraging in centre of thick acacias (especially pollarded) or feeding at ends of branches, *frequently hanging upside down*; tail slightly cocked and fanned most of time. Usually occurs in pairs.
Voice: various sudden harsh or mewing fluty whistles 'piiuu-ptyii-ptii', 'tchak-tsak-tiiv-huit', scolding 'skee' and rolling 'tschee-tchee' followed by whistles of high and low pitch. Song soft, slow but quite melodic, varied and often sustained, warbling (usually from concealed perch).
Status: see map. Resident.
Habitat: mountain hillsides, rock faces with tangled vegetation, acacia wadis and juniper scrub, lightly wooded cultivated valleys, 1,500–2,900 m. Nest undescribed.

Fan-tailed Warbler *Cisticola juncidis*

Identification: 10 cm. See PMH.
Status: see map. Resident with some dispersal, being a rare winter visitor to Libya and Syria and vagrant Kuwait and Oman.
Habitat: wet and dry localities, grainfields, grassy plains, often along streams, marshes. Purse-shaped nest suspended in bush, long grass or corn.

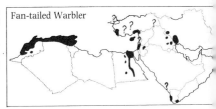

Graceful Warbler *Prinia gracilis*   Plate 31

Identification: 10 cm. Sexes alike. Tiny warbler, with *long, graduated tail, frequently held cocked and slightly fanned.* Upperparts grey-brown, noticeably but narrowly streaked darker on crown, mantle and back; *very indistinct pale supercilium.* Underparts off-white with greyish-buff wash on flanks and *without breast streaking* of most races of Scrub Warbler; *tail blackish above, pale below with black and white tips to graduated feathers.* Short bill appears very slightly decurved; rather long legs pinkish-brown; iris sandy-brown to reddish-brown. Flight weak and jerky; seldom flies far. Though it does skulk, usually tame and active. Very similar in shape and size to Scrub Warbler, from which distinguished by streaked upperparts, unstreaked underparts and indistinct supercilium; nearly always in vegetation and unlike Scrub Warbler rarely seen on ground.
Voice: song a 'rolling', continuous 'trrirrl-trrirrl-trrirrl' or 'tzeee-bit, tzee-bit', the second note lower; calls include trills, often recalling prolonged House Martin's call.
Status: see map. Resident.
Habitat: scrub and low vegetation, in arid regions; cultivated areas, patches of waste-ground in villages and towns. Domed nest in low bush or thick grass.

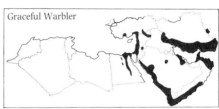
Graceful Warbler

Scrub Warbler *Scotocerca inquieta*   Plate 31

Identification: 10 cm. Sexes alike. Small, similar in general shape to Graceful Warbler but plumper, with *long, constantly manoeuvred, scarcely graduated tail, usually held cocked, white supercilium and finely-streaked breast.* Tail blackish with white tips to underside of outer feathers. *Most frequently seen on the ground.* Plumage tones vary. In the race *inquieta* (NE Egypt, Near East, N Saudi Arabia) upperparts grey-brown virtually unstreaked but with fine black streaking on pale crown; underparts buff-white with warmer grey-brown flanks and fine, dark streaks on throat and breast. The darkest race *buryi* (SW Arabia) smoky brown above with heavier streaking on crown and particularly on breast; underparts greyer with warm brown or dark rufous belly; pale tips to undertail less obvious. Conversely, *saharae* (N Africa) paler and sandier with fainter streaking on crown and breast and pinky-buff wash to flanks of white underparts. Often skulks and then can be very difficult to flush; on other occasions obvious, hopping on ground or through low vegetation with long cocked-up tail often waved from side to side or up and down; rarely flies far. In spring and summer usually seen in family parties.
Voice: song variable, fine, thin 'di-di-di-di-di', descending 'di-di-di-de-de' also dry 'dzit, dzit' followed by warbling 'toodle toodle toodle'. Various calls including short 'drzip', 'dri-dirrirri', and loud rolling, 'tlyip-tlyip-tlyip', which is sometimes fast and descending, also scolding rasping 'prrt'; alarm-note, sharp piping 'pip', often repeated.
Status: see map. Resident. Probably breeds S Syria.
Habitat: rather barren, stony hillsides, semi-deserts and sandy plains with patches of low scrub, up to 2,600 m. Nests in low bush or scrub.

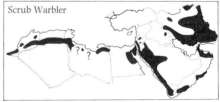
Scrub Warbler

Grasshopper Warbler *Locustella naevia*

Identification: 13 cm. See PMH.
Status: may breed NW Iran. Uncommonly recorded or rare passage migrant in region generally, being especially rare Near East and Arabia. Some winter Morocco and perhaps Algeria.
Habitat: thick moist vegetation, dense bushes, thickets near streams, reed-beds.

River Warbler *Locustella fluviatilis*

Identification: 13 cm. See PMH.
Status: a passage migrant, rarely seen anywhere in the region, with scattered or casual records extending from Turkey, Iran and Arabia to Algeria and Morocco.
Habitat: thick vegetation, dense bushes and swampy thickets.

Savi's Warbler *Locustella luscinioides*

Identification: 14 cm. See PMH.
Status: see map. Summer visitor. Passage migrant Turkey, Iran, Israel, Egypt and NW Africa. Vagrant or rarely recorded passage widely elsewhere in Near East, Arabia and N Africa.
Habitat: swamps, reed-beds, tall grass-fields, grassy bushy wadis.

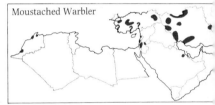

Moustached Warbler *Acrocephalus melanopogon*

Identification: 13 cm. See PMH.
Status: see map. Formerly bred Tunisia. Resident and partly migratory or dispersive; has occasionally been recorded away from breeding areas in winter in most parts of the region except SW Arabia; now wintering regularly in Kuwait.
Habitat: reed-beds and swampy thickets. Nests in reeds or low bushes above shallow water.

Aquatic Warbler *Acrocephalus paludicola*

Identification: 13 cm. See PMH.
Status: passage migrant Morocco and Algeria, rare Tunisia. Vagrant Turkey, Cyprus and Jordan.
Habitat: swampy thickets, marshes, reeds or low vegetation near water.

Sedge Warbler *Acrocephalus schoenobaenus*

Identification: 13 cm. See PMH.
Status: see map. Summer visitor. Passage migrant across N Africa, Turkey, Cyprus, Near East, Iran; uncommon Iraq, most of Arabia.
Habitat: reed-beds with sallows and lush vegetation near water, swampy thickets, crops; may occur in drier habitats on passage. Nests in low, dense vegetation.

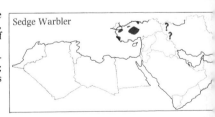

Paddyfield Warbler *Acrocephalus agricola*   Plate 31

Identification: 12 cm. Sexes similar. Very similar to but slightly smaller than Reed, Marsh or Blyth's Reed. Differs in shape from all three in its *shorter bill*, generally *shorter, more rounded wings* (has shorter wings than Reed or Marsh, but some overlap may occur in Blyth's Reed)

194

and rather long, ample tail, which is most apparent on ground or on landing, when often held slightly raised and constantly flicked. Feathers on fairly flat crown sometimes raised. In fresh plumage upperparts vary from greyish-brown with slight olive tinge to light rufous-brown with greyish wash on head, and darker, grey-rufous wings. Rump always rufous. Tail olive with rufous tinge; *prominent whitish-buff supercilium from bill to well behind eye* where most conspicuous; often slight darkening above supercilium at sides of crown. Underparts off-white to sandy-buff with warmer wash to lower flanks and undertail. By autumn, adult wears paler, more greyish-olive-brown with paler rufous-brown rump. Bill brown with flesh-coloured lower mandible but distal part often darker (never so in Blyth's Reed); legs flesh or pale brown and iris pale brown. Worn birds require distinction from some worn Booted Warblers; however, lack of traces of white in sides of tail, bolder supercilium and much longer undertail-coverts (contra short ones in genus Hippolais) should be looked for.

Voice: call 'chik, chik'. Song similar to Marsh Warbler's but softer and more pleasant, lacking harsh notes.

Status: see map. Summer visitor; on passage in SE Iran. Vagrant Oman, E Turkey.

Paddyfield Warbler

Habitat: river, marsh and lakeside vegetation, from large thickets to low scrub and reed-beds; on passage also in gardens and parks. Nests usually in sedges or reeds.

Blyth's Reed Warbler *Acrocephalus dumetorum*   Plate 31

Identification: 12.5 cm. See PMH. Sexes alike. Unstreaked *Acrocephalus* warblers present one of greatest identification problems throughout their range. Blyth's Reed very similar in structure to Reed and Marsh Warbler; also shows similarities to Paddyfield (which see). Differs structurally from Reed and Marsh in having shorter, more rounded, wings and *short primary projections*; bill frequently appears longer and more tapering. Other important features identifying Blyth's Reed are *uniform upperparts with little or no rump contrast* and *no contrasting pale fringes on wing feathers* (Reed has rufous wash to rump, Reed and Marsh have pale fringes to tertials and usually darker alula); *short supercilium which characteristically bulges in front of eye* but can be hard to see, and short dusky eye-stripe. Underparts whitish with greyish-buff suffusion on breast-sides and flanks. Bill dark grey with flesh-coloured bases to lower mandible (Marsh has palish bill). Legs usually grey (paler in Marsh). Can have *active flicking and even fanning tail-movements* (not shown by Marsh and Reed). *Carriage usually horizontal*, with head and bill often inclined upwards and tail cocked to give a *'banana' posture* (not shown by Marsh and Reed). *Call notes* (see voice) *also important for identification.*

Voice: song (often from high perch) musical and very imitative. Differs from Marsh Warbler in slower speed and more hesitant nature, with each phase repeated 5 times or more in Song Thrush-like manner. Many individuals have characteristic high-pitched phrase 'lo-ly-lia'. Frequently utters 'tjeck-tjeck' note between phrases. Contact call is frequently uttered, soft 'thik', or 'chck'.

Status: on passage E Iran (where may breed in NE). Rare migrant Kuwait, Oman. Vagrant Israel, Cyprus, Bahrain.

Habitat: thick moist bushy vegetation, but also hedges bordering agriculture, light woodlands bordering marshes.

Marsh Warbler *Acrocephalus palustris*

Identification: 13 cm. See PMH.

Status: see map. Summer visitor. Passage migrant through Turkey, Cyprus, Egypt, Israel, Arabia; uncommonly recorded elsewhere in Middle East. Vagrant Tunisia, Morocco and Iran away from breeding area.

Marsh Warbler

Habitat: dense low vegetation in ditchs, thickets, stream-banks, etc. On passage in almost any thick cover. Nests in low vegetation.

195

Reed Warbler *Acrocephalus scirpaceus*

Identification: 13 cm. See PMH.
Status: see map. Summer visitor. Passage migrant throughout.
Habitat: reed-beds and water-side vegetation. On passage in almost any thick cover, including gardens and parks. Nests in scattered colonies in reeds.

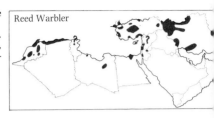

Clamorous Reed Warbler *Acrocephalus stentoreus*   Plate 31

Identification: 18 cm. Sexes alike. Very similar to Great Reed Warbler but slightly smaller and slimmer with *longer bill* and *proportionally longer, more rounded tail*; tail length accentuated by *short wings, with only 4–5 primary-tips showing beyond exposed tertials.* Generally colder grey-brown above than Great Reed, with the *off-white supercilium stretching from bill to just behind eye* and usually less pronounced than in Great Reed. Two races occur in the region, *stentoreus* (resident Palestine and Egypt) averages paler in Egypt than Great Reed, but those from Palestine warm dark brown above, dirty pale brown below (darker than Great Reed), often with yellowish tinge to undertail-coverts. In *brunnescens* (breeds Iran, migrates eastwards) upperparts olive-brown, slightly paler than Great Reed and buff-white underparts are also paler. Bill dark slaty with yellowish-horn basal two-thirds of lower mandible; legs steely-grey or slate-brown (pale brownish in some Great Reeds).
Voice: call a loud 'chack' or 'ptchuk' often continuously repeated, also 'kchrr' and 'kark'. Song, which is probably best aid to identification, similar in tempo to Great Reed but less raucous, more melodious, most phrases being repeated 3 or 4 times, e.g., 'weet-a-weet-a-weet, scratchy, scratchy, scratchy, would-you?, would-you?, would-you?, too-too-too,' etc, *and what appears to be particularly characteristic* 'rod-o-petch-iss', (sometimes only 'petch-iss') final syllable higher, squeakier and slightly emphasised.
Status: see map. Resident and winter visitor Egypt and Near East; summer visitor with some wintering Iran, Iraq, Oman and lower Arabian Gulf. Probably resident SW Arabia.
Habitat: frequents and nests in reeds and water-side vegetation, including mangroves; also cultivated cropland near water, such as bean, sugar cane.

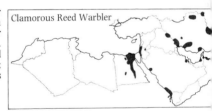

Great Reed Warbler *Acrocephalus arundinaceus*   Plate 31

Identification: 19 cm. See PMH.
Status: see map. May breed Tunisia; has bred Cyprus. Summer visitor. Passage migrant throughout almost all the region.
Habitat: tall reeds bordering open water; on passage also bushy areas, vineyards, crops, sometimes away from water. Nests, colonially, in reeds.

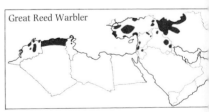

Olivaceous Warbler *Hippolais pallida*   Plate 31

Identification: 12.5 cm. Sexes alike. Very similar in size and shape to Melodious but normally lacks any yellow or greenish colouration. Crown flat (feathers often raised when singing), bill long, wings short extending to just beyond tips of undertail-coverts. Upperparts olive-brown, with slight greyish wash (noticeable in strong sunlight) on head and mantle, and pale, rather indistinct, supercilium; brown wings and tail, latter having inconspicuous whitish margins and barely visible whitish tips on outer feathers; sometimes shows faint pale edgings to secondaries. White throat, and rest of underparts buffish-white, or occasionally with slight, yellow wash. Bill brown with pale flesh or orange lower mandible; legs usually grey. Distinguished from greyish immature (and some adult) Icterines by shorter wings and lack (or virtual lack) of wing-panel. (Melodious Warbler has more rounded crown, usually prominent yellow wing-panel and deep yellow underparts.) An energetic warbler, even when singing; tail frequently flicked both up and down. Comparison with Booted given under that species.

Voice: call a continuous 'chuck-chuck-chuck' or 'ch-ch-ch-ch-ch' frequently merging into a long 'churr'; also single 'chuck' or 'tec'. Song, which appears hurried on first impression (rather like Sedge Warbler), has insistent and characteristic rhythm, with groups of phrases regularly repeated.

Status: see map. Summer visitor. Passage migrant throughout. Recorded rarely in winter in Turkey, Arabia (W and central Gulf), Egypt.

Habitat: scrub, gardens, many areas with trees and bushes, oases; on passage/winter also wadis with acacia and tamarisk. Nests in bush or small tree.

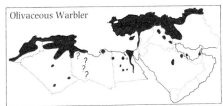

Booted Warbler *Hippolais caligata*   Plate 31

Identification: 11.5 cm. See PMH. Active warbler, slightly smaller and usually shorter winged than Olivaceous, the only *Hippolais* with which it is likely to be confused. *Call important in identification.* Upperparts grey-brown, spring plumage appearing darker than pale olive-brown of Olivaceous, and brown *wings extend to tips of upper tail-coverts*, and *usually lack palish edges to secondaries* shown by that species, (though some Booted can show diffuse panel). Underparts off-white frequently with some darker smudging at sides of breast. Pale buffish and rather indistinct supercilium (at least in spring plumage) from bill to just behind eye, inconspicuously bordered darker above. In fresh plumage, bill, which is usually slightly shorter and less deep than that of Olivaceous, appears all-dark with pale base to lower mandible. *Legs, when seen close, flesh-brown and contrast with very dark feet. Lacks downward flick of tail* characteristic of Olivaceous, and rarely raises feathers of domed crown, as does that species when singing. Moves through undergrowth with upward flick of tail and wings. Small Olivaceous with short wings and bill can be difficult or even impossible to distinguish from Booted in the field.

Voice: song longer and more hurried than that of Olivaceous but with little or no repetition of phrases so characteristic of that species. Sometimes has the quality of Marsh Warbler, but quieter and lacks mimicry. Call a constant 'tick-tick-tick-tick' or 'chek, chek, chek' recalling Lesser Whitethroat, but softer and weaker; also cicada-like 'skee, skee, skee'.

Status: see map. Summer visitor. Passage E Arabian Gulf, increasingly irregular to head of Gulf; vagrant W to Israel, W Arabia.

Habitat: bushes, cultivated land with trees and cover; on passage in any bushy country, wadis, gardens, parks. Nests in tamarisk and other bushes.

197

Upcher's Warbler *Hippolais languida*   Plate 31

Identification: 14 cm. Sexes alike. Resembles Olivaceous, but larger, with *rounder head*, steeper forehead and crown often peaking just before eye; carriage may recall a *Sylvia*. Most distinctive feature is *longish, frequently manoeuvred sooty-brown tail* (much darker than rest of plumage), usually showing *conspicuous white tips and outer webs of outer tail-feathers*, unless very worn. Remaining upperparts brownish-grey, washed-out on mantle and head with faint white supercilium (generally weaker than in other *Hippolais*) and eye-ring; wings with pale panel except in very worn birds. Underparts greyish-white with darker suffusion on flanks. Pale flesh-horn or yellow bill fairly long and deep. Legs light flesh-brown or grey. Juvenile buffer above than adult with distinct pale wing-panel. Rather sluggish but not skulking. *Tail loosely and repeatedly waved up and down, and in circular movement from side to side*, as if on unco-ordinated hinge, especially noticeable after alighting or during breaks in movement through vegetation; also has typical *Hippolais* downward tail-flicking; often forages on ground.
Voice: song similar in rhythm to Olivaceous but more musical, with fluty and mellow notes often introduced by long series of stuttering notes; Call 'tack', much less forceful than Olivaceous.
Status: see map. Summer visitor. Passage migrant throughout Near East and Arabia south of breeding range, generally scarce.
Habitat: scrub from plains to mountain valleys, up to 2,000 m; also in gardens and more wooded areas; on passage also wadis with acacia and tamarisk. Nests in bush.

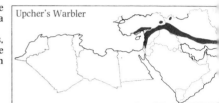
Upcher's Warbler

Olive-tree Warbler *Hippolais olivetorum*   Plate 31

Identification: 15 cm. See PMH. Sexes alike. Large brownish-grey *Hippolais* warbler with *prominent wing-panel and large yellowish-looking bill* (as long as some Great Reed Warblers); longish wings and square-ended tail. Shape of head recalls that of Icterine Warbler; crown feathers often raised. Upperparts brownish-grey, head, cheeks and ear-coverts often a little darker, wings dark brownish-grey with distinct whitish edgings to secondaries forming extensive streaked panel. Tail dark with whitish edging to outermost tail feather and tips of outer pair. Pale supercilium to behind eye. Underparts buffish-white with off-white throat which contrasts with head colour. Bill pale yellowish-flesh with darker tip; legs bluish-grey. Flight (somewhat reminiscent of shrike or Barred Warbler) strong, with glide up to perch. Differs from all other *Hippolais* in larger size, greyish plumage with pale wing-panel, and very long, dagger-like bill. Confusion more likely with young Barred Warbler, but latter has rather short bill, dark feather-edgings to undertail-coverts, uppertail-coverts tipped whitish, and longer, rounded tail.
Voice: song similar in rhythm to Olivaceous but slower, louder, lower-pitched, less scratchy and less regular phrases. At times rather like Great Reed Warbler. Call, loud 'tuc, tuc'.
Status: see map. Status uncertain Syria and Lebanon but might breed. Summer visitor. Passage Israel (where may breed in north), elsewhere recorded occasionally in Cyprus, Egypt, rarely Arabia.
Habitat: patches of scrub, olive-groves, oak-woods, usually on edge of cultivation; on passage also acacia wadis. Nests in tree or tall bush.

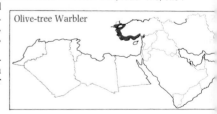
Olive-tree Warbler

Icterine Warbler *Hippolais icterina*

Plate 31

Identification: 13 cm. See PMH and Melodious Warbler text (below).

Status: see map. May occasionally breed NW Turkey. Summer visitor. Passage migrant mainly through central N Africa, west to Algeria though commoner in Libya (spring); scarce Turkey and W Iran, rare in Near East and Arabia. Vagrant Morocco.

Habitat: gardens, parks, wood thickets etc. On passage where trees and bushes exist. Nests in scrub, hedge or low in tree.

Icterine Warbler

Melodious Warbler *Hippolais polyglotta*

Plate 31

Identification: 13 cm. See PMH. Sexes alike. Typical *Hippolais* (longish, broad-based yellowish bill, short undertail-coverts and square-ended tail) resembling Icterine Warbler *but less elongated* with *short wings and short primary-projection*, latter being half as long as distance from wing-tip to tip of tail (Icterine has longer wings and primary-projection, latter about same length as exposed tertials; primary-projection covers uppertail-coverts and is about as long as distance from wing-tip to tip of tail). In Melodious, *head more rounded* with steeper forehead and, when singing, crown peaking above or just before eye (Icterine has flatter forehead with crown peaking behind eye). In adult, upperparts greyish greenish-brown, generally like Icterine, but brighter, less greyish; entire underparts warm yellow, with breast warmest coloured (but underparts can sometimes be pale lemon-yellow like Icterine or, more rarely, pale creamy-buff or dirty-white in both species). Melodious *lacks distinct uniform whitish-yellow panel on secondaries* of Icterine; some Melodious in spring may show narrowly pale-edged secondaries, but these rarely form solid panel so conspicuous in spring Icterine; in autumn, Melodious lacks any panel, as often does abraded adult Icterine. Short, ill-defined yellowish supercilium, mostly in front of eye and thin whitish eye-ring, but *no dark loral or eye-streak in either species*. Tail of both species has *no clean white on outer feathers* (though pale edges seen from below in Melodious); legs brownish-grey not lead- or bluish-grey of Icterine (but often hard to see). First autumn juvenile lacks pale wing-panel (has only narrow brownish-yellow edges on tertials) while similar Icterine has clear buffish-yellow wing-panel. Underparts often pale creamy-white (rarely in Icterine). Melodious without yellow underparts (and with greenish tinge on upperparts suppressed) separated from Olivaceous (which has similar primary-projection) by *shorter bill, steeper forehead* (rather flattish in Olivaceous) and by *absence of white edges of outer tail feathers*. Similarly washed-out Icterine separated from Upcher's (which also has fairly long primary-projection) *by absence of white sides and tips of outer tail-feathers* and lack of distinctive tail-movements.

Voice: song superficially resembles Icterine's, but faster and with individual notes less clear and more predictable, though often imitates other species, particularly at start of song. Lacks Icterine's characteristic 'gliee', sliding violin-like notes. Sometimes makes short song-flight. Call, a harsh rattling, not unlike sparrow's 'trrrr' (quite unlike Icterine's 'di-de-ro-id'); also 'tchret-tret'; call-notes sometimes inserted in song.

Status: see map. Summer visitor. Occurs on passage in NW Africa; vagrant Libya.

Habitat: woods, thickets and dense vegetation often near water. Nests in bush, rarely tree.

Melodious Warbler

Marmora's Warbler *Sylvia sarda*

Identification: 12 cm. See PMH.

Status: possibly a rare resident in Tunisia with some autumn dispersal; but mainly immigrant from Europe in winter when it also occurs in Algeria and Libya. Vagrant Egypt, Morocco.

Habitat: thick cover, macchis and other scrub in open country.

Dartford Warbler *Sylvia undata*

Identification: 13 cm. See PMH.
Status: see map. Resident with some south-ward dispersal in winter; may breed Tunisia, where winter visitor. Vagrant Libya.
Habitat: hillsides with low cover, often dense, frequently with scattered low pines and oaks. In winter also semi-desert with low dense vegetation. Nests in scrub near ground.

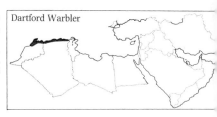

Tristram's Warbler *Sylvia deserticola*   Plate 32

Identification: 12 cm. Sexes rather similar. Size and shape resemble Dartford Warbler, with features of that species and Spectacled Warbler. Upperparts of male deep blue-grey, with *chestnut wings* and long, dark brown tail with white outer feathers. *Underparts deep vinous-pink*, with off-white belly and undertail-coverts. *Vinous extends onto throat and is separated from dark grey ear-coverts by ill-defined whitish moustachial streak, though much less con-spicuous than in Subalpine. Noticeable white eye-ring;* flesh-brown to straw legs. Adults in fresh plumage in winter are paler above and dull whitish below. Male Spectacled has similar chestnut wing but less blue upperparts, white throat (like Whitethroat) and pale underparts, although with pinker wash than Whitethroat. Male Dartford Warbler darker, and lacks chestnut wings and white eye-ring. Very active, moving through scrub with tail constantly cocked.
Voice: call, sharp 'chit' or 'chit-it', quite unlike Dartford's deep note; weak sparrow-like 'chip' or 'chirrup'.
Status: see map. Partial resident, dispersing in winter southwards to northern Sahara, including Libya.
Habitat: valleys or open scrub in hilly country, often with variety of trees, eg, juniper and evergeen oak, mostly above 1,000 m. In winter also semi-deserts with low scrub south of breeding range. Nests in bush.

Spectacled Warbler *Sylvia conspicillata*

Identification: 13 cm. See PMH.
Status: see map. Resident or partial migrant. In winter found also in Libya where may breed in west. Recorded rarely in Lebanon and Jordan. Vagrant Turkey, Iraq.
Habitat: chiefly in *Salicornia* on coastal flats often near lagoons, salty plains and semi-deserts with low scrub. Nests in low bush.

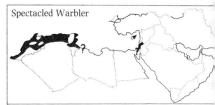

Subalpine Warbler *Sylvia cantillans*

Identification: 12 cm. See PMH.
Status: see map. Summer visitor. A common spring migrant throughout N Africa, fewer Cyprus and W Turkey, and uncommon in Near East and W Saudi Arabia. In autumn seen from Libya westward, rarely further east. Vagrant N Yemen.
Habitat: scrub and thickets; also open woodland. On passage also wadis with acacia or dense scrub. Nests in thick bush.

200

Ménétries' Warbler *Sylvia mystacea* Plate 32

Identification: 12.5 cm. Sexes differ. An active scrub warbler with dark head (in male) and rather long blackish *tail constantly waved* from side to side and up and down as if on an unco-ordinated hinge. Male has grey crown with darker lores and ear-coverts, but less dark nape; upperparts brownish-grey to slaty, with sandy fringes to wing-feathers and often prominent black bastard wing. Tail black with white outer feathers and adjacent pairs tipped white – a feature visible from below when tail is waved or when spread on landing. *White moustachial area contrasts with dark cheeks and with rest of underparts which are suffused with salmon-buff* to deep vinous though in abraded plumage (mid-summer) entire underparts appear rather whitish. Female resembles small, pale, washed-out Whitethroat: upperparts, including crown and ear-coverts, sandy-grey with black bastard wing; underparts silky off-white faintly suffused buff on flanks. Young and fresh-plumaged birds in autumn are similar to females but often have faint salmon wash on underparts. Eye brown to dull deep red in male, mud-coloured in female, both with *narrow straw-coloured eye-ring, though varying from whitish to pale orange*; legs vary from dark brown to pinkish-straw (the latter usual). Females and young birds confusable with females and young of Sardinian and Subalpine Warbler; active tail-movements of Menetries' an important feature for separation. Also, Subalpine has paler tail (quite dark in Menetries') and warmer buff sides of throat and breast; adult female often with centre of throat and breast tinged pinkish to orange-buff, with white moustachial streaks. Compared to Sardinian, Menetries' has slightly shorter tail (longer, more rounded in Sardinian), shorter bill, and is paler above and whiter below, Sardinian having brownish wash on breast and flanks. Active, seeks out low scrub and herbs, often on ground with tail slightly raised and nearly always waved.

Voice: calls considerably softer and less rattling than those of Sardinian. Most frequent a low, harsh, buzzing 'chrrr' or 'cheee', sometimes quite long. Other calls include a short chatter 'chik-chik-chik-chik-chik' or 'cha-cha-cha-cha-cha' with notes merging, or with each note separated. Song rather quiet and quick in tempo with Whitethroat-like quality, a mixture of melodious and soft grating notes, not unlike Tree Sparrow.

Status: see map. Mainly summer visitor. Winters Iran, sometimes Egypt and widely in Arabia, always in small numbers; occasional Oman. Passage migrant Arabian Gulf area, scarcer rest of Arabia, irregular Egypt, rare Lebanon and vagrant Israel, Jordan.

Habitat: scrub and small thickets, gardens, patches of cover along rivers, often in broken country. Nests in thick bush.

Sardinian Warbler *Sylvia melanocephala*

Identification: 13 cm. See PMH.

Status: see map. Resident or partial migrant. Passage noted in Turkey, Cyprus and Near East, rarely elsewhere. Recorded as a winter visitor in Libya, Egypt, Cyprus, the Near East. Vagrant W Arabia.

Habitat: dry, fairly open bushy scrub, thickets, pine and evergreen oak forest, etc. In winter wherever scrub exists, including acacia-wadis and desert edges, oases. Nests in low bush or undergrowth.

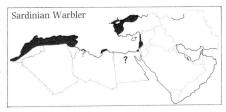

Cyprus Warbler *Sylvia melanothorax* Plate 32

Identification: 13 cm. Sexes differ. Similar size and structure to Sardinian (see PMH), though tail less rounded. Male unmistakable, having *white underparts heavily blotched with crescent-shaped blackish bars*, or occasionally pipit-like streaking, densest on lower breast. In autumn/early winter, throat white but by following spring, when feather-tips worn, becomes finely barred or almost uniform black, with contrasting white moustachial stripes. Similar to Sardinian above, with black head, dark grey upperparts but pale panel in wing (like Rüppell's but absent in Sardinian), and longish black tail with white edge to outers. Warm straw-coloured legs; dull chestnut iris with red orbital-ring and white outer orbital-ring. Female like female Sardinian, though more uniform above and usually dark crescent markings on throat and breast, and faint whitish moustachial stripe. Eye as male, but outer orbital-ring narrower and less white; pale reddish-brown legs. Juvenile like juvenile Sardianian or Rüppell's, being plain sooty or dirty brownish-grey above, dirty greyish-white below with whiter throat; lacks pale edgings to tertials until into first winter plumage. It then invariably shows a few black feathers on underparts, and mottling on undertail-coverts; in males, black starts to appear on head and white eye-ring starts to show.

Voice: call hard, harsh, stuttering 'tscha-tscha-tscha', etc (like Sardinian), also bunting-like 'pwit' and Wren-like rattling. Weak song, resembling that of Sardinian, a low warbling mixed with call notes.

Status: see map. Resident and partial migrant. Passage and winter visitor Israel, uncommon Lebanon, and vagrant Turkey, Egypt and NW Saudi Arabia.

Habitat: well-vegetated rocky slopes and foothills, dense scrub country. In winter also acacia wadis. Nests in low bush.

Cyprus Warbler

Rüppell's Warbler *Sylvia rueppelli*

Identification: 14 cm. See PMH.

Status: see map. Summer visitor. Passage migrant Cyprus, Near East, NW Saudi Arabia, Egypt and Libya (noted mainly in spring). Vagrant Algeria, Iran.

Habitat: low scrub with bushes and often rocky outcrops; on passage also acacia wadis. Nests in bush.

Rüppell's Warbler

Desert Warbler *Sylvia nana*   Plate 32

Identification: 11.5 cm. Sexes alike. Small, rather featureless, *pale greyish-sandy to golden-buff* with tail, bill and eye colour the most useful field-marks. Two races occur in region; *nana* (Asia), pale greyish-sandy upperparts; *deserti* (N Africa), pale golden-buff above. Both have brown wings with pale edgings to secondaries and blackish-centred tertials which may have a warm pale rufous-brown wash. Rump, uppertail-coverts and *tail bright rufous with white outer feathers and tips to penultimate pair*; colour only obvious when spread or in flight, when fairly contrasting darker (brownish) central tail-feathers and diffuse terminal band can be seen. Underparts creamy-white but may fade to greyish-white. Bill fine, *yellow with dark tip; iris pale yellow* and, at close range, palish area around eye may be discernible. Legs very pale straw-yellow. Generally skulking; creeps and hops on ground usually close to bushes, often with tail half-cocked and 'waved' from side to side; flies low and 'disappears' into even the smallest bush; but often will allow close approach.

Voice: dry, weak purring 'drrrrrrr' with stress on 'd' descending and fading out; also 'chrr-rrrr' and rapid high-pitch 'chee-chee-chee-chee'. Song which may be uttered in Whitethroat-type song-flight starts with purring call, followed by short, clear, very melodious lark-like trill.

Status: see map. Resident (Morocco and Algeria) and migratory (N Iran). Perhaps irregular Libya, rare in Tunisia but may breed in both countries. Passage and winter S Iran, and Arabia including Oman and Yemen, scarce Israel. Rare migrant Egypt and Jordan, and vagrant Cyprus.

Habitat: open desert and arid hillsides with low vegetation and scattered bushes. On passage/winter also flat semi-desert with low saline bushes. Nests in small bush.

Desert Warbler

Arabian Warbler *Sylvia leucomelaena*   Plate 32

Identification: 14.5 cm. Sexes alike. Large warbler, similar in size to Orphean but with comparatively longer, *graduated tail* (almost square-ended on Orphean), and shorter bill. Sooty-black to sooty-brown crown, ear-coverts and nape, and grey-brown upperparts (usually grey in birds occurring in Israel); off-white fringes to secondaries and tertials sometimes not obvious. Tail black *with very inconspicuous white fringes to outer webs of outer feathers* (when only slightly worn, not seen) and white tips to underside of outer three pairs, which can be noticeable when tail is spread on alighting. Underparts off-white with pure white chin and throat (and sometimes breast). Bill black, legs dark brownish or greyish, eye dark, sometimes with inconspicuous pale eye-ring. Juvenile greyer than adult on upperparts. Rather heavy and Orphean Warbler-like in movements; *tail constantly flopped downwards, in circular movement,* and occasionally upwards. Feeds amongst foliage of trees and on ground, occasionally hanging upside down, rather clumsily. Most closely resembles Orphean both in structure and plumage, but most important differences are graduated tail, inconspicuous white fringes to outer webs of outer tail-feathers (much white on whole length of outer tail-feathers in Orphean, above and below) and white spots on tips of outer undertail-feathers. Both species give typical Sylvia tail-flick but Arabian can manoeuvre its tail with more versatility, almost like Upcher's. Furthermore, Arabian tends to adopt a more upright stance. Finally, in Arabian Warbler, iris dark and there may be whitish eye-ring, but in Orphean, iris can be whitish in western races, dark in eastern races, but it never shows an eye-ring; however, care is necessary to distinguish iris from eye-ring.
Voice: song variable but usually a rather slow warbling, with short phrases interspersed with pauses and some scratchy notes. At times reminiscent of several species including Blackbird, Barred Warbler, Blackcap and Garden Warbler. Some phrases broken by drawn-out babbler-like 'pift'. Calls include 'tscha-tscha-tscha' and short churring rattle 'chir-rr-rr-rr-rr'.
Status: see map. Resident. Vagrant Sinai.
Habitat: thorn bushes and particularly acacias in semi-desert and in wadis and, in SW Arabia, rocky hills usually up to 1,500 m. Nests in tree, usually acacia.

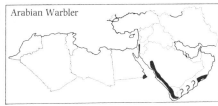

Orphean Warbler *Sylvia hortensis*

Identification: 15 cm. See PMH.
Status: see map. Summer visitor; passage migrant almost throughout, though scarce in E Arabia, rare Jordan, few winter records Iran, UAE. Oman.
Habitat: chiefly arboreal, bushy hillsides, deciduous thickets, orchards, parkland, olive-groves. On passage also acacia. Nests in bush or low tree.

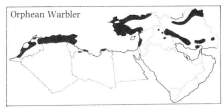

Barred Warbler *Sylvia nisoria*

Identification: 15 cm. See PMH.
Status: see map. Summer visitor. Passage most parts of SW Asia but rarer E Arabia, Syria, Egypt.
Habitat: thorny thickets and hedges, wood clearings. Nests in bush.

203

Lesser Whitethroat *Sylvia curruca curruca*   Plate 32

Identification: 13.5 cm. See PMH. In addition to European birds *S. c. curruca*, two subspecies (considered by some to be full species) occur in region which may be identified in field: *S. c. minula* (Desert Lesser Whitethroat) and *S. c. althaea* (Hume's Lesser Whitethroat). They are treated below.

Status: see map. Summer visitor. A passage migrant from Libya eastwards throughout, sometimes abundant in spring in the Near East and Egypt. In winter scarce, scattered in E and SW Arabia, Egypt, rarely Near East. Vagrant Tunisia, Algeria and Morocco.

Habitat: trees and dense bushes. Nests in bush or tangled vegetation.

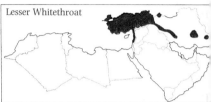

Hume's Lesser Whitethroat *Sylvia curruca althaea*   Plate 32

Identification: 14 cm. Fractionally larger than European birds with stouter bill and darker plumage; more closely resembling European bird than *minula*. Very dark grey crown merges into dull earth-brown back, with slaty and at times bluish wash; near-black ear-coverts. Wing panel formed by lighter feather edgings as in some European birds (but absent in *minula*). Underparts show dirty wash on sides of breast, and throat white.

Voice: subdued hard 'tek, tek' very similar to call of *curruca*; also melodious 'wheet-wheet-wheet' (sometimes preludes song) and *Sylvia*-like 'churr'. Song, pleasant Blackcap-like warble, lacking rattle of *curruca*.

Status: see map. Summer visitor, with some wintering in S Iran and perhaps reaching Iraq. Has been observed in E Arabia. Vagrant Israel.

Habitat: sub-alpine scrub and juniper forest, 2,500 m. On passage/winter in trees and scrub at lower altitudes. Nests in low bush.

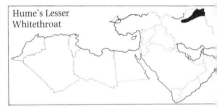

Desert Lesser Whitethroat *Sylvia curruca minula*   Plate 32

Identification: 13 cm. Fractionally smaller than European birds with smaller bill, shorter tail and paler plumage. Upperparts washed-out grey-buff or sandy-brown with buffish-grey crown and darker ear-coverts; underparts clean sandy-white with white throat. European birds darker and greyer, and often show pale chestnut edgings to wing-feathers. *minula* more active, frequently flicking tail; particularly favours acacias and has characteristic call (see Voice).

Voice: variety of churring calls which resemble, at least in part, calls of Sardinian Warbler, Blue Tit and Willow Tit, 'ch chrrr chrr ch', 'ch ch chrr', 'chrrr', or 'ch ch ch ch'; some calls are fast and buzzing, others slower. Quiet pleasant song comprises varied warbling notes.

Status: winter visitor, or passage migrant, occuring often commonly in most parts of Arabia including the south, also S Iran. Vagrant Israel.

Habitat: trees, especially acacia in savanna, semi-deserts and rocky hillsides.

Whitethroat *Sylvia communis*

Identification: 14 cm. See PMH.

Status: see map. May breed Tunisia. Summer visitor. Migrant throughout the region. Has been recorded in Arabian Gulf, Oman, in winter.

Habitat: fairly open country with scrub and patches of dense vegetation. Nests in low cover.

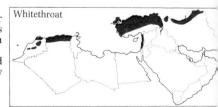

204

Garden Warbler *Sylvia borin*

Identification: 14 cm. See PMH.
Status: see map. Summer visitor. Also passage migrant throughout much of the region though scarce in most of Arabia. Vagrant Yemen.
Habitat: woods with abundant undergrowth, thickets; on passage anywhere with bushes or trees. Nests in low bush or brambles.

Blackcap *Sylvia atricapilla*

Identification: 14 cm. See PMH.
Status: see map. Resident and partial migrant in N Africa. Summer visitor to breeding areas in Turkey and N Iran. Common on passage most areas but scarce Tunisia and Arabia (although frequent N Yemen). Small numbers winter throughout Mediterranean region and occasionally east to Iran, but in Arabia apparently only in Yemen.
Habitat: woodland with undergrowth, old gardens, parks. On passage almost wherever thickets and trees exist, or in cultivation. Nests in bush.

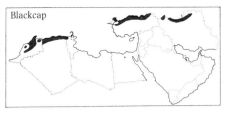

Brown Woodland Warbler *Phylloscopus umbrovirens*   Plate 32

Identification: 11 cm. Sexes alike. Can be told from other *Phylloscopus* by combination of small size, *brownish colouration with tawny wash on flanks* and *yellowish-green fringes to flight- and tail-feathers*. Slightly smaller and dumpier than Chiffchaff with brown (or olive-grey-brown) upperparts and obvious yellowish-green edgings to primaries, secondaries and outer webs of tail-feathers. Underparts buff-grey to off-white (and often rather greyish on sides of throat and breast) with whiter throat; quite noticeable tawny-buff wash on flanks and ventral region. Supercilium buffish, rather indistinct but more noticeable behind eye. Dark horn bill with pale flesh or orange-yellow lower mandible; dull blue-grey legs. Very active and frequently in pairs.
Voice: song loud and explosive, including trilling series of Coal Tit and Marsh Tit-type notes of variable speed and pitch, often with rising inflexion on last note: 'titititititi-wit', slower 'vuit, vuit, vuit, wit-wit-wit-wit tu-vi, tu-vi, tuvi-twit'; song may end with Willow Warbler-like descending 'diu-diu-diu, diu', but as a fast trill. Call, descending metallic long 'dzziieep'; also low 'psew' and 'swee-vik' alarm notes.
Status: see map. Resident.
Habitat: hillsides and wadis with trees and bushes, junipers, lush gorges, 1,600–2,600 m. Domed nest built near ground.

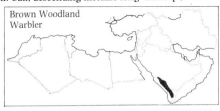

Green Warbler *Phylloscopus nitidus* Plate 32

Identification: 11 cm. Very similar to Greenish, and unless good view obtained or song or call heard, differentiation may be impossible, especially when green and yellow colouration of Green Warbler modified by light conditions. Upperparts olive-green (less yellow-green than Wood Warbler), but in dull light can appear grey-brown, even in fresh plumage; Turkish birds seem particularly dull. Underparts suffused with yellow, but sometimes discernible in the field only on chin and throat (in some may disappear in autumn). Narrow yellowish-white wing-bar on tips of greater coverts (frequently with suggestion of a second wing-bar on median coverts in fresh plumage), very similar to Greenish, as is narrow, prominent, pale yellowish supercilium of fairly even width, though in Greenish often uptilted behind eye. Tips of outer two tail-feathers off-white, though may be difficult to see in field. Dark greyish-brown legs. Confusion also possible with Yellow-browed Warbler of race *humei* (which see).

Voice: contact call and alarm, loud 'tss-eurp' or 'chirr-irip', almost like quieter version of White Wagtail call; also cheerful 'chi-wee'. Loud song of about 10 notes, in two parts, first 5 notes like those of slurred Cetti's Warbler flowing into second 4 or 5 notes, more Coal Tit-like. Usually stationary when singing (Greenish changes perch frequently).

Status: see map. Summer visitor; also passage in Iran, scarce Oman. Vagrant Lebanon, Bahrain.

Habitat: mixed coniferous and deciduous woods, usually with scrub layer on mountain slopes 1,500–2,000 m. Nests on ground.

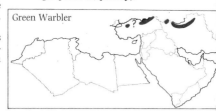

Green Warbler

Greenish Warbler *Phylloscopus trochiloides* Plate 32

Identification: 11 cm. See PMH.
Status: vagrant or rare passage Iran, doubtfully Turkey, reported Israel.
Habitat: on passage in bushes and trees.

Arctic Warbler *Phylloscopus borealis* Plate 32

Identification: 12 cm. See PMH.
Status: vagrant E Saudi Arabia, Oman.
Habitat: on passage in bushes and trees.

Yellow-browed Warbler *Phylloscopus inornatus* Plate 32

Identification: 10 cm. See PMH, which does not however cover duller, greyer race *humei* (breeding central Asia south to NW Himalayas) which probably constitutes majority of birds occurring in the region. Compared to *inornatus* (race usually seen in Europe), crown generally greyer, practically lacking green, supercilium buffish white rather than yellowish, indistinct in front of eye and not connected over forehead; upperparts less bright green, more greyish-olive; breast, showing little or no yellow, tinged buffish like throat and ear-coverts. Upper wing-bar often narrow and short, also tends to be buffer, less yellow; flight-feather margins less bright green. Bill darker throughout, dully pale at extreme base of lower mandible where *inornatus* has paler, more extensive yellowish area.

Voice: call, loud ringing 'tiss-yip'; also 'te-wie-esp', lower-pitched than *inornatus*, with last syllable dropping.

Status: winter visitor SE Iran and few Oman. Rare passage Iraq, E Arabia, Israel. Vagrant to Libya, Egypt, Cyprus and Turkey where may winter in SW.

Habitat: on passage/winter in bushes and trees.

Radde's Warbler *Phylloscopus schwarzi*

Identification: 13 cm. See PMH.
Status: vagrant Israel.

Dusky Warbler *Phylloscopus fuscatus*

Identification: 12 cm. See PMH.
Status: vagrant Morocco, N Yemen.

Bonelli's Warbler *Phylloscopus bonelli*

Identification: 12 cm. See PMH.
Status: see map. Also apparently breeds
Lebanon. Summer visitor. Passage throughout N Africa, Near East, Cyprus and Turkey,
scarce NW Saudi Arabia. Vagrant Iran, E
and SW Arabia.
Habitat: deciduous or mixed woodland, pine-
woods, evergreen oaks, or even scattered
trees up to tree-limit. On passage in trees and
bushes. Nests on ground in undergrowth
under tree.

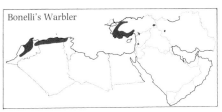

Wood Warbler *Phylloscopus sibilatrix*

Identification: 13 cm. See PMH.
Status: passage mainly spring, from Morocco extending through N Africa to W Iran, but very
scarce in Jordan, W, central and E Arabia.
Habitat: on passage in woodland and tall trees, also scrub.

Plain Leaf Warbler *Phylloscopus neglectus*   Plate 32

Identification: 8.5 cm. Sexes alike. Tiny, short-tailed *Phylloscopus*, lacking any obvious markings,
and unmistakable with its *Goldcrest-like size and proportions*. Colouration like Chiffchaff with
olive brown upperparts, indistinct pale supercilium, off-white underparts with creamy wash
especially on flanks. *Lacks any distinct trace of green or yellow*. Often seen in flight as it moves
about sparse hillsides that it frequents.
Voice: call, quiet, harsh 'chick', in winter also harsh 'churr'. Song, short phrase of 4 to 5
syllables recalling Goldfinch 'pt toodla toodla', from bush or flight between perches.
Status: see map. Short-distance migrant.
Winters Iran south of breeding range, a few
also recorded in Gulf States and Oman;
vagrant Jordan and possibly N Yemen.
Habitat: sparse low mountain scrub (deciduous
or evergreen) with occasional trees, 2,000–
3,000 m. Nests low in bush.

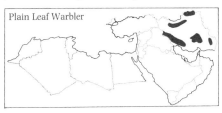

Mountain Chiffchaff *Phylloscopus sindianus*   Plate 32

Identification: 11 cm. Sexes alike. Very similar in structure to Chiffchaff but appears slightly
smaller and more active. Plumage similar to eastern forms of Chiffchaff (e.g. *P. c. tristis*),
being *without yellow* except for pale yellow on bend of wing, and sometimes underwing-
coverts. Upperparts *warm* brown to grey-*brown* without any greenish tinge on rump (but
tristis also lacks greenish on rump in worn plumage), wing-coverts or edges to wing and tail-
feathers. Underparts off-white with buff suffusion on breast and flanks. Bill blackish-brown
with yellowish-brown base to lower mandible (like most *phylloscopus* in this group) and
blackish-brown legs.

Voice: song resembles Chiffchaff, but less vigorous and not so rhythmic. Call, loud 'tiss-yip'; (also single 'psew' at least from birds in NE Turkey – see below).

Status: see map. Summer visitor. (Breeding range and wintering/passage areas not fully understood due to identification difficulties, see *Note* below). Vagrant Iraq.

Habitat: mountain forest with scrub in sub-alpine zone in breeding season.

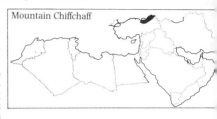

Mountain Chiffchaff

Note: this form of Chiffchaff is given separate specific status in Voous's *List of Recent Holarctic Bird Species*, which we have followed unless convinced otherwise, and so it is included here. Nevertheless, we have doubts that this is the correct treatment for this bird. Williamson gives it as breeding to north of region, from Caucasus eastwards, and it occurs in the region, perhaps not regularly, in winter. It closely resembles Chiffchaffs of Siberia, likewise birds breeding in Turkey and Iran which most taxonomists seem to regard as a race of Chiffchaff *P. collybita*, whose song (in Turkey at least) sounds inseparable from that of Chiffchaffs of Europe.

However, during past decade, some field-observers in Turkey have concluded that 'chiff-chaffs' which breed as fairly common summer visitors in NE Turkey are identical with, or effectively inseparable from Mountain Chiffchaff, whereas birds of NW Turkey are perhaps closer to Chiffchaff. Are the differences racial or specific? It is to be hoped that the systematic position of these various populations can be satisfactorily established before long.

Chiffchaff *Phylloscopus collybita*

Identification: 11 cm. See PMH.
Status: see map. Partial migrant, also occurs on passage or as winter visitor almost throughout the region.
Habitat: deciduous, mixed or sometimes coniferous woodland. On passage/winter almost anywhere with bushes and trees. Nests usually just above ground in vegetation.

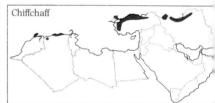

Chiffchaff

Willow Warbler *Phylloscopus trochilus*

Identification: 11 cm. See PMH.
Status: a passage migrant throughout region.
Habitat: bushy areas, woodland edges, gardens, parks.

Goldcrest *Regulus regulus*

Identification: 9 cm. See PMH.
Status: see map. Resident. Also winter visitor to Turkey, Cyprus, and uncommonly to Iran, Near East, Algeria and Tunisia. Vagrant Morocco, Libya, Egypt.
Habitat: coniferous or mixed woodland; in winter also hedges and undergrowth. Nests in conifer.

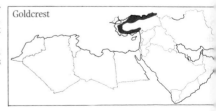

Goldcrest

Firecrest *Regulus ignicapillus*

Identification: 9 cm. See PMH.
Status: see map. Resident. Also winter visitor to NW Africa, rare Libya, Lebanon and vagrant Egypt, Cyprus.
Habitat: as Goldcrest, but less partial to coniferous woods; more often in low undergrowth, but also in higher mixed forest. Nests in tree.

Firecrest

Blue and White Flycatcher,
male (left), female (right)

Blue and White Flycatcher *Cyanoptila (Muscicapa) cyanomelana*

Identification: 17 cm. Sexes differ. The 'blue-and-white' flycatchers of E and SE Asia can be confusing. This is the only species recorded in region, but others could occur as vagrants. Blue and White Flycatcher resembles Spotted in size and shape but is larger, with larger squarer-sided head, longer tail and slightly heavier bill. Male has *dark blue upperparts, shining blue on crown, with throat, sides of head and breast darker, nearly black and sharply demarcated from white belly*. White bases to outer tail-feathers usually only visible in flight. Female, dark olive-brown above, paler brown below with distinct *creamy throat-patch* and *white belly and undertail-coverts*; indistinct buffy eye-ring. First-winter similar to female but male has bright blue rump and tail, the latter tipped black and with white sides ar base. Wings also bright blue with black-tipped primaries. Underparts can be more mottled than females, but still with creamy throat-patch and white belly, and under-tail coverts. Eye large and black, bill dark in adults but can be pale in young birds. Upright stance with frequent slow movements of tail and flicks of wings; swoops to ground to feed, then returns to perch.
Voice: grating 'tchack' or 'tek tek'.
Status: vagrant Oman and UAE, from E Asia.
Habitat: any area with trees, on passage.

Spotted Flycatcher *Muscicapa striata*

Identification: 14 cm. See PMH.
Status: see map. Summer visitor; recorded on passage throughout the region.
Habitat: gardens, parks, edges of woods, plantations and scrub near cultivation. Nests on or in building, against tree-trunk, foliage against wall, etc.

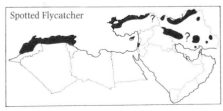

Spotted Flycatcher

209

Gambage Dusky Flycatcher *Muscicapa gambagae* Plate 33

Identification: 12 cm. Sexes alike. Rather small, brownish flycatcher, near size of Red-breasted with domed crown and small bill. Spotted Flycatcher larger with longer wings, more upright stance, flatter crown and longer bill. Generally resembles Spotted in plumage but browner; light *sooty-brown upperparts virtually lack any streaking on forehead and crown* (where noticeably streaked in Spotted) and *silky-white underparts have soft, indistinct vermiculations* on breast (more pronounced streaking in Spotted). Small bill has pale base to lower mandible (all-dark bill in Spotted). Like Spotted, white edgings to greater coverts, tertials and secondaries. Juvenile, darker brown upperparts with buff spots and streaks; underparts dirty white and much more strongly streaked than adult. Divides time between sitting on exposed perch from which sallies are made, or amongst upper foliage of small trees.

Voice: very soft creaking 'tchee, tchee', also Robin-like 'ptik, ptik'. Song, thin and sibilant, consisting of quiet high-pitched squeaking mixed with rusty, creaking notes and short trills.

Status: see map. Summer visitor.

Habitat: wooded highlands, bushy areas particularly acacia scrub, up to 2,500 m. Nests in hole, usually in dead stump or tree.

Gambage Dusky Flycatcher

Red-breasted Flycatcher *Ficedula parva*

Identification: 12 cm. See PMH.

Status: see map. Summer visitor. Recorded commonly on passage in Turkey and Iran. Scarce passage migrant in Libya, Egypt, Cyprus, N and E Arabia and Israel (where has wintered). Vagrant Lebanon, Tunisia, Algeria and Morocco.

Habitat: usually deciduous forest. On passage anywhere with trees. Nests in hole in tree, also against tree-trunk.

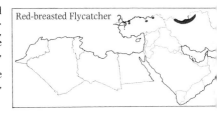

Red-breasted Flycatcher

Semi-collared Flycatcher *Ficedula semitorquata* Plate 33

Identification: 13 cm. Sexes differ. Size, shape and actions as Collared or Pied Flycatchers (see PMH). Male easily mistaken for latter species, being basically black above and white below, with conspicuous white panel on wing. Most differ, however, in having *white half-collar from white throat to sides of neck* (easily overlooked at a quick glance), *greater expanse of white in wing*, especially at base of primaries, even forming a square patch (in Pied, white fleck or narrow streak), as well as pure white tips to median coverts in spring birds (exceptionally in Pied), and *grey rump* sometimes flecked with white. White on forehead usually more extensive than on Pied. Semi-collared also shows more white in outer tail-feathers than Collared. Female and juvenile doubtfully distinguishable from Pied or Collared in field, but pure white tips to median coverts in spring females (and adults of both sexes in autumn) useful.

Voice: call, sharp 'chick' or 'tchik', indistinguishable from Collared or Pied.

Status: see map. Summer visitor. Recorded on passage through Asian area but scarce or rare Arabia; also Egypt (fairly common spring, rare autumn) and Tunisia. Vagrant Morocco.

Habitat: woods, parks, orchards and large gardens. On passage will occur in areas with trees. Nests in hole in tree.

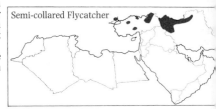

Semi-collared Flycatcher

210

Collared Flycatcher *Ficedula albicollis*

Identification: 13 cm. See PMH.
Status: passage migrant North Africa (but vagrant Morocco), Near East, Cyprus, Turkey. Vagrant Gulf States, Saudi Arabia.
Habitat: on passage will occur in areas with trees.

Pied Flycatcher *Ficedula hypoleuca*

Identification: 13 cm. See PMH.
Status: see map. Summer visitor. Recorded on passage throughout North Africa (where has been recorded in winter in Tunisia), Turkey, Cyprus, Israel, Lebanon, Syria and Iran (where uncommon).
Habitat: deciduous, mixed or coniferous forest and large gardens. On passage anywhere with trees. Nests in hole in tree or wall.

African Paradise Flycatcher *Terpsiphone viridis*   Plate 33

Identification: male 30–36 cm (including long tail); female 20 cm. Sexes differ. Large, bulbul-size, *with very long chestnut* (sometimes white) *central tail-feathers* in adult male, though these sometimes worn or broken. Unmistakable, with *chestnut upperparts, glossy blue-black slightly tufted head and breast* (sometimes extending to belly), slate-grey below and large white wing-patch, though this can vary in size and may often be absent. Female similar to male but less rich on mantle, and graduated tail lacks long streamers. Blue eye-ring and black bill. Slow, wavering and rather heavy, flycatching flight; when perched often slowly flicks tail. Secretive, often seeking densest shade. *A white phase*, rare in Arabia, has white back, rump, tail and wing-coverts.
Voice: harsh 'tsveit' or 'scheep'; also hoarse 'tscaeae-tscaeaet'. Song, with pleasant Blackbird-like quality, 'twee, twoo, twoo, twoo, twoo', uttered from perch with tail fanned, bird jerking from side to side with wings slightly spread.
Status: see map. Resident.
Habitat: well-vegetated semi-tropical wadis with trees, 1,000–2,400 m. Nests in fork of tree or bush.

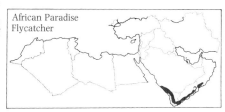

Bearded Tit *Panurus biarmicus*

Identification: 17 cm. See PMH.
Status: see map. Only regularly recorded in Turkey where its status is uncertain, being a resident or partial migrant. Elsewhere rare or irregular winter visitor to Iran, Cyprus and Israel; vagrant Morocco.
Habitat: extensive reed-beds. Nests low down near edge of wet reed-bed.

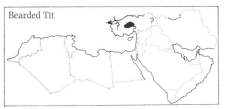

211

Iraq Babbler *Turdoides altirostris* Plate 30

Identification: 22 cm. Sexes alike. Babblers are brownish, thrush-like, with long graduated tails, short wings and stout, curved bills; gregarious habits – often in groups of up to 10 birds; sometimes skulking, at other times more obvious, even inquisitive, often hopping on ground with tail raised, or flying 'follow-my-leader' from bush to bush in low-level, rather laboured flight with straight-back appearance, and wing-beats interspersed with glides on stiffly-held wings. Iraq Babbler similar in structure to Common Babbler (which overlaps its range) but slightly smaller, with shorter stouter bill. Adult very similar in plumage to Common but warmer, *more uniform, lacking streaking on sides of rufous-buff breast*, with much finer streaks on upperparts (quite distinct streaks in Common) and only visible at close range. Legs dull brownish (dull yellowish in Common). Juvenile apparently quite distinct from juvenile Common, being paler above with creamy-buff cheeks and underparts, white chin and vent.
Voice: no information.
Status: see map. Resident.
Habitat: chiefly reed-beds, riverine thickets, palm groves, cultivated fields.

Iraq Babbler

Common Babbler *Turdoides caudatus* Plate 30

Identification: 23 cm. Sexes alike. Drab, sandy grey-brown, very similar to Iraq Babbler. *Conspicuous dark striations on crown and upperparts* and faint suggestion of rufous wash on cheeks. Pale fawn below, with whiter chin and throat, *and light streaking on sides of breast*. Blackish or yellowish-brown iris and dark, slightly decurved bill with base of lower mandible often yellow; *legs dull yellow*. Usually rather furtive and presence often revealed by piping calls. Distinguished from Iraq Babbler by more distinct streaking on sides of breast, which is greyer (less rufous), longer bill and dull yellow legs and feet.
Voice: high-pitched 'pee-pee-pee-pee-pee-pee', etc; also series of piping notes slowing and descending at end.
Status: see map. Resident.
Habitat: cultivated and dry regions with scattered bushes and trees. Nests in tree.

Common Babbler

Arabian Babbler *Turdoides squamiceps* Plate 30

Identification: 26 cm. Sexes alike. Large babbler, geographically isolated from other three species of region. Upperparts grey-brown, with darker centres to feathers of slightly greyer crown, nape and ear-coverts, giving a rather 'moth-eaten' look; some dark streaking on upper mantle. Underparts slightly paler grey-brown, with warmer tone to flanks and faint darker mottling on throat and breast. Bill blackish-brown with paler base to lower mandible. Legs brownish (often orangy-brown) to dark grey and feet usually darker. Iris colour variable from brownish to yellowish-orange and bluish-white. Birds in lowlands of North Yemen have variable white/whitish face and area surrounding eye, with bill varying from red through orange-red to yellowish-orange. Habits similar to Iraq Babbler, which see.
Voice: wide vocabulary but most typical call is high piping 'piu-piu-piu-piu-piu', etc, decelerating towards end.

212

Status: see map. Resident.
Habitat: dry areas with scrub and scattered trees (especially acacia), wadis, palm groves and savanna from below sea level to 2,400 m. Nests usually in acacia.

Fulvous Babbler *Turdoides fulvus* Plate 30

Identification: 25 cm. Sexes similar. Warm-coloured babbler, unstreaked except occasionally on crown and nape. *Upperparts warm sandy-brown*, pale below with whitish throat and *almost orange wash on flanks*. Bill blackish, with pale gape in male.
Voice: song, piping succession of 6 drawn-out notes, 'peeoo-peeoo-peeoo-peeoo-peeoo-peeoo', perceptibly descending; also soft rippling trill and short 'pip' flight-note.
Status: see map. Resident.
Habitat: sandy plains with scattered scrub, often dense, desert edges, oases, olive-groves. Nests usually in thorny bush.

Long-tailed Tit *Aegithalos caudatus* Plate 33

Identification: 13 cm. See PMH. The two races illustrated, *tephronotus* (Turkey) and *passekii* (Iran, except Caspian region), differ from European birds; *tephronotus* has a grey back (lacking pink of European birds), small sooty-black throat-patch and greyish-white underparts, with fine sooty streaking on cheeks becoming very faint on breast and upper flanks; *passekii* similar, but much paler both above and below and, like European birds, lacks sooty-black bib.
Status: see map. Resident with some winter dispersal within Turkey and Iran. Vagrant Morocco and Tunisia.
Habitat: bushes, hedgerows and other undergrowth, both in open country and within woodland. Nests in bush.

Marsh Tit *Parus palustris*

Identification: 12 cm. See PMH.
Status: see map. Resident.
Habitat: deciduous woods, thickets. Nests in hole in tree.

Sombre Tit *Parus lugubris*

Identification: 14 cm. See PMH.
Status: see map. Resident.
Habitat: lowland plains and mountain slopes
with mixed woods, scrub, and rocky
outcrops. Nests in hole in tree, occasionally
among rocks.

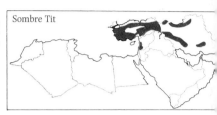

Crested Tit *Parus cristatus*

Identification: 12 cm. See PMH.
Status: vagrant Morocco.
Habitat: usually pine woods.

Coal Tit *Parus ater*   Plate 33

Identification: 10.5 cm. See PMH. Most races occurring in region similar to European birds;
however, three are distinct and illustrated. The race *atlas*, which occurs in Morocco, has
greyish-green mantle, black on throat extending onto upper breast and smoky-grey flanks.
Cyprus race *cypriotus*, has brown back, more black on head than European birds extending
onto upper mantle, and very dark underparts with rufous-brown flanks. Race *ledouci* of
Algeria and N Tunisia, has whole plumage strongly suffused with bright yellow.
Status: see map. Resident, slight dispersal.
Habitat: mainly coniferous woodland but also
oak and cork-oak; mainly in mountainous
areas. Nests low in stump or hole in tree,
bank or ground.

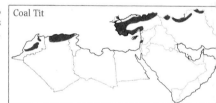

Blue Tit *Parus caeruleus*   Plate 33

Identification: 11 cm. See PMH. Races in region show subtle variations, but all similar to
European birds. Those in N Africa have slaty-blue backs as typified by Moroccan and Tunisian
race, *ultramarinus*, illustrated. Races in Turkey and Middle East have greenish backs, more
typical of European birds. Race in S Iran, *persicus*, also illustrated, is palest, being pale bluish
grey-green above and very pale yellow below.
Status: see map. Resident. Vagrant Syria
(where has bred), Lebanon.
Habitat: woodland, gardens, thickets, plantations, sometimes also oases. Nests in hole
in tree, wall, etc.

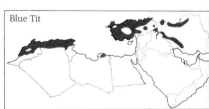

214

Azure Tit *Parus cyanus*   Plate 33

Identification: 13 cm. See PMH. Only the race *carruthersi* (illustrated) recorded in region. Differs from European birds in having dusky-grey (not white) head and throat, darker, greyer underparts, broad pale yellow band on breast, and rest of underparts less pure white. Juvenile quite strikingly tinged with yellow throughout plumage.
Status: vagrant Iran.
Habitat: trees and bushes (notably willow), invariably near water.

Great Tit *Parus major*   Plate 33

Identification: 14 cm. See PMH. Grey race *intermedius*, illustrated, which occurs in E Iran differs markedly from European birds, being blue-grey above (only hint of green being on upper border of mantle) and whitish below; head and breast markings, however, are similar. All other populations similar to European birds though hybridization occurs with *intermedius* on borders of its range. For differences between *intermedius* and very similar Turkestan Tit, see that species.
Status: see map. Resident.
Habitat: anywhere with trees (mixed woods, gardens, etc.) but not at high altitudes. Nests in hole in tree, wall, etc.

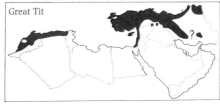

Turkestan Tit *Parus bokharensis*   Plate 33

Identification: 15 cm. Sexes alike. Very similar to grey race of Great Tit *intermedius* which occurs in the same area. Differs in slightly smaller size, proportionally slightly longer tail, larger *more fan-shaped, white cheek-patch, stouter bill, narrower black line down centre of belly* and *more noticeable blue-grey fringes to primaries and secondaries*. Otherwise blue-grey above and whitish below, without any trace of green or yellow in plumage; *intermedius* Great Tit, seen close, shows faint green wash on upper mantle.
Voice: no information.
Status: see map. Resident.
Habitat: riverine thickets in lowlands. Nests in hole in tree, wall etc.

Krüper's Nuthatch *Sitta krueperi*   Plate 34

Identification: 12 cm. Sexes alike. *Small*, with *large red-brown patch on breast* which distinguishes it from geographically separated Algerian and Corsican Nuthatches *Sitta whiteheadi* (see PMH); black forehead and crown (less extensive in female) divided from black eye-stripe by white supercilium. Upperparts blue-grey, with small white corners to tail; chin to breast-patch white, rest of underparts dirty white with rufous tinge on vent. Juvenile much dingier, with black on head reduced or absent, buffer below and with paler, more diffuse breast-patch. Separated from Nuthatch and the two Rock Nuthatches by smaller size, black on head, distinct white supercilium and, in adults, by red-brown breast-patch. Very active; will catch insects in flight.
Voice: can be very vocal; common call, harsh Jay-like note, sometimes continuing into scolding, rippling chur; also Nuthatch-like 'veet-veet-veet'; 'pip pirrup pirrup pip pip'; horn-like 'ue-ue-ue'; woodpecker-like 'keck'; Greenfinch-like 'dweij' and soft 'pwit', recalling Willow Warbler.

215

Status: see map. Resident.

Habitat: pine forest, cedars and junipers, from sea-level to tree-limit, but typically between 1,200–1,700 m. Nests in hole in tree without mud-plastering.

Algerian (Kabylian) Nuthatch *Sitta ledanti*   Plate 34

Identification: 12 cm. Sexes sometimes differ. Recently discovered species in Algeria resembling Corsican Nuthatch (see PMH) but larger with longer bill. Upperparts blue-grey with darker flight-feathers; blackish tail with small white patches at sides. Underparts vary from warm buff to creamy. Male has black forehead and crown (nape black in Corsican), white supercilium, bordered below by black eye-stripe (sometimes mottled behind eye). Female similar to male but sometimes lacks black on crown and eye-stripe. Bill bluish-grey, legs lead-grey. Juvenile resembles female but always lacks black head-markings, has ill-defined whitish eye-brow and paler buff underparts, notably from breast upwards; bill yellowish and legs paler than adult.

Status: see map. Resident.

Habitat: relict mixed woodland of fir, cedar and oak, 2,000 m. Nests in hole in tree.

Nuthatch *Sitta europaea*   Plate 34

Identification: 14 cm. See PMH. Race *persica* (illustrated), of SW and S Iran, distinctly paler grey on upperparts and whiter on underparts than others in Middle East, all of which resemble European birds; also white forehead band and supercilium more pronounced.

Status: see map. Resident.

Habitat: large deciduous trees in woods and parks. Nests in hole in tree, plastering entrance hole or crevices with mud.

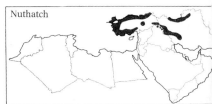

Eastern (Great) Rock Nuthatch *Sitta tephronota*   Plate 34

Identification: 19–20 cm. Sexes alike. Similar plumage to Rock Nuthatch (which see) but appreciably larger with more 'neck', *longer, more powerful bill and much broader and longer black eye-stripe, which curves and often broadens down side of neck* (particularly developed where bird overlaps some Iranian races of Rock). Upperparts clean pale grey, throat to upperbreast white, flanks and lower belly orange-buff, sometimes quite faint. Behaviour as Rock Nuthatch, but more frequently on trees or bushes.

Voice: very noisy; louder, deeper and slower than Rock Nuthatch, far less piping with noticeable gaps between each note, 'peep-peep-peep-peep', etc; also ringing and rather musical 'kwut-up', repeated 4–6 times; a 'kewk' repeated 4 times, yelping, trilling and quite tuneful. In winter 'tuk-tuk-tuk-trrruck'; also totally different, nasal 'whee-whee'.

Status: see map. Resident.
Habitat: rocky gorges, mountain sides, cliffs and semi-desert edges, sometimes with scattered trees. Nests on rock surface, often overhung, mud construction with hole near top.

Eastern Rock Nuthatch

Rock Nuthatch *Sitta neumayer*   Plate 34

Identification: 14 cm. See PMH. Race *tschitscherini* (illustrated; NW Iraq, western and southern Iran) distinctly paler than European birds, being almost whitish-grey above; black eye-stripe is reduced, in some very diffuse; race *plumbea* (also illustrated; SE Iran) bluish-grey above, has similarly reduced black eye-stripe, underbody ashy-grey, not white or creamy-white as other races. (Eastern Rock Nuthatch, which see, is larger, has stronger and longer bill and much broader and longer black eye-stripe, which curves down sides of neck).
Voice: call higher-pitched than Eastern Rock's, much more rapid, dry, flatter and less ringing.
Status: see map. Resident.
Habitat: rocky gorges, mountain sides, cliffs. Nests in protected cranny in rock; built of mud, with protruding tunnel entrance.

Rock Nuthatch

Wallcreeper *Tichodroma muraria*

Identification: 17 cm. See PMH.
Status: see map. Resident with some winter dispersal outside breeding range. Winters also in Cyprus, Syria, Israel (where may have bred), perhaps also Lebanon. Vagrant Morocco and Algeria.
Habitat: rocky ravines, earth cliffs, ruins, from 2,000 m to snowline. In winter rocky valleys and foothills, but also coastal cliffs. Nests in deep crevice on cliff-face, rocks, occasionally buildings.

Wallcreeper

Treecreeper *Certhia familiaris*

Identification: 13 cm. See PMH.
Status: see map. Resident, with some dispersal in winter, (e.g. to S Turkey).
Habitat: mixed mountain woodland up to 3,000 m. Nests behind loose bark, or in split trunk.

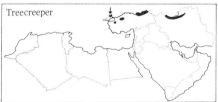

Treecreeper

217

Short-toed Treecreeper *Certhia brachydactyla*

Identification: 13 cm. See PMH.
Status: see map. Resident.
Habitat: large gardens, parks, pines and cedar woods, from sea-level up to 1,500 m (occasionally higher). Nests in slit or hole in tree or wall.

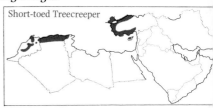

Penduline Tit *Remiz pendulinus*   Plate 33

Identification: 10.5 cm. See PMH. Adults of races in Iran, *macronyx, nigricans* and *coronatus* (last two illustrated) differ markedly from European birds which are similar to other races elsewhere in region. *Macronyx* (South Caspian) has *all-black head* (chestnut tinge at close range) extending well down onto throat and *separated from chestnut mantle by a white collar; nigricans* (Seistan area) similar to *macronyx* but *lacks white collar*, black on the head extending onto mantle; *coronatus* (NE Iran) more similar to European birds but has broad black coronal band which joins across nape and is separated from chestnut mantle by white collar; amount of black on crown variable, in some whole crown black with white forehead; in others, crown white with diffuse dark streaking. Juvenile similar to European birds.
Voice: song, short musical rippling 'ti-ti-ti-ti-ti', resembling quality of Great Tit, rather quiet and soft. Calls include 'seeoo-teeoo-teeoo', 'tseeoo tseeoo', sweet liquid 'tloo-tloo-ti' and short rippling rattle; all calls rather soft and quiet.
Status: see map. Resident and dispersive with winter records from Israel, Egypt, Cyprus (where may breed), Lebanon, Syria (where has bred), NW, central and E Arabia. Vagrant Oman, Tunisia and Morocco.
Habitat: trees (especially willows, poplars and tamarisks) and reed-beds, always near water, including coastal marshes and oases. The oval-shaped nest with tube entrance at side near top is suspended (usually over water) from outermost branch of tree.

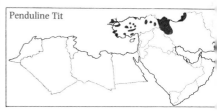

Nile Valley Sunbird *Anthreptes metallicus*   Plate 34

Identification: 10 cm (male in summer 15 cm). Small, with *short, only slightly decurved bill.* Sexes differ in breeding season, when male has *elongated central tail-feathers,* bright yellow lower *underparts,* purple breast-band (often looking black) and *dark green upperbreast.* Upperparts metallic-green with purple band across rump and uppertail-coverts; wings black and tail bluish-black. Female and juvenile greyish-brown above with whitish throat, rest of *underparts washed yellow* which, together with short bill, distinguish it from female Palestine and Shining Sunbirds; in female Purple (different distribution), darker underparts also washed yellow, and bill longer and more decurved. Male, in non-breeding plumage, lacks elongated tail-feathers and resembles female, but may be more yellowish below and may retain some metallic wing-coverts and body-feathers; in winter, some have blackish-grey centre of chin and throat. Often flicks wings and spreads tail.
Voice: soft, fine, high-pitched song consists of thin silvery trilling and hissing notes 'pruiit-prruiit-pruiit-tiririri-tiririri'; also thin hoarse 'veeii-veeii-veeii', a 'ptscheeiii', repeated 'cheeit-cheeit', and 'tee-weee' with upward inflexion on last note.
Status: see map. Resident.
Habitat: gardens, acacia and dry scrub in savanna and wadis; from sea-level to 2,500 m, but commonest at low altitudes. Nest is an oval structure suspended from twig.

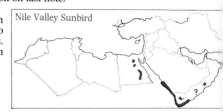

218

Purple Sunbird *Nectarinia asiatica*   Plate 34

Identification: 10 cm. Sexes differ. *Resembles Palestine Sunbird* but different distribution and *scythe-shaped bill slightly shorter and less decurved.* Male *metallic blue-black on upperparts, throat and breast, washed darker green* than in male Palestine, *a narrow reddish-brown breast-band sometimes seen.* Often looks black in rapid, dipping flight, or perched. Tufts at sides of breast yellower than in Palestine, but seldom seen. Female has mouse-brown upperparts with wings and tail darker; *underparts washed yellow* (pale grey in female Palestine). Male in eclipse (mainly September-December) like female but underparts yellower, and blue-black median line down centre of throat and breast. Short-tailed, hummingbird-like appearance, feeding largely on nectar from flowers.
Voice: song, excited 'cheewit-cheewit' repeated 2–6 times, with Willow Warbler-like cadence. Male in eclipse often utters low, continuous, twittering subsong; call, 'dzit-dzit' not unlike that of Fan-tailed Warbler; also 'tsweet'.
Status: see map. Mainly resident, some dispersal south in autumn.
Habitat: large trees in gardens, cultivation, tamarisks along river beds, thorn scrub and dry forest. Nest pear-shaped, suspended on bush.

Purple Sunbird

Shining Sunbird *Nectarinia habessinica*   Plate 34

Identification: 13 cm. Sexes differ. Medium-sized with longer, fuller tail than Palestine and long decurved bill. Male has bright metallic green head, back and upper breast (much greener than smaller Palestine which usually appears much bluer), blue-black tail, and *broad but inconspicuous scarlet-red band across lower breast* (absent in Palestine); narrow blue band bordering lower edge of red breast-band and violet crown not easily seen; bright yellow tufts at sides of breast normally hidden by wings; rump and tail deep metallic blue, but look blackish. Female, *dark sooty-grey with blue-black tail* and slightly paler underparts (female Palestine much paler greyish below); *white fringes to feathers of ventral region* (absent in Palestine). Juvenile male resembles female but has black centre of throat, often with clear-cut or diffuse black breast-patch, whitish fore-supercilium and moustachial stripe (all plumages much darker below than Palestine). Male in non-breeding plumage resembles female, but green feathers often show through on head, back or breast. Larger size, rather pronounced *slow gentle flicking of longer, broader tail* and, *in flight, long, deeper undulations* also help separation from Palestine.
Voice: song, fast strong fluty whistles combined into trilling and whirring notes, e.g. 'tuu-tuu-tuu-tuu, vita-vita-vita-vita, du-du-du-du', often ending in long trill, reminiscent of Wren. Subsong fast and rambling whispering warble; various calls include hard 'tshak', 'dzit' and 'chewit-chewit'; also fast, dry 'tje-tje-tje-tje'.
Status: see map. Resident.
Habitat: wadis and slopes with dense, often luxuriant vegetation, also in dry savanna scrub; 250–2,500 m, but mainly lower and middle altitudes. Nest bottle-shaped, suspended in tree or bush.

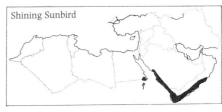
Shining Sunbird

Palestine Sunbird *Nectarinia osea*   Plate 34

Identification: 11 cm. Sexes differ. Small, with short tail and medium-long, decurved bill. Male, in breeding plumage, dark blue-black *with metallic violet-blue* (metallic green in some lights) *on upperparts, breast and forehead,* and dark brown wings. *Orange tufts at sides of breast difficult to see.* At distance looks all-blackish, whereas male of larger Shining Sunbird looks mainly metallic green with blackish wings and tail. Female Palestine, dark grey-brown with paler, *greyish underparts lacking yellow* (female Purple Sunbird, from which normally geographically separated, is yellowish below). Male in eclipse (July to November/February) resembles female but can retain traces of breeding plumage. Flicks tail, but movements flatter and quicker than in Shining Sunbird, and rapid flight has irregular, short, dipping undulations (longer and deeper in Shining).

Voice: song, fast rambling, high-pitched trilling 'dy-vy-vy-vy-vy-vy', or a rising 'tveeit-tveeit-tveeit', etc, or 'veet-tji, veet-tji, veetji', accelerating and often ending in Serin-like trill. Varied calls include thin 'ftift', Siskin-like 'tiu', hard 'tsak', and loud, sharp 'te-weeit, te-weeit' with rising inflexion on stressed second syllable.

Status: see map. Resident, with slight dispersal in winter, reaching Lebanon and Syria.

Habitat: in well vegetated areas, rocky wadis, river banks, acacia steppe or savanna, gardens in towns; from sea-level up to 3,200 m. Nest suspended on tree or bush.

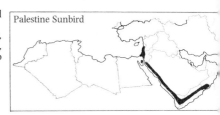

Palestine Sunbird

White-breasted White-eye *Zosterops abyssinica* Plate 33

Identification: 11–12 cm. Sexes alike. Small, plump warbler-like with *conspicuous white eye-ring*, and short, fine bill. All upperparts fairly dark greyish-green, chin and throat pale yellow, breast and belly smoky-white (flanks sometimes greyish), vent and undertail coverts pale yellow (but rear of underparts may occasionally lack yellow). Bill dark with paler base to lower mandible. Juvenile similar to adult but duller. Very active, tit-like, often in small groups, constantly on move, feeding usually in trees, exploring branches for insects, but will come to the ground; can probe flowers like sunbirds. Light, slightly undulating flight.

Voice: call, soft, fine and high-pitched 'tiiu' or 'teuu', not unlike that of Siskin or Coal Tit, but higher; occasionally, fine purring trill, not unlike Snow Bunting's call. Also, short, deep low 'waouw'.

Status: see map. Resident, with some seasonal movement.

Habitat: in trees (especially acacia), gardens with or without thick cover, wooded mountain slopes or wadis, 300–3,100 m, but usually at middle to higher altitudes. Builds cup-shaped nest in outer branch of tree.

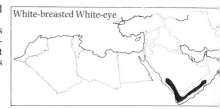

White-breasted White-eye

Golden Oriole *Oriolus oriolus*

Identification: 24 cm. See PMH.

Status: see map. Has bred Israel and attempted breeding in E Province of Saudi Arabia. Summer visitor. Recorded on passage throughout the region.

Habitat: essentially arboreal; parks with tall trees, riverine and other woodland; bird seldom in the open, except sometimes on passage. Nest usually slung between horizontally forked branches.

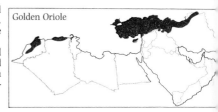

Golden Oriole

Black-headed Bush Shrike *Tchagra senegala*   Plate 35

Identification: 22 cm. Sexes similar. Unmistakable, thrush-sized but with rather large head and long graduated tail. Upperparts greyish with *chestnut wings* and *conspicuous white tips to all but central feathers of dark tail* (most noticeable in flight). *Striking head pattern* with black crown and eye-stripe *separated by long, broad, white supercilium.* Underparts pale greyish on breast and flanks. Bill black, heavy, with slight hook to tip. Fairly secretive and presence usually indicated by song or call. Movements rather clumsy and Magpie-like; when active, will hop on ground with tail raised or fly from bush to bush with long glide before alighting, when tail cocked and flicked. Occurs singly or in pairs.

Voice: song, from perch or in flight, fluty, melodious and far-carrying, comprising some 10 clearly separated notes, the second half descending; given mainly in early morning and evening. Starts song-flight by flying upwards in low arc, wings making soft 'pop, pop, pop', noise; at top of arc glides down singing. In addition, characteristic 'truit-truit-drirиririvivir', trill being long and rising and falling. Call, harsh 'shrrrr'.

Status: see map. Resident.

Habitat: dense, dry scrub with scattered trees. Nests in low tree or bush.

Black-headed Bush Shrike

Rosy-patched Shrike *Rhodophoneus cruentus*   Plate 35

Identification: 23 cm. Sexes differ. Slim, *very long-tailed shrike*, slightly smaller than Great Grey. Male has grey-brown upperparts, rosy tinge to top of head, and *conspicuous rosy-red at base of lower back* particularly noticeable in flight; *broad white tips to black tail-feathers*, especially obvious below. Underparts whitish with *creamy-buff sides of body and ventral region, with rosy-red patch from throat down centre of breast to mid-belly.* Female similar to male, but *black necklace on lower throat and upper breast*; throat white or rosy. Bill black, legs pale grey. Often occurs in noisy family parties and can be very tame; usually cover-seeking like babblers. Juvenile resembles adult, but lacks crimson on throat or breast, although juvenile female has variable blackish spot on side of throat. Greyer on head than adult with buff edges to crown feathers; quite broad pale buff edges to secondaries and wing-coverts, which form two distinctive wing-bars.

Voice: melodious, rather thrush-like song.

Status: see map. Resident.

Habitat: thorn bush or open acacias in arid regions. Nests in low bush.

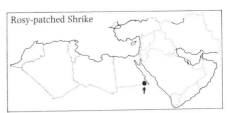

Rosy-patched Shrike

Isabelline Shrike *Lanius isabellinus*   Plate 35

Identification: 18 cm. Sexes differ. A variable, usually pale shrike, size of Red-backed but tail longer. Several races occur in east of region, ranging from darker (*speculigerus* and *phoenicuroides*) to paler (*isabellinus*). Darker males usually have distinct black mask from bill to sides of nape, and *distinct white patch at base of dark primaries*. Upperparts grey-brown or grey-buff, with crown and sometimes nape either rufous-brown or pale greyish; *rump and uppertail rufous-brown to almost rusty-red, latter often darkening towards tip.* Underparts unbarred whitish-buff. Male *isabellinus* paler and greyer or creamier above with mid-brown flight-feathers, primary-patch buffish or absent, mask browner, underparts creamier and tail paler rufous. Females of the two darker races pale earth-brown above with *rusty-brown uppertail and rump,* and creamy underparts with *fine, well-spaced barring on sides of neck, breast and flanks;* dark

221

mask paler grey-brown; *undertail tinged pale chestnut*; some show small buff primary-patch. Female *isabellinus* paler and sandier with very faint barring below. Bill blackish, pale, or pale-based in all races, female and immature often showing pink tinge. First-autumn bird has pale-based bill, poorly developed mask and black subterminal edgings to tertials and greater coverts; upperparts more or less barred and a buff primary-patch may be visible. Female and first-autumn birds best separated from similar Red-backed (which can also have rufous-brown uppertail but contrasting less with mantle) by *fine, sparse barring on sides of breast and flanks* (much more extensive in juvenile Red-backed), and by undertail toned rufous (generally greyish in Red-backed); tail-sides more gingery (Red-backed has clearer, whiter fringes). Juvenile Isabelline typically paler, more buffy above with faint barring (similar Red-backed, pale grey-brown to dark rufous and usually prominently barred); however, some first-year *phoenicuroides* very similar to first-year Red-backed, though slightly paler, greyer and less heavily barred above. Perches in typical conspicuous shrike-like manner, frequently man-oeuvring tail up and sideways.

Status: see map. Summer visitor. Passage migrant in Iran, Iraq, and throughout Arabian peninsula but uncommon in Israel. Vagrant Egypt, Turkey. Also scarce to uncommon wintering bird from S Iran, through Iraq and Arabia becoming commoner further south.

Habitat: bushes in dry steppes, semi-deserts or barren mountains. On passage/winter also in cultivation. Nests in bush.

Isabelline Shrike

Red-backed Shrike *Lanius collurio*

Identification: 17 cm. See PMH.

Status: see map. May breed Lebanon. Summer visitor. Recorded on passage in Turkey, Iran, Near East, Libya, Egypt and whole of Arabian Peninsula. Vagrant Morocco, Algeria and Tunisia.

Habitat: bushy wasteland, thickets, lightly wooded areas and uncultivated corners of farmland. Nests in dense bush or small tree.

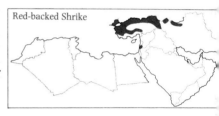

Red-backed Shrike

Bay-backed Shrike *Lanius vittatus*   Plate 35

Identification: 18 cm. Sexes fairly similar. Plump-bodied and long-tailed, superficially resembling Black-headed Shrike in colour. Immediately identified by combination of *deep chestnut back and scapulars, soft grey head and nape with black band from ear-coverts broadening across forehead, and grey rump grading to white on uppertail-coverts*. Wings black with white flash at base of primaries showing as prominent wing-bar in flight; *tail also black with white on outers and tips to all but central feathers*. Underparts off-white with light buffish wash, and golden-chestnut flanks. Female similar to male but slightly duller with less black wings and paler flanks. Immature (first-winter) superficially like adult but duller with some dark wavy barring on flanks and upperparts; forehead usually lacks black. Juvenile has rufous tail with darker subterminal lines and pale tips and faint wing-flash, thus very similar to Isabelline Shrike but greater coverts and tertials are rufous and lower rump grey.

Voice: grating call. Song quiet and pleasant, often imitating other species; can ramble on for long periods.

Status: see map. Resident but some dispersal as indicated by occasional records in Gulf States and Oman.

Habitat: open, often rocky country with scattered trees and low scrub. Nests in bush.

Bay-backed Shrike

222

Black-headed (Rufous-backed) **Shrike** *Lanius schach*   Plate 35

Identification: 24 cm. Sexes alike. Similar in size and structure to Great Grey and noticeably larger than Bay-backed which it resembles in colouration. Head and mantle pale grey merging into *orange-buff scapulars, lower back, rump and uppertail-coverts* (back deep chestnut and rump and tail-coverts pale greyish in Bay-backed). *Black eye-mask joins narrowly over forehead* (broad in Bay-backed); blackish-brown wings with narrow, buffish-white edges to tertials and small (sometimes absent) inconspicuous white patch at base of primaries (larger in Bay-backed). *Long, graduated tail black with buff outers – only shrike in region so patterned* (Bay-backed has white on outer tail-feathers). Underparts off-white with orange-buff wash on flanks and to lesser extent on undertail-coverts (very similar to Bay-backed). Immature has dark grey vermiculations on duller, darker head and mantle, duller blackish-brown secondaries and coverts edged buffish, rufous barred uppertail-coverts, dark, duller face-mask, less black forehead and even less whitish at base of primaries; underparts, which have less orange-buff on flanks, covered with dark wavy barring at sides; bill less black than adult's; (similar-aged Bay-backed has chestnut on back and scapulars and grey rump).
Voice: call, rough 'guerlek, guerlek', followed by barked 'yaon-yaon'. Song, rarely heard, *Acrocephalus*-like, rather slow and imitative.
Status: formerly bred in NE Iran. Vagrant Israel and Oman.
Habitat: open scrubland and cultivated regions. Nests in bush.

Lesser Grey Shrike *Lanius minor*

Identification: 20 cm. See PMH.
Status: see map. Summer visitor. Passage migrant through Turkey, Cyprus, Iran, Egypt, Near East and Arabian peninsula where often scarce. Occasional in Libya.
Habitat: fairly open cultivated country with scattered trees and bushes. Nests fairly high in tree.

Great Grey Shrike *Lanius excubitor*   Plate 35

Identification: 26 cm. See PMH, but it must be noted that most Great Grey Shrikes in region (unlike European birds) show little or no white supercilium, and consequently lack of supercilium cannot be taken as indication of Lesser Grey Shrike. Moreover the three races illustrated are similar to European birds in their grey, black and white plumage, but vary mainly in shade of grey on upperparts, size of white wing-panel, colour of underparts or presence of black line over bill. Those races with salmon-pink underparts, black line over bill or small white wing panel can be confused with Lesser Grey Shrike in quick or poor view. Lesser Grey, however, is smaller, with tip of shorter tail closer to wing-tip, very extensive black on forehead (except first winter birds) and stouter, less hooked bill.

pallidirostris (of N Iran, wintering S to Arabia) has pale grey upperparts, broad white wing-bar, white underparts (rarely tinged pink) and horn-coloured (not black) bill.

elegans (of S Tunisia, non-coastal Libya, Egypt and S Palestine) a very pale race, being pale grey above and white below, with large white wing-bar and black joining over bill in a thin line.

algeriensis (of NW Africa, south to Sahara) quite a dark race, greyer than *elegans* with grey wash on underparts and narrow white wing-bar.

The two races breeding in Arabia not illustrated; *aucheri* (Arabia, Iraq, Syria and Iran) similar in colour-tones to *elegans*, but slightly broader black line over bill, small amount of white in wing and always grey wash on flanks; *buryi* (of mountain regions in North Yemen) darkest race of all, dark grey above, grey below with white confined to centre of belly and small white wing-bar.

223

Status: see map. May breed Lebanon and probably more widespread in N Saudi Arabia than map indicates. Resident; also passage migrant and winter visitor throughout much of the region but generally rather scarce in Turkey.

Habitat: anywhere with patches of scrub and trees adjoining open areas. Nests in bush or small tree.

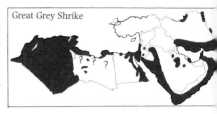
Great Grey Shrike

Woodchat Shrike *Lanius senator*

Identification: 17 cm. See PMH.

Status: see map. Summer visitor. Passage through most of the region but irregular in Oman. Wintering recorded in Algeria, Kuwait and SW Arabia.

Habitat: dry open country, olive groves, orchards, bushy wasteland, oases, hedges in cultivated areas, occasionally open woods. Nests in tree.

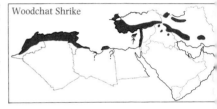
Woodchat Shrike

Masked Shrike *Lanius nubicus*   Plate 35

Identification: 18 cm. See PMH. Sexes differ slightly. Fractionally smaller than Woodchat Shrike, but longer tail and finer bill. Adult male and female not easily confused with other shrikes, the former having *white face with black mask, jet-black upperparts, white scapulars*, white patch at base of primaries, white outertail-feathers, and strong orange wash on flanks. Similar female duller, black suffused with brown or brownish-grey, often markedly so, and white flanks less obviously washed with orange. Care needed over juvenile which resembles young Woodchat. Both show light shoulder-patch (almost lacking in youngest juveniles), white patch at base of primaries (except *badius* Corsican race of Woodchat), whitish edgings to secondaries and tertials and whitish underparts variably barred. Young Masked distinguishable by *whitish forehead* (lacking in Woodchat) and, usually, *whitish eyebrow which accentuates dark mark through eye*, distinctly *grey upperparts* (more sandy-brown in Woodchat) and *rump concolorous with back* (paler rump in Woodchat). Frequently perches on bushes with long tail slightly cocked and waved up and down, a feature that also helps separate young Masked from Woodchat.

Voice: harsh scolding 'krrrr'. Song, rather tuneless jumble of quiet notes.

Status: see map. Summer visitor. Passage Turkey and Iran and all countries south including Arabia and Egypt, though generally scarce. Vagrant Algeria, Libya. Winters in small numbers in SW Arabia.

Habitat: olive-groves, parkland, cultivation with scattered trees and scrub, also in lowlands and foothills; on passage may occur in almost any group of low trees and bushes. Nests in tree.

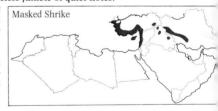
Masked Shrike

Black Drongo *Dicrurus macrocercus*   Plate 36

Identification: 30 cm. Sexes alike. Upright, rather slender, thrush-sized and all-black (glossy blue-black in sunlight), with long, deeply-forked tail, curving out towards end; brown, semi-translucent primaries revealed in flight. Juvenile has belly barred or flecked with white and care should be taken not to confuse with White-bellied Drongo *Dicrurus caerulescens* (not recorded in region), which is much smaller, with wholly white lower breast, belly and undertail-coverts. Sits upright on perch (tree, wall, animal's back, etc), whence makes aerial sally to pursue insects, with bee-eater-like glides and heavy flycatching manoeuvres. Often occurs in loose gatherings, particularly when hawking and going to roost.

Voice: call, harsh, throaty 'schweep-schweep' and loud 'pink'.
Status: formerly bred in SE Iran but no records this century.
Habitat: cultivated lowlands, particularly abundant near water; frequently near habitation and even edges of towns.

Jay *krynicki*

Jay *Garrulus glandarius*

Identification: 33 cm. See PMH. A number of races occur in the region. All are broadly similar to European birds but differ mostly in colour of crown (black in several races, streaked or strongly streaked in others), extent of white on face, and colour and uniformity of upperparts (vinous or grey, with nape matching or not matching mantle). An example of black-crowned form (*krynicki* of N Turkey) is illustrated.
Status: see map. Resident, slight dispersal outside breeding range.
Habitat: coniferous, oak or mixed woodland. Nests in tree.

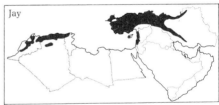

Magpie *Pica pica*   Plate 36

Identification: 46–50 cm. See PMH. Race *mauritanica* (NW Africa) identical to European birds except for turquoise blue, tear-shaped mark through eye; it often breeds in small colonies. Isolated *asirensis* (Western Arabia) is longer than European birds and has a particularly heavy bill.
Status: see map. Formerly bred Tunisia, and may still do so. Resident with some dispersal outside breeding range in winter, eg to S Iraq, also occasionally S Lebanon.
Habitat: bushy or open country with tall trees, scattered woods, pine and juniper-covered slopes, up to 2,900 m. Builds domed nest, in tree or large bush.

Pleske's Ground Jay *Podoces pleskei*   Plate 36

Identification: 24 cm. Sexes alike. Ground Jay aptly describes this shy, Hoopoe-sized bird which is not unlike that species in general colouration; *long, fine, decurved bill* and broad rounded wings help to accentuate this impression. Plumage warm cinnamon-buff with paler chin and face, black streak up to and behind whitish-ringed eye, *black wings with two white bars*, jet-black tail and prominent *narrow black patch on throat and upper breast*. Black bill and pale legs.

225

Elusive and rarely seen except when perched on bush-top, with slight flaunt of tail, to give one or two bursts of calls before dropping steeply to ground again; runs swiftly if approached. In flight, white wing-patches flash conspicuously.
Voice: song, rapid (10 notes per second) high, weak, flat-sounding 'pee-pee-pee-pee-pee' not unlike distant Rock Nuthatch.
Status: see map. Resident eastern Iran.
Habitat: steppe, liberally sprinkled with bushes 1–2 m high. Nest undescribed.

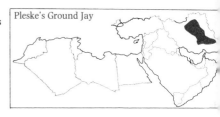
Pleske's Ground Jay

Nutcracker *Nucifraga caryocatactes*

Identification: 32 cm. See PMH.
Status: vagrant Turkey and N Iran.
Habitat: coniferous and deciduous woods.

Alpine Chough *Pyrrhocorax graculus*

Identification: 38 cm. See PMH.
Status: see map. Resident, extending into Syria in winter.
Habitat: Mountains at high altitude; rarely descends to lowlands. Nests colonially in rocky cliffs or ruins.

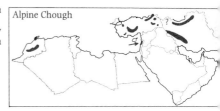
Alpine Chough

Chough *Pyrrhocorax pyrrhocorax*

Identification: 39 cm. See PMH.
Status: see map. May breed Mt Hermon (Near East). Resident.
Habitat: mountains, locally cliffs and rocky outcrops near the coast. Nests colonially in rock clefts, cliff-ledges, caves.

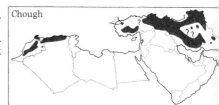
Chough

Jackdaw *Corvus monedula*

Identification: 33 cm. See PMH.
Status: see map. Bred formerly in Tunisia. Mainly resident. In winter more widespread in Syria and Iraq.
Habitat: towns, villages, parkland, farmland and mountain cliffs. Nests colonially in holes in cliffs, buildings or trees.

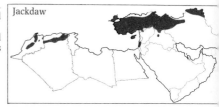
Jackdaw

226

House Crow *Corvus splendens*   Illustration p. 229

Identification: 43 cm. Sexes alike. Grey and black crow, slightly smaller than Carrion/Hooded but with *proportionately longer, deeper bill and more domed crown*. Can look thin, scrawny with attenuated neck and long legs when alert. Plumage shows similarities to Jackdaw and Hooded Crow: *black crown, face and throat abruptly joining grey nape, neck and breast*, the latter merging into dull slate underparts; back, wings and tail glossy black; bill black. Gregarious, fairly tame though wary; often with other scavenging birds around rubbish-tips and carrion.

Voice: quieter and higher-pitched than Carrion Crow, 'kwar, kwar, kwar', or 'waaa, waaa, waaa'.

Status: see map. A recent colonist, probably by introduction. Has bred but not always established Kuwait, E. Saudi Arabia, Bahrain, Gulf of Aqaba.

Habitat: mainly coastal towns and villages, rubbish dumps, picnic sites, palm-groves. Nests in tree or man-made structure.

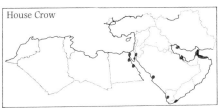

Rook *Corvus frugilegus*

Identification: 46 cm. See PMH.

Status: see map. Mainly resident. Passage through Turkey. In winter reaches SW Iran and S Iraq, Syria and irregularly Cyprus and Israel. Rare Egypt. Vagrant Algeria, Kuwait.

Habitat: agricultural land with trees. Nests and roosts in colonies in trees.

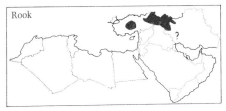

Carrion Crow *Corvus corone* (*corone* group)

Identification: 47 cm. See PMH.

Status: vagrant Morocco, Turkey, perhaps Iran.

Hooded Crow *Corvus corone* (*cornix* group)

Identification: 47 cm. See PMH.

Status: see map. Resident. In winter S Iraq. Vagrant Tunisia and Libya.

Habitat: wide range of habitats notably open country with scattered trees, edges of woods, parks and towns. Nests in tree, sometimes on cliff.

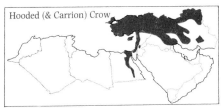

Jungle Crow *Corvus macrorhynchos*   Illustration p. 229

Identification: 43–50 cm. Sexes alike. Glossy black crow, about size of Carrion but slimmer, with proportionately *longer and slightly wedge-shaped tail; black bill longer, heavier and with more decurved culmen*, looking rather out of proportion, which rounded head and steep forehead accentuate. Noticeably smaller and sleeker than Raven with no shaggy throat-feathers,

227

though confusion possible with Raven in worn plumage. Generally less gregarious than House Crow.

Voice: most typical call is fairly deep 'hroarr-hroarr', deeper than call of House Crow, but not Raven-like.

Status: recorded in Iran last century as breeding in SE coastal area.

Habitat: edges of towns and villages, but mainly well-wooded countryside. Nests in tree.

Pied Crow *Corvus albus*

Identification: 45 cm. Sexes alike. Glossy black crow with *broad white collar around neck and across breast, black underwings* and no grey in plumage. (Rather similarly patterned Hooded Crow grey and black, grey more extensive on back and underparts as well as covering upper- and underwing-coverts; moreover, Hooded always dingier, even in Iraq and W Iran where birds can show strikingly pale grey parts.) Gregarious, often feeding with other scavengers including vultures and Black Kites.

Voice: croaking 'raark', Rook- or even Raven-like, but less deep.

Status: vagrant Libya, Algeria.

Habitat: usually near towns, villages, rubbish-tips, etc.

Brown-necked Raven *Corvus ruficollis*

Identification: 50 cm. Sexes alike. Slightly smaller than Raven (see illustration) with *slightly longer, slimmer wings, longer head and slimmer bill*, the latter frequently held drooped in flight; these features, together with longish wedge-shaped tail, at times recall Lammergeier. Central tail feathers protrude slightly beyond tail outline, whereas Raven has more even wedge-shape. At rest, *longer wings often reach tip of tail*, while in Raven they usually fall well short of tip (though overlap occurs). All glossy black with *bronzy-brown sheen on nape and neck*, difficult to see unless at close range. Juvenile as adult but lacks brown on neck.

Voice: similar to Raven but higher-pitched, less croaky and less varied.

Status: see map. In central Iran population shows characteristics intermediate between this species and Raven. Resident with some unclarified seasonal movements. Vagrant Syria. SE Turkey.

Habitat: desert and semi-desert, artemesia-steppe, savanna, rocky areas and wadis; in S Arabia from sea level to highest mountains (over 3,000 m). Nests on cliff, old building, occasionally in tree.

Raven *Corvus corax*

Identification: 64 cm. See PMH.

Status: see map. Resident. Reaches S Iraq in winter. Rare Lebanon.

Habitat: mountains with or without trees. Nests on cliff, or occasionally tree.

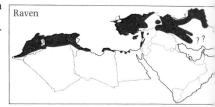

Fan-tailed Raven *Corvus rhipidurus*

Identification: 47 cm. Sexes alike. Stout, all-black, crow-sized raven with strong bill, shorter than Ravens' but stronger than Crow's. *Very short tail makes it unmistakable in flight*, and even on ground; *wing-tips extend beyond tip of tail*. May show bronze tinge to plumage and, when circling overhead in sunlight, very black coverts contrast with slightly paler, browner

228

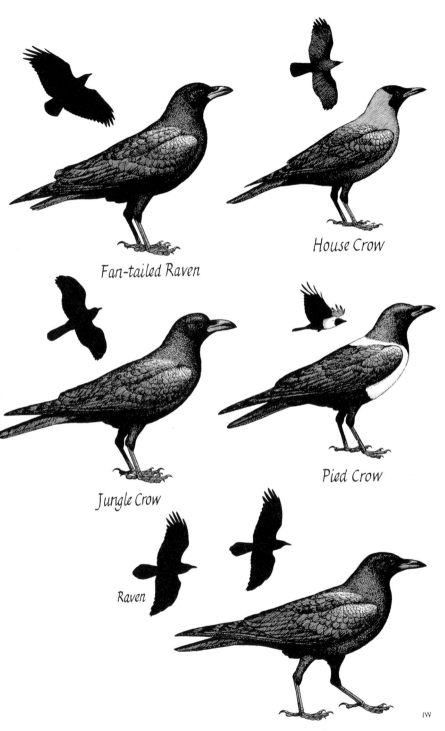

Fan-tailed Raven

House Crow

Jungle Crow

Pied Crow

Raven

Brown-necked Raven

IW

flight-feathers; also, pale greyish soles to feet show against dark plumage. Large groups frequently congregate and may then soar, raptor-like, in thermals. On ground often pants with open bill.

Voice: loud, high-pitched croak, rather gull-like.

Status: see map. Resident.

Habitat: desert, semi-desert, crags, cliffs from below sea level to over 3,000 m in mountains; often close to human habitation where flocks collect around rubbish tips. Nests on rock face or hole in cliff.

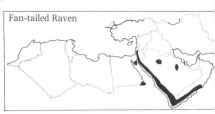
Fan-tailed Raven

Tristram's Grackle *Onychognathus tristramii* Plate 36

Identification: 25 cm. Sexes differ. *Black plumage with prominent rusty-orange primaries in flight* and loud echoing calls rule out confusion with any other species. Male glossy black, shining blue-violet in certain lights. Primaries bright rusty (above and below) conspicuous in flight and with narrow, brown hind-border. Secondaries below, dark grey. Eye reddish, bill black and legs dark grey. Duller female resembles male but has greyish black-brown head, neck and breast, streaked darker (rather like juvenile Blackbird), duller orange wing-patches and (always?) dark eye. Juvenile similar to female. Usually in flocks and fairly tame; a party will alight on a tree to feed noisily in manner of Rose-coloured Starlings.

Voice: parties keep up constant conversation of 'wolf-whistle' notes: 'dee-oo-ee-o'; 'o-eeou'; often loud and echoing round rocky panoramas, also mewing 'vu-ee-oo'.

Status: see map. Resident, slight winter dispersal.

Habitat: wild, rocky hills and ravines, semidesert, also rocky edges of well-vegetated wadis, often congregating around patches of cultivation, from below sea level to 3,000 m. Nests among rocks.

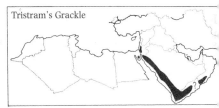
Tristram's Grackle

Amethyst Starling *Cinnyricinclus leucogaster* Plate 36

Identification: 18–19 cm. Sexes differ. Male unmistakable, with *iridescent violet-purple upperparts, head and breast, white on rest of underparts* and black wings. Female *dark brown above, white below, with dark brown speckling*; closer views reveal brown throat with faint white streaks and heavy spotting on breast, though belly virtually unmarked. Eye yellow in male, apparently yellow or chestnut in female and dark in juvenile; legs and bill dark. Most frequently seen in trees and fairly shy; often in small parties. Fast, direct, Starling-like flight.

Voice: call a long, ringing, grating, musical squeal with rising inflexion ending in quiet chuckle. Soft chuckle when flushed. Song, loud, metallic, gurgling warble.

Status: see map. Probably breeds in N Yemen. Summer visitor. Vagrant Israel.

Habitat: plains, hills and wadis with trees and other vegetation, mainly 500–2,000 m. Nests in hole in tree.

Amethyst Starling

230

Starling *Sturnus vulgaris*

Identification: 22 cm. See PMH.
Status: see map. Resident and winter visitor. Winters most of the region, but scarce or irregular in southern parts of N Africa, S Arabia (vagrant Yemen) and S Iran.
Habitat: towns and villages, but also woods or groups of old trees. In winter also farmland. Nests in hole in tree or building.

Spotless Starling *Sturnus unicolor*

Identification: 22 cm. See PMH.
Status: see map. Resident.
Habitat: cliffs, towns or villages, locally wooded regions or around isolated farms, or in olive-plantations. Nests in hole in tree, cliff, ruin, wall, etc.

Rose-coloured Starling *Sturnus roseus*

Identification: 22 cm. See PMH.
Status: see map. May breed erratically C and E Turkey. Summer visitor. Passage Turkey, N and W Iran and Iraq; scarce and irregular Cyprus, Near East, Arabian Gulf and Oman but vagrant in rest of Arabia and N Africa west to Tunisia; irregular in winter Oman.
Habitat: open country, agricultural land, cliffs, slopes. Nests colonially in holes among stones on open ground, in walls or wood-stacks.

Wattled Starling *Creatophora cineracea*   Plate 36

Identification: 21.5 cm. Sexes differ. Slightly larger than Starling but similar shape. Adult male variable; old males, in breeding season, unmistakable with *bare yellow head and fleshy black wattles* on forehead, crown and throat; otherwise plumage an even pale grey or buffish grey with glossed green-black wings and tail and *creamy-white rump*; white primary coverts form wing-patch in flight. Outside breeding season, male loses wattles and head becomes feathered pale grey. Pale, yellow-flesh bill; legs pinkish or flesh-brown. Female and non-breeding male pale sandy grey with whitish-buff greater coverts, black wings and tail and *whitish rump*; primary coverts black, sometimes showing fleck of white on leading edge. Diffuse blackish loral spot and moustachial streak, with yellow patch around and behind eye. Juvenile which is most likely to occur in region, cold grey-brown above (browner in female) with pale fringes to coverts and tertials. Underparts paler with grey-brown wash on upper breast. Bill broader-based than Starling, dull straw-yellow, often with blackish tip and culmen. In flight, shows *buffish panel on upperwing-coverts and sandy-grey rump*.
Voice: soft but rather squeaky whistle.
Status: rather scarce and irregular visitor Oman and S Yemen (mid-summer to winter); vagrant N Yemen. Nomadic from Africa.
Habitat: open bush and savanna.

231

Common Mynah *Acridotheres tristis* — Plate 36

Identification: 23 cm. Sexes alike. Resembles plump Starling in shape, and similarly short-tailed. Head glossy black merging into *deep vinous-brown or maroon breast, flanks and upperparts.* Centre of belly to undertail-coverts white, rounded tail blackish tipped white, broadly so at corners. In flight, reveals large white panel on upper and underwing, formed by *white primary-coverts* and white bases to blackish-brown flight-feathers. *Rich yellow bill*, legs and *wattle below and behind eye.* Tame, bold and rather vociferous, usually in pairs or small flocks, though sometimes large parties congregate. Often seen feeding on ground or perching on buildings.
Voice: very noisy. Mixture of strident and rough calls and liquid 'kiky-kiky-kiky, chour, chour, kok, kok, kok', last notes accompanied by nodding of head. Song imitative and repetitive. Alarm-note, 'traaahh' somewhat Nutcracker-like.
Status: see map. Resident in Iranian Baluchistan; small colonies in E Arabia and Jedda, Saudi Arabia, probably originated from captive birds.
Habitat: as Bank Mynah. Nests in hole in tree, under eaves, etc.

Common Mynah

Bank Mynah *Acridotheres ginginianus* — Plate 36

Identification: 20 cm. Sexes alike. Apart from slight crest on forehead, similar size and shape to Common Mynah, but *body plumage pale slate,* including chin and throat (unlike Common Mynah); head and throat black with *orange-red bare patch round eye* (yellow in Common Mynah), orange-yellow to pale reddish-flesh bill, yellow legs; undertail-coverts and vent rusty-buff. In flight, shows white patch at base of primaries, *and rusty-buff patch on adjoining primary-coverts also on tips of short rounded tail above* (these rusty areas being white in Common Mynah); below, *wing-coverts also rusty-buff.* Usually in small parties and can be fairly tame. Juvenile has head and neck brown, with remaining upperparts more brown-tinged than adults, also rusty-buff wing-patch and tip of tail buffish-white.
Voice: variety of chuckling notes, some quite musical, like Common Mynah but softer.
Status: one colony at Abu Dhabi, UAE, probably originated from introduced birds.
Habitat: towns, villages, fields, grassy areas, dumps, rivers; roosts in trees or reeds. Nests in holes in banks, masonry, etc.

Saxaul Sparrow *Passer ammodendri* — Plate 37

Identification: 15 cm. Sexes differ. Male superficially resembles similar-sized male House Sparrow but *paler sandy-grey,* and *entirely lacks chestnut.* Further separated by *black crown and nape,* bordered below by *long rich ochre supercilium* (white in front of eye), *broadening on sides of nape,* and black eye-stripe. *Black patch on lesser coverts* and two white wing-bars, the top one very broad; flight-feathers fringed whitish, and *sandy-grey mantle has distinct, but narrow black streaks.* Cheeks and underparts pale greyish, with large black bib. (Male House Sparrow has chestnut lesser coverts, warm buffish fringes to flight-feathers, no white bar on greater coverts, much broader black streaks on mantle and different head-pattern). Black bill turns brown in winter, when blacks of head and mantle obscured by pale buff feather-fringes. Female, much less contrasted than male, paler than female House Sparrow, with top of head paler and supercilium buffer at rear; paler *sandy-grey mantle has distinctly thinner dark brown streaks,* and strong white wing-bar; some have obscure, dull darkish bib.
Voice: no useful information.
Status: isolated old record Iran. Range Central Asia.
Habitat: sandy deserts and oases. Nests in bush, poplar or crevice.

232

House Sparrow *Passer domesticus*

Identification: 15 cm. See PMH.
Status: see map. Resident.
Habitat: built-up areas and cultivated land, seldom far from human habitation. Nests in hole or crevice in buildings, but sometimes builds in tree.

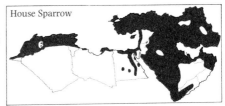

Spanish Sparrow *Passer hispaniolensis*

Identification: 15 cm. See PMH.
Status: see map. May breed some years N Saudi Arabia. Summer visitor and resident Morocco and Turkey, mainly resident elsewhere. Passage Turkey, Cyprus, N and SE Iran; winters Turkey, S Iran, Iraq, Near East, NW Saudi Arabia and Egypt, reaching western Gulf States but scarce further east to Oman; also central Libya.
Habitat: not restricted to houses, preferring woodland, fruit groves and stands of palms, tamarisks, eucalyptus, etc. In winter also open cultivation. Nests in foundations of large nest (eg storks), hole in wall or builds bulky ball-shaped nest in tree; singly or colonially.

Sind Jungle Sparrow *Passer pyrrhonotus*   Plate 37

Identification: 12.5 cm. Sexes differ. Small sparrow, closely resembling House Sparrow but male has *narrower black bib which does not reach upper breast, and chestnut lower back and rump* (greyish in House); band behind eye redder chestnut and greater coverts less rufous-chestnut. Female closely resembles small version of female House Sparrow, though spot behind eye darker and ear-coverts more ashen. Similar-sized female Dead Sea Sparrow has supercilium and particularly sides of neck tinged yellowish. Often in small groups.
Voice: like House Sparrow but clearer.
Status: see map. Resident SE Iran.
Habitat: along rivers and swamps with tamarisk, acacia and thorn bushes in which it nests.

Dead Sea Sparrow *Passer moabiticus*   Plate 37

Identification: 12 cm. Sexes differ. Small sparrow. Colourful male has distinct head-pattern, with *dark grey cheeks, long whitish supercillium* (which turns *yellow-buff behind eye*), whitish moustachial stripe (which becomes *rich yellow-orange at side of neck*) and narrow black bib. Crown greyish, upperparts sandy-brown, streaked black on mantle; wing-coverts chestnut with two buff bars, and blackish flight-feathers fringed pale buff. Underparts greyish-white in race *moabiticus* (Near East, E Iraq and SW Iran) or yellowish in *yattii* (E Iran) and undertail-coverts dotted brownish. Female, which lacks black bib and chestnut in wings, sandy-brown above, streaked darker on mantle and pale greyish-white below; female *yattii* underbody suffused yellowish. Resembles female House Sparrow but smaller; may show yellowish tinge in superciliary stripe and at sides of throat. Often gregarious; wary.

Voice: song, rolling 'tri-rirp, tri-rirp' or 'tlir-tlir-tlir' more tuneful and rhythmic than House Sparrow (rhythm not unlike Graceful Warbler's). Call, high-pitched 'trrirp'.

Status: see map. Resident Iran, Iraq; but apparently summer visitor Cyprus and N Israel breeding areas.

Habitat: near water in bushes or thick scrub of tamarisk or poplars, in which it nests, often colonially.

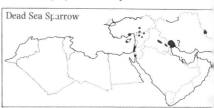

Desert Sparrow *Passer simplex*   Plate 37

Identification: 13 cm. Sexes differ. Pale, fairly large-headed sparrow which appears long-legged on ground. Male has *unstreaked pale grey upperparts and paler rump*, conspicuous dark-bordered light wing-patch in flight (formed by whitish-buff secondaries framed by dark primaries and tertials) and two broad, white wing-bars. Chin, throat and facial mask black (latter more evident in eastern greyer race *zarudnyi*), sides of head and underparts whitish; tail blackish-brown with broad light edges at sides. Female lacks black head-pattern; upperparts plain sandy-buff; less contrasting pale wing-patch and buffish wing-coverts have diffuse pale bars, but obvious dark centres to bastard wing, median and outer greater coverts. Bill yellowish-horn though normally black in adult male. Juvenile resembles female, but young male develops some adult-features by mid-summer, such as dark lores and sometimes black bill.

Voice: subdued and repeated 'chu'; also 'chip-chip', higher-pitched than House Sparrow's.

Status: see map. Mainly resident but some south movement in winter. No records this century Iran.

Habitat: sandy deserts and semi-deserts, frequently near habitation, oases, tamarisks, palms, cereal crops. Nests in hole in wall, edge of well, top of palm, foundations of Raven's nest, etc.

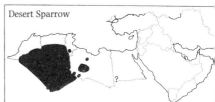

Tree Sparrow *Passer montanus*

Identification: 14 cm. See PMH.

Status: see map. Has bred Morocco, where otherwise vagrant. Resident, occasionally reaching Iraq, Cyprus and Israel in winter; vagrant Algeria, Tunisia, Egypt and Gulf States.

Habitat: trees, usually near habitation. Nests in hole in tree, but sometimes builds a domed nest.

234

Sudan Golden Sparrow *Passer luteus*   Plate 37

Identification: 13 cm. Sexes differ. Male unmistakable with striking *lemon-yellow, unstreaked head, neck, rump and underparts, chestnut mantle* and *two whitish wing-bars on black coverts*; broad rufous or buff edges conceal blackish secondaries, but blackish centres obvious on tertials; pale spot sometimes visible on lesser coverts but often hidden by chestnut scapulars. Ventral feathers sometimes fringed blackish, (never in Arabian Golden Sparrow). Dark grey tail-feathers narrowly edged whitish-buff. Bill blackish but pale brown outside breeding season. Female is *unstreaked, washed-out yellowish-buff*; wings similar to male but black replaced by dark grey and feather-edges buffish; whitish wing-bars less striking and lesser coverts buff-brown. Juvenile resembles female but usually has pale yellow-buff supercilium. Bill of female and juvenile pale horn-brown; legs flesh in all plumages, and dark eye appears large. Highly gregarious.
Voice: song recalls House Sparrow, 'chirp-chirp-chirp'; flight-call also sparrow-like but faster, with Redpoll-like rhythm, 'che-che-che' repeated 7–8 times.
Status: see map. Resident in SE Egypt (Gebel Elba).
Habitat: arid thorn bush country often near cultivation. Nests in thorn tree or bush, colonial.

Arabian Golden Sparrow *Passer euchlorus*   Plate 37

Identification: 13 cm. Sexes differ. Smaller than House Sparrow, with *domed head, large blackish eye* and relatively long tail. Male's *unstreaked golden-yellow head, upperparts and underparts, and broadly whitish- or sandy-buff fringes to blackish flight- and tail-feathers* separate it from other birds within its range (golden-yellow male Rüppell's Weaver has dark chestnut and blackish face, and always streaked mantle). In non-breeding season, mantle and wing-coverts much greyer and *head often tinged cinnamon or rufous*. Bill black in breeding season, otherwise pale horn-brown or pinkish. Female, pale buffish-grey or sandy; has unstreaked upperparts with head and nape often buffer and underparts paler, often with greyer breast and flanks; wing-coverts with some dark centres, and fringes to dark flight- and tail-feathers creamy sandy-grey; bill fleshy horn. Juvenile resembles female but can show slight mottling on mantle, but never bold streaks of larger female Rüppell's Weaver and House Sparrow. Highly gregarious; often quite independent of human habitation. Sometimes regarded as conspecific with Sudan Golden Sparrow, but geographically separate.
Voice: flocks utter constant twitter, recalling House Sparrow, but of more whispering quality; apparently lacks Sudan Golden's 'che-che-che' Redpoll-like call.
Status: see map. Resident but some local movement.
Habitat: arid thorn and acacia savanna and neighbouring cereal crops. Nests colonially in trees, typically acacia.

Pale Rock Sparrow *Petronia brachydactyla*   Plate 37

Identification: 14 cm. Sexes alike. *Rather featureless, sandy grey-brown* above, pale greyish-fawn to sandy-white below. Long wings darker with *two whitish wing-bars*, narrow, but usually conspicuous white panel on inner secondaries and creamy tips to primaries; short dark *tail has white tip* (except on central feathers), most evident on undertail in flight. Further features are faint whitish eye-brow, whitish throat bordered by faint dark malar and whitish moustachial streak, and strong pale bill. General drabness hinders identification but important points are white on inner secondaries, long wings, especially in flight, white tip to tail and *bright translucent-looking brownish-orange legs*. Immature slightly paler. Separated from larger and heavier Rock Sparrow by unstreaked plumage. See also Yellow-throated and Lesser Rock Sparrow.

Voice: song distinctive, buzzing, monotonous and persistent 'tss tss tss-tseeeeeeeei', superficially recalling Corn Bunting. Flight call, soft trill or churr, strongly recalling distant Bee-eater; also 'twee-ou'.

Status: see map. May breed Oman. Summer visitor. Passage in variable numbers in Arabia (especially SW), also Jordan; winter visitor W Saudi Arabia. Vagrant Egypt and Yemen.

Habitat: rocky and scrubby areas at moderate altitudes; in winter also plains and semi-deserts, sometimes in cultivation. Nest low in small bush.

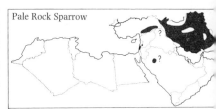

Pale Rock Sparrow

Yellow-throated Sparrow *Petronia xanthocollis*   Plate 37

Identification: 13 cm. Sexes differ. Can resemble female Chaffinch or Pale Rock Sparrow, but cleaner grey-brown on head and back, and distinctive *stout-based long and fine-pointed bill*. Male has *black bill* in breeding season, otherwise pinkish-flesh or pale brown like female, fine dark eye-line and *extensive, yellow lower throat-spot*, below whitish upper throat framed by greyish lower cheeks. *Chestnut patch on lesser coverts* (sometimes hidden by greyish shoulder feathers), bordered below by broad whitish wing-bar (with narrower whitish wing-bar on greater coverts). Lacks white edges of inner secondaries and white tip of tail of Pale Rock. Upperbreast and flanks buffish-grey, merging into buffish or silky white on rest of underparts; grey legs (translucent bright pale brown in Pale Rock). Female and juvenile lack chestnut shoulder-patch and yellow on throat; generally rather featureless grey-brown but female has *Chaffinch-like off-white wing-bar on median coverts*, diffuse buffish fringes to greater coverts and *distinctive bill shape*. Perches freely in trees; finch-like movements on ground; rather pipit-like dipping flight. Different habitat from Pale Rock Sparrow.

Voice: quiet chirruping song, obviously sparrow-like, but softer, more melodius and rhythmic than House Sparrow, with faster tempo. Call, sparrow-like 'cheep', 'chilp' or 'chirrup' but softer, more liquid and tuneful.

Status: see map. Summer visitor. Passage includes Kuwait and S Oman; vagrant E Province of Saudi Arabia, Bahrain and Israel. Occasional in winter Oman.

Habitat: open dry woodland, date groves, gardens, villages, river bottoms with some trees, cultivated areas. Nests in hole or crevice in tree.

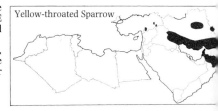

Yellow-throated Sparrow

Lesser Rock Sparrow (Bush Petronia) *Petronia dentata*   Plate 37

Identification: 13 cm. Sexes differ. Small, sparrow-like, with deep-based but *longish, pointed bill*. Male has *unmarked brown mantle*, brownish-grey crown bordered by *broad ill-defined chestnut supercilium* from eye backwards, often curving downwards behind ear-coverts; dark greyish or brownish sides of face and neck frame *creamy or whitish-grey throat with small yellowish spot* on *lower throat* (often hard to see); breast greyish merging into off-white below; tail dark brown. Bill black in breeding season, but otherwise lower mandible horn-coloured. Female brownish above streaked darker on mantle, with prominent *off-white supercilium* and *two creamy-white wing-bars* being most obvious features. Greyish on cheeks and ear-coverts, surrounded by *buffish area which extends onto sides of narrow white throat* (sometimes with yellowish spot at base) bordered by greyish upper breast. Dark horn bill has fleshy or horn lower mandible. Legs dark bluish-grey or dark brown. Juvenile resembles female but supercilium pale rusty-buff, broad above eye, then narrowing but curving upwards at rear; richer buff surrounds dark cheeks and ear-coverts; narrow bib white, framed below by diffuse longitudinal dark spots across foreneck and upper breast. Rather bounding flight; sits quietly, often flicking tail. Pale Rock Sparrow, the only other *Petronia* in SW Arabia, has white-tipped tail, lacks head- and throat-pattern of Lesser Rock. is always unstreaked, and has bright translucent fleshy-orange legs.

Voice: song consists of 4–6 fast, rolling notes 'triup-triup-triup-triup' which have tone like cross between House Sparrow and Budgerigar; also more bunting-like 'chu-chu-chu-chu', etc, rising in middle but ending on even pitch. Also, soft sparrow-like flight-note, 'chewee'.

Status: see map. Resident; recorded S Yemen and may breed there.

Habitat: wadis and terraced slopes with scattered trees; 650–1,700 m. Nests in hole or crevice in tree.

Lesser Rock Sparrow

Rock Sparrow *Petronia petronia*   Plate 37

Identification: 14 cm. See PMH.

Status: see map. Resident, but summer visitor to extreme NW Iran; in winter recorded E, SW Iran, Iraq. Vagrant Cyprus.

Habitat: rocky mountain slopes, stony ground, ruins, also dry river beds and farmland; seldom among houses though sometimes among trees. Nests in crevice in rock, building or tree.

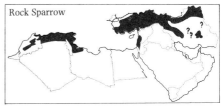
Rock Sparrow

Snow Finch *Montifringilla nivalis*   Plate 37

Identification: 17 cm. See PMH. Race *alpicola* (E Turkey to W Iran) has top of head brownish (ash-grey in nominate race), almost concolorous with back, which is clearly paler than European birds.

Status: see map. Resident, with altitudinal movements in winter. Vagrant Egypt.

Habitat: bare mountain-tops above 2,000 m, lower in winter; visits mountain huts and camps. Nests in rock crevice, wall, etc.

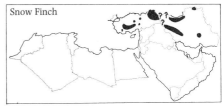
Snow Finch

Rüppell's Weaver *Ploceus galbula*   Plate 37

Identification: 14–15 cm. Sexes differ. Only weaver breeding in SW Arabia. Similar size to House Sparrow but longer stouter bill, shorter tail and shorter, more rounded wings. Male in breeding season has black lores and bill surrounded by *deep chestnut face looking blackish at distance; rest of head and underparts golden yellow;* mantle and rump yellow-green, the former streaked darker; wings brown, feathers fringed yellow; tail olive-brown fringed greenish-yellow. During part of non-breeding season loses chestnut on face, while crown and nape become yellowish-green, uniform with mantle. Bill black in breeding season, otherwise browner; eye chestnut. Female olive-brown above, streaked darker on mantle; underparts buffish-white with yellowish-buff on throat and breast; wings olive with paler fringes and two whitish wing-bars (fainter on greater coverts); tail olive, fringed paler. Bill pale flesh or horn-coloured. Female distinguished from female Arabian Golden Sparrow by larger size and bill, shorter tail and streaked upperparts; from female House Sparrow by yellowish-buff breast and olive-tinged upperparts. See also Streaked Weaver, feral in Nile Delta. Gregarious, often forming large flocks.

Voice: song, wheezy chatter which ends in insect-like hissing sounds. Call, dry 'cheee-cheee'.

Status: see map. Resident. Birds nest-building at Riyadh originated from escapes.

Habitat: crops, palm groves, savanna or wadis with acacia, tamarisk and other bushes from sea-level to 2,000 m but commonest at lower altitudes. Nest suspended from acacia or other large tree, telephone-wire, etc; colonial.

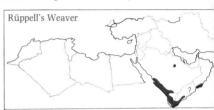

Rüppell's Weaver

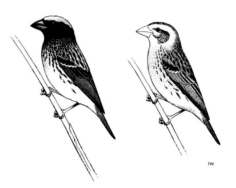

Streaked Weaver, male, summer (left), female and winter male (right)

Streaked Weaver *Ploceus manyar*

Identification: 15 cm. Sexes differ. Size of House Sparrow but bill much heavier and wings and tail shorter. Male in breeding plumage has *bright yellow crown and forehead, distinct broad black mask* on side of head and throat and buff-white underparts with conspicuous *blackish streaks on breast and flanks*. Upperparts whitish- or fulvous-buff, conspicuously streaked blackish; blackish median coverts show broad pale wing-bar; blackish tertials distinctly fringed whitish. Bill black in breeding season, otherwise pale flesh. Female has dark grey-brown top of head, cheeks and ear-coverts, latter framed by *long broad yellow supercilium which curves down behind them*. Upperparts fulvous, streaked blackish-brown; underparts buffy- or yellowish-white with some *dark streaks on flanks*; pattern of tertials and wing-bar much as male, and shows large buffish patch on closed wing. Bill yellow to pale flesh, legs flesh. Immature male resembles female but gradually develops blackish and yellow mottling on sides of head, and upper head becomes yellow with variable thin dark streaks or speckles on crown. Rüppell's Weaver (different distribution and habitat) lacks streaks on underparts in all plumages.

Voice: song from colony recalls House Sparrow flock; 'chack' call reminiscent of Wheatear.

Status: resident Nile Delta, Egypt, from escaped birds.

Habitat: dense reedy areas in which it nests colonially.

Red-billed (Senegal) Firefinch *Lagonosticta senegala*   Plate 38

Identification: 9 cm. Sexes differ. A tiny waxbill. Male unmistakable with *crimson head, breast and belly with minute white flecks on upper breast*, brown back and wings, latter without white spots of Avadavat; blackish tail with deep crimson rump and uppertail-coverts; yellow eye-ring and *red bill with blue base* (often looks mauve in field). Female much less distinct; sandy-brown above with crimson in front of eye, *warm sandy below with a few minute white flecks on upper breast*. Tail, rump, eye-ring and bill similar to male, though latter often red-pink with blue top to upper mandible. Juvenile resembles female but has greyish bill, lacks white breast-spots and red in front of eye. Very active; on ground frequently flicks tail upwards and has

238

constant side-to-side movement of bill through top soil, searching for seeds. Fast, direct flight.
Voice: weak 'tweet tweet'.
Status: see map. Probably resident. Vagrant Morocco.
Habitat: scrub and cultivation; often near human habitation. Nests in bush or hut.

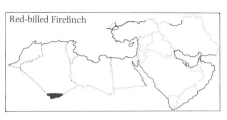

Arabian Waxbill *Estrilda rufibarba* Plate 38

Identification: 10 cm. Sexes alike. Very slightly larger than Zebra Waxbill. Upperparts grey-brown with *faintest of vermiculations*, only visible when close, and *dark crimson-red mask through eye*. Graduated tail and *rump black* with narrow white edges to outer tail-feathers, only visible from below. White cheeks and throat merge into very clean silky or whitish-buff underparts, sometimes showing dark vermiculations on flanks. Juvenile brown above with slightly darker wings, off-white below with buff wash to breast and especially belly and flanks. Grey-brown or *blackish mask through eye* (often creating black-capped appearance); usually dark greyish bill. Bill colour can vary, and although most adults have black bills (with red on sides and base at certain times) and immatures dark greyish bills, birds can sometimes show quite pale, even whitish bills; these colours are presumably linked with age, sex or season but are not fully understood. Often gathers in flocks; less shy than Zebra Waxbill with which it will associate. When perched often waves tail from side to side. Jerky flight.
Voice: conversational notes from group comprise hard buzzing 'dzit', 'dzeet', 'chzit' or 'chee', often developing into continuous buzzing chatter. Flight-call, buzzing high-pitched 'chee-chee', or 'chee-chee-chee-chee-chee' (no buzzing quality to call of Zebra Waxbill).
Status: see map. Resident
Habitat: wadis, rocky hillsides with cultivation and trees, patches of agriculture, also reeds and thick bushes, usually 250–2,400 m, often near water. Nest not described.

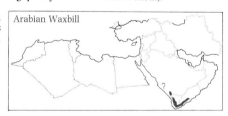

Avadavat *Amandava amandava* Plate 38

Identification: 9–10 cm. Sexes differ. Small, short-tailed finch-like bird originating from India. Male in breeding plumage *bright crimson-red* all over body, though wings browner and tail blackish; sides of neck, underparts *and wing coverts* show some *small white spots* (absent on wings of very similar Red-billed Firefinch, vagrant from Africa); lower belly dark brown. Female brown above with blackish lores, grey-buff throat and breast, belly fulvous-yellow; rump red, tail blackish. Male in non-breeding plumage resembles female, but throat and breast greyer. Bill coral red in both sexes all year, with ridge of culmen blackish. Juvenile similar to adult female but lacks red on rump, has two buff wing-bars and blackish-brown bill which soon changes to reddish-brown.
Voice: song, high-pitched but soft continuous twitter (from perch or in flight). Call, series of high-pitched chirps, uttered in flight; some notes not unlike call of Penduline Tit; also a squeak.
Status: see map. Also recorded Lebanon, Iran, UAE, Oman. All records originate from escapes.
Habitat: varied, often near water, sometimes near human habitation. Nests, low in bush.

Zebra Waxbill *Amandava subflava*   Plate 38

Identification: 9 cm. Sexes differ. Very slightly smaller than Arabian Waxbill which it otherwise resembles in shape. Male dull brown-grey above with paler cheeks and *strong orange-red to yellow-orange wash on underparts, but flanks barred black and white. A crimson-red eye-mask*, bordered black on lores. *Lower back, rump, upper- and under-tail coverts red*; dark tail narrowly bordered white. Small *conical bill waxy-red*. Female lacks red eye-mask, having palish diffuse eye-ring and supercilium; *red usually confined to rump; underparts have yellowish-buff wash* varying in intensity and *usually richer on rear body*: flanks less boldly barred than in male. Juvenile similar to female but lacks red on rump and barring on flanks, is browner above; bill usually dark brown. (Note that bill-colour can vary with sex, age and season from waxy-red through yellowish-orange to dark brown). Forms large flocks; often more difficult to observe when perched than Arabian Waxbill as it quickly 'disappears', sliding down cereal stems. Fast flight with short undulations.
Voice: piping 'ptik'; twittering flight-notes recall Silverbill, but sharper: 'tip' 'tif' or 'tith-tith'. Also hard, short metallic 'zzrrep', repeated 2–3 times.
Status: see map. Resident; apparently a fairly recent colonist; has been recorded in Riyadh, central Saudi Arabia.
Habitat: trees and cultivation including cereal fields. Nests near ground in vegetation, or uses old nests of other small birds.

Indian Silverbill *Euodice malabarica*   Plate 38

Identification: 11 cm. Sexes alike. Small brown and whitish finch-type, with pointed tail and large *conical-shaped, silvery, gunmetal-grey bill*. Very similar to African Silverbill, which see. Upperparts mouse-brown, *without vermiculations on wing-coverts and tertials. Whitish rump and uppertail-coverts*; blackish tail. Underparts greyish-white to silvery-white, merging into darker upperparts on sides of neck and head. Eye dark and quite prominent. Juvenile has pale edgings to wing feathers. Frequently in small cohesive parties; perches freely in low vegetation, often waving or half-spreading and flicking tail. Fairly tame, often sitting in groups, chattering. Short undulations in flight.
Voice: rapid 'cheet-cheet-cheet' flight-call, Linnet-like but more tinkling; short, sharp, high-pitched trilling 'zip-zip'; harsh 'tchwit', conversational 'seesip, seesip' and other weak chirping notes. Song, short trill.
Status: see map. Resident. Has occurred elsewhere on Arabian Gulf. The separation of Indian from African Silverbill is becoming complicated as their ranges are spreading, may soon overlap and hybridisation might occur. Apparently recorded Algeria.
Habitat: dry open grassland with scrub and thorn bush, also cultivated regions, palm groves, etc. Nest as African Silverbill.

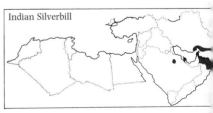

240

African Silverbill *Euodice cantans* Plate 38

Identification: 11 cm. Sexes alike. Very similar to geographically separated Indian Silverbill in all respects except in having *fine vermiculations on wing-coverts and tertials* (visible only at close range), and *black rump and uppertail-coverts*; may also show slight brownish on chin.
Voice: call notes similar to those of Indian Silverbill. Song, high-pitched trill of rapidly repeated single then double notes, each phrase descending then rising.
Status: see map. Resident. Isolated records Gulf States and Riyadh assumed to be escapes.
Habitat: as Indian Silverbill, but also in savanna. Nests in bush, crevice, old nest of weaver etc; will also build suspended nest with entrance hole at side.

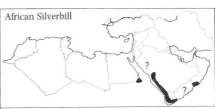

Red-eyed Vireo *Vireo olivaceus*

Identification: 15 cm. See PMH.
Status: vagrant Morocco.

Chaffinch *Fringilla coelebs* Plate 38

Identification: 15 cm. See PMH. North African races *africana* (illustrated) and *spodiogenys* similar to European birds (which also occur in N Africa in winter) but males have soft slate-blue head, including face and cheeks, with white half-circle round, and streak behind, eye; also green back and salmon-pink underparts. Often rather wary.
Status: see map. Resident, also winter visitor to N Africa, Near East and south to Iraq and SW Iran (but not SE Iran); irregular Kuwait, vagrant elsewhere in E Arabia; has reached S Egypt.
Habitat: trees, forests, gardens, orchards, plantations, thickets, palms. In winter often in cultivation, from sea-level to mountains. Nests fairly low in tree or bush.

Brambling *Fringilla montifringilla*

Identification: 15 cm. See PMH.
Status: scarce, irregular winter visitor to northern Morocco, Algeria, Egypt, more regular Near East; commoner Turkey and Iraq and common N and W Iran; rare E Arabia to central Oman; vagrant Tunisia and Libya.
Habitat: fields, farmland or other cultivation with trees and bushes nearby; also wasteland.

Red-fronted Serin *Serinus pusillus* Plate 38

Identification: 12 cm. Sexes alike. *Small, rather dark, stubby finch with sooty brown (near black) head and breast and 'luminous' orange circular patch on forehead.* Upperparts heavily streaked orange-brown and dark brown, with orange-ochre wash on coverts and rump and two pale wing-bars. Wings and tail blackish with yellow-orange feather edgings. Underparts below breast off-white with dark and buff streakings, particularly bold on flanks; sometimes yellow streaking on sooty breast. Stubby bill dark. In bouncing flight looks small and very dark above, pale below (including underwings) with dark head and breast. Juvenile *lacks sooty head and orange forehead*; instead, face, cheeks and throat washed-out orange-buff; birds moulting into adult plumage have rather *mottled dark head and breast*, Often feeds on ground and mixes with other finches, particularly Serins, Siskins and Chaffinches.
Voice: pleasant song not dissimilar to Serin, but not sibilant, having more of a Goldfinch quality and with powerful outpouring delivery. Call, Serin-like rippling note, 'drlllt-drlllt' or 'drillt-drillt'.

241

Status: see map. Mainly resident but at lower altitudes in winter, reaching S Iraq and rarely Syria, Lebanon and Israel; vagrant Cyprus, Egypt.

Habitat: rocky mountains and valleys, sometimes nearly barren, with junipers, conifers, willows, birches and open grassy areas; often near water. Usually 2,000–4,000 m, but much lower in winter. Nests in tree.

Red-fronted Serin

Serin *Serinus serinus*   Plate 38

Identification: 12 cm. See PMH.

Status: see map. Has been recorded Israel. Mainly resident. Also winter visitor to coastal N Africa, Cyprus, Near East. Vagrant W Iran.

Habitat: parks, gardens, vineyards, thickets, edges of woods and other similar cultivation. In winter also in wastelands, fields, etc near trees. Nests in tree (eg cedar, cypress), vine or small bush.

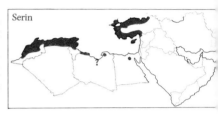

Serin

Syrian (Tristram's) Serin *Serinus syriacus*   Plate 38

Identification: 12.5 cm. Sexes differ slightly. Similar to Serin but less stubby, with longer tail and (all plumages) rather paler with greyer cast, *lacking bold streaks on underparts*. Male in summer told from Serin by *rich orange-yellow forehead and forecrown* (much more glowing and extensive than lemon-yellow of Serin), *lack of supercilium* (but yellow encircles and accentuates dark eye), bright golden-yellow greater coverts forming broad band (Serin has narrow yellowish wing-bar), more conspicuous yellow on flight-feathers and *yellowish-edged tail feathers* (not in Serin). Upperparts olive-yellow, faintly streaked darker (boldly in Serin), with olive-grey crown, hind-neck and cheeks and yellow rump. Underparts yellowish and unstreaked, with greyish flanks. In winter duller and greyer. Female olive-grey above, weakly streaked darker with greyish head and yellow forehead and area around eye (no orange tone). Underparts greyish-yellow, greyer on flanks and usually unstreaked, but sometimes (at least in winter) has two–three short dark flank-streaks. Juvenile sandy-brown showing no yellow except on margins of flight- and tail-feathers; has *ill-defined mottling on underparts* (young Serin crisply streaked below); washed-out yellow on forehead and rump appears in first-winter. Perches high in trees, also feeds on or near ground. Sociable, often forming flocks in winter.

Voice: flight-call drier, less ringing, less musical than Serin, 'tearrrrh', or 'tirrrrh' and 'tsirrr', also thin high nasal 'shkeep'. Often twitters (in flight or when perched) very low, soft 'tree-dar-dee', or 'tree-der-doo'. Song soft with Goldfinch and Linnet-like elements, with 'siou' notes and purring 'trrrr' cardueline trill. Usually sings from perch.

Status: see map. Apparently mainly resident, but extends to S Israel and Sinai in winter when remarkably also recorded in N Iraq.

Habitat: mountains with trees, eg cedars, junipers, but also deciduous including orchards; less restricted to trees outside breeding season. Nests in tree.

Syrian Serin

Citril Finch *Serinus citrinella*

Identification: 12 cm. See PMH.
Status: vagrant Algeria.

Arabian Serin *Serinus rothschildi*   Plate 38

Identification: 11.5 cm. Sexes alike. Similar size, structure and colouration to Yemen Serin, which see, but *stouter bill, darker colouration, dirtier throat, cheeks and upper breast,* and *hardly any streaking on crown.* Upperparts smoky-brown with faint pale eyebrow (obscure in Yemen Serin); ear-coverts and sides of throat mottled smoky, producing rather dirty look to head, with *no signs of even a faint moustachial streak* (present in Yemen Serin); chin buffish. Underparts off-white but breast often greyish-brown, with diffused darker streaks on breast and flanks (prominence of streaks can vary). Ill-defined olive rump (lacking in Yemen Serin) often difficult to observe. Strong bill, usually horn or grey, but can be dull pinkish, sometimes with small pale spot at base of lower mandible, absent in Yemen Serin. Less gregarious than Yemen Serin and often seen in pairs. *Spends most time in trees* (Yemen Serin is a ground or rock dweller) and when perched characteristic *gentle tail-flicking* may be noticed.
Voice: *call, quiet 'tsit-tsit', quite unlike Yemen Serin;* also short ripple. Song, rather slow, pleasant but plaintive 'ti-tiiu-tuiu', or 'ti-ti-tui-viu' or 'tsu-tsu-tsi-tsu' with rising inflexion, recalling thin, fine Rosefinch; song often starts with trill and occasionally ends with long varied musical jingle, more warbler- than finch-like.
Status: see map. Resident
Habitat: rocky hills and wadis, always with trees and bushes, often acacia, but also gardens, orchards, usually 1,500–2,600 m. Nests in tree.

Arabian Serin

Yemen Serin *Serinus menachensis*   Plate 38

Identification: 11.5 cm. Sexes alike. Small Serin-sized, rather nondescript, grey-brown with lightly streaked underparts and, at close range, *indistinct moustachial stripe in front of pale cheek-patch.* Rather similar to Arabian Serin, which see. Upperparts earth-brown with *distinct pale and dark streaks on crown* and broad indistinct streaks on back. Underparts greyish-white (paler than Arabian Serin) with light grey-brown streaks. Obscure buffish supercilium and half-ring under eye. Small, stout horn-coloured bill with pinkish hue to lower mandible (smaller, with less curved culmen than Arabian); dull flesh legs. May be seen in pairs or flocks and, unlike Arabian, feeds almost exclusively on ground, but may roost in flocks in trees. Differs from very similar Arabian Serin in cleaner, paler appearance, slightly shorter tail, and moustachial streak bordering pale cheek-patch (absent in Arabian Serin, which has ear-coverts and sides of throat mottled smoky); also absence of greenish-yellow rump (though beware, this feature not always apparent in Arabian), *lack of tail-movement when hopping on ground* (Arabian often flicks tail) and call. More of a flock-bird than Arabian Serin.
Voice: varied, flight-call, rather Redpoll-like 'che-che-che', also 'chwee', wagtail-like 'cheir-virp, cheir-virp', rolling twittering 'chirrip, chirrip', quiet 'che-che-che-che-che'; sonorous 'triurp-triurp', quickly repeated, and quick 'prlyit-prlyit' which may be repeated several times. Feeding flocks often keep up whispering but sonorous 'tleeit-tleeit', uttered constantly. Song, 'chew-chee-chee-chwee' in dipping song-flight and when perched.
Status: see map. Resident; has been recorded in S Yemen.
Habitat: high plateaux and rocky hillsides with patches of cultivation or bushes; also villages or on buildings in towns; trees not essential, sometimes in quite bare country; 2,000–3,200 m. Nests in hole in cliff, rocks, wall.

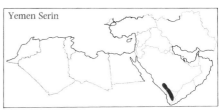

Yemen Serin

Golden-winged Grosbeak *Rhynchostruthus socotranus*   Plate 38

Identification: 14.5 cm. Sexes differ. Sparrow-sized, but plumper with larger head and *very stout bill*; readily identified by *prominent white cheeks* (vary in extent – sometimes just small white crescent) and *yellow patches on wings and tail* – especially noticeable in flight. Male has warm brown crown and nape, merging into brownish-grey back and greyish rump; underparts light grey, with rufous across upper breast extending to surround white cheeks; *lores and area around base of bill dark blackish-brown, intensifying size and colour of blackish-grey bill*; black wings with golden-yellow fringes to secondaries and coverts, off-white fringes to tertials; black tail with yellow fringes to feathers. Female similar to male but duller and without blackish area around base of bill. Juvenile brown with head and underparts streaked darker, streaking less extensive on lower belly and undertail-coverts. Rather inactive unless feeding. Flight bouncing, often flying some distance when disturbed.

Voice: song, liquid, musical and discordant; variable and quite loud. Generally starts with 'whit-whee-oo', 'sit-eeee-did-ee did-oo-ee' or 'tviit-te-vyt-te-viit', first and last notes longest, repeated and interspersed with notes of Linnet- and Goldfinch-like quality; song from concealed perch in top of tree (usually acacia) or in fluttering, bat-like display flight. Various calls include 'wip', 'wink', 'tzeee'; rippling 'tut-tut-tut-tut' and 'tlyit-tlyit', soft Goldfinch-like 'tlyit' and fast 'dy-dy-dy' followed by dry trill 'drrrt'.

Status: see map. Resident; recorded in S Yemen where probably resident.

Habitat: hills and wadis with Euphorbia, acacia, juniper, 1,200–2,000 m. Nest undescribed.

Greenfinch *Carduelis chloris*

Identification: 15 cm. See PMH.

Status: see map. Mainly resident but dispersive. Also winter visitor across coastal N Africa, Near East to SW Iran; uncommon NW Saudi Arabia, unrecorded rest of Arabia.

Habitat: gardens, parks, pine woods, farmland, olive plantations, orchards, oases. Nests in bush or small tree, particularly evergreen.

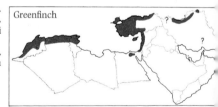

Goldfinch *Carduelis carduelis*   Plate 39

Identification: 12 cm. See PMH. Race occurring in E Iran, *paropanisi*, quite distinct from all other forms in region. Known as Grey-headed Goldfinch, it lacks familiar black and white 'Goldfinch' head pattern, being uniform *buff-grey on back and head* (down to breast) but retains red face-mask and black patch from bill to eye; plumage otherwise like European Goldfinch, but slightly larger with noticeably *longer and heavier bill*.

Status: see map. Mainly resident but dispersive. Also winter visitor NW Africa, Cyprus, Near East to S Iraq and SW Iran; reaches NW Saudi Arabia; rare Kuwait; vagrant elsewhere E Arabia.

Habitat: gardens, orchards, cultivated areas, also scrub and tree-covered hills and valleys, from sea-level to 2,200 m. In winter also in open country with tall herb vegetation, wasteland, etc. Nests in tree.

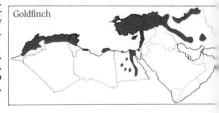

244

Siskin *Carduelis spinus*

Identification: 12 cm. See PMH.
Status: see map. Resident. Also winter visitor northern NW Africa (but rare Tunisia, Libya), N Egypt, Near East to N Iran; rare S Iran, E and central Arabia; vagrant Oman.
Habitat: coniferous woods, birches and alder thickets; in winter often in more open, cultivated areas but with trees or woods nearby. Nests high in conifer.

Linnet *Carduelis cannabina*

Identification: 13 cm. See PMH.
Status: see map. May breed Libya. Resident. Also winter visitor across northern N Africa to Near East and SW Iran; rarely to Kuwait and E Saudi Arabia; vagrant UAE.
Habitat: open country with thickets and plantations; in winter in wasteland, cultivation, marshes, coastal areas and other open ground. Nests sociably in bushy thickets, vines, low scrub, etc.

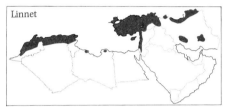

Yemen Linnet *Carduelis yemenensis*   Plate 39

Identification: 11.5 cm. Sexes differ. Somewhat resembles Linnet (from which geographically isolated) but with much more *conspicuous white wing- and tail-patches in flight*. Male has whole head, neck and breast grey (unlike Linnet) with, usually, faint, Linnet-like mark through dark eye. Back chestnut-brown, lightly streaked, and rump greyish and paler; wings brown with small white flash at base of primaries when perched, becoming fairly *broad white wing-bar in flight, particularly noticeable on underwing*. Prominent chestnut coverts. White underparts (below grey upper breast) have chestnut patches at side of breast. Notched tail black with obvious white inner webs to outer feathers. Female duller, lacking richness of male plumage, having washed-out pale grey head, with *chestnut confined to only lesser coverts.* Horn-coloured bill. Thus, both male and female differ from Linnet in having *broad white wing-bar, chestnut on wing-coverts* and *lacking red or streaking on breast and forehead.* Semi-colonial.
Voice: in flight, short, rather soft Goldfinch-like ripple, 'vliet'. Also musical *'chip-chip'*. Song, usually from concealed perch in small tree, is fast, melodious twittering, reminiscent of songs of Canary and Goldfinch.
Status: see map. Resident.
Habitat: highland regions, lightly wooded slopes and wadis, cultivation and scattered trees (eg juniper, acacia), from 1,700 to over 3,000 m. Nests in tree.

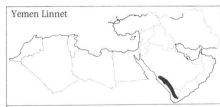

Twite *Carduelis flavirostris*   Plate 39

Identification: 13.5 cm. See PMH. Race *brevirostris* (illustrated) breeds in Turkey and Iran, differs from European birds in having paler, frosty edgings to feathers of upperparts, more conspicuous, pinker rump and whiter underparts with obvious dark patches on sides of breast (European Twite has tawny-buff underparts with dark streaks across breast.)

245

Status: see map. Descends and disperses from high breeding grounds in winter.
Habitat: mountain slopes; also plains in winter. Nests on ground under cover of vegetation or rock.

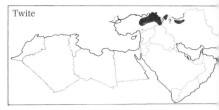

Redpoll *Carduelis flammea*

Identification: 13 cm. See PMH.
Status: vagrant Morocco, Turkey, Cyprus and perhaps Israel.
Habitat: lightly wooded regions, near cultivation and wasteland.

Crossbill *Loxia curvirostra*

Identification: 17 cm. See PMH.
Status: see map. Has bred Israel in recent years. Resident and dispersive; in Turkey also irruptive, and recorded on passage. Also winter visitor Morocco, Israel; vagrant Iran.
Habitat: coniferous woods in which it nests.

Crimson-winged Finch *Rhodopechys sanguinea*   Plate 39

Identification: 15 cm. Sexes differ slightly. Fairly large, ground-dwelling finch with horizontal carriage and stout bill. Rather non-descript until it flies and displays *rosy-pink wing-panel* and *white underwing-coverts*. Male has warm dark brown upperparts with feathers edged diffuse creamy-buff; black crown, creamy-buff supercilium, dark sandy-buff ear-coverts, rosy-pink patch at base of bill and around eye (absent in winter), and rosy-pink rump. Primary coverts and most of primaries and secondaries (except tips) rosy-pink, forming noticable panel in flight. Base of tail-feathers edged pink, tips white. Underparts whitish with dappled warm brown chin, throat, upper breast and flanks. Bill dull yellow in breeding season, but greyish-horn at other times. Female duller with less bright wing-panel, dark brown crown; buffish-horn bill in breeding season but, like male, greyish-horn at other times. In heavy indulating flight rather long-winged; shows white underwing-coverts, white tips to tail, rosy-pink wing-panel and edges to base of tail-feathers. Forms flocks outside breeding season. Racial variation occurs between birds of the Near-Middle East (*sanguinea*) and those of Morocco, (*aliena*) males of latter having paler upperparts, duller pink in wing, less white in tail, ashy-grey nape and whitish throat.
Voice: flight calls characteristic soft 'chee-rup', 'tureep, tureep', or 'dy-lit-di-lyt', rather Woodlark-like. Also House Sparrow-like 'chee chee'. Short, melodious trilling song often uttered in song-flight.
Status: see map. Resident, but moving to lower altitudes in winter
Habitat: rocky mountains and slopes, sometimes with scrubby areas usually above 2,000 m; at lower altitudes in winter, including cultivated fields or stony grassland. Nests under stone or bush.

246

Desert Finch *Rhodospiza obsoleta* Plate 39

Identification: 14.5 cm. Sexes differ slightly. *Pale, greyish-buff*, subtly plumaged Greenfinch-sized finch with *black bill in male* and *purring flight note*. Male has soft greyish-buff to sandy-grey head and upperparts, merging into light chestnut uppertail-coverts; slightly paler below, becoming white on belly and vent; flight-feathers *mostly black with pronounced white edgings and pink panel on coverts and base of secondaries*; tail black with white feather-edgings. Most obvious feature is *glossy black bill* (in breeding season) and *black lores and narrow area around bill*. Female drabber than male, with less pink, white and black in wing and lacking black face-patch; bill black to brownish horn. Outside breeding season, bill can be pale brownish, especially in female. Juvenile has straw-coloured bill. In flight, from below, pale greyish with *broad diffuse translucent panel on underwing*, and dark tail with white edgings often noted; flight pattern above shows white primary patch with *rose-pink on secondaries and greater coverts*. Usually perches in trees in upright posture; fairly tame. Forms small flocks in winter, often feeding on ground.

Voice: very soft purring 'prrryv, prrryv', or 'prrrt, prrrt', or 'turr' and also 'shreep' flight-note. Contact note, nasal 'hear'. Song quiet, pleasant and reminiscent of Greenfinch.

Status: see map. Mainly resident, some wandering in winter when recorded in E Iraq. Vagrant Egypt.

Habitat: open country with trees and bushes, orchards and vineyards; in winter also in cultivation with trees nearby. Nests in small tree: loosely colonial.

Desert Finch

Mongolian Trumpeter Finch *Bucanetes mongolicus* Plate 39

Identification: 13 cm. Sexes differ slightly. Small rather inconspicuous mountain-dwelling finch, resembling Trumpeter Finch. Male in breeding season differs from male Trumpeter in having *clear-cut rosy rump-patch* (ill-defined in Trumpeter), *rosy-red fringes to white-based greater coverts* (rosy-grey without white in Trumpeter), *whitish panel in wing* (absent in Trumpeter), *white fringes to tail-feathers* (rosy-grey in Trumpeter) and *rosy supercilium* (absent in Trumpeter). Bill slightly smaller with less angular lower mandible than Trumpeter's, brownish-yellow (never orangy-red or scarlet of breeding male Trumpeter); legs similarly coloured. Underparts have varying rosy-pink tinge on throat, breast and flanks with creamy-buff centre of belly. Female, in breeding season, duller version of male, less rosy with less pronounced rosy eyebrows, buffer brown sides of body, often ill-defined rump-patch and less brightly patterned wings. Separated from female Trumpeter by whitish area across base of rose-fringed greater coverts (all coverts more uniform in Trumpeter), cleaner, paler fringes on secondaries and more clear-cut fringes to tail-feathers (more diffuse in Trumpeter); also, when present, rosy rump-patch. In autumn, in fresh plumage, sexes similar and many characters useful in breeding season lost or subdued: sandy-brownish upperparts, less rosy below, more rosy (less whitish) fringes to flight-feathers, paler rosy fringes to diffusely whitish-based greater coverts, faint rose tinge to rump, more distinctly white-tipped flight-feathers and more creamy tinges to tail-feathers. Juvenile similar, but wing-coverts with pale sandy-brown fringes, underparts without any pink, breast and flanks tinged tawny. In non-breeding plumages distinguished from Trumpeter by sandy-cream fringes to secondaries, broad whitish fringes to blackish tail and smaller, less stout bill. Gregarious, feeding on ground in flocks; tame.

Voice: call, 'djou-voud' alternating with 'djoudjou-vou'. Song slowly executed 'do-mi-sol-mi'.

Status: breeding status in Iran uncertain, where may be a partial migrant with altitudinal movements in winter. Vagrant Bahrain.

Habitat: mountains, from 2,700 m upwards, in steep rocky sites; in winter at lower altitudes to 1,500 m, including desert plains. Nests on ground, in tussock or bush.

247

Trumpeter Finch *Bucanetes githagineus* Plate 39

Identification: 12.5 cm. Sexes differ. Small, rather inconspicuous, stubby ground-dwelling finch with *large head, stout bill* and rather short tail. Female and winter male *rather featureless smooth sandy grey-buff with slightly paler rump,* blackish-grey wings and tail with whitish feather-edgings, pale yellowish-brown bill. In breeding season male has pearl-grey head, blotchy *pinkish wash especially noticeable on underparts,* forehead and rump, and *bright orange-red bill.* Many females develop faint pink wash on lores, chin, throat and centre of breast in breeding season; some also have faint pinkish edgings to greater coverts and edges of primaries and secondaries, and some pink in rump and outer tail-feathers. Juvenile and first-winter birds have yellowish-buff lores and ear-coverts, otherwise similar to female. Legs orangy-flesh, and large eye black. On ground, moves with hops and scuffles amongst stones and rocks, and frequently adopts upright stance. In skipping flight, shows no obvious wing-bars or tail-markings. Usually seen singly or in pairs, but flocks form in autumn and winter. For differences from Mongolian Trumpeter Finch, see that species.
Voice: song, drawn-out wheezing nazal buzz 'cheeeee'; shorter conversational 'chee' or 'chit' by feeding parties.
Status: see map. Has bred S Turkey. Mainly resident, but dispersive outside breeding season. Status uncertain N Yemen and Oman where may be resident; rare Cyprus.
Habitat: bare rocky and stony hill-sides, plains and wild arid wadis, stony deserts and semi-deserts. Nests amongst rocks or under clump.

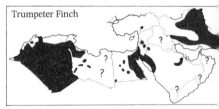

Scarlet (Common) Rosefinch *Carpodacus erythrinus*

Identification: 15 cm. See PMH.
Status: see map. Summer visitor. On passage common NE Iran; regular Oman; very scarce Israel, Egypt, UAE; otherwise vagrant to E Arabia, also Cyprus and Morocco.
Habitat: mountainous regions with damp woods, wet bushy streams and valley-bottoms. Nests low down in thick bush.

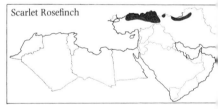

Sinai Rosefinch *Carpodacus synoicus* Plate 39

Identification: 14.5 cm. Sexes differ. Nervous, rock-dwelling rosefinch; male strikingly coloured with *crimson face* (deepest around base of bill) becoming less intense on cheeks, throat and especially crown, where fine silvery streaking can give more hoary, rose effect, *crown sometimes looking pale-capped.* Bright colours of head contrast with *fairly heavy grey bill;* eye dark. Back grey-brown with mauve tinge and pale grey fringes to darker wing- and tail-feathers. Underparts and rump deep rose-pink but some buff on lower flanks. Light pinkish-grey underwing in flight. Female and juvenile plain pale grey-brown above, very faintly streaked, with faintly darker shade on crown; buffish below, darker wings (with no wing-bars) and tail-feathers have pale greyish-buff fringes. Frequently shows gingery-brown wash to face, and ear-coverts may show faint bordering crescent – visible only at close range. Some females (old individuals) can resemble adult males, others can be decidedly greyish above. Unobtrusive but flighty, often occurring in small groups, especially in winter. Despite bright colour, male is easily 'lost' on the rocky hill-slopes it frequents and groups then best located by calls. Flight bounding. Differs in habitat from Scarlet Rosefinch, which see.
Voice: feeding flocks quite vocal in spells, especially when agitated, keeping up constant quiet 'tsweet' or 'ts-tsweet'. Also frequently-uttered 'chig', on ground and in flight. Usual flight-call fairly rich 'trizp', rather Tree Pipit-like; also Yellowhammer-like 'tieu', but not so sharp. Song varied and melodious; male gives buzzing sound during display.

Status: see map. Resident, but slightly dispersive.
Habitat: remote, barren rocky hills, cliffs, gorges, dry stony wadis with negligible vegetation, to 2,000 m. Nests in hole in rock face.

Sinai Rosefinch

Great Rosefinch *Carpodacus rubicilla*   Plate 39

Identification: 21 cm. Sexes differ. Large, thrush-sized high-dwelling rosefinch with stout bill. Male distinct with *bright crimson-red head and underparts*, deepest colour around base of bill; *crown and ear-coverts finely streaked with white giving hoary, rose appearance, while underparts have broader white flecks from throat to undertail coverts*. Wings brown with very faint pale wing-bar on greater coverts, and faint whitish fringes to tertials; brown tail also fringed whitish. Bill ivory-horn. Female pale greyish-brown with darker brown ear-coverts and sides of face and darker brown wings, similarly marked to those of male; head, upperparts and slightly paler *underparts lightly* (but noticeably at close range) *dark-streaked*. Juvenile similar to female but generally duller and browner. Feeds mainly on ground but also in low bushes.
Voice: soft 'dyyb' and 'dyuit', resembling Bullfinch.
Status: vagrant Turkey. (Status Iran uncertain).
Habitat: descends in winter, from high rocky alpine meadows, to 1,000–1,500 m.

Bullfinch *Pyrrhula pyrrhula*

Bullfinch

Identification: 15 cm. See PMH.
Status: see map. Mainly resident. Winter vagrant Morocco and Tunisia.
Habitat: chiefly coniferous forest with undergrowth, also more open regions with woods and thickets. Nests in bush or tree, usually evergreen.

White-winged Grosbeak *Mycerobas carnipes*   Plate 39

Identification: 21 cm. Large grosbeak, larger than Lesser Grey Shrike, but with proportions of American Cardinal *Richmondena cardinalis*, having big head, stout bill, comparatively slim body and long tail. Frequently perches in shrike-like upright stance on top of junipers on which it feeds. Male's *head, upperparts, upper breast and tail dull slate-black*. Rest of *underparts, rump and lower back yellowish-green* (like Green Woodpecker's rump-colour). Prominent *white patch at base of primaries*, and pale yellowish area on tertials, produce wing-bar and shoulder-patch in flight. *Gleaming, steel-grey bill*, rather paler than head. Female like washed-out version of male with head, mantle and upper back soft grey merging into greenish-yellow rump; tail grey. Underparts paler buff-grey, merging into greenish-yellow on belly and undertail-coverts; wing-bars also prominent. Flight bounding and purposeful, with regular wing-closures (yellow-green rump obscured). *Wing-bars and long tail obvious in flight*. Active, gregarious and at times very noisy, with far-carrying calls. Will also squat quietly with horizontal carriage 'munching' juniper berries, occasionally giving very soft calls; inconspicuous and quite approachable when feeding.
Voice: loud chattering and churring notes reminiscent of a distant Magpie; also 'schweeup, schweeup', very similar to call of Rock Sparrow.
Status: see map. Resident.
Habitat: mountain slopes with open juniper forest. Nests in juniper.

White-winged Grosbeak

249

Hawfinch *Coccothraustes coccothraustes*

Identification: 18 cm. See PMH.
Status: see map. Mainly resident, but dispersive in winter. Passage and winter visitor Turkey. Also scarce winter visitor Morocco, Algeria, Cyprus, Lebanon, Israel, recorded N Egypt; vagrant Libya, Iraq. Not recorded Arabia.
Habitat: chiefly arboreal, mixed woodland and parks. In winter in more open, lightly wooded country. Nests in tree, often in scattered groups.

Lapland Bunting *Calcarius lapponicus*

Identification: 15 cm. See PMH.
Status: vagrant Algeria.

Snow Bunting *Plectrophenax nivalis*

Identification: 17 cm. See PMH.
Status: vagrant Morocco and possibly Turkey.
Habitat: in winter in open coastal regions and fields.

Pine Bunting *Emberiza leucocephalos*   Plate 40

Identification: 16–17 cm. Sexes differ. Medium-sized, fairly long-tailed bunting. Male distinguished from other buntings by *black-bordered white crown* with black forehead, *white cheek-patch* with partial black margin; otherwise chestnut on head, including throat and broad band through eye. White underparts below throat have band of rufous speckles across lower breast, and diffuse rufous streaks on flanks; warm brown mantle streaked blackish but chestnut-brown rump virtually unstreaked; tail has white outer feathers. In autumn, white crown partly obscured by grey-brown, and chestnut throat has whitish fringes; full breeding plumage gradually achieved during winter. Female grey-brown above streaked blackish-brown; underparts whitish with blackish streaks across upper breast; rump as male; some females show a little white on top of head, chestnut on whitish throat and variable rufous speckles across breast; in some, top of head quite pale, streaked blackish with blacker border at sides of crown; most are patterned like female Yellowhammer but *lack any yellow in plumage.* Juveniles of both species rather similar, but Pine more often greyish-brown and Yellowhammer normally has some yellowish on belly. Juvenile Rustic Bunting smaller, with broad, pale buff supercilium and moustachial streak, bolder chestnut streaks on upper breast and flanks, chestnut scapulars and lesser coverts. Juvenile Rock Bunting has rufous-buff underparts. Behaviour as Yellowhammer with which it often hybridizes (in West Siberia) producing intermediates with white parts sullied yellow. See also White-capped Bunting.
Voice: song resembles short version of Yellowhammer's. Flight-call also similar to Yellowhammer.
Status: winter visitor Iran; scarce Israel; vagrant Turkey, Cyprus, Iraq and Saudi Arabia (Gulf).
Habitat: as Yellowhammer.

Yellowhammer *Emberiza citrinella*

Identification: 17 cm. See PMH.
Status: may breed W and extreme NE Turkey. Winter visitor Iran and Turkey; scarce Cyprus, Near East, Iraq. Vagrant Morocco, UAE.
Habitat: farmland, road-sides, open (often hilly) country with bushes.

Cirl Bunting *Emberiza cirlus*

Identification: 17 cm. See PMH.
Status: see map. Mainly resident, wandering a little in winter. Vagrant SW Iran and Egypt.
Habitat: scrubby broken country with scattered trees; in winter also farmland. Nests low in bush or tree.

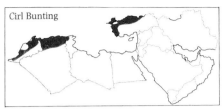

White-capped Bunting *Emberiza stewarti*　　　　　Plate 40

Identification: 14–15 cm. Sexes differ. Male readily identified by *whitish-grey head* (crown whiter when breeding) *and fore-body, black throat and line from bill through eye* and *broad chestnut lower breast-band* with chestnut streaks on flanks; mantle grey-buff with strong chestnut streaks and chestnut rump. Outer tail-feathers white. Bill dark, relatively small and fine, with straight or slightly curved culmen. Male Pine Bunting only other bunting with white cap (though partially concealed by dark feathers in autumn). However, it has quite different head-pattern with noticeable white cheek-patch, chestnut throat and supercilium. Female White-capped resembles small, neater dark-streaked female Pine (both have chestnut lower back and rump); upperparts duller brownish-grey with less conspicuous, neater dark streaks on mantle, and darker top of head with less noticeable blackish streaks. Underparts dirty white, more greyish at sides of neck and flanks; breast and flanks finer and neater-streaked than female Pine. Female distinguished from other buntings with chestnut rumps by combination of *chestnut scapulars* in brownish-grey surroundings and *rufous patch at sides of neatly streaked breast* (sometimes across breast as thin band), rather unpatterned head, finer bill and small size. Juvenile lacks rufous on sides of breast.
Voice: song recalls fast, jingling Cirl Bunting's 'dzyn-dzyn-dzyn-dzyn-dzyn'. Calls include sonorous 'tsik', characteristic rolling 'turrit', 'tjuriritt' or 'ru-ti-ti', recalling Linnet and Serin; also sharp 'tit' and 'tsip-ip'.
Status: vagrant E Iran.
Habitat: in winter open, dry hillsides with scattered bushes.

Rock Bunting *Emberiza cia*

Identification: 16 cm. See PMH.
Status: see map. Resident, but wanders to nearby lowlands in winter. Rare winter visitor Cyprus, Iraq; vagrant Kuwait.
Habitat: rocky and bushy slopes in mountains, with or without sparse trees. In winter at lower, more sheltered altitudes. Nests on or near ground, in crevice, among loose stones, rarely small bush.

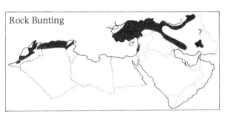

House Bunting *Emberiza striolata*　　　　　Plate 40

Identification: 14 cm. Sexes differ slightly. Smallish bunting with *rufous-brown upperparts*, warm yellow lower mandible and *rufous-edged outer tail-feathers*. Two races occur; male *striolata* (Near East and Arabia) has distinctly (though variably) striped head, *sometimes recalling African Rock Bunting*; well-marked males show whitish crown-streak, supercilium, white streak across cheeks and ear-coverts (of variable width) and whitish moustache, all separated by black; other males have ill-defined crown-streak and moustache and black replaced by dark ashy-grey; throat and upper breast greyish with blackish speckles; rest of underparts rufous. *Upperparts and wings bright rufous-brown*; dark streaks on mantle usually ill-defined

251

and variable dark centres or streaks to wing-coverts; dark-centred *tertials with broad rufous fringes*. Female duller, head-stripes much more diffuse, usually off-white and ashy-greyish; upper breast more dark-streaked. In *saharae* (North Africa), head-stripes much less obvious and, except at close range, *head looks greyish* (even duller in female); dark streaks on mantle and to centres of wing-coverts virtually absent. Juveniles of both races resemble female, but bill all-dark horn. Near Eastern House Buntings separated from Rock Bunting by yellowsh, not grey, lower mandible, by rufous back and wings with less bold blackish streaks and centres, respectively, and by rufous, not white outer tail-feathers. Very tame in North Africa (where frequently found in towns), rather more shy in some other parts of range.

Voice: song 'wi-di-dji-du-wi-dii', or 'witch witch a wee' with delivery resembling Chaffinch. Calls include nasal 'tzswee', thin, sharp, 'tchick' and 'sweee-doo'.

Status: see map. Resident. Some seasonal movements occur. Vagrant Kuwait.

Habitat: villages and towns on edge of cultivated land or deserts and oases; also wild desolate rocky wadis with very little vegetation. Nests in hole in building, crack in wall or rock crevice.

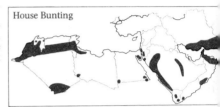
House Bunting

African (Cinnamon-breasted) **Rock Bunting** *Emberiza tahapisi*
Plate 40

16–17 cm. Sexes differ slightly. Medium-sized bunting with dull tawny underparts, black head and four white stripes (on crown, supercilium, cheeks and moustache). Mantle buff-brown, streaked blackish, wing-coverts with blackish centres and flight-feathers fringed buffish; blackish *tail narrowly fringed rufous-buff (no white)*. Female duller with blackish-grey head and throat and less pure white streaks on head. In both sexes dark horn bill has orange-yellow lower mandible. Juvenile resembles female but dark on head, throat grey-brown and pale stripes buffer; virtually no pale crown-streak, and dull grey-brown throat has fine blackish streaks extending onto upper breast. Separated from slightly smaller House Bunting of Near East and Arabia (where male can have similar head-pattern) by *blackish or dark grey throat* (greyish, flecked blackish in House, but juvenile African Rock rather similar to this), *sandy-buff ground-colour to upperparts and fringes of wing-coverts* and flight-feathers (rufous-brown in House), *bolder blackish streaks on mantle* and centres to wing-coverts (in House, mantle often poorly marked and some wing-coverts almost unmarked rufous). Rock Bunting (not normally so far south), has pale greyish throat, white outer tail-feathers and all-grey bill.

Voice: short song bunting-like 'dzit-dzit dzirera', or 'try-tri, tve-rerir', second and last notes higher in pitch; song sometimes followed by scratchy notes. Call soft metallic 'anh' and nasal 'daav'; alarm-call short metallic 'ptik'.

Status: see map. Resident, but seasonal movements Oman and SW Saudi Arabia. Vagrant Sinai.

Habitat: dry, rocky and stony hillsides with scattered vegetation, 300–2,500 m. Nests on ground at base of stone or bush.

African Rock Bunting

Cinereous Bunting *Emberiza cinerea*
Plate 40

Identification: 16.5 cm. Sexes differ. Male *greyish with unstreaked yellow throat and yellowish-green head*; ill-defined greyish malar streak bordering yellowish moustacial streak (not unlike pattern of Ortolan); ashy-grey hind-neck and variable band across unstreaked, yellow-tinged breast. Upperparts, including rump, greyish with dark-streaked mantle and two whitish wing-bars; outer tail-feathers white. Belly to undertail-coverts white in Turkish race, *cineracea*, yellowish in Iranian *semenowi*. Autumn male has greyer head and soft, dark streaks on breast. Female duller greyish- or olive-brown upperparts with dark streaks on grey- or yellowish-brown crown, on sides of neck, mantle and rear scapulars; chin and throat buffish-white or -yellow, malar region and sometimes throat generally finely streaked; breast pale brownish, finely streaked darker. Juvenile resembles female but slightly darker; browner scapulars and wing-coverts and more extensive dark streaking on ash-brown throat, breast and flanks; grey-brown rump moderately streaked; in autumn some may show slight sulphur wash on throat. *Narrow but conspicuous yellow-white eye-ring, bluish or horn-grey bill present at all ages.* Juvenile Cretzschmar's, Grey-necked and Ortolan Bunting also have pale yellowish or white eye-ring but their bills are largely pale pinkish or fleshy; in addition, Cretzschmar's and Ortolan have rufous and brownish rumps respectively (but Grey-necked has greyish-brown). Juvenile Red- and Black-headed Bunting have yellowish vent and undertail-coverts and no pure white in tail; juvenile Pine and Rock Bunting have chestnut-brown rump, latter with rufous-buff underparts, and these and juvenile Cirl Bunting lack distinct pale eye-ring; juvenile Cirl also has chestnut-brown scapulars.

Voice: call-note short metallic 'kjip'. Brief simple song consists of 5–6 notes of typical bunting character 'drip-drip-drip-drip-drie-drieh'.

Status: see map. Summer visitor. Very scarce or rare passage migrant SW and E Arabia (not Oman), Cyprus, Israel, Jordan and Syria. Vagrant Tunisia, Egypt, Lebanon.

Habitat: dry, rocky or stony slopes with sparse vegetation, up to tree-limit. On passage/winter also in semi-desert and bushy wadis. Nests on ground.

Cinereous Bunting

Ortolan Bunting *Emberiza hortulana*

Identification: 17 cm. See PMH.

Status: see map. Summer visitor. Widespread on passage (but rare Tunisia), scarcer NW and central Saudi Arabia, S Iran and Oman; rarely in winter Oman and N Yemen.

Habitat: broken lowland or hilly country, bare cultivation with scattered trees and scrub. On passage also in semi-desert regions. Nests on or near ground in vegetation.

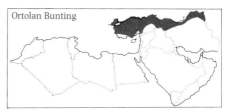

Ortolan Bunting

Grey-necked Bunting *Emberiza buchanani*   Plate 40

Identification: 16 cm. Sexes similar. Similar size and shape to Cretzschmar's and superficially similar plumage, sharing whitish eye-ring and pinkish bill with that species and Ortolan. *Underparts dull vinous-rufous* (lacking dark grey breast-band of Cretzschmar's) with whitish feather-fringes often creating mottled appearance; vent and undertail-coverts whitish or pale yellow-buff (rufous-buff in Cretzschmar's); moustachial streak whitish and malar streak greyish. *Head to hind-neck soft bluish-grey* (brighter in male Cretzschmar's) *mantle brownish-grey with inconspicuous fine dark streaks*, framed by chestnut scapulars (in Cretzschmar's, warm brown mantle broadly streaked blackish); lower back to *uppertail-coverts virtually unstreaked brownish-grey or grey* (rufous-brown in Cretzschmar's); tertials dark grey-brown with diffuse paler, dull creamy-brown edges (blackish-brown with more clear-cut and rufous-brown edges in Cretzschmar's); dark tail has white in outer feathers. Female similar but slightly duller and paler than male. Adult Ortolan has olive-grey head and breast-band, yellowish throat, boldly blackish-streaked mantle, grey-brown rump and blackish-brown tertials with clear-cut pale brown edges. Juvenile Grey-necked separated from juvenile Cretzschmar's by *absence of rufous tinge to rump and tail-coverts*, and by *pale buff* (not rufous-buff) *ventral region*; from juvenile Ortolan by *absence of pale yellow on throat*; from both young Cretzschmar's and Ortolan by *much less bold dark streaks on mantle and breast* and pale brownish flight-feathers with less contrasting pale edges (darker flight-feathers with contrasting pale edges in the other two species).

253

Voice: song quite loud and rich; typically 'di-di-dew, de-dew', penultimate note higher pitched and more emphasized; delivery can be fast or slurred and more like Ortolan's than Cretzschmar's. Flight-calls 'tip', 'tsip', or 'sik'. Perched calls 'chep' or 'tcheup'.

Status: see map. Summer visitor. Passage SE Iran.

Habitat: rocky, barren mountain hillsides and plateaux with sparse vegetation, usually above 2,000 m. Nests on ground.

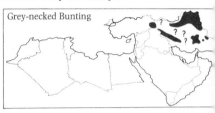

Grey-necked Bunting

Cretzschmar's Bunting *Emberiza caesia*

Identification: 16 cm. See PMH.

Status: see map. Summer visitor. Also passage migrant Cyprus, Near East to NE Egypt and NW Saudi Arabia; rarer SW Saudi Arabia; winter records from W Saudi Arabia. Vagrant Libya, Iran and Kuwait.

Habitat: bare rocky hill-sides, sometimes with bushes. On passage also in more cultivated areas, semi-deserts, etc. Nests on ground.

Cretzschmar's Bunting

Rustic Bunting *Emberiza rustica*

Identification: 15 cm. See PMH.

Status: perhaps rare migrant in Iran and Israel; vagrant Syria, Egypt, Kuwait, E Arabia, Oman and possibly Turkey.

Habitat: on passage generally in bushy or damp areas, sometimes near cultivation.

Little Bunting *Emberiza pusilla*

Identification: 13 cm. See PMH.

Status: rare migrant or vagrant in east of region, recorded Lebanon, Israel, Iran, Kuwait, E Arabia, Oman, and possibly Turkey; also recorded Algeria.

Habitat: on passage as Rustic Bunting.

Yellow-breasted Bunting *Emberiza aureola*

Identification: 14 cm. See PMH.

Status: rare migrant or vagrant in east of region, recorded Cyprus, Israel, N Iran, E Arabia, Oman and possibly Turkey.

Habitat: on passage in open country with thickets.

Reed Bunting *Emberiza schoeniclus*

Identification: 15 cm. See PMH.

Status: see map. Resident and partial migrant. Scarce winter visitor to all Mediterranean countries (but vagrant Egypt), also Near East, Iraq and Iran (common in north); rare E Arabia.

Habitat: reed-beds and swampy thickets. Nests in reeds and bushes.

Reed Bunting

Red-headed Bunting. *Emberiza bruniceps*   Plate 40

Identification: 16–17 cm. Sexes differ. Male has *chestnut head and throat, bright yellow underparts, hind-collar and rump*; mantle yellowish-green streaked blackish, wings and tail dark brown, narrowly edged greenish-yellow; *no white in outer tail-feathers* in any plumage. Female almost identical to female Black-headed (see PMH) with buffish-yellow underparts including undertail-coverts; mantle and back medium- or olive-brown *without rufous tinge on rump* of most Black-headed females, but a few are inseparable; rarely shows chestnut on fore-crown. Juvenile resembles female but yellow of underparts usually confined to vent and undertail-coverts; inseparable from juvenile Black-headed Bunting. Females of hybrids with Black-headed (found in SE Caspian region) indistinguishable in field.

Voice: song clear and far-carrying like Black-headed; starts quietly, then develops with characteristic descending end, 'tsit tsit tsi tsoo', or 'tsit tsit tsi tsee tsoo tsoo tsootooel'.

Status: see map. Summer visitor. Outside breeding range recorded as vagrant Turkey, Israel, NW Saudi Arabia, Kuwait and UAE.

Habitat: irrigated farmland and other open country with bushes, mainly in upland areas. Nests in bush close to ground.

Black-headed Bunting *Emberiza melanocephala*

Identification: 17 cm. See PMH.

Status: see map. Summer visitor. On passage Iran (widely), Oman (where recorded winter) and S Israel; scarce or irregular Gulf States, central Saudi Arabia. Rare Sinai; vagrant to N African countries.

Habitat: bushy, hilly or rolling country with or without cultivation; also fairly open farmland. Nests in vegetation close to ground.

Corn Bunting *Miliaria calandra*

Identification: 18 cm. See PMH.

Status: see map. Mainly resident but dispersal in winter to coastal Libya (where it may breed) and Egypt; also S Iran, S Iraq and E Arabia and Oman.

Habitat: open farmland, hillsides with scattered bushes. Nests in long grass or similar vegetation near or on ground.

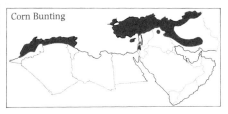

255

References

The following are some of the more useful publications giving information on birds occurring in the region.

Ali, S. and Ripley, S. Dillon 1983 *Handbook to the Birds of India and Pakistan.* Compact edition. Oxford University Press, Oxford.

Allouse, B. E. 1953 *The Avifauna of Iraq.* Iraq Natural History Society, Baghdad.

Archer, G. and Godman, E. M. 1937–61 *The Birds of British Somaliland and the Gulf of Aden.* Four vols. Gurney and Jackson, London; Oliver and Boyd, London.

Bannerman, D. A. 1953 *The Birds of West and Equatorial Africa.* Two vols. Oliver and Boyd, Edinburgh.

Bauer, K. M. and Glutz Von Blotzheim, U. N. 1966–82 *Handbuch der Vögel Mitteleuropas.* Band 1–9. Akademishe Verlagsgesellschaft, Frankfurt am Main.

British Birds. A monthly journal. Fountains, Park Lane, Blunham, Bedfordshire, UK.

Brown, L. H. and Amadon, D. 1968 *Eagles, Hawks and Falcons of the World.* Two vols. Country Life Books, London.

Brown, L. H., Urban, E. K. and Newman, K. 1982–86 *The Birds of Africa.* Vols. 1 and 2. Academic Press, London.

Bruun, B. and Singer, A. 1971 *The Hamlyn Guide to the Birds of Britain and Europe.* Hamlyn Feltham.

Bundy, G. 1976 *The Birds of Libya: an annotated checklist.* British Ornithologists' Union, London.

Cave, F. O. and Macdonald, J. D. 1955 *Birds of the Sudan.* Oliver and Boyd, Edinburgh.

Cramp, S. and Simmons, K. E. L. (eds) 1977–88 *The Birds of the Western Palearctic.* Vols 1–5 (6 and 7 in prep.), Oxford University Press.

Dementiev, G. P. and Gladkov, N. A. 1951–54 *The Birds of the Soviet Union.* (Moscow; English edition, Jerusalem 1966; 1st progr. Sci. Transl.).

Dresser, H. E. 1871–81 *A History of the Birds of Europe.* Nine vols. Published by the author, London.

Dutch Birding. A quarterly journal. Dutch Birding Association, Postbus 5611, 1007 AP Amsterdam.

Etchécopar, R. D. and Hüe, F. 1967 *The Birds of North Africa.* English translation. Oliver and Boyd, Edinburgh.

Etchécopar, R. D. and Hüe, F. 1983 *Les Oiseaux de Chine.* Two vols. Boubee, Paris.

Ferguson-Lees, I. J., Willis, I. and Sharrock, J. T. R. 1983 *The Shell Guide to the Birds of Britain and Ireland.* Michael Joseph, London.

Fitter, R., Parslow, J. and Heinzel, H. 1972 *Birds of Britain and Europe with the Middle East and North Africa.* Collins, London.

Flint, P. R. and Stewart, P. F. 1983 *The Birds of Cyprus: an annotated checklist.* British Ornithologists' Union, London.

Gallagher, M. and Woodcock, M. W. 1980 *The Birds of Oman.* Quartet Books, London.

Grant, P. J. 1986 (second edition) *Gulls: a guide to identification,* Poyser, Calton.

Harper, P. C. and Kinsky, F. C. 1978 *Southern Albatrosses and Petrels.* Price Milburn/Victoria University Press, Wellington, New Zealand.

Harrison, P. 1985 *Seabirds: an identification guide.* Croom Helm, Beckenham.

Hayman, P., Marchant, J. and Prater, T. 1986 *Shorebirds.* Christopher Helm, Beckenham.

Hüe, F. and Etchécopar, R. D. 1970 *Les Oiseaux du Proche et du Moyen Orient.* Boubee, Paris.

Inskipp, C. and T. 1985 *A Guide to the Birds of Nepal.* Croom Helm, London.

Jennings, M. C. 1981 *The Birds of Saudi Arabia: a checklist.* Published by the author. Wittlesford, Cambridge.

Jonsson, L. 1982 *Birds of the Mediterranean and Alps.* Croom Helm, London.

King, B., Woodcock, M. and Dickinson, E. C. 1975 *A Field Guide to the Birds of South East Asia.* Collins, London.

King, B. 1978 'April Bird Observations in Saudi Arabia'. J. Saudi Arab. Nat. Hist. Soc. 21: 3–24.

Mackworth-Praed, C. W. and Grant, C. H. B. 1952–55 *Birds of Eastern and North Eastern Africa.* Two vols. Longmans, London.

McLachlan, G. R. 1985 *Robert's Birds of Southern Africa.* Cape Town.

Meinertzhagen, R. 1930 *Nicoll's Birds of Egypt.* Two vols. Rees, London.

257

Meinertzhagen, R. 1954. *Birds of Arabia*. Oliver and Boyd, Edinburgh and London.

Mikkola, H. 1983 *Owls of Europe*. Poyser, Calton.

Nelson, B. 1973 *Azraq: desert oasis*. Allen Lane, London.

Nelson, J. B. 1978 *The Sulidae: gannets and boobies*. University of Aberdeen/Oxford University Press.

Ornithological Society of the Middle East. Sandgrouse, published annually.

Ornithological Society of Turkey. 1966–1973 Bird reports.

Peterson, R., Mountfort, G. and Hollom, P. A. D. 1983 *A Field Guide to the Birds of Britain and Europe*. Fourth edition. Collins, London.

Pizzey, G. and Doyle, R. 1980 *A Field Guide to the Birds of Australia*. Collins, Sydney.

Porter, R. F., Willis, I., Christensen, S. and Nielsen, B. P. 1981 *Flight Identification of European Raptors*. Poyser, Calton.

Prater, A. J., Marchant, J. H. and Vuorinen, J. 1977 *Guide to the Identification and Ageing of Holearctic Waders*. British Trust for Ornithology, Tring.

Roberts, T. J. and King, B. 'Vocalisations of the Owls of the Genus Otus in Pakistan'. In press, Ornis. Scand.

Scott, D. A., Hamadani, H. M. and Mirhosseyni, A. A. 1975 *Birds of Iran*. Dept. of the Environment, Teheran.

Serle, W., Morel, G. J. and Hartwig, W. 1977 *A Field Guide to the Birds of West Africa*. Collins, London.

Smythies, B. E. 1953 (second edition) *The Birds of Burma*. Oliver and Boyd, Edinburgh.

Svensson, L. 1984 *Identification Guide to European Passerines*. Roserberg, Stockholm.

Steyn, P. 1982 *Birds of Prey of Southern Africa*. David Philip, Cape Town and Johannesburg. Croom Helm, Beckenham, Kent.

Thomsen, P. and Jacobsen, P. 1979 *The Birds of Tunisia: an annotated checklist*. Jelling Aps, Denmark.

Udvardy, M. D. F. 1977 *The Audubon Society Field Guide to North American Birds: western region*. Knopf, New York.

Vaurie, C. 1959–65 *The Birds of the Palearctic Fauna*. Two vols. Witherby, London.

Vere Benson, S. 1970 *Birds of Lebanon*. Warne, London and New York.

Voous, K. H. 1960 *Atlas of European Birds*. Nelson, London.

Voous, K. H. 1973, 1977 List of recent Holearctic bird species (reprinted, amended from Ibis).

Wild Bird Society of Japan. 1982. *A Field Guide to the Birds of Japan*. Wild Bird Society, Tokyo.

Williams, J. G. 1964 *A Field Guide to the Birds of East and Central Africa*. Houghton Mifflin, Boston.

Williams, J. G. and Arlott, N. 1980 *A Field Guide to the Birds of East Africa*. Collins, London.

Williamson, K. 1976 *Identification for Ringers. Warblers*. Three vols. (revised). British Trust for Ornithology, Tring.

Witherby, H. F., Jourdain, F. C. R., Ticehurst, N. F. and Tucker, B. W. 1938–41 *The Handbook of British Birds*. Five vols. Witherby, London.

Readers wishing to keep in touch with ornithological developments in the area may wish to join the Ornithological Society of the Middle East (c/o RSPB, The Lodge, Sandy, Bedfordshire SG19 2DL, England) whose journal 'Sandgrouse' appears annually.

Checklist

This list includes all species covered by this book, though not all have necessarily been admitted onto national lists, where these exist. The sequence and nomenclature conform generally to those used by Prof. K H Voous in his *List of Recent Holarctic Bird Species* and by the Editors of *The Birds of the Western Palearctic*.

Ostrich *Struthio camelus*
Red-throated Diver *Gavia stellata*
Black-throated Diver *Gavia arctica*
Great Northern Diver *Gavia immer*
Little Grebe *Tachybaptus ruficollis*
Great Crested Grebe *Podiceps cristatus*
Red-necked Grebe *Podiceps grisegena*
Slavonian Grebe *Podiceps auritus*
Black-necked Grebe *Podiceps nigricollis*
Black-browed Albatross *Diomedea
    melanophris*
Shy Albatross *Diomedea cauta*
Fulmar *Fulmarus glacialis*
Schlegel's Petrel *Pterodroma incerta*
Soft-plumaged Petrel *Pterodroma mollis*
Bulwer's Petrel *Bulweria bulwerii*
Jouanin's Petrel *Bulweria fallax*
Cory's Shearwater *Calonectris diomedea*
Streaked Shearwater *Calonectris leucomelas*
Pale-footed Shearwater *Puffinus carneipes*
Great Shearwater *Puffinus gravis*
Wedge-tailed Shearwater *Puffinus pacificus*
Sooty Shearwater *Puffinus griseus*
Manx Shearwater *Puffinus puffinus*
Little Shearwater *Puffinus assimilis*
Audubon's Shearwater *Puffinus lherminieri*
Wilson's Petrel *Oceanites oceanicus*
Black-bellied Petrel *Fregetta tropica*
White-bellied Petrel *Fregetta grallaria*
White-faced Petrel *Pelagodroma marina*
Storm Petrel *Hydrobates pelagicus*
Leach's Petrel *Oceanodroma leucorhoa*
Swinhoe's Petrel *Oceanodroma monorhis*
Madeiran Petrel *Oceanodroma castro*
Red-billed Tropicbird *Phaethon aethereus*
Red-footed Booby *Sula sula*
Masked Booby *Sula dactylatra*
Brown Booby *Sula leucogaster*
Gannet *Sula bassana*
Cormorant *Phalacrocorax carbo*
Shag *Phalacrocorax aristotelis*
Socotra Cormorant *Phalacrocorax
    nigrogularis*
Pygmy Cormorant *Phalacrocorax pygmeus*
Long-tailed Cormorant *Phalacrocorax
    africanus*
Darter *Anhinga rufa*
White Pelican *Pelecanus onocrotalus*
Dalmatian Pelican *Pelecanus crispus*
Pink-backed Pelican *Pelecanus rufescens*
Great Frigatebird *Fregata minor*
Lesser Frigatebird *Fregata ariel*

Bittern *Botaurus stellaris*
Little Bittern *Ixobrychus minutus*
Night Heron *Nycticorax nycticorax*
Green Heron *Butorides striatus*
Squacco Heron *Ardeola ralloides*
Indian Pond Heron *Ardeola grayii*
Cattle Egret *Bubulcus ibis*
Western Reef Heron *Egretta gularis*
Little Egret *Egretta garzetta*
Intermediate Egret *Egretta intermedia*
Great White Egret *Egretta alba*
Black-headed Heron *Ardea melanocephala*
Grey Heron *Ardea cinerea*
Purple Heron *Ardea purpurea*
Goliath Heron *Ardea goliath*
Hamerkop *Scopus umbretta*
Yellow-billed Stork *Mycteria ibis*
Black Stork *Ciconia nigra*
Abdim's Stork *Ciconia abdimii*
Woolly-necked Stork *Ciconia episcopus*
White Stork *Ciconia ciconia*
Marabou *Leptoptilos crumeniferus*
Glossy Ibis *Plegadis falcinellus*
Bald Ibis *Geronticus eremita*
Sacred Ibis *Threskiornis aethiopicus*
Spoonbill *Platalea leucorodia*
African Spoonbill *Platalea alba*
Greater Flamingo *Phoenicopterus ruber*
Lesser Flamingo *Phoenicopterus minor*
Fulvous Whistling Duck *Dendrocygna bicolor*
Mute Swan *Cygnus olor*
Bewick's Swan *Cygnus columbianus*
Whooper Swan *Cygnus cygnus*
Bean Goose *Anser fabalis*
White-fronted Goose *Anser albifrons*
Lesser White-fronted Goose *Anser erythropus*
Greylag Goose *Anser anser*
Snow Goose *Anser caerulescens*
Barnacle Goose *Branta leucopsis*
Brent Goose *Branta bernicla*
Red-breasted Goose *Branta ruficollis*
Egyptian Goose *Alopochen aegyptiacus*
Ruddy Shelduck *Tadorna ferruginea*
Shelduck *Tadorna tadorna*
Spur-winged Goose *Plectropterus gambensis*
Cotton Teal *Nettapus coromandelianus*
Mandarin Duck *Aix galericulata*
Wigeon *Anas penelope*
American Wigeon *Anas americana*
Falcated Duck *Anas falcata*
Gadwall *Anas strepera*
Teal *Anas crecca*

Blue-winged Teal *Anas discors*
Cape Teal *Anas capensis*
Mallard *Anas platyrhynchos*
Pintail *Anas acuta*
Garganey *Anas querquedula*
Shoveler *Anas clypeata*
Cape Shoveler *Anas smithii*
Marbled Teal *Marmaronetta angustirostris*
Red-crested Pochard *Netta rufina*
Pochard *Aythya ferina*
Ring-necked Duck *Aythya collaris*
Ferruginous Duck *Aythya nyroca*
Tufted Duck *Aythya fuligula*
Scaup *Aythya marila*
Long-tailed Duck *Clangula hyemalis*
Common Scoter *Melanitta nigra*
Velvet Scoter *Melanitta fusca*
Goldeneye *Bucephala clangula*
Smew *Mergus albellus*
Red-breasted Merganser *Mergus serrator*
Goosander *Mergus merganser*
White-headed Duck *Oxyura leucocephala*
Honey Buzzard *Pernis apivorus*
Black-winged Kite *Elanus caeruleus*
African Swallow-tailed Kite *Chelictinia riocourii*
Black Kite *Milvus migrans*
Red Kite *Milvus milvus*
African Fish Eagle *Haliaeetus vocifer*
Pallas's Fish Eagle *Haliaeetus leucoryphus*
White-tailed Eagle *Haliaeetus albicilla*
Lammergeier *Gypaetus barbatus*
Egyptian Vulture *Neophron percnopterus*
Hooded Vulture *Necrosyrtes monachus*
Indian White-backed Vulture *Gyps bengalensis*
Griffon Vulture *Gyps fulvus*
Rüppell's Vulture *Gyps rueppellii*
Lappet-faced Vulture *Torgos tracheliotus*
Black Vulture *Aegypius monachus*
Short-toed Eagle *Circaetus gallicus*
Bateleur *Terathopius ecaudatus*
Marsh Harrier *Circus aeruginosus*
Hen Harrier *Circus cyaneus*
Pallid Harrier *Circus macrourus*
Montagu's Harrier *Circus pygargus*
Dark Chanting Goshawk *Melierax metabates*
Gabar Goshawk *Micronisus gabar*
Goshawk *Accipiter gentilis*
Sparrowhawk *Accipiter nisus*
Shikra *Accipiter badius*
Levant Sparrowhawk *Accipiter brevipes*
White-eyed Buzzard *Butastur teesa*
Buzzard *Buteo buteo*
Long-legged Buzzard *Buteo rufinus*
Upland Buzzard *Buteo hemilasius*
Rough-legged Buzzard *Buteo lagopus*
Lesser Spotted Eagle *Aquila pomarina*
Spotted Eagle *Aquila clanga*
Tawny Eagle *Aquila rapax*
Steppe Eagle *Aquila nipalensis*
Imperial Eagle *Aquila heliaca*
Golden Eagle *Aquila chrysaetos*
Verreaux's Eagle *Aquila verreauxii*
Booted Eagle *Hieraaetus pennatus*

Bonelli's Eagle *Hieraaetus fasciatus*
Osprey *Pandion haliaetus*
Lesser Kestrel *Falco naumanni*
Kestrel *Falco tinnunculus*
Red-headed Merlin *Falco chicquera*
Red-footed Falcon *Falco vespertinus*
Manchurian Red-footed Falcon *Falco amurensis*
Merlin *Falco columbarius*
Hobby *Falco subbuteo*
Eleonora's Falcon *Falco eleonorae*
Sooty Falcon *Falco concolor*
Lanner *Falco biarmicus*
Saker *Falco cherrug*
Peregrine *Falco peregrinus*
Barbary Falcon *Falco pelegrinoides*
Caucasian Black Grouse *Tetrao mlokosiewiczi*
Caspian Snowcock *Tetraogallus caspius*
Chukar *Alectoris chukar*
Barbary Partridge *Alectoris barbara*
Philby's Rock Partridge *Alectoris philbyi*
Arabian Red-legged Partridge *Alectoris melanocephala*
See-see Partridge *Ammoperdix griseogularis*
Sand Partridge *Ammoperdix heyi*
Black Francolin *Francolinus francolinus*
Grey Francolin *Francolinus pondicerianus*
Double-spurred Francolin *Francolinus bicalcaratus*
Grey Partridge *Perdix perdix*
Quail *Coturnix coturnix*
Harlequin Quail *Coturnix delegorguei*
Pheasant *Phasianus colchicus*
Helmeted Guineafowl *Numida meleagris*
Andalusian Hemipode *Turnix sylvatica*
Water Rail *Rallus aquaticus*
Spotted Crake *Porzana porzana*
Little Crake *Porzana parva*
Baillon's Crake *Porzana pusilla*
Striped Crake *Porzana marginalis*
Corncrake *Crex crex*
White-breasted Waterhen *Amaurornis phoenicurus*
Moorhen *Gallinula chloropus*
Allen's Gallinule *Porphyrula alleni*
Purple Gallinule *Porphyrio porphyrio*
Coot *Fulica atra*
Crested Coot *Fulica cristata*
Crane *Grus grus*
Siberian White Crane *Grus leucogeranus*
Demoiselle Crane *Anthropoides virgo*
Little Bustard *Tetrax tetrax*
Houbara *Chlamydotis undulata*
Arabian Bustard *Ardeotis arabs*
Great Bustard *Otis tarda*
Pheasant-tailed Jacana *Hydrophasianus chirurgus*
Painted Snipe *Rostratula benghalensis*
Oystercatcher *Haematopus ostralegus*
Black-winged Stilt *Himantopus himantopus*
Avocet *Recurvirostra avosetta*
Crab Plover *Dromas ardeola*
Stone Curlew *Burhinus oedicnemus*
Senegal Thick-knee *Burhinus senegalensis*
Spotted Thick-knee *Burhinus capensis*

Great Stone Plover *Esacus recurvirostris*
Egyptian Plover *Pluvianus aegyptius*
Cream-coloured Courser *Cursorius cursor*
Collared Pratincole *Glareola pratincola*
Black-winged Pratincole *Glareola nordmanni*
Little Pratincole *Glareola lactea*
Little Ringed Plover *Charadrius dubius*
Ringed Plover *Charadrius hiaticula*
Kittlitz's Plover *Charadrius pecuarius*
Kentish Plover *Charadrius alexandrinus*
Lesser Sand Plover *Charadrius mongolus*
Greater Sand Plover *Charadrius leschenaultii*
Caspian Plover *Charadrius asiaticus*
Dotterel *Charadrius morinellus*
Pacific Golden Plover *Pluvialis fulva*
American Golden Plover *Pluvialis dominica*
Golden Plover *Pluvialis apricaria*
Grey Plover *Pluvialis squatarola*
Spur-winged Plover *Hoplopterus spinosus*
Black-headed Plover *Hoplopterus tectus*
Red-wattled Plover *Hoplopterus indicus*
Sociable Plover *Chettusia gregaria*
White-tailed Plover *Chettusia leucura*
Lapwing *Vanellus vanellus*
Great Knot *Calidris tenuirostris*
Knot *Calidris canutus*
Sanderling *Calidris alba*
Little Stint *Calidris minuta*
Temminck's Stint *Calidris temminckii*
Long-toed Stint *Calidris subminuta*
Pectoral Sandpiper *Calidris melanotos*
Sharp-tailed Sandpiper *Calidris acuminata*
Curlew Sandpiper *Calidris ferruginea*
Purple Sandpiper *Calidris maritima*
Dunlin *Calidris alpina*
Broad-billed Sandpiper *Limicola falcinellus*
Buff-breasted Sandpiper *Tryngites
  subruficollis*
Ruff *Philomachus pugnax*
Jack Snipe *Lymnocryptes minimus*
Snipe *Gallinago gallinago*
Great Snipe *Gallinago media*
Pintail Snipe *Gallinago stenura*
Solitary Snipe *Gallinago solitaria*
Long-billed Dowitcher *Limnodromus
  scolopaceus*
Asiatic Dowitcher *Limnodromus semipalmatus*
Woodcock *Scolopax rusticola*
Black-tailed Godwit *Limosa limosa*
Bar-tailed Godwit *Limosa lapponica*
Whimbrel *Numenius phaeopus*
Slender-billed Curlew *Numenius tenuirostris*
Curlew *Numenius arquata*
Far Eastern Curlew *Numenius
  madagascariensis*
Spotted Redshank *Tringa erythropus*
Redshank *Tringa totanus*
Marsh Sandpiper *Tringa stagnatilis*
Greenshank *Tringa nebularia*
Green Sandpiper *Tringa ochropus*
Wood Sandpiper *Tringa glareola*
Terek Sandpiper *Xenus cinereus*
Common Sandpiper *Actitis hypoleucos*
Turnstone *Arenaria interpres*
Wilson's Phalarope *Phalaropus tricolor*

Red-necked Phalarope *Phalaropus lobatus*
Grey Phalarope *Phalaropus fulicarius*
Pomarine Skua *Stercorarius pomarinus*
Arctic Skua *Stercorarius parasiticus*
Long-tailed Skua *Stercorarius longicaudus*
Great Skua *Stercorarius skua*
Sooty Gull *Larus hemprichii*
White-eyed Gull *Larus leucophthalmus*
Great Black-headed Gull *Larus ichthyaetus*
Mediterranean Gull *Larus melanocephalus*
Laughing Gull *Larus atricilla*
Little Gull *Larus minutus*
Sabine's Gull *Larus sabini*
Black-headed Gull *Larus ridibundus*
Brown-headed Gull *Larus brunnicephalus*
Grey-headed Gull *Larus cirrocephalus*
Slender-billed Gull *Larus genei*
Audouin's Gull *Larus audouinii*
Ring-billed Gull *Larus delawarensis*
Common Gull *Larus canus*
Lesser Black-backed Gull *Larus fuscus*
Herring Gull *Larus argentatus*
Glaucous Gull *Larus hyperboreus*
Great Black-backed Gull *Larus marinus*
Kittiwake *Rissa tridactyla*
Gull-billed Tern *Gelochelidon nilotica*
Caspian Tern *Sterna caspia*
Royal Tern *Sterna maxima*
Swift Tern *Sterna bergii*
Lesser Crested Tern *Sterna bengalensis*
Sandwich Tern *Sterna sandvicensis*
Roseate Tern *Sterna dougallii*
Common Tern *Sterna hirundo*
Arctic Tern *Sterna paradisaea*
White-cheeked Tern *Sterna repressa*
Bridled Tern *Sterna anaethetus*
Sooty Tern *Sterna fuscata*
Little Tern *Sterna albifrons*
Saunders' Little Tern *Sterna saundersi*
Whiskered Tern *Chlidonias hybridus*
Black Tern *Chlidonias niger*
White-winged Black Tern *Chlidonias
  leucopterus*
Common Noddy *Anous stolidus*
Lesser Noddy *Anous tenuirostris*
African Skimmer *Rynchops flavirostris*
Indian Skimmer *Rynchops albicollis*
Guillemot *Uria aalge*
Razorbill *Alca torda*
Puffin *Fratercula arctica*
Lichtenstein's Sandgrouse *Pterocles
  lichtensteinii*
Crowned Sandgrouse *Pterocles coronatus*
Spotted Sandgrouse *Pterocles senegallus*
Chestnut-bellied Sandgrouse *Pterocles
  exustus*
Black-bellied Sandgrouse *Pterocles orientalis*
Pin-tailed Sandgrouse *Pterocles alchata*
Pallas's Sandgrouse *Syrrhaptes paradoxus*
Rock Dove *Columba livia*
Stock dove *Columba oenas*
Eastern Stock Dove *Columba eversmanni*
Woodpigeon *Columba palumbus*
Olive Pigeon *Columba arquatrix*
African Collared Dove *Streptopelia roseogrisea*

261

Collared Dove *Streptopelia decaocto*
Red-eyed Dove *Streptopelia semitorquata*
Red Turtle Dove *Streptopelia tranquebarica*
Turtle Dove *Streptopelia turtur*
Dusky Turtle Dove *Streptopelia lugens*
Rufous Turtle Dove *Streptopelia orientalis*
Palm Dove *Streptopelia senegalensis*
Namaqua Dove *Oena capensis*
Bruce's Green Pigeon *Treron waalia*
Ring-necked Parakeet *Psittacula krameri*
Alexandrine Parakeet *Psittacula eupatria*
Jacobin Cuckoo *Clamator jacobinus*
Great Spotted Cuckoo *Clamator glandarius*
Didric Cuckoo *Chrysococcyx caprius*
Klaas's Cuckoo *Chrysococcyx klaas*
Cuckoo *Cuculus canorus*
Yellow-billed Cuckoo *Coccyzus americanus*
Senegal Coucal *Centropus senegalensis*
White-browed Coucal *Centropus superciliosus*
Koel *Eudynamys scolopacea*
Barn Owl *Tyto alba*
Indian Scops Owl *Otus bakkamoena*
Striated Scops Owl *Otus brucei*
Scops Owl *Otus scops*
Senegal Scops Owl *Otus senegalensis*
Eagle Owl *Bubo bubo*
Spotted Eagle Owl *Bubo africanus*
Brown Fish Owl *Ketupa zeylonensis*
Snowy Owl *Nyctea scandiaca*
Little Owl *Athene noctua*
Spotted Little Owl *Athene brama*
Tawny Owl *Strix aluco*
Hume's Tawny Owl *Strix butleri*
Long-eared Owl *Asio otus*
Short-eared Owl *Asio flammeus*
Marsh Owl *Asio capensis*
Tengmalm's Owl *Aegolius funereus*
Plain Nightjar *Caprimulgus inornatus*
Nubian Nightjar *Caprimulgus nubicus*
Sykes' Nightjar *Caprimulgus mahrattensis*
Indian Nightjar *Caprimulgus asiaticus*
Nightjar *Caprimulgus europaeus*
Red-necked Nightjar *Caprimulgus ruficollis*
Egyptian Nightjar *Caprimulgus aegyptius*
Plain Swift *Apus unicolor*
Swift *Apus apus*
Pallid Swift *Apus pallidus*
Alpine Swift *Apus melba*
White-rumped Swift *Apus caffer*
Little Swift *Apus affinis*
Palm Swift *Cypsiurus parvus*
White-breasted Kingfisher *Halcyon smyrnensis*
Grey-headed Kingfisher *Halcyon leucocephala*
White-collared Kingfisher *Halcyon chloris*
Kingfisher *Alcedo atthis*
Malachite Kingfisher *Alcedo cristata*
Pied Kingfisher *Ceryle rudis*
White-throated Bee-eater *Merops albicollis*
Little Green Bee-eater *Merops orientalis*
Blue-cheeked Bee-eater *Merops superciliosus*
Bee-eater *Merops apiaster*
Roller *Coracias garrulus*
Abyssinian Roller *Coracias abyssinicus*
Indian Roller *Coracias benghalensis*

Lilac-breasted Roller *Coracias caudata*
Rufous-crowned Roller *Coracias naevia*
Hoopoe *Upupa epops*
Grey Hornbill *Tockus nasutus*
Wryneck *Jynx torquilla*
Grey-headed Woodpecker *Picus canus*
Green Woodpecker *Picus viridis*
Levaillant's Green Woodpecker *Picus vaillantii*
Scaly-bellied Woodpecker *Picus squamatus*
Black Woodpecker *Dryocopus martius*
Great Spotted Woodpecker *Dendrocopos major*
White-winged Woodpecker *Dendrocopos leucopterus*
Syrian Woodpecker *Dendrocopos syriacus*
Sind Pied Woodpecker *Dendrocopos assimilis*
Middle Spotted Woodpecker *Dendrocopos medius*
White-backed Woodpecker *Dendrocopos leucotos*
Lesser Spotted Woodpecker *Dendrocopos minor*
Arabian Woodpecker *Dendrocopos dorae*
Singing Bush Lark *Mirafra cantillans*
Black-crowned Finch Lark *Eremopterix nigriceps*
Dunn's Lark *Eremalauda dunni*
Bar-tailed Desert Lark *Ammomanes cincturus*
Desert Lark *Ammomanes deserti*
Hoopoe Lark *Alaemon alaudipes*
Dupont's Lark *Chersophilus duponti*
Thick-billed Lark *Ramphocoris clotbey*
Calandra Lark *Melanocorypha calandra*
Bimaculated Lark *Melanocorypha bimaculata*
White-winged Lark *Melanocorypha leucoptera*
Black Lark *Melanocorypha yeltoniensis*
Red-capped Lark *Calandrella cinerea*
Short-toed Lark *Calandrella brachydactyla*
Hume's Short-toed Lark *Calandrella acutirostris*
Lesser Short-toed Lark *Calandrella rufescens*
Indian Sand Lark *Calandrella raytal*
Crested Lark *Galerida cristata*
Thekla Lark *Galerida theklae*
Woodlark *Lullula arborea*
Small Skylark *Alauda gulgula*
Skylark, *Alauda arvensis*
Shore Lark *Eremophila alpestris*
Temminck's Horned Lark *Eremophila bilopha*
Brown-throated Sand Martin *Riparia paludicola*
Sand Martin *Riparia riparia*
Banded Martin *Riparia cincta*
African Rock Martin *Ptyonoprogne fuligula*
Crag Martin *Ptyonoprogne rupestris*
Swallow *Hirundo rustica*
Wire-tailed Swallow *Hirundo smithii*
Red-rumped Swallow *Hirundo daurica*
House Martin *Delichon urbica*
Golden Pipit *Tmetothylacus tenellus*
Richard's Pipit *Anthus novaeseelandiae*
Tawny Pipit *Anthus campestris*
Long-billed Pipit *Anthus similis*
Olive-backed Pipit *Anthus hodgsoni*
Tree Pipit *Anthus trivialis*

Meadow Pipit *Anthus pratensis*
Red-throated Pipit *Anthus cervinus*
Water Pipit *Anthus spinoletta*
Yellow Wagtail *Motacilla flava*
Citrine Wagtail *Motacilla citreola*
Grey Wagtail *Motacilla cinerea*
White Wagtail *Motacilla alba*
African Pied Wagtail *Motacilla aguimp*
White-cheeked Bulbul *Pycnonotus leucogenys*
Yellow-vented Bulbul *Pycnonotus xanthopygos*
Common Bulbul *Pycnonotus barbatus*
Red-whiskered Bulbul *Pycnonotus jocosus*
Red-vented Bulbul *Pycnonotus cafer*
Waxwing *Bombycilla garrulus*
Grey Hypocolius *Hypocolius ampelinus*
Dipper *Cinclus cinclus*
Wren *Troglodytes troglodytes*
Dunnock *Prunella modularis*
Siberian Accentor *Prunella montanella*
Radde's Accentor *Prunella ocularis*
Arabian Accentor *Prunella fagani*
Black-throated Accentor *Prunella atrogularis*
Alpine Accentor *Prunella collaris*
Rufous Bush Robin *Cercotrichas galactotes*
Black Bush Robin *Cercotrichas podobe*
Robin *Erithacus rubecula*
Thrush Nightingale *Luscinia luscinia*
Nightingale *Luscinia megarhynchos*
Bluethroat *Luscinia svecica*
Red-flanked Bluetail *Tarsiger cyanurus*
White-throated Robin *Irania gutturalis*
Eversmann's Redstart *Phoenicurus erythronotus*
Black Redstart *Phoenicurus ochruros*
Redstart *Phoenicurus phoenicurus*
Moussier's Redstart *Phoenicurus moussieri*
Güldenstädt's Redstart *Phoenicurus erythrogaster*
Blackstart *Cercomela melanura*
Red-tailed Chat *Cercomela familiaris*
Whinchat *Saxicola rubetra*
Stonechat *Saxicola torquata*
Pied Stonechat *Saxicola caprata*
Isabelline Wheatear *Oenanthe isabellina*
Red-breasted Wheatear *Oenanthe bottae*
Wheatear *Oenanthe oenanthe*
Pied Wheatear *Oenanthe pleschanka*
Cyprus Pied Wheatear *Oenanthe cypriaca*
Black-eared Wheatear *Oenanthe hispanica*
Desert Wheatear *Oenanthe deserti*
Finsch's Wheatear *Oenanthe finschii*
Red-rumped Wheatear *Oenanthe moesta*
Red-tailed Wheater *Oenanthe xanthoprymna*
Eastern Pied Wheatear *Oenanthe picata*
Mourning Wheatear *Oenanthe lugens*
South Arabian Wheatear *Oenanthe lugentoides*
Hooded Wheatear *Oenanthe monacha*
Hume's Wheatear *Oenanthe alboniger*
White-crowned Black Wheatear *Oenanthe leucopyga*
Black Wheatear *Oenanthe leucura*
Little Rock Thrush *Monticola rufocinerea*
Rock Thrush *Monticola saxatilis*

Blue Rock Thrush *Monticola solitarius*
Siberian Thrush *Turdus sibirica*
Yemen Thrush *Turdus menachensis*
Ring Ouzel *Turdus torquatus*
Blackbird *Turdus merula*
Eye-browed Thrush *Turdus obscurus*
Dusky Thrush *Turdus naumanni*
Black-throated Thrush *Turdus ruficollis*
Fieldfare *Turdus pilaris*
Song Thrush *Turdus philomelos*
Redwing *Turdus iliacus*
Mistle Thrush *Turdus viscivorus*
Cetti's Warbler *Cettia cetti*
Yemen Warbler *Parisoma buryi*
Fan-tailed Warbler *Cisticola juncidis*
Graceful Warbler *Prinia gracilis*
Scrub Warbler *Scotocerca inquieta*
Grasshopper Warbler *Locustella naevia*
River Warbler *Locustella fluviatilis*
Savi's Warbler *Locustella luscinioides*
Moustached Warbler *Acrocephalus melanopogon*
Aquatic Warbler *Acrocephalus paludicola*
Sedge Warbler *Acrocephalus schoenobaenus*
Paddyfield Warbler *Acrocephalus agricola*
Blyth's Reed Warbler *Acrocephalus dumetorum*
Marsh Warbler *Acrocephalus palustris*
Reed Warbler *Acrocephalus scirpaceus*
Clamorous Reed Warbler *Acrocephalus stentoreus*
Great Reed Warbler *Acrocephalus arundinaceus*
Olivaceous Warbler *Hippolais pallida*
Booted Warbler *Hippolais caligata*
Upcher's Warbler *Hippolais languida*
Olive-tree Warbler *Hippolais olivetorum*
Icterine Warbler *Hippolais icterina*
Melodious Warbler *Hippolais polyglotta*
Marmora's Warbler *Sylvia sarda*
Dartford Warbler *Sylvia undata*
Tristram's Warbler *Sylvia deserticola*
Spectacled Warbler *Sylvia conspicillata*
Subalpine Warbler *Sylvia cantillans*
Ménétries' Warbler *Sylvia mystacea*
Sardinian Warbler *Sylvia melanocephala*
Cyprus Warbler *Sylvia melanothorax*
Rüppell's Warbler *Sylvia rueppelli*
Desert Warbler *Sylvia nana*
Arabian Warbler *Sylvia leucomelaena*
Orphean Warbler *Sylvia hortensis*
Barred Warbler *Sylvia nisoria*
Lesser Whitethroat *Sylvia curruca curruca*
Hume's Lesser Whitethroat *Sylvia c. althaea*
Desert Lesser Whitethroat *Sylvia c. minula*
Whitethroat *Sylvia communis*
Garden Warbler *Sylvia borin*
Blackcap *Sylvia atricapilla*
Brown Woodland Warbler *Phylloscopus umbrovirens*
Green Warbler *Phylloscopus nitidus*
Greenish Warbler *Phylloscopus trochiloides*
Arctic Warbler *Phylloscopus borealis*
Yellow-browed Warbler *Phylloscopus inornatus*

Radde's Warbler *Phylloscopus schwarzi*
Dusky Warbler *Phylloscopus fuscatus*
Bonelli's Warbler *Phylloscopus bonelli*
Wood Warbler *Phylloscopus sibilatrix*
Plain Leaf Warbler *Phylloscopus neglectus*
Mountain Chiffchaff *Phylloscopus sindianus*
Chiffchaff *Phylloscopus collybita*
Willow Warbler *Phylloscopus trochilus*
Goldcrest *Regulus regulus*
Firecrest *Regulus ignicapillus*
Blue and White Flycatcher *Cyanoptila cyanomelana*
Spotted Flycatcher *Muscicapa striata*
Gambage Dusky Flycatcher *Muscicapa gambagae*
Red-breasted Flycatcher *Ficedula parva*
Semi-collared Flycatcher *Ficedula semitorquata*
Collared Flycatcher *Ficedula albicollis*
Pied Flycatcher *Ficedula hypoleuca*
African Paradise Flycatcher *Terpsiphone viridis*
Bearded Tit *Panurus biarmicus*
Iraq Babbler *Turdoides altirostris*
Common Babbler *Turdoides caudatus*
Arabian Babbler *Turdoides squamiceps*
Fulvous Babbler *Turdoides fulvus*
Long-tailed Tit *Aegithalos caudatus*
Marsh Tit *Parus palustris*
Sombre Tit *Parus lugubris*
Crested Tit *Parus cristatus*
Coal Tit *Parus ater*
Blue Tit *Parus caeruleus*
Azure Tit *Parus cyanus*
Great Tit *Parus major*
Turkestan Tit *Parus bokharensis*
Krüper's Nuthatch *Sitta krueperi*
Algerian Nuthatch *Sitta ledanti*
Nuthatch *Sitta europaea*
Eastern Rock Nuthatch *Sitta tephronota*
Rock Nuthatch *Sitta neumayer*
Wallcreeper *Tichodroma muraria*
Treecreeper *Certhia familiaris*
Short-toed Treecreeper *Certhia brachydactyla*
Penduline Tit *Remiz pendulinus*
Nile Valley Sunbird *Anthreptes metallicus*
Purple Sunbird *Nectarinia asiatica*
Shining Sunbird *Nectarinia habessinica*
Palestine Sunbird *Nectarinia osea*
White-breasted White-eye *Zosterops abyssinica*
Golden Oriole *Oriolus oriolus*
Black-headed Bush Shrike *Tchagra senegala*
Rosy-patched Shrike *Rhodophoneus cruentus*
Isabelline Shrike *Lanius isabellinus*
Red-backed Shrike *Lanius collurio*
Bay-backed Shrike *Lanius vittatus*
Black-headed Shrike *Lanius schach*
Lesser Grey Shrike *Lanius minor*
Great Grey Shrike *Lanius excubitor*
Woodchat Shrike *Lanius senator*
Masked Shrike *Lanius nubicus*
Black Drongo *Dicrurus macrocercus*
Jay *Garrulus glandarius*
Magpie *Pica pica*

Pleske's Ground Jay *Podoces pleskei*
Nutcracker *Nucifraga caryocatactes*
Alpine Chough *Pyrrhocorax graculus*
Chough *Pyrrhocorax pyrrhocoroax*
Jackdaw *Corvus monedula*
House Crow *Corvus splendens*
Rook *Corvus frugilegus*
Carrion Crow *Corvus corone corone*
Hooded Crow *Corvus corone cornix*
Jungle Crow *Corvus macrorhynchos*
Pied Crow *Corvus albus*
Brown-necked Raven *Corvus ruficollis*
Raven *Corvus corax*
Fan-tailed Raven *Corvus rhipidurus*
Tristram's Grackle *Onychognathus tristramii*
Amethyst Starling *Cinnyricinclus leucogaster*
Starling *Sturnus vulgaris*
Spotless Starling *Sturnus unicolor*
Rose-coloured Starling *Sturnus roseus*
Wattled Starling *Creatophora cineracea*
Bank Mynah *Acridotheres ginginianus*
Common Mynah *Acridotheres tristis*
Saxaul Sparrow *Passer ammodendri*
House Sparrow *Passer domesticus*
Spanish Sparrow *Passer hispaniolensis*
Sind Jungle Sparrow *Passer pyrrhonotus*
Dead Sea Sparrow *Passer moabiticus*
Desert Sparrow *Passer simplex*
Tree Sparrow *Passer montanus*
Sudan Golden Sparrow *Passer luteus*
Arabian Golden Sparrow *Passer euchlorus*
Pale Rock Sparrow *Petronia brachydactyla*
Yellow-throated Sparrow *Petronia xanthocollis*
Lesser Rock Sparrow *Petronia dentata*
Rock Sparrow *Petronia petronia*
Snow Finch *Montifringilla nivalis*
Rüppell's Weaver *Ploceus galbula*
Streaked Weaver *Ploceus manyar*
Red-billed Firefinch *Lagonosticta senegala*
Arabian Waxbill *Estrilda rufibarba*
Avadavat *Amandava amandava*
Zebra Waxbill *Amandava subflava*
Indian Silverbill *Euodice malabarica*
African Silverbill *Euodice cantans*
Red-eyed Vireo *Vireo olivaceus*
Chaffinch *Fringilla coelebs*
Brambling *Fringilla montifringilla*
Red-fronted Serin *Serinus pusillus*
Serin *Serinus serinus*
Syrian Serin *Serinus syriacus*
Citril Finch *Serinus citrinella*
Arabian Serin *Serinus rothschildi*
Yemen Serin *Serinus menachensis*
Golden-winged Grosbeak *Rhynchostruthus socotranus*
Greenfinch *Carduelis chloris*
Goldfinch *Carduelis carduelis*
Siskin *Carduelis spinus*
Linnet *Carduelis cannabina*
Yemen Linnet *Carduelis yemenensis*
Twite *Carduelis flavirostris*
Redpoll *Carduelis flammea*
Crossbill *Loxia curvirostra*
Crimson-winged Finch *Rhodopechys sanguinea*

264

Desert Finch *Rhodospiza obsoleta*
Mongolian Trumpeter Finch *Bucanetes mongolicus*
Trumpeter Finch *Bucanetes githagineus*
Scarlet Rosefinch *Carpodacus erythrinus*
Sinai Rosefinch *Carpodacus synoicus*
Great Rosefinch *Carpodacus rubicilla*
Bullfinch *Pyrrhula pyrrhula*
White-winged Grosbeak *Mycerobas carnipes*
Hawfinch *Coccothraustes coccothraustes*
Lapland Bunting *Calcarius lapponicus*
Snow Bunting *Plectrophenax nivalis*
Pine Bunting *Emberiza leucocephalos*
Yellowhammer *Emberiza citrinella*
Cirl Bunting *Emberiza cirlus*
White-capped Bunting *Emberiza stewarti*

Rock Bunting *Emberiza cia*
House Bunting *Emberiza striolata*
African Rock Bunting *Emberiza tahapisi*
Cinereous Bunting *Emberiza cineracea*
Ortolan Bunting *Emberiza hortulana*
Grey-necked Bunting *Emberiza buchanani*
Cretzschmar's Bunting *Emberiza caesia*
Rustic Bunting *Emberiza rustica*
Little Bunting *Emberiza pusilla*
Yellow-breasted Bunting *Emberiza aureola*
Reed Bunting *Emberiza schoeniclus*
Red-headed Bunting *Emberiza bruniceps*
Black-headed Bunting *Emberiza melanocephala*
Corn Bunting *Miliaria calandra*

Index of English names

Index of scientific names

277